W9-BZF-957

NEWMAN

His Life and Spirituality

CARDINAL NEWMAN
from the painting by W. W. Ouless

NEWMAN

His Life and Spirituality

by

LOUIS BOUYER

of the Oratory

With a Preface by the Very Reverend
MONSIGNOR H. FRANCIS DAVIS

P. J. KENEDY & SONS

NEW YORK

This translation from the original French, Newman: Sa vie; sa spiritualité (*Les Editions du Cerf, Paris*), *was made by*
J. LEWIS MAY

NIHIL OBSTAT: ANDREAS J. MOORE, L.C.L.
CENSOR DEPVTATVS
IMPRIMATVR: ✠ GEORGIVS L. CRAVEN
EPISCOPVS SEBASTOPOLIS
VICARIVS GENERALIS
WESTMONASTERII: DIE XIII FEBRVARII MCMLVII

Library of Congress Catalog Card No. 58-5667
Printed in Great Britain

PATRI DESIDERATISSIMO
HENRICO TRISTRAM
ORATORII S. P. N. PRESBYTERO
CVIVS ANIMA IN REFRIGERIVM

PREFACE

BY MGR H. FRANCIS DAVIS

FR BOUYER was kind enough to be pleased that I was to introduce his book to English readers. When people meet over Newman, they remain life-long friends. For Newman was one of those personalities who attract friends. One of his earliest acts of thanksgiving to God was for the "Blessings of friends, which to my door, unask'd, unhoped, have come." He did not seek them, he tells us. They came, as though sent by God. And still they come. Many who read this book will feel they have gained a friend. Fr Bouyer and I met around the Newman shrine at the first great post-war international gathering, which was held at Beaumont College in memory of Newman's conversion a hundred years earlier.

Ever since the book appeared in France, people have been asking: "When will it come out in England?" We had a great international Congress at the hospitable invitation of Luxembourg in 1956; and then the same question was asked, along with the other recurring query, "Is anything happening about the Newman cause?" I suppose Fr Bouyer's interest is the greater in that he came to the Catholic Church from the Huguenots, just as the illustrious English convert had a mother of the same stock. He says Newman-study has been the fondest and most enduring interest of his life.

Though books on Newman appear almost monthly in either English, French, or German, and though most books on Newman are an event to those who have been caught in the Newman net, this book is a special event, and will interest not merely the specialists, but the general English-reading public. A little over a century ago, one of Newman's Oxford friends spoke of his name as "a passport to the hearts and a secure claim on the intellectual respect of his countrymen both within and without the church." It is now many years since that reverence and respect have extended far beyond the bounds of Newman's countrymen, and one wonders whether there are any important languages unprovided with a Newman literature.

I do not think I could do better in this preface than repeat words I used about this book when it appeared a few years ago in France. "I do not think that any book as yet produced has done so much to depict Newman's life in its true proportions as Father Louis Bouyer's *Newman*. The author clearly wishes to give his personal vote for Newman's sanctity, while duly submitting his judgment to that of the Church. He endorses Father Przywara's declaration many years ago that, as St Augustine was the great apostle of the early period of the Church, and St Thomas of the Middle Ages, so is Newman that of modern times." The saintly Bishop Hedley was as convinced as is Fr Bouyer of this sanctity. When the monumental life by Wilfrid Ward appeared, with its first publication of so many private Newman documents, he wrote:

> We had been so accustomed—I speak for the generation of Catholics which was young in 1850—to look upon him as a hero, a sage, and a saint, that his biography has certainly found us unprepared to believe that he could ever have had trouble in his own interior life with such unworthy feelings as disappointed vanity, the ambition of success, or petty personal dislike. Let me hasten at once to say that, in spite of his own confessions, no one, it seems to me, will think him less of a sage and a saint. There is nothing finer in all the lives of the Saints than the expression we here find, not only of his joy and peace in the Catholic faith, but of his perfectly and intimately Catholic apprehension of the deepest ascetic principle, on humility, human applause, earthly success, true charity, sincere obedience, and conformity to the most holy Will of God. He feels the depressing temptations indicated above—but, except that he cannot help recognizing what he considers facts, he humbly and resolutely, and with absolute reliance on Divine Grace, strives to guard his heart from them and stands firm in refusing to allow them to influence his will, or his behaviour. His own temperament and the circumstances of his position and history as a Catholic entitle us to say that his trial was exceptionally severe and his spiritual battle nothing less than heroic.[1]

These words from one who is acknowledged the greatest of our nineteenth-century Bishops, "a Prince in Israel," as *The Tablet* called him at his death, who "knew no fear, save that of offending God", and who was Newman's acknowledged disciple, must still have great authority.

Fr Bouyer's book has given great stimulus to the growing desire that the Church would consider Newman's cause. He is not primarily concerned with Newman's intellectual reputation. Clearly he is in full agreement with those who see in Newman one of the great modern Catholic thinkers. But his book is more concerned with Newman's personal life. He does not attempt to cover all the events of that century-long life. Rather he emphasises those events and aspects which

[1] *Ampleforth Journal*, April 1912, pp. 288–9.

throw light on his inner life. Even as a record of the inner life, it does not attempt to be exhaustive. More exhaustive monographs will undoubtedly appear in the time to come. But he does give us, in the proportions required by the ordinary reader, an account of that life's origins and development.

The reader will be greatly helped in his estimate of Newman by Fr Bouyer's account of the meaning and importance of Newman's "conversion" at the age of 15. In his judgment—that it was this conversion which gave Newman his abiding sense of God's presence and ever-watchful providence—Fr Bouyer has given us a most valuable key to the appreciation of his whole life. It is significant that the last-named, who from his own Calvinistic upbringing, ought to know, refuses to regard this "conversion" as normally Calvinistic, as has sometimes been said. Fr Zeno, the devoted Dutch student of Newman's spiritual life, has reached very similar conclusions to Fr Bouyer in this.[1]

This view of Newman's childhood "conversion" enables us to understand his "introspectiveness". Many who speak of this introspectiveness forget that, for him, there were always *two* luminous beings before his conscience, not *one*. In other words, he lived in the presence of God, even more than in the presence of his own soul. It was an intuitive outlook which was partly temperamental, partly encouraged by his trials, partly, doubtless, God's grace acting in his delicate conscience, which made him, in this respect, like St Augustine, or the two St Teresas. Newman could not conceive a self-centredness which excluded God, or even which put self in any way before God. That such a psychological state was found among men Newman would be the first to admit; but he would have found it difficult to conceive of their state. "I am a Catholic," he wrote in the *Apologia*, "by virtue of my believing in a God; and if I am asked why I believe in a God, I answer that it is because I believe in myself, for I feel it impossible to believe in my own existence (and of that fact I am quite sure) without believing also in the existence of Him, who lives as a Personal, All-seeing, All-judging Being in my conscience." Like St Teresa of Avila, who found God in the innermost recesses of her soul, Newman found Him never so certainly as when he was driven back into his own loneliness. Whenever he was tempted to feel lonely, he quickly recovered, as he saw God's hand detaching him from creatures. He consoled his sister in this way: "I am not more lonely than I

[1] Cf. Fr Zeno, O.F.M., *Newman's Inner Life*, I.E.R., 1952, p. 274.

have been a long while. God intends me to be lonely; He has so framed my mind that I am in a great measure beyond the sympathies of other people and thrown upon myself. . . . God, I trust, will support me in following whither He leads." It was indeed because all his life seemed to him so bound up with God that he felt he must keep the records of what he saw to be God's daily providence. Take the following passage, recorded by Fr Zeno from the MSS: "Misericordias Domini in aeternum cantabo. I am loath to destroy altogether the record of God's great mercies to me, of the wonderful things He had done in my soul, and of my early moral and spiritual history." It was his same intense feeling of God's presence and holiness and his own unworthiness that made him exclaim in his old age, like St Paul and so many of the saints: "I cannot but repeat words which I think I used in a memorandum book of 1820, that among the ordinary mass of men, *no one* has sinned so much, *no one* has been so mercifully treated, as I have; no one has such cause for humiliation, such cause for thanksgiving." It is very unrealistic to believe Newman in his repeated confessions of sin and unworthiness, unless one recognises the humility and God-fearing sincerity which prompts them, and his deep sense of God's mercy in forgiving them.

Fr Bouyer's book will also help us to see in correct perspective Newman's sensitiveness. Some people have exaggerated this beyond bounds, and seen a serious blemish in his character. I wrote on the French appearance of this life: "Since when, asks Fr Bouyer, has sanctity been a matter of temperament? Since when are the robust, insensitive, healthy temperaments an exclusive seedground for sanctity? Surely sanctity consists in merit, and merit depends upon what one does with one's temperament under the influence of grace, not upon any natural qualities." Certainly both Anglicans and Catholics did a great deal—though unintentionally—to give Newman a sense of frustration. In this respect, Newman seems to qualify for one of the marks of sanctity mentioned by Benedict XIV, that the servant of God who is being examined must have passed through trials and tribulations, such as God has in the New Testament promised to His elect, and such as we actually find in the lives of most of the saints. Benedict XIV reminds us of the words of the Psalmist, which every servant of God can to some extent apply to himself: "Had some enemy decried me, I could have borne it patiently; some open ill-wisher, I could have sheltered myself from his attack. But thou, my second self, my familiar friend! How pleasant was the companionship we shared, thou and I." To how many of the saints have not these words applied, in that they suffered innumerable trials from their friends, often indeed from good men? And, though the servant of God must not give way under the strain, it does not surely detract essentially from his sanctity, even if he felt with keen sensitiveness, as did the Psalmist, these heaven-sent trials. Mr St John Stevas recently put his finger on Newman's real difficulty. He was "a man of action forced by circumstances to become a man of letters". In the days of the Oxford Movement he had a chance to show his practical nature. "Let us be up and doing", he would say. "Speak I must," he wrote in the first *Tract for the Times*, "for the times are very evil, yet no one speaks against them. Is not this so? Do we not 'look upon one another', yet perform nothing? Do we not all confess the peril into which the Church is come, yet sit still, each in his own retirement, as if mountains and seas cut off brother from brother?"

What is said in the above paragraph, and indeed in this whole preface, about Newman's sanctity, is, of course, purely the writer's personal conviction, and is entirely subject to the judgment of the Church.

The need of Newman's to be "up and doing" was an aspect of his intense realism. True education, he would say, consists in unlearning life's poetry, and learning its prose. Superficial education, which is at all times so widespread, was the substitution of appearances for reality. Newman was never happy about "society"; for, full as it appeared of gentlemanly virtues, it lacked true depth. Everything was sacrificed for the sake of decent appearances. "*To seem* becomes *to be*." The religion of society is a religion of outward appearance, which offends no one, and gets nowhere. Polite society could not understand the religion of the inward heart, the acceptance of difficult creeds, and the dedication of one's real, everyday life to the pursuit of sanctity. It was not that Newman was opposed to poetry or culture. He was only opposed to the substitution of these for the hard facts of human existence. His eventual rejection of the Oxford *Via Media* was on the grounds of its unreality.

You will catch in this life by Fr Bouyer a glimpse of the inner workings of grace in Newman's active and tormented soul. Perhaps also you will learn something of the secret of his intuitive mind, so un-Victorian in its farseeing prophecies of the temptations and dangers of twentieth-century man. His inability to write straightforward technical treatises on the numberless subjects that filled his mind comes from the unceasing demand of his nature for action. A paradox to us who admire and study him—this man of action who yet was so unusually sensitive and intuitive! Yet to read his own autobiographical *Memoirs* is to realise that he never could have remained a recluse. When one activity after the other was denied him, he had to fulfil his vocation to teach, preach, and evangelise by writing. Every one of his important writings, including even the *Grammar of Assent*, was written for an evangelical or educational purpose. "Looking ahead," writes Mr St John Stevas, "—and it is this that makes Newman so astonishingly modern—he prophesied that the abandonment of belief would finally lead to a lowering of moral standards, uncertainty about human destiny, and hence to the insecurity and anxiety which are the hallmarks of contemporary man."[1] With a faith so deep that his whole world was seen under the aspect of God and the soul, and convinced that true belief about Christ translated into life was the meaning of Christianity, he dedicated the efforts of his ninety years to bringing his fellow countrymen to a realisation of this. This he expressed by saying that all his life he had fought liberalism. This gospel he proclaimed in season and out of season. For God has spoken, he would say, and if God speaks man must listen; and if man listens, he must believe and obey. Any other way lies rebellion.

If I might once more quote from my remarks of four years back, in this book Fr Bouyer "steadily removes one after another of the more important misunderstandings. He shows how the decree of the Pope's infallibility was as much a triumph for the attitude of moderation represented by Newman as it was for the extreme attitude of Manning. He shows us the wisdom and charity of the method of apologetics which Newman all his life preferred, rather recognising the sincerity of the non-Catholic and the plausibleness of his case—a case wrong rather by its incompleteness than by its positive error. Heresy, he used to say, is right in what it affirms, wrong in what it denies. His vocation he always felt to be primarily against rationalism; and, though he believed firmly that the Catholic Church was the one true Church for all, he knew that all were not ready to take that step; and he found it impossible to hope for the destruction of the Church of England, as long as it saved people from unbelief who were not yet ready for Catholicism. . . . Merely destructive tactics may easily lead to agnosticism, giving them nothing in its place. It is unfortunate that the group of Catholics, from whom Newman hoped to build up a

[1] *Time and Tide*, Jan. 26, 1956.

constructive school of Apologetics, as well as an enlightened Catholic literature, though not lacking intelligence, lacked the reverence for authority and prudence in reform, which were so characteristic of Newman himself."

This book will do much for the cause dear to Newman's heart if it succeeds in preparing the ground today for a greater sense of the apostolate of truth, as well as a sounder understanding of Newman's ambitions for the growth of the deep, sincere, inward holiness and sense of God's presence and providence in the weary, anxious, materialist world of the later twentieth century.

H. F. D.

conjecture school of apologetics as well as an enlightened Catholic literature, though not lacking intelligence, lacked the reverence for authority and prudence in reform which were so characteristic of Newman himself.

This book will do justice to the same ideal as Newman's heart if it succeeds in preparing the ground today for a greater sense of the apostolate of truth, as well as a sounder understanding of Newman's ambition for the growth of the deep, strong, inward holiness and sense of God's presence and providence in the weary, anxious, materialist world of the later twentieth century.

H. F. D.

CONTENTS

AUTHOR'S NOTE

WHATEVER the merits or demerits of the present work, it can at least be claimed for it that, in it, the documents will tell their tale without suppression, alteration or addition. Even so, it will owe such value as it may possess not so much to me as to Father Henry Tristram, who, not content with furnishing the documents, with unparalleled generosity permitted me to benefit by the fruits of the immense labours he had bestowed upon them.

Next to him, and to the Oratorian community at Edgbaston, there is no one to whom I am more deeply indebted than to Mr Julien Green. I know not whether I have profited as much as I might from his comments and criticism and from his advice regarding the form my book should take. At all events he gave me the most timely and tactful encouragement in a task in which I, more than anyone, was conscious of my shortcomings.

I am also greatly indebted to Mgr H. Francis Davis and Mgr Philip Hughes whose comments have enabled me to correct a number of mistakes in the original edition.

I

CHILDHOOD AND ADOLESCENCE

No one in the last century was more conscious than Newman of the need to preach a Christianity that should detach us from the world, and lead us straight to Christ, to Christ who redeems us from the world before calling the world to judgment. There is consequently a touch of irony in the circumstance of Newman's being born in the very heart of what we may call the business stronghold of Victorian England. It was in Old Broad Street, which seems today to be made up entirely of banks, that John Henry Newman, the son of a banker, was brought into the world, on the 21st February, 1801. The church of St Benet Fink, where he was baptised on the 9th of the following April, no longer exists. The number of parishioners having dwindled to a mere handful, it was demolished to make room for the new Royal Exchange.

Like many Londoners, Newman, though born in the centre of the metropolis, had his roots in the country and, indeed, beyond it. His father, John Newman, came of a Cambridgeshire family that had settled in London only a generation before. His mother, Jemima Fourdrinier, was descended from some Huguenots who had taken refuge in London on the revocation of the Edict of Nantes. It would be vain and unnecessary to go searching farther afield for the ancestry of this most English of Englishmen. The notion that he was of Jewish descent, which rests on nothing more substantial than the contour of his nose and his father's line of business, may be dismissed as the purest fantasy. No need to seek elsewhere for his forebears than those good, honest tillers of the glebe and those humble French bourgeois who, by this time, were thoroughly absorbed into the British population around them. None of those far-fetched conjectures about his heredity contribute anything so valuable to our understanding of him as the things we know, and know for certain, about his upbringing.

His father seems to have been a thoroughly typical example of the late-eighteenth-century Englishman. In politics he was a Whig, and in religion enough of a free-lance to interest himself in Quaker literature, but, at the same time, too averse to "ticketing" himself, too impatient of "enthusiasms" of any kind, to profess himself a member of any particular religious body or sect. He gives us the impression of being the sort of business man who is more of an optimist than a success, or, should we say, more courageous than capable. First a banker, then a brewer, he wasn't afraid to swop horses while crossing the stream, but, maybe, he was no more fitted for brewing than he was for banking. At all events, the family fortunes, though never exactly desperate, showed but little sign of improvement. It looks as if there were some chronic instability about the man. At any rate, continual "flittings" are a conspicuous accompaniment of Newman's young days. As to the paternal change of occupation, its immediate cause was the precarious position of the bank, brought about, or perhaps merely hastened, by the economic unsettlement that followed the conclusion of the Napoleonic wars.

Mr John Newman was evidently a man of Johnsonian culture, and definitely superior in this respect to most of his class. To his eldest son he bequeathed a profound admiration for Shakespeare, and a passionate love of music. This latter predilection, however, derived from an earlier generation. The grandfather, another John Newman, was an oil-and-colour merchant who had come from somewhere near Cambridge to set up in business in London, and his musical tastes and talents were proverbial in the family.

Mrs Newman presents perhaps a somewhat more conventional personality. At any rate, she was of a more placid, more accommodating disposition than her husband. The many letters we have of hers betray the somewhat elaborate airs and graces that would have been the natural fruit of what, in those days, would have been considered a first-rate education. They give evidence, too, these letters, of warm-heartedness and delicacy of feeling, and of a more serene temperament than we find in the rather overbearing epistles of her husband, but with nothing to suggest, in her any more than in him, the least tendency to an exaggerated idealism. This is not to say that she was devoid of religious feeling, or that he too was not genuinely, if somewhat coldly, religious. Still, her religion was far removed from the rigid Calvinism which had doubtless been professed by her exiled family; as far removed from that, as it was from the evangelical fervours of the Rev. John Newton, the rector of St Benet Fink's, a spiritually enlightened gentleman who grated terribly on the nerves of Mr John Newman. The religion of both of them in its plainness, its power, and, perhaps we should add, in its poverty, was the middling Protestantism, the more or less colourless Anglicanism, which centred round the Bible and the Book of Common Prayer. We shall see, however, later on, what a more eager soul than either of these worthies was able to discover in it.

The Newmans did not have the Rev. John Newton for their pastor for very long after the birth of John Henry. The latter's earliest recollections were, not of Old Broad Street, but of Ham, near Richmond, whither his parents had removed some time before the battle of Trafalgar. Though John Henry was then but four years old, he told his sister Jemima, in a letter he wrote to her in 1861, that he remembered lying in his cot and gazing at the lighted candles that had been set in the windows in celebration of the victory of Trafalgar. This is perhaps the earliest of those cherished memories which he retained, with all their details clear-cut and undimmed, throughout the whole of his long life. Grey's Court, as the house at Ham was called, was vacated by the Newmans as early as 1807, yet few places, if any, left a deeper or more lasting impression on the child's mind. In the letter to his sister to which we just now referred, he declared that he could pass an examination on the house, although it was fifty-four years since he had been there. This accuracy of memory is the reflex of a correspondingly warm and profound attachment. The house at Ham, he tells his sister, had been ever in his dreams. Years afterwards, when he came to portray the typical humanist, one of the interlocutors in an imaginary dialogue on intellectual culture, the setting in which he framed him was none other than the beloved old house, called back to life by the mingled magic of memory and imagination.

The house, with its spacious garden, has been kindly dealt with by the passing years, and enough has been spared by devouring time for us to recognise and understand the magic charm of its old-world aspect. The place is now a school, but that in no way disturbs the childhood memories with which Newman peoples it for us. Though spacious and attractive, the Georgian mansion has no air of mystery about it, yet there is something in its clear and luminous symmetry that prepares us for the more appealing, more pensive, beauties of the enchanted garden. When Newman knew it, it lay amid beautiful country, stretching away from the soft-flowing river. Today, overtaken by the gangrenous excrescence of the ever-spreading metropolis, the place still retains enough of its old-fashioned grace to enable us to share in the visionary charm which the recollection of it never failed to awaken in Newman's mind. The magnificent plane-tree, on which the boy used to swing till his head began to turn, his gaze fixed on the patch of sky glimpsed between the luxuriant branches, still lives on, but it is bigger now than when he knew it. Later on, during the nightmares which haunted him at the end, the all but tragic end, of his sojourn in Sicily, the memory of those woods and copses, with their friendly and familiar ghosts, came back to him to comfort and console. That house and that garden were for him, all through his life, the enchanted home of a visionary childhood, even as the Lake Country was for Wordsworth; but with a charm more directly personal, more intimate, because of its narrower compass. When his thoughts turned to that far-off summer morning when he lay in bed listening to the ring of the scythe on the dewy lawn, it seemed to awaken in his mind thoughts of Paradise, of the Garden that would never fade.

Early memories like these, such a faculty for deriving from them, or reading into them, spiritual impressions such as that, reveal what an exceptional nature was his, even as a child. He himself has told us at the beginning of his *Apologia* of the ideas, not a little strange, that haunted him in his childhood days:

> I used to wish the Arabian Tales were true: my imagination ran on unknown influences, on magical powers and talismans. . . . I thought life might be a dream, or I an Angel, and all this world a deception, my fellow-angels, by a playful device, concealing themselves from me, and deceiving me with the semblance of a material world.

It is not only an innate power of imagination that those striking words reveal; it is, as it were, a direct and spontaneous vision of the invisible, more real to him even then, child though he was, than the visible; close to it, and discernible both in and beyond it.

This sense of the mysterious nature of the world, of the loneliness and isolation of the soul, was more than a mere poetic fancy. Far from that, the remarkable child was already aware of maleficent presences about him, and his ideas implied far more than the ordinary childish fears. "I was very superstitious", he tells us, "and for some time previous to my conversion (when I was fifteen) used constantly to cross myself on going into the dark." Very characteristic, too, is the tendency to fear (but for his religious faith it might have culminated in panic), with which he dwelt on the mystery, at first so alluring, of the fairy world.

From this green paradise, already threatened, the child was soon to be snatched away. In September 1807 the Newmans went to Brighton, but in the following February they were back in London, this time at

No. 17 Southampton Street. They had just settled in, when John Henry got the measles, and that meant quarantine. Soon after he was about again, he was sent, with his brother Charles, to a private school at Ealing, where he was to remain till December 1816. From Ealing he passed straight on to the University, so that he never had any experience of life at a Public School. He appears to have thought, judging by something he once said to his brother-in-law Thomas Mozley, that his Latinity, in consequence, suffered a little in ease and elegance. If so, it was made up for on the moral side. The brutality, to use no stronger term, which characterised the lives of schoolboys in some of the most highly reputed centres of education in those days, Newman was never fated to experience. Had he been called upon to do so, his sensibilities might possibly have become blunted enough to enable him to endure it. What is not so certain is that the process would not also have robbed him of some of that transparent delicacy which was one of his many lasting and distinctive characteristics.

The gifted child who, before he was five, was able to read the first letter—and a long one it was—which he received from his father, and who was evidently able to write, since, in the said letter, his father promised to send him a nice copy-book, soon came to be looked on as the "flyer" of the school. Its then headmaster, the Rev. George Nicholas, D.C.L., of Wadham College, Oxford, had greatly enhanced its reputation. That fact, and its being close to Richmond, where they had formerly lived, no doubt decided Mr and Mrs Newman to send their son there.

There, their eldest child, who was now seven years old, was just as shy and scared as any small boy of his temperament, suddenly thrust into a crowd of youngsters he did not know, and mostly older than himself, was likely to be. Hardly had his parents departed, when the headmaster found him in tears at the chaff he had endured, or expected to endure, from the other boys. The shyness remained, but it did not prevent him from quickly making his mark among his fellows, and displaying those qualities of leadership and charm which never left him.

Dr Nicholas afterwards used to say that no other pupil of his had ever run through the school curriculum at such a pace. In 1874 we find Newman amusing himself by assigning dates to the successive stages of his school career. By the 25th May, 1810, he was doing Ovid and the Greek grammar. By November he had gone on to Virgil. A day or two before his tenth birthday he started on Latin verse-composition and, about the same time, on the violin. Next year, after the Greek Testament, Homer swam into his ken, followed, in 1813, by Herodotus.

Although he much preferred to be alone with a book to joining in any of those games which the ordinary English schoolboy considers so important, we soon find him playing the ringleader, we might almost say the agitator, among his comrades. He must have been somewhere about eleven when he started a club, and a new magazine called *The Spy*, a variation, presumably his own, though not altogether a happy one, of Addison's *Spectator*. But—and here we see how loth he was to be shut up in one shell—he secretly brought out a rival, the *Anti-Spy*, alleged to be the organ of an opposing faction. A file in his room at the Oratory still contains a juvenile caricature drawn by a member of the opposing party. It represents a diminutive Newman, but already recognisable by his prominent nose, haranguing, notes in hand, a group of his adherents. Newman was very fond of speechifying after the parliamentary manner, a taste which his club gave him plenty of opportunities to indulge. He also conceived, at a very early age, a marked liking for the theatre. Every year, from 1813 till he left school, one of his greatest and most absorbing interests was the part he had been given to work up, and was in due course to enact, at the end of term. Successively sustaining the roles of Hegio in the *Phormio*, Pythias in the *Eunuchus*, Cyrus in the *Adelphi*, and Davus in the *Heautontimorumenos*, he acquired a love of Terence which he retained undiminished even in his very old age. The venerable Oratorian of the eighteen-sixties would spend many an hour coaching his pupils at Edgbaston in the parts he himself had played as a boy. Nor was he above imitating the style and language beloved of Erasmus when composing a prologue with topical allusions. Like many another stage-struck youngster, Newman was not content with seeing other people act, or even with acting himself. When he came home for the holidays, he persuaded all his brothers and sisters to take some part or other in plays and comedies of his own composition. In his fourteenth year he went one better; a complete comic-opera, of which words and music were both his own, was enacted by this little company of brothers and sisters.

After John Henry, five other children had been born in quick succession; Charles Robert in 1802, Harriet in 1803, Francis in 1805, Jemima in 1807, and Mary Sophia in 1809. Newman's whole life was so closely interwoven with these brothers and sisters of his that a few words about them, before we go any farther, may not be amiss. It was not merely on the stage that the eldest of them played the lead, nor was the influence of his precociously brilliant personality confined to the members of his own family. Wherever he went, people were swayed by it, whether they were aware of it or not. This is not to say there were not revolts in some quarters, some manifestations of resentment which, because they had been a long time smouldering, were all the more violent, all the more astounding, when they did break out. Francis, almost before his elder brother was in the grave, poured forth all the venom of his nature, a nature which his brother's brilliant reputation, the world-wide admiration with which he was regarded, had slowly turned to bitterness and gall. A strange production indeed, this book of Francis Newman! In it the meanest jealousies, the shoddiest envy, are found side by side with outbursts of reluctant admiration and gratitude, with here and there, a ray of searching and sagacious insight, the whole lumped together in a clumsy hotchpotch in which good sense and good taste are alike conspicuous by their absence. Though Francis was undoubtedly a great humanist, this piece of preposterous and unseemly invective seems to hint at some hidden flaw or gap in his practical, mundane mental equipment. The other boy, Charles Robert, a fantastic, unpredictable, unbalanced creature, fated to be the only matter of common concern between his two brothers, exhibited from time to time, in outbursts bordering on insanity, an incurable instability of which the germ was very possibly to be traced to the father. John Henry's extraordinarily delicate sensibility, and the singular gift of self-detachment which, paradoxically enough, went with it, may have been qualities of which the envy and malice of the one brother and the maladjusted disposition of the other were but the dark reverse.

As for the sisters, they present a set of temperaments of a charm in inverse ratio to their ages. Harriet, refined and lady-like, but not a little disposed to lay down the law, even to scold, and distinctly narrow-minded, was at once the most brilliant and the least attractive of the three. The fair and delicate Jemima was destined to be his staunchest friend, which made her subsequent inability to understand why he acted as he did all the harder to bear. Of Mary, as yet but a baby, we shall have more to say as our narrative proceeds. She was the first of those "angel faces" "loved long since, and lost awhile", of which Newman was to speak in that last mysterious line of his most moving poem.

If, picturing to ourselves Newman amid his home surroundings, we seek to discover what terms of affection and endearment passed between him and the other members of the family, we shall be disappointed. His schoolboy diary gives us little more than explosions of glee at the coming of the holidays; all very natural, but not very revealing. He himself preserved whole piles of the letters he had written home. Produced with scrupulous attention to penmanship, and couched in terms of becoming respect for his elders, they only tell us about the places he had been to, his school excursions, and even that in disappointingly impersonal terms. Apart from that, all we have relating to this period are some notes addressed to his sisters, rather superior in tone, the superiority being certainly no more than half-ironic, typical enough of the sort of thing a brother might write to his younger sisters in an average middle-class family, but not at all typical of Newman.

About his relations with other children, we know little; about his school friendships, nothing at all, not even whether he had any worth mentioning. But a few entries in his school-diary about one of the masters reveal a sensitiveness which he was at great pains to hide, and which he hid most successfully when he put on the air of the off-hand satirical pupil:

> 31st August: Laurie [the master in question] turned me east. For what? Ask him. 11th December: I and Mr Laurie very good friends. He took me up for a reward.

And a few days later, he writes a little song, in which he has a friendly dig at this same Mr Laurie. Of what little schoolboy drama have we here the hardly perceptible traces? An over-sensitive child afraid that he has been unjustly treated, or misunderstood, by his master; then the sudden outburst of joy when his fears are dispelled, and he gains, or maybe regains, the sympathy he has been longing for.

This is the first time we catch a glimpse of the tenderness of feeling that lay concealed beneath the mental agility, the delicacy of perception, the sparkling facility, the amazing depth of thought that characterised this reticent and possibly secretive lad.

Now, almost at the end of his schooldays, something was to happen to him, a sudden crisis was at hand, which was to lay bare the innermost soul of the young John Henry, to determine the path he was to take, and to leave its seal upon him for ever. It was what he himself used to call in after years his "conversion". He never ceased to regard this experience as the undoubted turning-point in his career.

II

THE CONVERSION OF 1816

THE year 1816 was one of bitter trial for the Newman family. One after-effect of the economic and financial upheaval which followed the termination of the Napoleonic wars was to compel the Banking House of Messrs Ramsbottom, Newman & Co. to stop payment. Many years later, Newman, hearing his friend Bowden alluding somewhat tactlessly to what he called the Bank's failure, reproved him rather sharply, pointing out that there had been no question of "failure". The Bank did suspend payment; that, he agreed, was true enough; but only for a time. Eventually, all the creditors were paid in full. That gives us some idea of the moral trials the Newmans had to bear, not to mention the material anxieties which beset them all through that spring. The letters exchanged between Mrs Newman and her sister-in-law Elizabeth afford eloquent testimony of the tribulations she had to endure.

Certainly, the creditors were quickly paid off, and the family, so far as money-matters were concerned, was soon on its feet again. At this juncture, however, Mr Newman took it into his head to give up banking and become a brewer. That meant yet another change of houses, and so, from the lanes of Norwood, off they go to Alton, so as to be near the brewing works of which the *paterfamilias* was now to take over the management. One result of all this unsettlement was that the Newmans found it convenient to leave their son at his boarding-school all through those summer holidays. The void of that solitary vacation was to be filled by his conversion. How that came about he himself has described in the autobiographical memoir of which Anne Mozley availed herself in preparing his letters for publication. The passage runs thus:

> On my conversion how the wisdom and goodness of God is discerned. I was going from school half a year sooner than I did. My staying arose from the 8th March. Thereby I was left at school by myself, my friends gone away.[1] That is, it was a time of reflection, and when the influences of Mr Mayers would have room to act upon me. Also I was terrified at the heavy hand of God which came down upon me.

[1] *Letters*, Vol. I, p. 17. Anne Mozley has cancelled what follows.

That last rather cryptic phrase is apparently the only piece of evidence there is to support a conjecture advanced by Maisie Ward. In her view, the words imply that Newman had been prepared for his conversion by the mental distress which the family misfortunes had caused him, and that, it must be confessed, seems to be the most plausible interpretation to put upon them, though there is nothing to corroborate it. At all events, what he himself considered most expressly providential about the whole affair was that it had resulted in his being left by himself at Ealing in close contact with Mr Mayers, thus bringing him under an influence which, if things had taken a different turn, he would never have experienced. The Rev. Walter Mayers, of Pembroke College, Oxford, was a master at the school. So far, all that had happened between him and his pupil was that the latter had collided rather sharply with the master's Evangelical brand of Christianity in various discussions they had had together, discussions which were enlivened for the pupil by his somewhat mischievous satisfaction in putting a "poser", when he could, to a master more pious than brilliant. Thoroughly to understand how, in the course of those lonely weeks, the clergyman came to be the means of bringing about so radical a change in the boy's mind, we must go back and look a little more closely into Newman's early religious training and endeavour to find out exactly where his own unaided reflections had brought him by the time with which we are dealing.

We have said that Mr Mayers was an Evangelical, and it has sometimes been assumed that the Newmans belonged to the same party. Nothing could be farther from the truth. A few years later they became acquainted with a Miss Giberne, a young woman who at that time was a typical Evangelical. Throughout her life, and it was a long one, she was to remain a true friend of the future Cardinal. However, the sort of impression we get from her first encounter with the Newmans gives a vivid idea of the gulf there was between them and herself.[1] This musical, literary, and, from her point of view, worldly family had nothing in common with her own ideals, notwithstanding the immediate liking she had taken to John, Francis, and their sisters.

What exactly are we to understand by the term "Evangelical"? To answer that question, we must try to get some sort of general idea of the Anglican Church as it was in the early part of the last century. From the seventeenth century onwards, it had been exposed to two divergent tendencies: the one, High Church; the other, Low

[1] See Maisie Ward's *Young Mr Newman*, p. 122.

Church. The High Church party set great store by Tradition—that is to say, by the Catholic, and by what, in those days, may have been still more important, the Royalist element which the term connotes. The others—the Low Church party—were all for the stark, uncompromising Protestantism of the Puritans and the Presbyterians, yet not going to the length of actually parting company with the Establishment. When the Deists were at the height of their power, it looked as if both parties were going to fuse together into a sort of religion which was hardly more than a vague philanthropy, but which still adhered to those conservative ideas of which the Church of England seemed to be the natural stronghold. Athwart this atmosphere of stagnation and inertia the voices of Wesley and Whitefield rang like a trumpet-call to arouse the people from their slumber. Had it not been for them, all definite belief, all religion in the strict sense of the word, might well have disappeared from England, and with it the State Church itself. Perhaps the most conspicuous characteristic of Wesleyanism in its early days was the overwhelming conviction that Christianity implied a new life. Hence the transcendent importance attached by the Methodists, as they came to be called, to "conversion". But conversion, new life, might be taken to mean merely such a moral reform as a man might bring about by his own efforts. What is distinctive about Wesleyanism is that it is concerned with an experience, a religious experience and one clearly recognisable from the nature of its onset. At a first glance, Methodism would appear to be a return to the Christianity of the Gospel as contrasted, not merely with rationalism but with the humanistic and philanthropical ideas then prevailing. Looked at from another angle, it reveals a close affinity with the sentimentalism that was so marked and so general a feature of the late eighteenth century. Still, it cannot be denied that in one way or another it links up with a Christian tradition dating back far earlier than the Reformation; with the love of the religious folk of the Middle Ages for the person of Jesus Christ. Viewed against a Moravian background, compared with the German Pietists and certain manifestations of primitive Lutheranism, Wesley's religion will be seen to have had more in common with Saint Bernard or with Saint Francis of Assisi than with the Scottish Calvinists or the English Puritans, for it is from a direct encounter of the soul with Jesus, with the Christ of the Gospels, that conversion is looked for. It was not a matter of a mere moral reform, which a man might claim to have brought about by his own efforts, but a gift bestowed by God. It is from Jesus, from Jesus acknowledged to be in the fullest sense the Son of God, the Saviour of the World, that the gift is to proceed.

It cannot therefore be denied that, notwithstanding its intrinsic intellectual insufficiencies, there is a core of sound doctrine at the heart of Methodism. But this cannot be dissociated from a particular kind of spiritual experience characteristic of the period. It is in the contemplation of Jesus as loving us and as shedding His blood for us that the Wesleyan gives himself to Him, and it is during an intense and passionate outpouring of the emotions that he attains to what he calls faith, by which he means the certain conviction that the blood of Jesus was shed for him, that it has cleansed him from his sins and made him a new man.

It was partly by force of circumstance, partly from their indifference to everything save this spiritual experience, far rather than from any definite separatist resolve, that the Wesleyans, after Wesley, and in spite of his desires, eventually cut themselves off from the Established Church. This, however, they did not do without leaving their own indelible mark upon it. The Evangelical party within the Church were a lasting witness to the effect Wesley had had upon it, and Wesley's influence still endures, albeit modified in various ways to bring it into closer harmony with the more traditional, less emotional, elements in Anglicanism.

For Evangelicals, conversion did not necessarily involve any of those violent paroxysms of emotion to be seen at the usual revivalist meetings. Emotion there was, but by conversion was generally signified the gradually growing conviction, the belief taking ever deeper and deeper root, that one had been saved by Jesus Christ. Such had been the experience of Thomas Scott, with whose writings Newman was now shortly to become acquainted, and of whom he declared many years later that he almost owed him his soul. Such, too, was conversion as understood by Mr Mayers, who was now to initiate his pupil into his own particular school of religious belief. Nothing, however, was more remote from the ideas in which Newman had been reared than this sentimental religiosity, even in the modified and milder form in which he was now to encounter it. How his family looked on the Christian religion he has described in a few words in the *Apologia*:

> I was brought up from a child to take great delight in reading the Bible; but I had no formed religious convictions till I was fifteen. Of course I had a perfect knowledge of my Catechism.

If we want to get a clear idea of what was in Newman's mind when he penned that brief *résumé*, it is perhaps conveyed at least implicitly, in the following passage, which we take from the *Grammar of Assent*:

> "Bible Religion" is both the recognised title and the best description of English religion. It consists not in rites or creeds, but mainly in having the Bible read in Church, in the family, and in private. Now I am far indeed from undervaluing that mere knowledge of Scripture which is imparted to the population thus promiscuously. At least in England, it has to a certain point made up for great and grievous losses in its Christianity. The reiteration again and again, in fixed course in the public service, of the words of inspired teachers under both covenants, and that in grave majestic English, has in matter of fact been to our people a vast benefit. It has attuned their minds to religious thoughts; it has given them a high moral standard; it has served them in associating religion with compositions which, even humanly considered, are among the most sublime and beautiful ever written; especially, it has impressed upon them the series of Divine Providences in behalf of man from his creation to his end, and, above all, the words, deeds, and sacred sufferings of Him in whom all the Providences of God centre.[1]

There we have without doubt the basis of Newman's religion: a high moral standard, a standard hallowed by the idea of Providence—that is to say, as Newman understood the word, by the presence of God, the all-seeing Witness and sovereign Actor in every circumstance of our daily lives. But as that is drawn wholly from the Bible, the reading of the Bible lends it an atmosphere of light and colour of a very special character, and what exactly that was we must endeavour to understand.

It is difficult for anyone who has never experienced it to form even a remote idea of what a religious training, founded wholly and solely on a study of the Bible, really is. For a thoughtful and imaginative child it results in a kind of supernatural humanism quite unique in its character. The world, human history, the life of mankind are bathed in a light that nothing henceforth avails to dim or extinguish. The presence of God, everywhere active, all-powerful, reigns over all things, animate and inanimate. Then there are those countless figures of Patriarchs, Prophets, Kings and Apostles, Saints and Sinners, or rather of sinners called to repentance, of Saints conscious of their sin, who, for such as are familiar with them, seem more real than the folk we meet every day.

Let us make no mistake about it, we have here the underlying

[1] Bk. 56–57.

stratum of Newman's spiritual nature, the lasting soil from which its fairest blossoms, its choicest fruits were to spring.

However all this may be the case with Protestant children in general, Newman adds two important particulars regarding himself. It was not any sort of Bible in which he was taught as a child to take delight. His Bible was King James's Bible, the celebrated Authorised Version, the outstanding landmark of English prose. He dwells on the grave majesty of its language, thus accounting for the incomparable and sacred charm which the Bible, merely as literature, never ceased to have for him from his childhood onwards. No doubt the Bible is the Word of God, and is always so, no matter into what tongue it is rendered. Nevertheless, those golden periods were well calculated to make him see in them the confirmation of the Bible's sacred character. Hence for him, as for many another, the fusion of Christianity with that Biblical humanism of which the Latin countries have scarce a notion, but which is so natural and so real an experience for the Anglo-Saxon and Germanic peoples. Finally, Newman gives us this additional indication of what Bible-reading is for an Anglican; it is not confined to a few passages selected in the light of individual fancy, nor does it range haphazard over the whole of the sacred text without scheme or plan. Thanks to the Prayer-Book lectionary it is Scripture in its entirety gradually unfolded in harmony with the rhythm of the Christian year. From the Cradle to the Cross, from the Cross to the Celestial Abode, the scene unfolded itself to the child John Henry like a pageant of unforgettable splendour.

If, over and above this general view of the matter, we would learn something of the more particular manner in which Newman was affected by his experience, we may profitably take note of what Anne Mozley has to tell us in an essay of no little insight and delicacy. In all probability it was not without guidance from Newman himself that she went gleaning among his sermons for the passages to which she refers, passages every one of which is unmistakably the record of some personal experience of his own. It is not always easy to determine how far Newman's sermons are to be regarded as the autobiography, or, shall we call it, the diary, of their author. Here, however, is a passage that can scarcely leave us in doubt:

> At first children do not know that they are responsible beings; but by degrees they not only feel that they are, but reflect on the great truth, and on what it implies. Some persons recollect a time as children when it fell on them to reflect what they were, whence they came, whither they tended,

> why they lived, what was required of them. The thought fell upon them long after they had heard and spoken of God; but at length they began to realise what they had heard, and they began to muse about themselves.[1]

Concerning this first discovery of the Divine Word, of the appeal it makes, is it not the child we hear speaking, though the words are the words of the man?

Let us consider this consciousness of self, which begins with a sense of being dependent on God, the sudden outcome of the patient pleading of God's words, in which the child's soul had bathed before its awakening. To the significant passage just quoted, Anne Mozley added another, and, in the whole of Newman, there is hardly one which we should be more inclined to describe as Proustian. It is of peculiar interest to us at this juncture because it shows us the belief which Newman was not only to retain, but steadily to develop, the belief in the spiritual treasure inherent in those childish experiences. From the mere contact with the Bible, the dawning soul, touched all unawares by Grace, is enriched with a treasure which, as long as life shall last, it will never lose or exhaust. One's thoughts revert, not only to Proust, as we ponder these things, but to Wordsworth and his *Ode on Intimations of Immortality drawn from Recollections of Early Childhood*. But with Newman the whole is set in a different key. For him, the invisible world is not substituted for the visible, but added to it, and hopes, hitherto vague and undefined, are now steadily focused on the expectation of the Divine Vision.

> Such are the feelings with which men often look back on their childhood, when any accident brings it vividly before them. Some relic or token of that early time, some spot, or some book, or a word, or a scent, or a sound, brings them back in memory to the first years of their discipleship, and then they see, what they could not know at the time, that God's Presence went with them and gave them rest. Nay, even now perhaps they are unable to discern fully what it was which made that time so bright and glorious. They are full of tender, affectionate thoughts towards those first years, but they do not know why. They think it is those very years which they yearn after, whereas it is the Presence of God which, as they now see, was then over them, which attracts them.[2]

We shall have occasion to return to this experience, so vivid in Newman's case, of Memory and of the Presence of God through it perceived. For the moment, we would remark that Wordsworth's sad lines about his passing from childhood to adolescence are equally applicable to Newman:

[1] *Parochial and Plain Sermons*, Vol. VI, p. 98.

[2] *Ibid.*, Vol. IV, p. 262.

Heaven lies about us in our infancy,
Shades of the prison-house begin to close
About the growing boy.

What, then, was it that had happened to this fifteen-year-old lad? The answer is precisely what was to happen or fail to happen again in the young man of ten years later. It was that the growth, the activity of his intellectual powers, had stifled his religious life. It was not that the intellect had seized on any particular argument against religion. It was rather a case of an intellectual attitude, a mental climate, inimical to that immediate sense of God as being Sovereign Lord of All, which afterwards came to be, and thenceforth always remained, an outstanding feature of Newman's faith. The youthful mind, confidently relying on its own powers, instinctively shrinks from the idea of any such dependence. The acceptance of a mystery beyond his comprehension, and that he feels, none more clearly, to be the whole of religion, strikes him as something he has grown out of, and left behind him. In the *Apologia* we read:

> When I was fourteen, I read Paine's Tracts against the Old Testament, and found pleasure in thinking of the objections that were contained in them. Also, I read some of Hume's Essays; and perhaps that on Miracles. So at least I gave my Father to understand; but perhaps it was a brag. Also I recollect copying out some French verses, perhaps Voltaire's in denial of the immortality of the soul, and saying to myself something like, "How dreadful, but how plausible."

Be it noted that this semi-scepticism, which had taken hold of the young lad's mind, was of a purely intellectual order. Morality was in no way questioned. Quite the reverse, in fact. The proud intellectual self-sufficiency which thus put God out of the picture, seems to go hand in hand with a corresponding self-reliance on the moral side. The autobiographical memoir records a note of an earlier day which makes that point quite clear:

> I recollect, in 1815 I believe, thinking that I should like to be virtuous, but not religious. There was something in the latter idea I did not like. Nor did I see the meaning of loving God. I recollect contending against Mr Mayers in favour of Pope's "Essay on Man". What, I contended, can be more free from objection than it? Does it not expressly inculcate "Virtue alone is happiness below".[1]

These entries are of the highest importance, not only as explaining the nature of his conversion, but for the light they throw upon his

[1] *Letters*, Vol. I, p. 19.

apologetical writings, from the *Oxford University Sermons* to the *Grammar of Assent*. When, sixty years later, Newman received the Red Hat, he summed up his life's work in a single phrase, when he said he had always fought against liberalism. What he meant by that term was the claim of man to do without God, to act by himself and for himself, whether it be a matter of comprehending the Universe or ordering his own life. The "reason" which, in the *University Sermons*, is contrasted in so definite a manner with "faith", is reason in which self-reliance amounts to pride, and which refuses, on principle, to rely on any power external to itself. It was reason in this sense of the word, and reason very much alive in the boy John Henry, that led him to turn away from Christ, not indeed in order to live a life of sensual indulgence, but rather to entrench himself in a virtuous independence that refuses to bow to anything or anybody.

How, then, are we to account for its bowing to the very ordinary intellectual gifts of the worthy ecclesiastic over whom, it is only too clear, the dialectical prowess of the child of genius scored some very easy victories. Newman has not explained (how, indeed, could he have explained?) the process by which his ideas, in this particular instance, underwent so complete a change. He does, however, give us to understand that it was not so much by his sermons or exhortations that Mayers influenced him, as by the books he gave him to read during those long weeks of inactivity in the year 1816.

We may take it, then, that Mayers impressed him more by his character than by his discourse, more by what he was than by what he said. Those victories which the pupil, doubtless too brilliant, too adroit for his master, had scored in their arguments, did not delude him. He who put virtue before religion must have recognised in a mind of a humbler order than his own, virtue of a different order from his own. And that probably is what led him to attach to Mayers' words an importance that his arguments as such would certainly not have earned them. That it was, as well as the necessity of finding something to fill up the time, that led the boy to tackle the somewhat austere books that were put into his hands. How these books of Mayers' affected him, Newman in a few succinct and striking words tells us in the *Apologia:*

> I fell under the influence of a definite Creed, and received into my intellect impressions of dogma, which, through God's mercy, have never been effaced or obscured.

Those words whet our curiosity still more to learn what books these were that were thus offered to this young, enquiring mind. And now a paradox awaits us. Of the first of them, Newman tells us that the main doctrine contained in it struck him very forcibly and at once commanded his assent. But he adds that he came to discard it later on, and long before his conversion to Catholicism. A few lines farther on he adds that he retained it till he was twenty-one, when it gradually faded away. The book alluded to was by Romaine, one of the few rigid Calvinists that were still numbered in the Evangelical fold. It will not surprise us to learn that the doctrine in question was that of final perseverance, conversion being regarded as a sudden consciousness, on the part of the convert, of his predestined salvation.

If it was a doctrine that converted him, how came Newman, who stressed the doctrinal and dogmatic character of his conversion, to write of it—of his conversion, that is to say—a few lines farther on, "I am still more certain of it than I am of having hands and feet"? Here we have a problem which, up to now, does not appear greatly to have exercised his biographers. Nevertheless, it must be evident that the importance ascribed by Newman to this conversion, definite and permanent as it was, cannot be satisfactorily explained so long as this problem remains unresolved. How could Newman attach such importance to a conversion which he himself describes as doctrinal in its nature, if the very doctrine by which he was converted was soon, despite the terms in which he had just alluded to it, to fade, and at last totally to disappear, from his mind? The answer to this question is implicitly conveyed in the very page of the *Apologia* which gave rise to it. In order, however, to make this clear, we must interpret the words of the *Apologia* in the light of a passage contained in the *Memoir*. We have now once again to hark back to an earlier period—as far back, in fact, as 1826.

> In the matter in question, that is conversion, my own feelings were *not* violent, but a returning to, a renewing of, principles, under the power of the Holy Spirit, which I had already felt, and in a measure acted on when young.

If we carefully bear that statement in mind, the passage from the *Apologia* which we shall now quote will need no explanation.

> I received it [the doctrine of final perseverance] at once, and believed that the inward conversion of which I was conscious (and of which I am still more certain than that I have hands and feet) would last into the next life, and that I was elected to eternal glory. I have no consciousness that this belief had any tendency whatever to lead me to be careless about pleasing God. I retained it till the age of twenty-one, when it gradually faded away;

> but I believe it had some influence on my opinions, in the direction of those childish imaginations which I have already mentioned, viz. in isolating me from the objects which surrounded me, in confirming me in my mistrust of the reality of material phenomena, and making me rest in the thought of two and two only absolute and luminously self-evident beings, myself and my Creator;—for while I considered myself predestined to salvation, my mind did not dwell upon others, as fancying them simply passed over, nor predestined to eternal death. I only thought of the mercy to myself.

We have already adverted, in the course of our narrative, to an idea very strange in a small child—the idea, namely, that he thought he might be an angel and all this world a deception, his fellow-angels by a playful device concealing themselves from him and deceiving him with the semblance of a material world. That passage readily recurs to our mind when Newman himself tells us that in the spring of 1816, reading a book by Isaac Watts which spoke of saints unrecognised by the world, he took it to be an allusion to that early notion of his, as if Watts was speaking of angels living in the world, but disguised. The first of the two passages we have quoted seems to furnish the clue to the second, and to explain its apparent contradictions. If the 1816 conversion, all-important though it was, was but a return to beliefs which he had already held as a child, if, rather, it was a revival, a renewal of them, we may well understand how it was that Romaine's doctrine took such a hold on him and affected him for so long, destined though it was gradually to fade and finally to disappear from his mind. The truth is, as he clearly indicates, that Romaine's doctrine merely acted as a catalytic, reviving in the mind of the adolescent a conviction, an idea prematurely implanted in the mind of the child. The sense of God's immediate and sovereign presence had been obliterated by the consciousness of his own growing intellectual powers. But now, behold! into a mind rendered mysteriously receptive by the solicitations of Divine Grace, there comes, to resuscitate that conviction, a wholly different doctrine operating in a manner that none but Newman could perceive. It would not only reawaken, it would transform, what, in the child, was merely a passive impression, into a reasoned belief that was destined to remain an enduring factor in the life of the man.

How can this be explained? The truth is that, in some degree, we read into a book what we bring to it ourselves. This is especially the case with young people of exceptional endowments. The books they read, particularly the things that fire their liveliest enthusiasm, are as often as not misunderstood by them. But these misinterpretations bear rich fruit. These young people have within them riches which, to begin with, they are unable to realise, to take account of; but a sentence, even a single word, will often avail to bring them to light. Thus it comes about that they think they have found something in a book which, later on, when they have had more experience of real life, they will, to their grievous disappointment, be quite unable to rediscover in it. The truth is that what they thought they had found in the book was something which they themselves had brought to it. The book and what it set forth was the steel which struck the spark from the flint; but the spark was theirs, and theirs alone.

So, no doubt, it was with Newman, and the call to a conversion conceived as the intuitive consciousness of an indefectible election was interpreted by him in his own way. Giving definite shape to a conception of the Universe hitherto vaguely floating in the subconscious imagination of the child, it suddenly projected it into the consciousness of the adult, now arrived at maturity.

The young man's intellectual powers were displaying themselves in all their sovereign pride, notwithstanding the importance he ascribed to virtue. Disquieted, it may be, by the obscurity which overhung the destiny of man, he was soon to be still more deeply moved by the truly Christian witness of his master, which he found strangely in harmony with the memories of his far-off childhood.

Those memories needed but the touch of some external stimulus to bring them once more to the surface and to be interpreted in the light of his now maturer understanding. The young man, in the fullness of his intellectual pride and self-sufficiency, now becomes aware of something, of some power, which he had dimly guessed at, even when he turned away from it. Something, Someone, stronger and more wise than he, Someone who subdued him to His will, even in the proudest hour of his intellectual self-reliance. To that other Power, the mind, be it never so proudly confident, must needs defer. The very clearness with which he recognises this is a token that he has already surrendered.

Interpreted thus, and we see no other way of doing equal justice to all the various views of it that he has given us, it is, to begin with, quite clear that his was no conversion after the Evangelical pattern. His association with an Evangelical of the milder type, his reading of Evangelical books may have been the means of bringing his conversion about, but, in its nature, it never really belonged to what was its occasion rather than its cause. This break in the chain of logical sequence escaped the notice of hasty or superficial observers. The docility displayed by the boy Newman in adopting the characteristic mode of speech and thought of those to whom his conversion was due, may to some extent account for the error, an error which was his own to begin with, the rest merely following suit. But with him, and in spite of Bremond, an error it was, and as such it must be recognised[1]:

> And in truth, much as he owed to the evangelical teaching, so it was, he never had been a genuine evangelical. The evangelical teaching, considered as a system and in what was peculiar to itself, had from the first failed to find a response in his own religious experience, as afterwards in his parochial. He had indeed been converted by it to a spiritual life, and so far his experience bore witness to its truth; but he had not been converted in that special way which it laid down as imperative, but so plainly against rule, as to make it very doubtful in the eyes of normal evangelicals whether he had really been converted at all.[2]

To put it briefly, what is principally notable about the conversion which thus robs him of his independence, is the independence which it nevertheless betrays. Just as it points, not so much to a change, as to a releasing, a rising to the surface, of something hidden in the profoundest recesses of his being, so too it shrinks instinctively from adopting all such fixed and definite forms as may suggest themselves or be suggested to him.

As a boy of fifteen most certainly would, he expresses his ideas and his feelings in the sort of terms he hears used by the people about him, at the same time adapting them to suit what he has in his own mind. As soon as experience shows him how inadequate they are, there will be nothing to prevent his dropping them. So far from that weakening his impression of what he has experienced, it will strengthen it. Let us now enquire more closely into the nature of that spiritual experience. What was it that was so personal about it, so peculiar to himself? And what rendered it so indifferent to the strongest influences brought to bear on it, even to those which were, or seemed to have been, its exciting cause?

But here a twofold snare awaits us. Either we may pass over the condensed and pregnant passage in the *Apologia* without fully penetrating to the precious metal within, or we may be tempted, as Newman himself may have been, to read into the experience of the boy all the things that entered into the maturer reflections of the man. This latter would be the lesser evil. There is no doubt that the extract in question, revealing as it does Newman's striking originality, also exemplifies the continuity of personality, its normal concomitant. Borrowing again

[1] Cf. Bremond, *The Mystery of Newman, passim.*

[2] *Autobiographical Memoir*, III, in *Autobiographical Writings*, Sheed & Ward, 1956, p. 79.

from Wordsworth, he seems to have been an outstanding example of those of whom it is said, "The Child is father of the Man." It is this independence, this pronounced individualism, which, before everything else, we must stress, and, if possible, define. Of all his various characteristics, is it not this that first demands our attention? It and it alone explains the mystery of his acceptance, so complete, so spontaneous, of Romaine's Calvinism; an acceptance which was, in fact, much rather an unconscious annexation. Moreover, we have here our first opportunity of examining Newman's undoubted individualism. If, taking it at its source, we succeed in avoiding any misapprehension of the goal at which it aimed, we may hope to avoid distorting it when, later on, we find it enriched but possibly subtilised by experience.

In the story, or rather the balance-sheet, presented by the *Apologia*, one phrase stands out beyond all others, "Making me rest in the thought of two and two only absolute and luminously self-evident beings, myself and my Creator."

"Myself and my Creator"—that theme, what elaborate variations Bremond composed on it! Variations that have found a responsive echo in the hearts of all who are unable to resist the spell of the enchanter. Alas! giving play to his gift for improvisation, Bremond began with the effect the words had on him, not, as he should have done, if he wanted to interpret them correctly, with the circumstances in which Newman came to utter them. If we now go back and take the only road permitted to the historian, we may find the enchanter vanished, and only a conjurer in his place. Still, the real Newman may even yet be disentangled from those verbal arabesques which were at least as well calculated to bury as to adorn him.

We do not hesitate to stress this point. The whole *Mystery of Newman* idea, which led Bremond to make of him a figure so engaging and so unreal, depends entirely on the interpretation put on those words. What he called in Newman "the Poet", "the Voluntary Recluse", and some others, less flatteringly, "the Misfit", "the Incurable Egoist", all arises from that interpretation. Were there any grounds for the idea, or did Bremond simply invent them? The enquiry to which we propose to address ourselves will go some way towards elucidating that crucial question. The state of mind in which this fifteen-year-old youth found himself at the beginning of summer in the year 1816 shows us that this apparent emphasis on "Myself" and the implied disregard of others, far from being centred in his religious experience had, in fact, no connection with it. On the contrary, it was the outcome, gradually set free, of all that was purely natural and, in the last analysis, a-religious in his personality. That there was in Newman a strong notion of self, of independence, of self-reliance cannot be denied; but to confuse this basic characteristic with his religious experience is to condemn oneself *a priori*, to a misunderstanding of the latter.

This consciousness of self, more astonishing, when we come to think of it, in the child than in the adolescent, has, no doubt, something disquieting about it, but let us not call it irreligious or immoral. It comes under the category of the "natural" in the strict sense of the word. It is, perhaps, that which constitutes the peculiar genius of Newman, if genius be an exceptional concentration, a more than ordinarily intense glow, in something that is no more than a natural attribute, or faculty, of the human mind. But that there is in it, from the religious, the Christian, point of view, an element of danger, of temptation, particularly in the case of one such as Newman, there is no denying. Let us remind ourselves of Goethe, who resembles him so closely in this respect. Was it not the firm resolve of his *daimon* to assert its independence and not to capitulate or bow to anyone or anything that at last drew him away from religion which, round about the year 1770, was attracting him so powerfully?

With Newman, things took a different course. What *he* found was that, when this independent spirit, this innate self-reliance of his, was brought into the presence of Another, of God, it meant nothing more nor less than the negation of meaning. How, then, did it come about that this "self", so adamant in its nature, was suddenly projected into the "self" of that Other and became wholly obedient to Him? That no doubt is the crux, the mysterious element in this conversion. Still some gleams of light are thrown on it in what Newman tells us and always held.

Let us now picture to ourselves this boy of fifteen, strong in the possession of an intelligence that enables him to expose fallacies, to detect sophistries and faulty reasoning, all those specious arguments by which ordinary folk are impressed, but which lack the hall-mark of indubitable truth. It does not appear that he was now, or that he ever had been, in any danger of falling into scepticism. An instinctive conviction, but a conviction confirmed by his intelligence, put the claims of morality beyond all question. If for a time he thought he could dispense with God, it never entered his head that he could disregard the Good, or the True.

Now whence came this moral sense? Evidently it was the fruit of his training, of the way he had been brought up, and especially of that Biblical instruction which taught him to connect truth and goodness by connecting both with God, with God to whose Word he listened. But now his intellect took hold, as part of its own belongings, of this union of truth and goodness. This union was now one with his affirmation of self. It was at this time that he fell in with a man, and heard words and read books, in which this twofold union in God reappears. Its effect was to make him recognise that what belonged to his consciousness, belonged in the first place to God; to put it plainly, it was the presence of God within himself; and this he realises even when, though not denying Him, he turns away from Him. Romaine speaks to him of predestination, of conversion, which implies the recognition that God is concerned with each one of us, and that from His purposes regarding us there is no escape. Little matters the system of which that is a part. What took hold of Newman and continued to hold him was the revelation that God was there, within him, in those very gifts (for they were His gifts, personal gifts, inseparable from the Giver), in those gifts which were his strength and support. It was as a ray of light amid the shadowy region from which his mind was emerging.

If it be true, as he was now beginning to feel that it was, that all complete consciousness of self is moral consciousness, he realised that moral consciousness is the consciousness, the awareness, of Someone, of God.

Let us ponder that well. Of that, even as a child, he had caught glimpses. Let us recall again the passage recently quoted, the passage about the child who suddenly became aware of religious truths on which he had been living without knowing it. Once more, as he himself bears witness, his conversion did not proceed from anything newly discovered. It was rather a rediscovery of something he had already known, something he thought he had left behind him, but which now, in the light of his maturer understanding, appeared as something fully, because freely and independently, thought out and established. Thus the words "Myself and my Creator" imply no more than the recognition that the soul only escapes from what is harmful to it, from what has been vainly endeavouring to enslave it, by discovering that it belongs wholly to God, and that it is truly itself only in the light of God's presence, God being its master, and the soul His, and His alone.

If this be a true account of what happened, if we may say of this unforgettable experience of this fifteen-year-old boy in a phrase which an old Oxford scholar applied to him some years later, in allusion to his love of solitude, *Nunquam minus solus quam cum solus*, we shall see that Newman in no way claimed to have been vouchsafed any sort of incommunicable intuition of God. On the contrary, the God who revealed Himself to him in solitude was the God defined by dogma in a course of teaching now for the first time fully understood, clearly recognised, the God of Holy Writ. With that Word he had been long familiar, though he had never been able to fathom its full meaning till he became aware of himself in the light of it. Thus it was not a mere discovery or rediscovery of God that he bore in remembrance. He tells us that God took possession of him in this direct and intimate manner, personal in the fullest sense implied by the words "Myself and my Creator", bringing him thus to realise and embrace defined dogma.

For it is as person to person that God reveals Himself.

It is as a person that God reveals Himself; it is in deeds in which He takes part, deeds which are destined to bring about a renewal of our own lives. It is as a duologue which enlightens us concerning our own existence by revealing on whom that existence depends. To discover God as the soul's Creator is, then, for Newman to recognise that that revelation is visible to us in His Son who is at the very heart of the Bible. It amounts to accepting, not as abstract ideas but as vital truths, the doctrine of the Incarnation and the Redemption, themselves dominated by the revelation of the Trinity. For it is thus that God becomes Someone for us, Someone to whom we belong, Someone who has given all, even His Son, to save us from our own disobedience.

As for the other concomitant of his conversion, the objective counterpart, without which the subjective considerations which have hitherto been engaging us would make the whole narrative seem like a dialogue with one of the speakers left out, there were the works of Thomas Scott. These provided him with something more lasting than the idea he got from Romaine. "To Scott," he says, "humanly speaking, I almost owe my soul."

Referring to his book, *Force of Truth*, which captivated him straight away, Newman enlarges better than we could do on all that he owed to this autobiography. It implanted in him the ineradicable conviction that fidelity to the living truth must naturally result in the acceptance of Christianity in all its gradually unfolding plenitude. Scott, in fact, tells us how, beginning as an unbeliever, he came to realise that without disobeying God and disregarding the dictates of conscience, he could not avoid traditional Christianity, the Church (which for him meant the Church of England), or belief in the Trinity. Was it not all like a preliminary sketch, or adumbration, of that *Odyssey*, or perhaps we should call it that spiritual *Æneid*, that was to be Newman's own story, when his guide and help were those prophetic words uttered by him during the illness that struck him down in Sicily, words to which before long we shall again recur—"I have not sinned against the light".

On that same page of the *Apologia*, a page whose wealth of significance it is hardly possible to exhaust, Newman confesses that what attracted him in Scott and in his account of his eventual acceptance of a progressively integrating Christianity, was what he calls his "bold unworldliness, and vigorous independence of mind". It is curious to note how the dearest aspirations of the adolescent, and those the most spontaneous, found their echo in this book, as he interpreted it. Scott became his hero. Such a spiritual adventure fascinated him as offering an example of that virile independence of mind at which he himself aimed—that, and a standard of moral rectitude which was destined to remain with him all his days. What exactly is it that he means by "this bold unworldliness"? It is precisely that intellectual freedom, on which his young mind had set such store, transferred to the ethical plane. It is the conviction, at once instinctive and reasoned, that the only way of maintaining complete spiritual and intellectual independence in this unintelligible and deceptive world lies in uncompromising fidelity to the voice of conscience.

How all things meet together and link up here! The free and independent quest for truth, unhesitating obedience to the voice of conscience, acceptance of the teaching of Christianity. This helps us to understand his joy at finding himself in accord with the essential elements in Scott's religion, as one by one he unfolded them.

They appeared to him, as to Scott himself, to be the pure and simple expression of the process which was destined to bring him also to the same religious goal: "Holiness rather than peace", and "Growth the only evidence of life".

In the sequence to which we referred just now—that is to say, the intellectual conscience, the moral conscience, and the recognition of God's sovereignty over the *ego*—we have, in embryo, the whole of Newman's apologetic. And now, in those two closely connected *motifs* of unworldliness and the search for perfect truth, as set forth under the twofold device, "Holiness rather than peace", "Growth the only evidence of life", we have something still better—we have, if not the whole, then at all events the kernel, of his spiritual being. Inasmuch as we shall meet with these ideas many a time hereafter, we shall refrain from elaborating any farther here our commentary on the spiritual experience which made that summer of 1816 ever memorable for Newman. The lengthy and minute analysis to which we thought it behoved us to submit those two pages of the *Apologia* will, we trust, at least have shown that Newman was under no delusion when, in after years, he declared that experience to have been the turning-point in his career.

And now the time had come for him to say good-bye to Ealing, and to take his leave of the worthy Mr Mayers. Bearing within him wealth thus acquired at the eleventh hour, it was to take him a lifetime gradually to enter into full and effective possession of the riches that now were his. He also took with him, as food for the journey, other books whose substance he was to assimilate in the course of the years to come. One of these was Milner's *Church History*, concerning which he says, "I was nothing short of enamoured of the long extracts from St Augustine, St Ambrose, and the other Fathers which I found there." Another, Newton *On the Prophecies*, which he read simultaneously with Milner, was to fill him with a profound abhorrence of Rome and the Papacy. As he himself confesses, these two books, though he did not suspect it at the time, were the seeds, the origin, of the first and greatest antinomy of his career. The attraction which Catholic Tradition had for him was henceforth fated to wage a secret conflict with the repulsion he felt for the institution which one day—and that day was not far off—he was to acknowledge as that Tradition's authentic guardian.

Before we prepare to set out with Newman on his journey from Ealing to Oxford, we must touch briefly on another matter concerning his inward life, an experience that followed hard upon his conversion. It is a matter about which Newman showed the greatest reserve. This, in the *Apologia*, is the only reference he makes to it:

> I am obliged to mention, though I do it with great reluctance, another deep imagination, which at this time, the autumn of 1816, took possession of me,—there can be no mistake about the fact; viz. that it would be the will of God that I should lead a single life. This anticipation, which has held its ground almost continually ever since, with the break of a month now and a month then, up to 1829, and after that date without any break at all,—was more or less connected with the notion, that my calling in life would require such a sacrifice as celibacy involved; as, for instance, missionary

work among the heathen, to which I had a great drawing for some years. It also strengthened my feeling of separation from the visible world, of which I have spoken above.[1]

We must not be misled by the brevity of that statement. The connection between his ideas about celibacy and his conversion is obvious, and the importance of its bearing on his subsequent spiritual evolution needs no emphasising. If Newman deals with the matter thus summarily, we must always bear in mind that the *Apologia* is not a book of confessions, a form of composition which his extreme reserve would have led him to regard with the utmost repugnance. The *Apologia* is, and claims to be, no more than a history of his religious opinions. But that he himself was perfectly aware of the importance of a decision, then more than provisionally contemplated, a passage in the original draft-manuscript of the *Apologia* makes abundantly clear. It consists of an explanatory passage of some length which Newman never sent to the printer. We give it in full. After the initial sentence of the passage just quoted, the manuscript continues:

> This anticipation has held its ground almost continuously ever since, and it has been closely connected with that feeling of dissociation from scenes about me, of which I have already spoken. I had a strong persuasion that offences against the rule of purity were each of them visited sharply and surely from above: I have still extant prayers and memoranda of the years 1816 and 1821, showing my distress at the thought of going to dances or to the theatre.
>
> This imagination, which I will speak of once for all, and then dismiss, was not founded on the Catholic belief of the moral superiority of the single life over the married, which I did not hold till many years afterwards, when I was taught it by Hurrell Froude. It arose from my feeling of separation from the visible world, and it was connected with a notion that my mission in life would require such a sacrifice as it involved. When I was first on the Oriel foundation it was associated in my mind with Missionary employment, or with duties at Oxford.

Here we omit a few lines. We shall give them later. They refer solely to his Oxford days, and have no bearing on his sixteenth year.

Evidently, this question of a celibate life, so early envisaged by Newman, has a twofold aspect. So profound, on the one hand, was his resolve to give himself wholly to God, that his earlier idea of entering on a missionary career recurred to him after his conversion almost as a matter of course. The idea of a missionary life, quite apart from strictly religious considerations, seemed necessarily to involve the

[1] *Apologia*, p. 7.

celibate state. But there was another side to the matter, which he himself mentions at the outset, and that was that celibacy was in harmony with that yearning for complete separation from the world which he appears to have experienced so spontaneously and so soon. Thus, the conviction that it would be a practical necessity for him to live a solitary life, reacted on the earlier sentiment, deepening it, and finally fixing it in his mind. Even now, however, we suspect that we are far from having plumbed the full depths of Newman's psychology.

III

THE OXFORD UNDERGRADUATE

No sooner had Newman finished his schooling at Ealing than his father decided to send him to a University. But which University? That was the question. The chaise, Newman tells us, was already at the door and still his father had not made up his mind whether to tell the postboy to make for Hounslow, or for the first stage on the road to Cambridge. The matter was settled at the last moment in favour of Oxford by the Rev. John Mullins, a curate of St James's, Piccadilly, who was accompanying them, and who hoped to secure John Henry's admission to his own college, Exeter. But at Exeter there was no vacancy. Consequently, on the advice of some friends of his, Mr Mullins took his two companions across to the other side of Broad Street, and very soon afterwards the young man was matriculated by Dr Lee, then Vice-Chancellor of the University, at Trinity College, of which he was President.

Back again next day at Ealing, he told his masters what had been decided on more or less by chance. If they had had any doubts as to the wisdom of their proceeding, Dr Nicholas at once dispelled them. "Trinity?" he said. "A most gentlemanlike College. I am much pleased to hear it."

Some people have been tempted to speculate as to what might have happened if Mr Newman had decided to send his son to Cambridge. Encountering there the Rev. Charles Simeon, who, from the pulpit of the University Church, was exerting the same sort of influence on the student population as Newman himself was later to exert at Oxford, would not the young man have been won over by the great Evangelical? If such had been the case, would there ever have been, we will not say an Oxford Movement, but any sort of Catholic revival at all in the nineteenth-century Church of England? It is not easy to say, but we may be permitted to doubt whether Newman's deep-rooted individuality, which even then was markedly evident, would have so readily succumbed. Be that as it may, the die was cast. Oxford, as he seemed to divine, almost as soon as he arrived there, was to be the inspirer of all his thoughts, of all his work. However, he was not at Oxford yet.

He had been duly entered at Trinity, but he was obliged to wait another six months before the place reserved for him became available.

The interval, he spent at home with his family, but we know little of what he did with his time during that period. What, however, is clear is that he was able to absorb at leisure the books which Mr Mayers had lent him. He did his best, not without success, to adopt the bearing and attitude of mind of a thoroughgoing Evangelical.

That this was not precisely suited to the tone of the family circle, and that a little tension occasionally resulted, an entry in his diary, almost certainly relating to this period, seems pretty clearly to reveal. It had reference to the worldly distractions in which, even according to the Evangelicals of the milder sort, such as Mr Mayers, "converted" people could not take part. The Newman family, though one could hardly call them frivolous, were evidently strangers to such rigid scruples.

> Although it is far from pleasant to give my reasons, inasmuch as I shall appear to set myself up, and to be censuring recreations and those who indulge in them, yet when I am urged to give them, I hope I shall never be ashamed of them; presenting my scruples with humility and due obedience to my parents; open to conviction, and ready to obey in a matter so dubious as this, and to act against my judgment if they command, thus satisfying at once my own conscience and them. . . . I have too much sense of my own weakness to answer for myself. The beginnings of sin are small, and is it not better, say, to be too cautious than too negligent? Besides, I know myself in some things better than you do; I have hidden faults, and if you knew them, so serious a protest would not appear to you strange. . . . I think those things of importance to myself; but I hope I am not so enthusiastic as to treat it as a concern of high religious importance.[1]

Reading between the lines, we seem to discern in these subtleties a hint that the outward and visible signs which denoted the inward and spiritual change were not always very warmly received at home. We imagine that there were counter-arguments, and that Mr Newman, in enunciating them, did not mince his words. But we also observe that John Henry, willing, nay eager, as he may have been to put into practice the lessons which had been inculcated upon him, did so with a certain amount of discretion and restraint. To take it for granted that, when he was thrown amongst Evangelicals, he immediately and completely adapted himself to the tone and manner of those about him would be undoubtedly an error.

So, too, the letters he wrote to Mr Mayers about the things he was

[1] *Letters*, Vol. I, pp. 19–20.

reading make it clear that, submissive as he may have been, his docility by no means obliterated his critical sense. One of the books which Mayers gave him was the *Private Thoughts* of Bishop Beveridge (1638–1708). Newman preserved the letter with which Mayers accompanied this present.[1] It seems to convey a hint of irritation on the part of the writer at having to deal with so argumentative a pupil. In giving him Beveridge, a seventeenth-century theologian who flourished long before Wesley, he designed to show him that Evangelical teaching in its essence was far from being a novelty, or having anything strange about it. The Bishop of St Asaph, even in his day, betrayed the same gravity of demeanour, the same sense of belonging to God, and of the obligations thereby entailed. Newman's reply shows that the book was likely to succeed in its purpose only too well. If Beveridge did, in fact, convince him that such things had been permanent features of Christianity at all times, he also directed his readers' attention to other elements of traditional Christianity which were far from finding favour with the Evangelicals. Newman instanced Baptismal regeneration. For the first time, it seems to have been borne in upon him that the gift of the Holy Spirit was not confined to conversion, in the Methodist sense, but that it might be bestowed, apart from any special individual experience, through the normal channels of Grace, the Sacraments. So great, in fact, was the enthusiasm which Beveridge aroused in him that, some sixty years later, we find him setting down the following remarks in the copy which had been given him by Mr Mayers, and in which the letter originally sent with it was still preserved.

> No book was more dear to me, or exercised a more powerful influence over my devotion and my habitual thoughts. In my private memoranda I even wrote in its style.

A subsequent note, appended to the remains of his youthful diary, comments with pitiless severity on that style.

> The unpleasant style in which it is written arises from my habit, from a boy, *to compose*. I seldom wrote without an eye to style, and since my taste was bad, my style was bad. I wrote in style as another might write in verse, or sing instead of speaking, or dance instead of walking. Also my evangelical tone contributed to its bad taste.

Apart from these notes and letters, the only products we have of this period of waiting, which must have been trying enough, are the

[1] The letter is printed on pp. 114–115 of the *Correspondence of J. H. Newman with Keble and others*, 1917.

drafts of the sermons which Newman composed at the beginning of 1817; these, too, are in the Beveridge style. We have but to read them over to catch the mingled flavour of an austerity rather suggestive of the neophyte (the neophyte of sixteen!), not only of a resolve to think and act for himself, as he had a right to do, whatever his parents might say, but also of a resolute determination to avoid what his father scornfully termed "enthusiasm". These are the texts in question:

1. Whoso eateth and drinketh unworthily.
2. Great things doeth He which we cannot comprehend.
3. These shall go into everlasting punishment.
4. Man is like to vanity, his days are as a shadow.
5. Let no one despise thy youth.
6. Let not sin therefore reign in your mortal bodies.
7. Thou, when thou fastest. . .[1]

The extremely grave tone of these titles recalls what Newman in the *Apologia* tells us of the influence Calvinism, with its sharp division between the elect and the world, exerted on him at this period. A conviction was implanted in him which he continued to regard as essential to Catholic Christianity, and that was the gulf that must necessarily exist between the "world" and the Christian community, an adumbration of the final and irrevocable choice between Heaven or Hell. In the same passage, he tells us how this impression was deepened and confirmed by his reading of Law's *Serious Call*. This work, by one of the most penetrating minds, one of the purest mystics, one of the foremost traditionalists in the Anglican Church, was among those which Mayers had recommended to him when he gave him Beveridge. In this way, his master had designed to impress him with the genealogical credentials of Evangelicalism which, however, Law, even more than Beveridge, led him to discard. However, it must be confessed that the freshman who, at last, went into residence at Trinity College in June 1817, must have cut a figure not a little out of the ordinary. To begin with, in spite of his prolonged wait, he was still little more than a child, but a child with powers of mind extraordinarily developed. Then again, his personality, so quickly matured, was fortified by the feeling that he had made his final choice between the warring powers which rend the world asunder. Adopting, with juvenile exactitude, the Augustinian scheme (or to put it simply, the Evangelical theory)

[1] *Letters*, Vol. I, p. 20, n.l. Note that at the end of No. 7, the text reads "Anoint thy head and wash thy face". Evidently it was quoted to shun all pharisaical ostentation.

of things—that is to say, the irreconcilable and unending conflict between the City of God and the City of the Evil One—the boy who found himself that June day in the lovely green quadrangle of Trinity, had thoroughly made up his mind to make no concession to the enemy.

Whatever stiffness, whatever constraint or self-opinionatedness there may have been in the young doctrinaire, the magic of Oxford came most opportunely to mitigate. Of course, he was going to yield nothing on matters of principle. Nevertheless, he instantly fell under the spell of his surroundings. At once, a new air, purer, ampler, an atmosphere full of grandeur and of beauty, was to charm him out of himself. Whatever trace of narrowness and sectarianism his religious fervour may have caught from the hearth at which it had been kindled, the enchanting city was soon to consume in the glow of its Attic radiance.

It is difficult now to give an idea of the charm that invested the Oxford of those days. That Oxford is there no longer. The encroachment of the industrial district of Cowley, the invasion of the omnibus, the formidable increase in the number of students, the progressive, though still incomplete, laicisation of the University itself—all these causes contribute to leave the city little more than the faint shadow of what it was in Newman's day, and, indeed, long after that. What is left, however, suffices to awaken, in any one who has been there, a nostalgia of such intensity as no other place evokes. Everything in this sanctuary of religion, of culture, and of art reaches a perfection that no other city can rival. In saying this, we must assign to those words a significance which perhaps they nowhere else convey. The beauty of the buildings and gardens of Oxford belongs to one of those rare and happy periods when art, all the arts, were blended into a single one, viz: the art of living. The setting, we grant, is perfection, provided always we divest the word of any suggestion of artifice. It were nearer the mark to say that it is a world apart, a world in which all things are so completely humanised that they seem to be the shrine of a spirit; that same spirit being, as it were, the sap, or quintessence, of an exquisite culture. The spirit of Antiquity and the spirit of Christianity are so subtly commingled there that it is not easy to determine what part is from Christ and what part the mind and experience of man have long and patiently outpoured upon it. Vittorino da Feltre, or Marsilio Ficino, or Erasmus would have found there a fulfilment of his wishes far more consonant with his desires than he would have discovered in the pagan luxuriance of Florence, or the chaotic grandeur of Rome.

The precious and tiny jewel which was the Oxford of old days was set within the bow-like curve of two hallowed streams, the Isis and the Cherwell. Halting along the straight line St Giles and St Aldate's, its buildings scarcely extended beyond the confined rectangle enclosed within the parallel thoroughfares of High Street and Broad Street. The vision of its towers and pinnacles, its cloisters, its gracious fanes, diversified with lawns enclosed by lofty trees fringing the river-line, all rose up from a beautiful landscape of wooded hills and valleys. At a dip in the road along the Thames, the traveller coming from London, like young Newman that fine June day, would catch sight of this city of the mind, without suburbs, almost without any private dwellings, nestling, like a jewel, in a setting of woodland, stream, and meadow.

As he crossed the bridge over the Cherwell, he would be greeted by the tall square tower of Magdalen, from whose summit, every May-day morning, a choir of boys chant a motet of Byrd's, saluting, like the children of Athens at the Thargelia, the coming of Spring and Summer.

Sicut lilia in transitu aquae, the lovely buildings of Magdalen, Gothic or Palladian, merge, on the one side with the broad parkland where the tame deer wander at will; on the other, they are bounded by the High Street, whose curve, as we make our way along it, discloses to view, successively, the somewhat grandiose colonnade of Queen's College, next, the elegant twin towers of All Souls, then the lofty, richly decorated spire of St Mary's, and beyond that again, the cupola of the Radcliffe Camera.

Opposite St Mary's, Oriel Street, a quiet narrow lane leads to the new quadrangle of Christ Church, whose symmetrical proportions remind one of Versailles. On the other side of the street stand the unpretentious buildings of Oriel College, which was destined to be Newman's second home; while, behind Oriel, stands the fine square tower of Merton which, though not so elegant as Magdalen's, rears itself majestically amid the surrounding verdure of Christ Church.

Wolsey's great college, where the stone carving of a Cardinal's hat recalls the memory of its founder, contains in its great, but still unfinished, cloister, the refectory, more spacious and more ecclesiastical-looking than a chapel, and the chapel itself, the chapel which is also the Cathedral, where Newman was, in due time, to receive his Anglican orders. On the other side of the quadrangle, which is enlivened by a fountain soaring up from a basin of Florentine design, we see the familiar outlines of Wren's Tom Tower from which the curfew is nightly rung. Passing through the porch, we come to St Aldate's, which leads across the High straight into Broad Street, and there we come upon St John's, an exquisite gem in the Renaissance style, which you might almost imagine had been transported from the banks of the Loire, so bright its radiance, and looking to some of us quite as much French as Elizabethan. Behind, stands Balliol, massive and stolid; then the main gate of Trinity.

There is, in the whole of Oxford, no college where you seem to find yourself more readily at home, more promptly at your ease. The graceful classical buildings, the chapel, half-covered with ivy, trees planted at irregular intervals, there is here an unstudied elegance which you will not find elsewhere. No sooner had Newman settled in and made himself at home, than he dashed off a letter to his people in tones bubbling over with almost boyish glee. After the long mental and spiritual strain of the last few months, it is a relief to find him so light-hearted, so readily delighted with the sights and experiences that come thronging so thick and fast upon him.

Everything enchanted him in this college life. There was his undergraduate's gown which, it seems, he thought a little too big. However, the tailor assured him it couldn't have been a better fit if it had been made for him. Besides, added the wily tradesman, he would go on growing. Then there was the first friend he made there. Little did he guess that he would turn out to be perhaps the best friend he ever had. John William Bowden was his name. His tutor, the Rev. Thomas Short, had sent Bowden along to instruct the newcomer in the ways of college life. He adds, incidentally, that from what Bowden told him about Short, he thought he was lucky to fall into his hands, Short being considered the most serious-minded of all the tutors (an impression which, as the future will show, was perhaps not wholly justified).

However, we have to confess that what most profoundly impressed this budding ascetic about the whole set-out was the decorum and the profusion of the dinners in Hall.

> At dinner I was much entertained with the novelty of the thing. Fish, flesh, and fowl, beautiful salmon, haunches of mutton, lamb, etc., fine strong beer; served up in old pewter plates and misshapen earthenware jugs. Tell Mama there were gooseberry, raspberry, and apricot pies. And in all this the joint did not go round, but there was such a profusion that scarcely two ate of the same. Neither do they sit according to their rank, but as they happen to come in.[1]

[1] *Autobiographical Memoir*, I, in *Autobiographical Writings*, p. 31.

Meanwhile, notwithstanding these excitements and distractions, he did not neglect his work. Indeed, he displayed an enthusiasm, in that respect, which, as he was soon to find out, was not one of the outstanding characteristics of the place, although Trinity happened at the time to be one of the colleges in which the intellectual level was relatively high. It must be borne in mind that he had not come up until the term was all but finished. The examinations were beginning, and the lectures were over. His own tutor had departed for the holidays without having had time to tell him what books to start on. In his innocence, the shy youth betook himself straight to the President, to ask his advice. After a prolonged and at first fruitless wait, he at last obtained an audience of this exalted personage. Amused at the eagerness of this student, who must have struck him as little more than a child, Dr Lee treated him not only with courtesy but with cordiality, though not, it may have been, without a touch of condescension. However, regarding what the young man had come about, he referred him to the tutors. That was all very well; but where *were* the tutors? His own had already gone, the others, if they had not followed him, were busy packing. So the novice went wandering about the college *quaerens quem devoret.* The day before his own departure, he encountered a don booted and spurred and already in the saddle, just heading for the country, whom he accosted. With the same easy urbanity as the President had displayed, this gentleman told him that he, too, was just off, but referred him to one of his colleagues who, it appeared, was not in such a desperate hurry. From him he obtained the information he was seeking.

His first encounters with his fellow-undergraduates were no less disconcerting, though in a different way. On the 16th June, four days later than the letter just quoted, he wrote to say, among other things, that the occupant of the adjoining rooms had asked him in to spend the evening. The one and only entertainment was wine-bibbing, a typically fashionable amusement in English upper-class society at the time, but not one calculated to commend itself to our young friend. He was thankful when the bell went for prayers, and he was able to hurry down to Chapel. There he discovered one of the prevalent failings of Oxford learned society at that period. Of certain dons the undergraduates used to say you could tell how much tipple they had swallowed in the Common Room by the fervour of their responses in Chapel.[1]

[1]*Loss and Gain*, p. 57.

On the 19th he had something of a more edifying character to report. From a favourable seat in the Sheldonian Theatre he managed to get a fine view of the Academic ceremonial:

> Tell Charles he would have liked to have seen the noblemen's dresses, as also the I-do-not-know-what-they-were—very fat men, I suppose DD's in red robes or scarlet, and the Proctors with sheep-skins. Mr Peel was made a Doctor of Laws by the Vice-Chancellor.[1]

All these splendours prelude the arrival of the vacation. On the 27th, another letter gives the news that he had presided at table, he being the only person present.[2] The same letter adds that he had already been taken some notice of, which rather scared him. The astonishing young man, landed there at the end of the year and forthwith plunging into his studies with an almost exaggerated ardour, was clearly not the sort of person to escape attention. He confessed to his parents that he had tired his eyes so much at the start that he simply could not read any more. The family scolded him about it, but now he assures them that he goes to bed early and is soon asleep. His stock of candles is so far almost intact.

If some things had not quite come up to his expectation in these early experiences of his, this did not prevent him from leaving Oxford after these preliminary weeks there, completely enamoured of the place. Later on, in his novel *Loss and Gain*, he was evidently recalling his own recollections when he wrote thus of his hero Charles Reding:

> When he came to Oxford, he came there with an enthusiasm so simple and warm as to be almost childish. He reverenced even the velvet of the Pro.; nay, the cocked hat which preceded the Preacher had its claim on his deferential regard. Without being himself a poet, he was in the season of poetry, in the sweet spring-time, when the year is most beautiful, because it is new. Novelty was beauty to a heart so open and cheerful as his; not only because it was novelty, and had its proper charm as such, but because when we first see things, we see them in a "gay confusion", which is a principal element of the poetical. As time goes on, and we number and sort and measure things—as we gain views—we advance towards philosophy and truth, but we recede from poetry.[3]

It was not until he went up again after the vacation that University life began for him in real earnest. At Trinity, as formerly at Ealing, it soon became evident that an exceptionally gifted person had come among them.

[1] Letter quoted by Maisie Ward, *Young Mr Newman*, p. 40.
[2] *Ibid.*
[3] *Loss and Gain*, p. 18.

On the 13th November, a letter home, a little quizzical in style, said that Mr Short, having been pretty off-hand with him to start with, was becoming increasingly impressed with his ability. He, Mr Short, said that his knowledge of mathematics, far from being below standard, put him well in front of the men he had to teach. Similar success attended his Latin composition.

Nor are picturesque details lacking. He had again so promptly and so completely buried himself in his studies that the death of a royal princess had taken place without his being aware of it. The whole University was supposed to go into mourning, but of that he had to be informed by a visit from his tailor, who called on him with an eye to business. A week later, another letter. He has clearly won the esteem of Mr Short, who has lent him a book and actually invited him to breakfast, which, at Oxford, is the meal to which one usually asks one or two particularly intimate friends. Another week passes, and this time the tutor is apologising because he can't provide him with a course of lectures up to his level. The advanced class which he got together out of the pick of his pupils, was soon reduced to two, Newman and one other; the other being that same Bowden who had been the first to call on him when he came up.

Newman and he very soon became fast friends. Their birthdays fell on the same date, but John William Bowden was three years Newman's senior. Francis once said of him that he was perhaps too tall for an Apollo, but the gentleness and modesty of his expression bespoke a Christian beauty such as he had never seen on the Greeks in the British Museum. From then onward, Newman and he were practically inseparable, taking their meals together, reading, walking, boating—nay, visiting each other's home in the vacations. On the day before his friend's untimely death in 1844, Newman wrote to Keble, "He is my oldest friend. I have been most intimate with him for about twenty-seven years. He was sent to call on me the day after I came into residence; he introduced me to college and University; he is the link between me and Oxford, I have ever known Oxford in him. In losing him I seem to lose Oxford."[1] He adds, "We used to live in each other's rooms as undergraduates, and men used to mistake our names and call us by each other's. When he married, he used to make a like mistake himself, and call me Elizabeth and her Newman."

Bowden was still more advanced in mathematics than Newman, and their association proved an additional stimulus to the latter's

[1] Quoted by H. Tristram, *Newman and his Friends*, p. 56.

studies. But, more than that, he helped him to find in Oxford the mental relief of which he stood so much in need, after the intellectual and spiritual cramming, so to call it, of his last year at Ealing and London. With Bowden, Newman enjoyed that familiar pleasure of Oxford men boating on the Cherwell, when reading, talking, or just idly meditating, amid those quiet, restful surroundings, is quite as much a part of the enjoyment as the rowing itself. They also frequently went bathing at Holywell. Francis, with a frankness not uncommon in brothers, would have it that John Henry did more paddling than swimming.

It was providential that Newman made friends with Bowden as soon as he came up, for his relations with the other undergraduates would have disheartened many a youth less shy than he. As soon as the new term began, they were at him again, doing their best, though unsuccessfully, to persuade him to join their drinking bouts. They tried to get him away from his work by bursting into his room and creating a wild uproar. They ragged him unmercifully about his fiddle-playing, which was pretty well his sole distraction. At last, his calmness, his self-control and his firm determination to be himself and to go his own way, wore down and put an end to these rowdy tactics. He had won. For some time after that no particular notice was taken of him, till, a little later, his success in the examinations made him at once the pride and the hope of the college.

There is no denying that at the end of the eighteenth century and the beginning of the nineteenth, Oxford was sunk in a deep conservative slumber, and blissfully unconscious of what was going on in the world outside. The system of studies had not been overhauled for ages. Not only that, but the tutors themselves took almost as little interest in the work as the pupils, who thought it quite enough if they acquired that tincture of classical culture that was expected of a gentleman, and resolved to have as good a time as possible in acquiring it. Those who had any interests outside the ordinary Common Room topics were few and far between. The majority were content with talking politics, Tory politics, emphasising their loyalty to the Establishment, or it may be discussing the college finances, salting their discourse with varying doses of Johnsonian wit. Dr Routh, the President of Magdalen, an antiquary and a first-rate scholar, was something of a phenomenon, and there is no denying that this dignitary, who went about from morning till night in full academicals, who, at the age of sixty-five or rather more entered into the bonds of matrimony, and who continued to discharge his duties as Head of his College till he departed this life in his hundredth year, was indeed a personage to excite remark.

Trinity, however, it was that was the first, or one of the first, to give signs of a desire to set its house in order. Newman soon became aware of this, and on the 28th November we find him writing home about it in a vein of proud satisfaction:

> If anyone wishes to study much, I believe there can be no college that will encourage him more than Trinity. It is wishing to rise in the University, and is rising fast. The scholarships were formerly open only to members of the College; last year, for the first time, they were thrown open to the whole University. In discipline it has become one of the strictest of the colleges. There are lamentations in every corner of the increasing rigour; it is laughable, but it is delightful to hear the groans of the oppressed.[1]

The scholarships, to which Newman alludes, were for sixty pounds a year for a period of nine years, and were supposed, in theory, to give the student a superior status. The cut of his gown distinguished him from the ordinary undergraduate. The fact was, however, that in the early part of the century, when studies were held in small esteem, scholars were more looked down on than honoured, their comrades regarding the monetary reward as a sort of charity; but the line taken by Trinity, as reported by Newman (who tells us also that Mr Short was at the back of it all), suggests a very different view of the matter.

Seeing the high opinion Short had so early conceived of this very young freshman, it is not surprising that he was anxious for him to try his luck. Newman, in principle, was quite ready to do so, and his own idea was to go in the following year; but one morning in early April, when he was having breakfast, and barely three weeks before the examination, he was sent for by his tutor. He found that gentleman in close conversation with another don, Wilson, who soon afterwards became President of Trinity. Both insisted that the young man, who was very much taken aback, should go up at once. At first he did not seem to think he stood a chance. All the same, he wrote home for his baptism certificate so that he might comply with the formalities imposed on all candidates. Meanwhile, he said nothing about his intentions, not wishing to raise false hopes.

Four competitors were in against him, one of whom, a Worcester man, was generally considered the favourite. The day arrives, and now behold him being put through his paces in Mathematics, English

[1] *Autobiographical Memoir,* I, in *Autobiographical Writings* p. 35.

Composition, Latin verse, translation and essay, a chorus from Euripides, passages from Plato, Lucretius, Xenophon, Livy. A letter written a day or two later describes the terrible suspense he felt waiting to hear the result. Trinity Monday arrives; the dons deliberate and cast their votes. At last, John Henry Newman is sent for by the Dean. Very pale, with beating heart, he went to present himself before the dread assembly. His mathematics, it appeared, had put the Worcester man completely in the shade. His head in a whirl at this unexpected success, he listened to the President delivering one of those solemn Latin orations which invest with a quasi-sacramental character each successive stage in an Oxford career. Then the same dignitary solemnly harangued the abashed but radiant youth. After that, the other dons shook hands with him, and he took his leave in the best of spirits.

With boyish glee he hurried off to the tailor's to purchase the scholar's gown which he was now entitled to wear. But hear what he himself says in a letter to his Mama: "Going out, before I had changed my gown, one of the candidates met me, and wanted to know if it was decided. What was I to say? It was. Who has got it? Oh, an in-college man. And I hurried away as fast as I could. On returning with my newly-earned gown, I met the whole set going to their respective homes. I didn't know what to do; I held my eyes down."

The rest of the letter shows how glowing were the vistas that this brilliant success opened up before him. Already he sees himself elected to a fellowship, when his scholarship has expired. This initial triumph set the seal on his allegiance, his lifelong allegiance, to Oxford. When the day came for him to bid farewell—an everlasting farewell, he then believed—to the beloved City, he thought on the snapdragon which grew in such profusion on the walls outside his freshman's rooms at Trinity; he recalled how he had then beheld in it an emblem of his perpetual residence, even unto death, in his university.[1]

However, that same Trinity Monday, in the year 1818, which had beheld his victory, was not only election day for fellows and scholars, it was also the College Gaudy. It was the custom that, the day before, all the college should attend Holy Communion; but there was another custom, no less firmly established, and that was, that on the evening of the same day all the men should be dead drunk.

Newman made his first Communion soon after he came up to Oxford, and he recorded the event in a special note in his diary:

A.C. Dec. Prid. Mane Eucharist. Sacr. accipio.

[1] *Apologia*, p. 237.

It will be remembered that, the year before, he had written, for his own personal edification, a whole sermon on "Unworthy Communions". We may well understand, therefore, how shocked and scandalised he must have been to see what he regarded as a glaring act of profanation repeated again and again, year in and year out. In 1819, he wrote Mr Mayers a letter on the subject, by far the most "Evangelical" he had ever penned.

All we need say is that the place and its principles, or lack of principles, had done nothing to change the young man's sentiments, or to blunt his conscience. Later on, when he became a don and a power in the place, his determination to put an end, if he could, to the perpetuation of this desecration, showed how profoundly he was moved by the scandalous nature of such proceedings. So deeply were his feelings stirred that, as we shall see later on, the ardour of his protest brought him for the first time into sharp collision with the Anglican authorities.

All this notwithstanding, this first academic success of his held out for Newman, at least for a time, a bright prospect of worldly advancement. The gleeful delight of the family circle at his intellectual prowess, contrasting so markedly with the frigidity with which they had regarded his "conversion", played a part in all this. Before the letter he had written announcing his success arrived at Alton, whither the family had now removed, the good news had already reached them, and his letter crossed with one from his mother to him. This read as follows:

> My dear Scholar,
>
> By this address you are informed that your mysterious news has flown to us . . . My mind is such a chaos of surprise, pleasure and hope that I can scarcely write to you.[1]

Quite possibly, too, Bowden's example encouraged him to pursue the mundane path. Bowden, who eventually obtained an important post in the Treasury, was now planning his career on definitely secular lines, although he fully shared the religious views and convictions of his friend. Moreover, it was in the hope that his son would choose an honourable calling for himself, preferably the Bar, that Mr Newman had sent him to Oxford. This preliminary success appears to have led the young man to acquiesce in his father's ideas, at least for a year or so. Early in 1819, he put his name down at Lincoln's Inn, During the same year, he attended professorial classes in modern history, simply because he had heard that the names of those present were passed on to

[1]Quoted by Maisie Ward, *Young Mr Newman*, p. 45.

the ministry. The years ahead, years of ambition, were to be also years of more strenuous toil than ever before; too strenuous, alas! for they were to end in a disastrous breakdown.

However, that was not yet. During the period of calm which followed his scholarship examination, he and Bowden went in for a few months of the sort of intellectual browsing which many students are accustomed to allow themselves after the strain of an exacting contest, and Newman read and studied without appearing to have any definite object in view. Gibbon and Locke were his great discoveries in the Long Vacation of 1818. The tragedies of Aeschylus, Aristotle's *Poetics*, a learned work on Herodotus, completely absorbed him.

His taste for personal essay-writing, a taste which we may almost call congenital, was now given full rein, though at that time the essay was not included in the examination syllabus. Thus it was that, purely for his own pleasure, he wrote an account of his views on Aeschylus, judged in the light of Aristotle's *Poetics*.

But he was to wander still farther from the prescribed track. In the winter of 1818–1819, jointly with Bowden, he started on a kind of versified romance in which Bowden was to be responsible for the historical and picturesque parts, and he for the theological. Whatever its merits or demerits as poetry, one thing it made clear, and that was the strength of his Protestant convictions at the time. But more than that, have we here a revival of that twofold taste for journalism *cum* mystification which had inspired the *Spy* and the *Anti-Spy* in his Ealing days? At any rate, in February 1819, the pair of them were busily engaged bringing out anonymously the first number of a new periodical which they called *The Undergraduate*. It was printed and offered for sale by an Oxford bookseller. However, someone divulged the identity of the editors. That gave the alarm, and the venture was abandoned. The same year, he became deeply interested in geology and, at the suggestion of Kinsey, then Dean of Trinity, he attended Buckland's lectures, though geology was not a subject he had to get up for his examination.

However, music was still, and was always to remain, his chief diversion. Apparently a taste for music was unusual in university circles in those days. But in England, however eccentric your tastes may be, you may be sure of finding someone to share them. He is to be found, with other enthusiasts, at chamber-music gatherings, and takes part in the performances. St John's College was the headquarters of the group. Writing to Harriet in February 1820, he tells her he has come across a don so devoted to music that they spent a whole evening, from seven o'clock to midnight, practising together.

He read a number of books that had nothing specifically academic about them. As far back as his Ealing days, he had been passionately devoted to Sir Walter Scott, eagerly devouring the Waverley Novels as they appeared (*Ivanhoe* belonged to those days). The early poets of the romantic school, such as Crabbe and, in particular, Southey, excited, strangely enough, his enthusiastic admiration.

Amid all this intellectual expansion, purely on the human plane as it is, the extraordinary power of inward vision, or rather the power of discerning the invisible through the visible, which had been his from childhood, gives a promise of what it was to become when he had had experience of life. Under date 21st March, 1819, the young man—he is now eighteen—enters this note in his diary:

> Sunday evening bells pealing. The pleasure of hearing them. It leads the mind to a longing after something, I know not what. It does not bring past years to remembrance; it does not bring anything. What does it do? We have a kind of longing after something dear to us, and well known to us—very soothing. Such is my feeling at this minute as I hear them.

But the B.A. examination was drawing near, and he must needs concentrate on matters of more immediate concern. During the summer of 1819, he started working without intermission. In order to carry out his programme, he scarcely left Oxford all through the vacation. When October came, he was already working eleven or twelve hours a day, allowing himself one hour for walking and one hour for dinner. He went on working at this rate, and even harder, up to the very eve of the examination which he was due to take in November 1820:

> I stayed in Oxford during the vacations, got up in winter and summer at five or six, hardly allowed myself time for my meals, and then ate, indeed, the bread of carefulness.[1]

This sort of thing was not very wise. The astonishing part about it is that his tutor, Mr Short, should have been so lax in supervising, and so ineffective in preparing, his pupil for the examination. It was not a mere pass, but an honours degree he was aiming at. This honours degree was instituted at the beginning of the century and was designed to qualify the candidate who obtained it for a high-ranking post, whether in the University itself, or in the Government service. Newman was extremely correct in all the references he makes in his autobiographical

[1] *Autobiographical Memoir*, I, in *Autobiographical Writings*, p. 46.

memoir to Mr Short; nevertheless, as Maisie Ward sees clearly enough, the latter gave him practically no useful advice as to what he should work at, and as to how he was to go about it. The manuscript explained that, as none of the Trinity tutors belonged to the Board of Examiners, their guidance was always more or less vague.

And yet, what hopes Mr Short entertained of this young, this exceptionally young, candidate! A reference to the matter in a note preserved by Newman calls it to mind:

> At Easter 1818 my Father came to Oxford and took me home with him. When we got to London, he determined to go with me to Dr Nicholas at Ealing, for he was quite overcome with Short's warmth about me. He said Short went to meet him as an old friend, and holding out his hands said, "O, Mr Newman, what have you given us in your son?" or words to that effect. This was before I got the scholarship.

Not only did this esteem persist, but it spread throughout the College. A stimulus it may have been, but for a highly strung person like Newman, it engendered a feeling of strain that must have been anything but helpful to one preparing for a difficult examination. We may judge his state of mind from a letter he wrote to Mayers in the autumn of 1820:

> The very few honours that have been taken by men of our college, the utter absence of first classes for the last ten years, the repeated failures which have occurred, and the late spirit of reading which has shown itself among us, render those who attempt this, objects of wonder, curiosity, speculation and anxiety. Five of us were going up for first classes this term; one has deferred his examination, one most likely goes up for no honours at all; one is expected to fail; one—whom I think most certain of success—may before the examination remove to another college; one remains. "Unless", I am told, "success at length attends on Trinity this examination, we have determined it is useless to read."
>
> The high expectations, too, that are formed of me; the confidence with which those who know nothing of me put down two first classes to my name; the monstrous notions they form of the closeness of my application, and, on the other hand, my consciousness of my own deficiencies—these things may create a smile, in my future life, to think I feared them, but they are sufficient to dismay me now. I fear much more from failure than I hope from success.[1]

We have only to remember the agony of suspense he went through at the previous examination to get an idea of what must have been his feelings on this occasion. Was it not a testing-time of far greater import to his future, seeing that it would make or mar him once for

[1] *Ibid.*, p. 47.

all, and that there was no second chance? It is, indeed, remarkable that the tutor, or tutors, who had so keenly urged him to aim as high as possible, should have lent him now such little and ineffectual aid. It appears, indeed, that, right up to the end, when he was putting such an incredible strain upon himself, he was working entirely unaided. Surely, the delicacy of his nervous system should, one would have thought, have prompted someone who was alive to the situation to intervene and persuade him to take things a little easier. A fainting fit which he had in chapel very soon after he came up might have warned people of what might happen to so delicate a constitution subjected to so severe a strain.

In this period of suspense, these days of alternating hopes and fears, it is deeply moving to observe the profound seriousness, but also the unfailing serenity, with which the youth, now insensibly emerging into manhood, regarded his ambitions before God. In August 1820, when he was reading his hardest at Oxford, he wrote this revealing and highly characteristic letter to his brother Francis:

> Here at Oxford I am most comfortable. The quiet and stillness of everything around me tends to calm and lull those emotions which the near prospect of my grand examination, and a heart too solicitous about fame and too fearful of failure, are continually striving to excite. I read very much, certainly, but God enables me to praise Him with joyful lips when I rise, and when I lie down, and when I wake in the night. For the calm happiness I enjoy I cannot feel thankful as I ought. How in my future life, if I do live, shall I look back with a sad smile at these days! It is my daily, and I hope heartfelt, prayer that I may not get any honours here if they are to be the least cause of sin to me. As the time approaches and I have laboured more at my books, the trial is greater.[1]

Writing at the same time to one of his sisters, he laid yet greater stress on his fear of thinking too much about success. He ended,

> I will not therefore ask for success, but for good.[2]

And then, just three weeks before the examination, still more anxiously and still more openly, since it was for his eyes alone, he penned the following note in his diary:

> The time draws near. I have had anguish in my mind. Yes, and all owing to my former sins. My soul would have been light and cheerful, I could have rested in the loving-kindness of the Lord, I should have been of good courage, but He seems to be threatening retribution, and my enemy takes occasion to exult over his prey.

[1] *Ibid.*, p. 46. [2] *Ibid.*

Yet, through the thick cloud of heaviness which is on my heart, the gracious Lord at intervals darts His beams and shows that He has not forsaken me.

However, on the eve of the fateful day, pitiless self-analyst that he was, he wrote these words to Mayers, in concluding the letter before quoted,

Still may I continue to pray, "Give me no honours here if they are to be the slightest cause of sin to my soul.'

But, while saying this, I often find that I am acting the part of a very hypocrite; I am buoyed up with the secret idea that, by thus leaving the event in the hands of God, when I pray, He may be induced, as a reward for so proper a spirit, to grant me my desire. Thus my prayer is a mockery.[1]

After all this, after so many ill-directed efforts, after so prolonged and severe a mental strain, small wonder that the unhappy John Henry found himself at the end of his tether when the day came round. He got his pass easily enough, on the 25th November. But honours, that was the thing; and here his exhaustion ended in a complete breakdown. The result was that his name appeared in the lower division of the second class. He had done his utmost to overcome his weakness all through the examination, but his brain seemed paralysed, and at last he had to give up the hopeless struggle.

The blow was a crushing one, at any rate to begin with. However, a few days later, this hyper-sensitive soul had got his emotions completely under control. A will flexible, but as unbreakable as steel, went through what it was to go through many and many a time later on in the course of his long and often sorely tried existence. Without trying to smother, or even to minimise, the severity of the blow, his will soon asserted its firm and unfaltering mastery over his emotions.

His first letter to his father—it is dated the 1st December—affords us an idea of what his feelings were, but it shows, too, how he had already made up his mind to put his troubles behind him.

It is all over, and I have not succeeded. The pain it gives me to inform you and my Mother of it, I cannot express. What I feel on my own account is indeed nothing at all, compared with the thought that I have disappointed you. And most willingly would I consent to a hundred times the sadness that now overshadows me, if so doing would save my mother and you from feeling vexation. I will not attempt to describe what I have gone through, but it is past away, and I feel quite lightened of a load. The examining masters were as kind as it was possible to be; but my nerves quite forsook me and I failed.[2]

[1] Maisie Ward's *Young Mr. Newman*, p. 52.

[2] *Letters*, Vol. I, p. 40.

The letter continues with a touch of irony for himself, to assure them that his reputation is safe.

Knowing only too well what his feelings must be, his mother wrote off at once to comfort him, telling him that the only thing that troubled them was that he himself should be troubled. With a spirited gesture of manly courage, the young man, pained to think he had let his feelings get the better of him, wrote back immediately:

> I am ashamed to think that anything I have said should have led you to suppose that I am at all pained on my own account. . . . I am perfectly convinced that there are few men in the college who do not feel for me more than I feel for myself. . . . I am sure success could not have made me happier than I am at present. . . . Very much I *have* gone through, but the clouds have passed away. . . . Since I have done my part I have gained what is good.[1]

The self-control of which these letters give evidence is the more remarkable seeing that that sensitive nature of his could never before have been so painfully and deeply stirred. Not every young man of nineteen would recover such complete serenity of mind within a week of sustaining so rude a shock. The feat implies an extraordinary degree of self-control, a singular power of self-detachment, very remarkable in one who has so often been portrayed as an example of morbid sensibility and incurable egoism.

But that is not all. Not only did he succeed in subduing his inward perturbation, but he forthwith set to work again, with a calmness and a clarity of vision and, more important still, a boldness to which his recent set-back seemed to have imparted all the more vigour. His failure made it doubtful whether he would be well advised to pursue the career his father had planned for him, and in which, for the time being, he had acquiesced. Now, however, his ideas definitely turned back towards the kind of religious work which had appealed to him at the time of his "conversion", and, in particular, some post, part clerical, part educational, at Oxford.

On the 11th January, 1821, he makes the following entry in his diary:

> My father this evening said I ought to make up my mind what I was to be, . . . so I chose; and determined on the Church. Thank God, this is what I have prayed for.

At the same time, in view of the fact that his scholarship had still

[1] *Letters*, Vol. I, p. 41.

several years to run, he determined, since affairs at home showed no sign of improvement, to take pupils as a private tutor. His younger brother Francis might be one, and in this way he hoped to relieve his parents of the whole burden of the boy's education. Mr Short was going to find him another pupil, at a hundred a year, and Bowden was to let him and his brother have some rooms which he himself had occupied. They were in a small house in the town, and had a restaurant attached, so that they would not have to go out to meals.

All this was thought out and definitely arranged in the early part of 1821, and came into operation in the ensuing October, as soon as the new term began.

It is remarkable, indeed surprising, to see how calmly, how serenely Newman comported himself during those months of waiting. In the first place, he took things quietly, occupying his mind with a variety of subjects, without, apparently, having any definite object in view. Then, when he was fully restored, when his mind and his nerves were again in proper working order, he quietly made up his mind as to what his next object should be. Compared with this latest enterprise, his trying for an honours degree was a matter of trivial importance. It was a University post he was aiming at. But what was it? Not by any means a Trinity fellowship, which he had once had in mind, and which, as a Trinity scholar, he might reasonably hope to gain from a board of understanding and well-disposed examiners. Not that. No; what he had his eye on was a College enjoying the highest intellectual reputation in all Oxford; a College where he was quite unknown, or known only as an unsuccessful competitor in an examination which, when all is said and done, was not after all such a formidable affair. No; what he had in mind, and what he was determined to try for, was an Oriel fellowship.

If, the year before, his friends and acquaintances had entertained extravagant hopes about him, hardly anyone thought he had the ghost of a chance this time. Nor was he himself under any illusion as to the forces arrayed against him. But he had the will to succeed, and he surveyed the situation with perfect equanimity. This so-called neurotic, this alleged creature of impulse, now bore himself with a coolness and a courage that did honour alike to his mental sagacity and to his moral determination.

The 12th April, 1822, was marked by an event at once the most auspicious and the most decisive that ever befell him. In a trice, the ill-starred student found himself in the company of the foremost men in Oxford, foremost, if not in their official position, at all events in intellectual prestige. Simultaneously, from three towers, the bells rang out proclaiming, far and wide, that John Henry Newman had just been elected a fellow of Oriel.

IV

THE FELLOW OF ORIEL

NEWMAN has described in detail the various circumstances that led him to try for an Oriel fellowship and how he triumphed in the end in a contest where everything seemed against him. We need not follow him in all these particulars, but it is important that we should profit by the light they throw on the attitude of mind which made Oriel and himself so mutually attractive to each other.

We have already remarked on the vital and, in a measure, instinctive wisdom which, in the months immediately following his reverse, led Newman to give rest to his mind and his nerves by taking up subjects of a more or less miscellaneous description. Now, in the course of the spring and summer, just as he had done after winning his Trinity scholarship, he devotes himself to whatever takes his fancy, without any idea as to whether, now or hereafter, it is going to serve him in an examination. Mineralogy, chemistry, the elements of musical composition take their turn, together with his first intensive and systematic study of the Scriptures.[1]

In this we may see, besides the salutary reaction of a mind anxious to regain its normal health and equilibrium, a further manifestation of that intellectual independence which always rendered any rigidly defined course of study distasteful to him. Whether it was the classics or theology that was in question, Newman was always the first to acknowledge that he was no expert. We should not interpret that as mere modesty or humility. If he was not an expert, it was because he had not wanted to be one. His genius was too free and, as it was soon to reveal itself, too creative, to endure the restrictions, the rigidly defined frontiers, which are the price the scholar has to pay for his strict but limited exactitude. Of that technique he will acquire, when circumstances demand it, just as much as he needs, and when that happens, he will show himself a match for any specialist he may have to deal with, and on the specialist's own ground. But nothing was more alien to his nature than pedantry in any shape or form. The gentleman he was to describe later on as the fine flower of intellectual culture,

[1] *Autobiographical Memoir*, II, in *Autobiographical Writings*, p. 54.

corresponds very closely to what we in France call an *honnête homme*, and principally in this, that the *honnête homme*, like the gentleman, is not given to blowing his own trumpet. Culture, in Newman's view of it, far from being a sort of intellectual craze, is merely a means of shaping a man, of investing him with a richer humanity.

It was the merit of the Oriel men to whom Newman offered his candidature that they chose him precisely on that account, and it was a merit rarely to be met with in University circles. This Newman had felt in advance, and it inspired him with a hope which the event fully justified.

Against the general decadence to which we have alluded as marking the Oxford of those days, the keenness of the Oriel men for intellectual advancement stands out in strong relief. However, it was not in the scholar as such, but in the man of wide general culture and enlightenment based on qualities of character on a par with his intellectual endowments, that the Oriel men looked to find the sort of candidate of whom they were in search.

The system had its drawbacks, for it exposed its practitioners to the reproach of favouritism. However, none were more fully aware than they of the delicacy of the decisions they had to make, decisions based on factors superior to, and sometimes quite dissociated from, purely academic attainments. They were fully conscious of the danger of allowing their judgment to be warped by personal considerations. However, they accepted this risk, hoping at any rate to exclude from their company those plentifully qualified nonentities who are the *caput mortuum* of even the most flourishing universities. It was particularly to their credit that they took such a line that year of all others. *The Edinburgh Review*, the chief organ of the Liberals, had recently discharged a weighty broadside against stagnation at Oxford. Oriel, notwithstanding its high intellectual reputation, was singled out as a particular offender, as practising a system of favouritism that was a sure bar to all progress. The writer of the article was the kind of person described as "brilliant"—brilliant, and nothing more. When, the year before, he had presented himself as a candidate for a fellowship, the Oriel authorities, true to their principles, had declined to elect him.

Copleston, the Provost, in a vigorous reply to the attack, did not omit to draw attention to certain objective considerations which told in favour of the Oriel system. The assailant's identity, which soon became common property, made it easy to retort on him that he, too, was allowing himself to be influenced by the very kind of personal considerations he affected to deplore. Nevertheless, Copleston's retort did reveal the existence of some shortcomings in the sphere of Science, which Newman had noted on his coming up. Oriel was not free from reproach on this score, and this was the point on which the Edinburgh Reviewers, fired with zeal for "progress", concentrated their attack.

Such being the prevailing atmosphere, it said a great deal for the courage of the Oriel authorities, and for the strength of their convictions, that they elected Newman at this juncture. To select a man who had come to grief in the honours school, to choose him in preference to a number of others, highly distinguished academically, might have been judged, not so much brave as foolhardy. But twenty years later we find Copleston still valiantly sticking to his guns.

> That defect which I always saw and lamented in examiners, and in vain endeavoured to remedy, still seems not only to exist but increases—the quackery of the schools. Every election to a fellowship which tends to discourage the narrow and almost the technical routine of public examinations, I consider as an important triumph. You remember Newman himself was an example. He was not even a good classical scholar, yet in mind and power of composition, and in taste and knowledge, he was decidedly superior to some competitors who were a class above him in the schools.[1]

The Oriel position could not be more clearly stated; it gave that college an unparalleled reputation in nineteenth-century Oxford. Nevertheless, there is no gainsaying that it ran counter to the tendency generally prevailing in other universities and teaching bodies at the time—the tendency, that is, to put technical and specialised instruction before culture; and so generally was this the case that the very conception of culture had been all but lost sight of.

When he presented himself as a candidate for an Oriel fellowship, Newman was in a position to reap the benefit of the wide and varied range of study, outside the prescribed routine, to which he had devoted himself ever since his serious reading began. Certain, too, it was that he would find his early-acquired habit of essay-writing a very considerable resource. However, the great thing was that his signal native endowments, enriched by a wide and original culture, were certain to attract the attention of the Oriel examiners, possessing, as they did, a wonderful gift for recognising genius when they saw it.

However, as the stern reality of the examination drew nearer and nearer, fainter and fainter grew his hopes of success. Well: anyhow, he would go on. If he failed, he would fail with honour, and that would

[1] Quoted pp. 64–65 of Vol. I of the *Letters*.

do something towards reinstating him in public esteem; besides that, he could try again another year. He had small hopes of succeeding, yet, in his heart of hearts, he did not rule out the possibility. When, however, the day came and he sat down with his papers in front of him and saw exactly what he had got to do, he felt a wave of optimism come over him that at once calmed and encouraged him:

> I have several times been much comforted yesterday and today by a motto in Oriel hall (in a coat of arms in a window), *Pie repone te*. I am now going to bed, and have been very calm the whole evening.[1]

Notwithstanding all that, there were times, during those fateful days, when he felt his heart sink so low that he was almost tempted to throw the whole thing up. On the third day, Mr Short, who was going to be out of Oxford for a time, asked him to come and see him. He went, very depressed, for he thought he had done so badly in the *viva* that he was already out of the running. Little did he suspect that, at that very moment, Short had good grounds for entertaining the highest hopes, The fact was he had just had a confidential visit. The examiners had been so favourably impressed with the way the unknown candidate had acquitted himself that three dons, acting on behalf of the others, had turned up at Trinity to try to find out something about the "dark horse" who had displayed such engaging capabilities. Short, though bubbling over with excitement, had, of course, to keep his mouth shut. He managed, however, to get Newman to give him some sort of an account of what he had written and said so far, and did his best to put fresh heart into him, not only by his encouraging words, but by making him sit down, then and there, to an excellent meal. Those lamb-cutlets came very opportunely to make up for his almost complete neglect of the inner-man during the ordeal. The upshot was that when Newman returned to his diary again, he was able to set down this simple sentence recording what was, perhaps, the happiest thing that had ever befallen him:

> This morning I have been elected fellow of Oriel.

He often told the story of how he received the great tidings. He was playing his fiddle when the Provost's butler came to make his portentous announcement. The messenger, thinking it appropriate to couch his message in terms that might have suited a character out of Dickens, said he feared he had some disagreeable news to impart, it was that Mr Newman had been elected a fellow of Oriel and that his presence

[1] *Letters*, Vol. I, p. 61.

was required there immediately. Newman, resenting what he considered a piece of unwarrantable familiarity, answered curtly, "Very well," and went on with his fiddling. The worthy butler, already considerably surprised at an occupation he had never yet seen indulged in by a fellow of Oriel, was so taken aback at this cool reception of his news, that he said he feared he had come to the wrong rooms. Quite calmly. Newman assured him that he had made no mistake. No sooner, however, had the butler, who, in all his long experience, had never seen or heard the like, taken his departure, than Newman flung down his fiddle, and a few moments later the shopkeepers in Broad Street, whom the sound of bell-ringing had brought to their doors, saw the tall, slender figure in cap and gown taking, for the first time, the road along which, for the next twenty years or more, he was so often to come and go.

The immense wave of delight that had swept over the young man to begin with, gave way to a feeling of timidity when, at the college—his own college now—he found himself being greeted as an equal by some of the most eminent men in Oxford. That same night he wrote to Bowden, saying:

> I could bear the congratulations of Copleston, but when Keble advanced to take my hand I quite shrank, and could have nearly shrunk into the floor, ashamed at so great an honour—however, I shall soon be used to this.

To his brother Charles he said:

> I took my seat in chapel, and dined with a large party in the Common Room. I sat next to Keble, and, as I had heard him represented, he is more like an undergraduate than the first man in Oxford; so perfectly unassuming and unaffected in his manner.

And, finally, to his father:

> I am absolutely a member of the Common Room; am called by them "Newman" and am abashed, and find I must soon learn to call them "Keble", "Hawkins", "Tyler".

Meanwhile, at Trinity, the excitement knew no bounds; it amounted to a sort of mass-hysteria. One man almost battered down his neighbour's door in his eagerness to proclaim the news. One elderly don frisked and capered like a young goat. People went rushing about all over the place shouting the news, and men who were reading hard for their examinations had to put aside their books for the rest of the day.[1]

When the first flush of victory was over, Newman wrote to his

[1] *Letters,* Vol. I, pp. 63–64.

aunt telling her the complete change which the event had brought about so suddenly in his circumstances:

> A month ago, everything was uncertain and dark as to my future prospects. I seemed to have no hopes in the University, I had few friends, no reputation, no provision for the morrow. I was sensible that everything I ate even, I had no idea how it was to be paid for. I knew that every day was adding to what was owing and I saw no quarter from which relief could come; as to getting a fellowship this year, when I examined it seriously and rationally, there seemed no chance. I had completely failed in the schools, I was looked down upon and nearly despised by those who heard I was a competitor for the Oriel Election. I had not been attending either to classics or mathematics the last year—the other candidates were men who had taken high honours and came *fresh* from the schools and scholastic reading. Yet by that Heavenly Arm before which the most difficult things are as nothing, I was in an instant secured in comfort and tranquillity. He rolled away every barrier, He dispelled every cloud. In the morning everything was uncertain, and by noon everything was sure and settled.[1]

The fact that his material position and his academic future were now assured was a great advantage; still greater, however, was the enrichment that would accrue to him from his association with Oriel, or, to put it in other words, from his integration into that intellectual and ecclesiastical society which was made up of the fellows of the College, and of which the Common Room was the customary rendezvous.

The last surviving relic, in the Europe of those days, of those intellectual monasteries, the collegiate establishments of the Middle Ages, the colleges of Oxford and Cambridge still retained their unique character. The furnishings of the Common Room had a sort of old-fashioned comfort about them. Here, from time out of mind, groups of intellectual bachelors had been accustomed to forgather, men of a type hardly to be met with elsewhere. At Oriel, in those days, the members of the Common Room were personalities of quite unusual distinction.

We have seen that it was Keble who made the deepest impression on the newly elected fellow, not so much on account of his academic attainments, brilliant as these were, as by the unselfishness with which, after a few years, he had given up his rooms in college to go and take over the duties of a small and remote country parish. That simplicity of character, by which Newman had been so struck, combined with an astonishing youthfulness of mind and heart, may have led him to behold in Keble one in whom the highest intellectual gifts and attain-

[1] Unpublished letter dated 28th April, 1822.

ments were ideally united with complete devotion to the inward and spiritual life, and to the cure of souls.

Nevertheless, during these earlier years, when Keble's visits to the College were few and of brief duration, it was not he, but a very different sort of personage, who had the greatest influence on Newman. Influence, perhaps, is hardly the word. It would be nearer the mark to say that he took him in hand and, to use his own expression, "licked him into shape". This mentor whom he had not seen the first day (most likely he was not there—he had recently married and was preparing to depart for some parish in Suffolk) was Whately, the future Archbishop of Dublin.

Oxford Common Rooms often harboured a strange assortment of personalities, people with queer idiosyncrasies which, however, were studiously respected. As a rule they were tempered and kept under control by social laws which, though unwritten, no one would have dreamed of transgressing. But Whately, with lofty composure, ignoring them all, wearing whatever sort of clothes took his fancy, talking in loud, penetrating tones in places accustomed to an almost cloistral silence, a great lover of dogs and horses, altogether alarmingly unconventional, had little or nothing of the typical don about him. Among the Provost and fellows, Copleston, Davison, Hawkins, Arnold (the famous Dr Arnold, who was shortly to go to Rugby, and whom Newman in fact succeeded), Whately stood out as the centre of a group, or clique, who had already come to be nicknamed the Noëtics. Equally critical, equally ironical at the expense of High Church or Low (the former, Whately called the Sadducees, the latter, the Pharisees), the Oriel Noëtics were to found a new party in the Church of England. Indeed, critical, aristocratic, and strongly attached to tradition though they were, they were destined, though no one then suspected it, to give rise to two new and divergent tendencies, the one Latitudinarian, the other Catholic. Sympathising, though distantly and condescendingly, with the Evangelicals in their endeavour to bring about a revival of religion, unsparing in their sarcastic references to the stiff and arid High and Dry, the Noëtics subjected every proposition to the most pitiless cross-examination. However, the questioners were too much given to self-criticism to acquiesce in a facile scepticism. There is something about this, about this penchant for a sort of enlightened traditionalism, that suggests an analogy with our Montaigne and his *Apologie de Raymond de Sebonde*. There is something that hints at a desire to gain credit by reverting, with strictly logical safeguards, to ideas which had come to be regarded as reactionary. Whately himself had composed, with a brand of humour decidedly British, a widely read work which, in the year 1819, appeared under the title, *Historical doubts concerning Napoleon Buonaparte*. The Higher Criticism of the eighteenth century (and of the nineteenth, too) is held up to ridicule in these pages with super-Voltairian derision. Whately pretends to demonstrate beyond all doubt that this Napoleon, who rises in the East and sets in the West, is nothing more nor less than the Sun, and the twelve Marshals, who attend him in his progress, the twelve signs of the Zodiac.

In ways strongly contrasting with these, the other members of the group were well qualified to rival him in shrewdness of judgment and originality of approach, in a wide diversity of subjects. It was impossible to make any statement in this company of profound thinkers and brilliant dialecticians, without its being held up to criticism from every point of view, and subjected to the most relentless of dialectical tests.

Launched thus abruptly into a *milieu* so different from any to which he had hitherto been accustomed, Newman, overcome with shyness, enveloped himself in a cloak of unvarying silence, which, seeing the cordial welcome they had given him, caused his colleagues some misgiving. His Evangelical tone and style, his odd taste for music combined with his uncouth taciturnity, led them to wonder whether they had not made a bad bargain after all.

Nevertheless, there was something about the place, about its whole atmosphere, that strongly appealed to him. If, as some people declared, it "stank of logic", the only intoxication to be found there was intoxication of the intellect. The Common-Room teapot was a byword all over Oxford, and undergraduates going down Oriel Lane used to shout out to the porter and ask him if the kettle was boiling.

It must be added that some of his other Evangelical scruples were not greatly appreciated. There is an entry in his journal to the effect that he will soon have to impress on his colleagues that he cannot agree to profane the Sabbath; which, in plain language, means, no doubt, that he feels he ought not to dawdle away his Sundays over cups of tea, talking at large about anything and everything. Then again at Oriel, as indeed in the other colleges, a pretty high standard of living, inherited from the eighteenth century, was kept up, and this may have caused Newman, with his plain middle-class upbringing, to feel a little like a fish out of water. At one of his first dinners—he had to attend them in knee-breeches—he received from the Provost, a typical specimen of the elderly church dignitary, learned and lordly, a stinging rebuke about the way he served the sweetbreads.

Things of that sort were hardly calculated to put at his ease a highly-strung introvert like Newman. But, quite apart from all that, his sudden introduction into a society of profound thinkers and brilliant talkers must have told for some considerable time on a mind that till then had always been more prone to meditation than to argument.

Whately, however, had taken his measure at a glance, and taken it accurately. It so happened that there was nothing he liked better than playing the part of Socrates—of course, his own reading of that character—delivering himself of home-truths, dealing not a few shrewd thrusts, but all with perfect good humour. When some of his colleagues suggested his taking Newman in hand, he set to work to lick him into shape, and teach him, as he put it, to let himself be held up by one leg without yelling, like dogs of King Charles's breed.

About his relations with Whately and their walks together by the Cherwell, their rides about the countryside, Newman afterwards said:

> While I was still awkward and timid in 1822, he took me by the hand, and acted towards me the part of a gentle and encouraging instructor. He, emphatically, opened my mind, and taught me to think and use my reason.[1]

Newman was a good listener. From the opening word or two, he grasped the speaker's drift, not only what he was saying, but even what he was going to say. An incessant talker, yet acutely sensitive to the slightest reactions of his listener, Whately declared himself delighted. He hardly knew anyone, he was soon telling his colleagues, with such a clear intelligence. His liveliness and "go", his good-humoured provocativeness, brought Newman completely out of his shell. Given this sort of good-natured shake-up, compelled to stand up for himself, taken up short at the first word or two, then forced to go on and say what was in his mind, this brusque handling braced him up and gave him more confidence in himself than he had ever felt before. A few years later, a treatise on logic appeared of which the greater part was written by Newman from material furnished by Whately, and the book did, in fact, come out under Whately's name. It was Whately who put Newman in the way of writing his earliest published works. He got him to write a series of articles for the *Encyclopaedia Metropolitana*, in particular, one on Cicero. While he was thus engaged, Newman worked his hardest to improve his own scholarship, and

[1] *Apologia*, p. 11.

before very long he had men reading for their examinations under his direction. Copleston, the author of some remarkable *Praelectiones* on Latin style, was a great help to him. Meanwhile, his own private pupils made him more keenly aware of his shortcomings than anything else could have done. Long afterwards, he noted down in the margin of his diary for the winter of 1822–1823, that "a little wretch aged 17" brought home to him how little he knew of Greek and Latin. Another instance of the delight young people take in pointing out the shortcomings of their teachers.

In those early years at Oriel, however, it was not Whately, too seldom present, that had the greatest influence upon him; still less the majestic Copleston, who, even in his unbending moments, had something august and remote about him. There was another don, Hawkins, to whom, as he freely avowed, he was indebted for some still more important acquisitions.

By his quasi-Socratic handling of him, Whately brought him out and enlarged his ideas. Hawkins gave them clarity and balance. Hawkins was twelve years Newman's senior. As he was Vicar of St Mary's, he had perforce to remain in Oxford throughout vacation time, just as Newman was obliged to do when, shortly afterwards, he became curate at St Clements. The pair of them, alone in hall and Common Room, could hardly help comparing notes, exchanging confidences. Newman's lack of experience in parochial work, and his need of someone familiar with such duties to instruct him, was quite enough to bring about a close relationship between the two men. Some problem or other connected with his work in the parish would prompt the young curate to mention the matter when they were having their cup of tea together. The Vicar, riper in years and experience, would readily respond, and so perhaps a whole evening would go by. Practical problems soon brought up theological ones, which they discussed in the course of their walks together. The upshot was that Hawkins, being the older man, became practically Newman's second tutor, and a far more profitable one than Sharp.[1]

Among the Noëtics, Hawkins, though not so conspicuous a figure as Whately, was no less remarkable in his way, and no one could have found the vagaries and eccentricities of the future Archbishop less to his taste than he. Some years later, he succeeded Copleston as Provost, and the story is told that, on word being brought to him that a man had met with a fatal accident in the quadrangle below, he

[1] *Autobiographical Memoir*, III, in *Autobiographical Writings*, p. 77.

stopped to put on his gown before going down to investigate. It will not therefore be surprising to learn that he counselled deliberation, caution and the need for taking a carefully balanced view of things—and all this on the man whom Whately had whisked away on the sort of intellectual steeplechase in which he himself loved to indulge.

> He was the first who taught me to weigh my words, and to be cautious in my statements. He led me to that mode of limiting and clearing my sense in discussion and in controversy, and of distinguishing between cognate ideas, and of obviating mistakes by anticipation, which to my surprise, has been since considered, even in quarters friendly to me, to savour of the polemics of Rome.[1]

Most important of all, Hawkins rendered him the invaluable service of criticising with the strictest severity his first literary productions. We may take it, therefore, that it is to Hawkins that we are largely indebted for that luminous simplicity, that unerring precision of expression, which distinguish Newman's prose in its great days, so far removed from the rhetorical embellishments of his earlier compositions.

But there is something else, something far more valuable than logical reasoning and elegant composition, that he got from Hawkins. He was the first personal and living influence to develop in him the notion of a religion richer and more world-embracing than Evangelicalism, though some foreshadowings of it had been awakened in him by his incursions into the works of Beveridge and William Law. The doctrine that Baptism is the fountain of grace within us (instead of the Methodists' "conversion"), which, it will be remembered, he had already encountered in Beveridge, was the first of those which Hawkins succeeded in fixing in his mind.

The first sermon Newman ever preached gave Hawkins his opening. Newman, a novice in the pulpit, and still a very young man, dwelt on the main doctrine he had derived from Mayers—the doctrine, namely, which divides the whole human race into converted and unconverted, the former being absolute Light, the latter absolute Darkness. Hawkins read the sermon, and immediately submitted it to some very drastic criticism. He showed its author how complex the state of mind of the vast majority of Christians really is, and added that of this his own practical experiences would soon convince him. He pointed out that St Paul never divided his flock into two separate categories, but considered them all "in Christ", "sanctified in Him" and as all "having the Holy Ghost in their hearts". That did not

[1] *Apologia*, p. 8.

prevent the Apostle from pointing out all manner of irregularities and scandalous defects among them. From this it was to be deduced that the gifts of grace were not the effect of a single, direct, and final psychological experience. No; the traditional doctrine of Baptismal Regeneration, of Grace conferred at Baptism and received wholly by faith, without any sensible manifestation of its coming, on the one hand, and calling for an effort continued through life on the other, was alike in conformity with the teaching of Scripture and the facts of experience. Next, to drive home what he had told him, Hawkins lent him the *Treatise on Apostolical Preaching* by Sumner, afterwards Archbishop of Canterbury. What he read there, and his talks with his colleague, combined with his early parochial activities and experiences, led to a complete revision of his views on Christianity.

The question of personal regeneration, so essential to the Protestant view, he came in due course, still thanks to Hawkins, to examine in relation to a still wider question, to which hitherto he had devoted no attention, and that was the Church.

With a foresight that does him credit, Hawkins was among the first of religious thinkers in England to realise what a serious blow the higher criticism of the nineteenth century was fated to deal at the Bible, or rather at the British view of the Bible. But prior to that, he indicated to Newman, as the only way to counter it, a view of the Bible that would take it from its "splendid isolation", and put it in its rightful setting—that is to say, the Church.

It was not only the principle of Tradition that the future Provost instilled into his young companion, but a personal and carefully considered conception of it, which became, and always remained, the basis of Newman's ideas on the subject. This conception he had set forth in a notable sermon which Newman in his undergraduate days had listened to without, at the time, realising its importance. Presented with a copy later on by its author, he studied it carefully, and no doubt discussed it with him. From this sermon he got this fundamental idea—the idea, namely, that the normal channel of Christian truth is not the Bible, but the Church. The Bible presupposes the existence of a teaching medium. The Bible furnishes that teaching-body with the necessary bases and *criteria*, but it can in no way take its place, or perform its functions.

These views, which Whately shared, widely as in many respects he differed from Hawkins,[1] were, as the years went on and his intimacy

[1] He indeed it was who had suggested to Hawkins his sermon on Tradition.

with Newman grew closer, to be still further developed by him. Whately was the first clearly to impress upon Newman the idea that the Church, founded by Christ, was not the *Civitas Platonica* of Saved Souls, but a visible and organised body. This, in common with the other elements of Catholic teaching which lead up to it, came to the Noëtics from the Anglican divines of the seventeenth century. What, however, was an original corollary of Whately's own, and very faintly implicit in the High Church traditions, was that the Church should be independent of the State, that she should brook no interference by the temporal power in her own affairs. This view was elicited by a vigorous and clear-sighted criticism of the lamentable state of things which the contrary doctrine of Hooker and other Anglican theologians had brought about. Newman was certainly not at fault in discerning therein the idea that was at the heart of the whole Tractarian Movement.

Tradition, a visible Church conceived as a purely religious institution, and certainly not as one Department of State among many others—all these ideas are to be traced back to one original source, the doctrine of Apostolical Succession. It was another fellow of Oriel, though one less in the foreground than those we have mentioned—the Rev. William James—who made him acquainted with it, probably about 1823. Long afterwards, Newman recalled how James had expounded it to him in a walk round Christ Church meadow, and how he had been rather impatient of the subject at the time. All these ideas, new to him, that were now called back to life by the strikingly characteristic treatment of the Noëtics, were to be pressed home to him still more effectively by an experience which he was now shortly to undergo. We have already touched upon it when commenting upon his first parochial appointment.

In May 1824,[1] Newman, anxious to undertake all the duties imposed by the Holy Orders to which he was now about to submit himself, took the post of curate at St Clement's, an outlying parish on the far side of Magdalen Bridge. On the 13th June, he received Deacon's Orders and at once went to place himself at the disposal of the octogenarian vicar. His immediate task was to try to get into touch with a number of parishioners who had transferred their allegiance to dissenting bodies of various kinds or, in some cases, to the public house, having found the Established Church not very forthcoming. Here it was, at St Clement's, that he preached those first sermons of his which he

[1] According to his *Memoranda*, the exact date was the 16th.

showed to Hawkins and which Hawkins so searchingly criticised. More important, however, than that, it was when paying his frequent visits to the general run of his parishioners, where he met with all manner of lukewarmness, half-belief and sectarian error, that the unreality of the Evangelical system was borne in upon him.

The result was that he now became fully aware of something he had already dimly apprehended, and that was that his own conversion was in no way bound up with any such artificial theory. What is more, he came to see how unreasonable it was to presume to gauge the spirituality of any Christian soul by deciding whether it had, or had not, passed through a psychological experience of a certain particular character. He came to know some whose claim to consider themselves saved was nothing but a monstrous delusion. On the other hand, he met with some in whom the workings of grace were plainly discernible, though they were far from having passed through any experience at all resembling the Evangelical notion of conversion. The Church, transcendent yet visible, the objectivity of the gifts of God proclaimed in the Gospel and made accessible to us through the sacraments—these new conceptions were borne in upon him at an opportune moment, replacing, as they did, a Christianity based on vague imaginings by a religion adapted to the world of realities, a world with all its meannesses, and all its grandeur, both alike unsuspected. In like manner the true Christian life began to reveal itself to him, not as the fruit of a single isolated spiritual experience, but as involving, day by day, a self-devotion constantly renewed in faith and obedience to a divine Word, independent of any human words.

The ideas he derived from these talks with his colleagues, confirmed and developed as they were by the books they lent him—all this, combined with his own experience in the cure of souls, and the practical nature of the Church's office—enabled him to distinguish his own religious intuitions from the nebulous Evangelicalism in which those intuitions had at first been merged. If for a long time an undefined but instinctive feeling had been leading him to realise that the two, the intuitions and Evangelicalism, had to be separated long before that impression was confirmed by circumstances, nevertheless, those circumstances, when at length they *did* arise, were slow in producing all the results that might have been expected from them. Here, we may aptly draw attention to the measured and deliberate evolution of Newman's ideas, as well as to what we may call its homogeneous character. Throughout the whole of his spiritual history there are manifest a profound continuity and necessity which arise from the fact that never did man more consistently combine a docile willingness to accept the teaching that came to him from without, with a downright determination to bring his whole mind and soul to bear on all matters in which the interests of truth were involved.

From the outset he had been apprehensive of a tendency, on the part of the Evangelicals, to adopt an air of superior enlightenment, combined with a sort of vague sentimentality. His father had done his best to put him on his guard against this kind of thing. Newman, while not agreeing with the sweeping condemnation pronounced by that worthy man, did feel a certain amount of sympathy with his disapproval of their exaggerated revivalistic displays. Of the discussions that took place after his reverse in the schools, discussions which resulted in his deciding to take Orders, his autobiographical memoir contains some piquant details. As a rule, when she encountered anything which she considered struck too personal a note, Anne Mozley was not sparing with the scissors; she was not sparing with them here. It will be worth while to restore her excisions.[1]

It appears that the whole affair arose from an article contributed by Newman to an Evangelical periodical, an article which had considerably stirred the parental bile:

> I understand, he said to his son, that you have been writing for the *Christian Observer*. Well; my opinion of the *Christian Observer* is that it is a humbug.

After such an arresting exordium, it may well be imagined that the succeeding discussion was not lacking in savour. The father blamed his son for yielding to a morbid sensibility, and to a state of mental irritability that might become dangerous. He earnestly advised him not to go compromising himself by saying things he might soon have cause to regret. He prophesied that in a year or two's time he would have completely changed his views. Newman, ironical at his own expense, notes that, when the conversation was over, after praying to be preserved from illusion, pride and uncharitableness, he wrote down in his diary:

> How good is God to give me the "assurance of hope"! If anyone had prophesied to me confidently that I should change my opinions, and I was not convinced of the impossibility, what anguish I should feel!

[1] *Letters,* Vol. I, p.111. Cf. *Autobiographical Memoir*, III, as given in full in *Autobiographical Writings*, p. 82.

Then he added:

> Yet a very few years passed, before, against his confident expectations, his Father's words about him came true.

At this point Anne Mozley thinks it her duty to cut him short. However, in the original, there follow these highly significant observations:

> His Father spoke from his general knowledge of the world, and had he known his son's character thoroughly, he would have had a still greater right to anticipate a change in the religious views of the youth whom he so much loved and was so anxious about. For, as has been said above, the critical peculiarities of evangelical religion had never been congenial to him, though he had fancied he held them. Its emotional and feverish devotion and its tumultuous experiences were foreign to his nature, which indeed was even conspicuously faulty in the opposite direction, as being in a way incapable, as if physically, of enthusiasm, however legitimate and guarded.

The importance of that passage is self-evident, self-evident from two points of view which, though different, are nevertheless complementary. It shows how profound was the cleavage which afterwards brought about his final break with the Evangelicals. But it also shows how profoundly aware Newman was—and, indeed, always remained—that it was owing to his association with these same Evangelicals that he learnt and grasped some of the elements of authentic Christianity. Hence the difficulty he experienced in breaking away from a system he had once accepted *en bloc*. All this goes to show how seriously, after his conversion, he was impressed by the things of God. No more question now of modifying his *Credo* for purely intellectual motives. For him to accept these, and to act upon them, they had to be more than merely intellectual conclusions, they had to be absorbed into the depths of his being and made one with his experience as a whole. Despite, therefore, the unsettling effect of the arguments of the Noëtics, we need not be surprised that it took him so long to throw off the ideas and general tone he had derived from Mayers and his school. Nothing could offer a more revealing commentary on those ideas, so slow to disappear, and on his reluctance to modify his very Protestant suspicion of anything that came from the High Church party, than the circumstances which marked the opening stages of one of his most eventful friendships.

A few months after Newman's election, another fellowship fell vacant at Oriel, and on the 4th April, 1823, Edward Bouverie Pusey was selected to fill it.

Pusey was but one year older than Newman, but he was one of

those men who seem never to have been young. His deeply religious nature, his impressive learning, as well, we may take it, as his obvious kindheartedness, at once drew Newman to him. About Pusey, however, there was nothing at all of the Evangelical. With unconscious condescension, Newman started praying for his conversion. Then, after a talk which had given him an insight into Pusey's sincerely religious character, he hurriedly jotted down this entry—it is dated the 17th May—in his diary, the *naïveté* and pathetically sectarian tone of which drew from him many years later a lively comment. This was the note:

> That Pusey is Thine, O Lord, how can I doubt? His deep views of the Pastoral Office, his high ideas of the spiritual rest of the Sabbath, his devotional spirit, his love of the Scriptures, his firmness and zeal, all testify to the operation of the Holy Ghost; yet I fear he is prejudiced against Thy children.

When they had met, a little over a month before, he began to pray that Pusey, evidently by conversion, might be brought "into the true Church", that is to say, into the invisible Church of the Elect. This time, however, he added:

> Let me never be eager to convert him to a *party* or to a form of *opinion*. Lead us both on in the way of Thy commandments. What am I that I should be so blest in my near associates?

That marked some progress, but if Whately could have seen those words of his young colleague, the word "Pharisee" would probably have again risen to his lips. However, on the 15th March of the ensuing year, after a number of walks with Pusey, when one of the favourite topics, and one always uppermost in Newman's mind, was that of a missionary career, one more conversation on the same theme was to dispose of his last remaining Evangelical prejudices.

> We went along the lower London road, crossed to Cowley, and, coming back, just before we arrived at Magdalen Bridge turnpike, he expressed to me. . . .

At this point Newman suppresses what he himself considered an over-intimate confidence. Then, he goes on:

> Oh, what words shall I use? My heart is full. How should I be humbled to the dust! What importance I think myself of! My deeds, my abilities, my writings! Whereas he is humility itself, and gentleness, and love, and zeal, and self-devotion. Bless him with Thy fullest gifts, and grant me to imitate him.

From this friendship, then, he learned that a High Churchman, albeit "unconverted", might be a saint; while his parochial experiences told him that a Methodist, calmly assured of his own salvation, might be the most complacent of self-deluded egoists. Now, then, the time was ripe for Sumner's book and Hawkins's words of counsel to gather in their fruit.

During the same period, while preparing for Orders, he became acquainted with a prominent member of the High Church party. This was Dr Lloyd, Regius Professor of Divinity and Canon of Christ Church. He had been to Pusey to some extent what Whately had been to him. Lloyd and Whately, however, were commonly held to represent the two most opposite types in Oxford. If Whately was all for striking out on a purely personal and independent line, Lloyd took a malicious pleasure in professing the most rigid and inflexible orthodoxy. This Whately countered with a typically daring jest. Orthodoxy, he declared, was your own doxy, heterodoxy was the other man's.[1]

Lloyd was deeply versed in Christian antiquity, and was undoubtedly a better scholar than Whately. Moreover, and this is still more noteworthy, his teaching method, whatever the subject, was no less Socratic, no less original than that of his public opponent. For those of his students who were preparing for ordination, he organised, in addition to the regular course of lectures, what might be called a study-group, or reading-circle. Passages were read out and then discussed, and everyone was not merely invited but peremptorily required to state his views on the matter at issue.

Well aware that Newman was reputed to be an Evangelical, this burly and decidedly John Bull-ish individual kept marching up and down among the students, his wig all awry, making the most dreadful but good-natured grimaces at Newman. Did he know, or did he not, how interested Newman had once been in the Fathers of the Church? Anyhow, he reawakened that interest and brought back to life all the old longing to know them at first hand. Between a couple of pinches of snuff, he would pretend to punch the heretic on the jaw, or to box his ears; but in the end he came to agree with Whately in his admiring recognition of his pupil's, as yet unelicited, talents. Nevertheless, it does not appear that these lectures, on whose highly technical character Newman remarks, started him off on any new principles, any more than did the mutual regard between them, which endured through the professor's episcopate, which his premature death brought to so untimely

[1] Newman repeated this quip with an indulgent smile. He did not know that in current slang, with which Whately was thoroughly well acquainted, "doxy" meant a drab.

an end. Moreover, it was through a book, and not through any direct personal influence, that Newman began to familiarise himself with the great school of Anglican traditionalism. It was in 1825, the year of his ordination to the priesthood, that he set himself to read Butler's *Analogy*. It is not easy, in a few words, to describe the scope of this work; still less to give the reader any idea of the effect it had, not only on Newman, but on most of those who took part in the Tractarian Movement.

Butler's great book, published in 1732, is one of those famous works which may be described as always up to date, or, better perhaps, as exempt from age. It breathes the very spirit of the theologians of the previous century, the Caroline divines, as they are called, and it contains in germ most of the ideas which, in their full development, were to constitute Newman's chief claim to originality. At the same time, though in no polemical tone, and without any specific reference to his own time, his real concern, from beginning to end, is with the eighteenth century's particular brand of incredulity. Furthermore, it is not one of those books of which it suffices to say that they have been long and carefully thought out. It would be more correctly described as the harvest of a lifetime of thought stored up bit by bit between the covers of a book; not in the least that it bears any resemblance to a mere compendium of miscellaneous ideas. The perfect regularity of its structure much rather suggests a complex unity, like a crystal formed little by little from its mother element.

Newman began on the book at what seems like a providential moment. Whately had succeeded in giving him back his freedom of conscience. Whately and Hawkins between them, leading him to abandon the Evangelical "closed shop", brought him into view of some of the main features of Catholic tradition in a rejuvenated and refurbished form. His parochial experiences, coinciding as they did with his inward convictions, pointed the way to a reassessment of all those spiritual intuitions, vague and confused as they still were, of his childhood and adolescence. A kind of pre-ordained consonancy between the hidden yearnings of his spirit and the progressive unfolding of Butler's ideas was to complete the process. This book, which had come to his notice at the psychological moment, provided him with a sort of profit and loss account for the past, and a sure foundation for the future.

A passage in the *Apologia* enumerates all the lasting gains which he deemed he owed to the *Analogy*. Of those new conceptions of Christianity which his colleagues had tossed at him pell-mell, he found in its pages the coherent and harmonious expression, "a visible Church, the oracle of truth and a pattern of sanctity, of the duties of external religion, and of the historical character of Revelation." And he says, "These are characteristics of the great work which strike the reader at once." He selects two points of which he says:

> They are the underlying principles of a great portion of my teaching. First, the very idea of an analogy between the separate works of God leads to the conclusion that the system which is of less importance is economically or sacramentally connected with the more momentous system, and of this conclusion to which I was inclined as a boy, viz. the unreality of material phenomena, is an ultimate resolution. At this time I did not make the distinction between matter itself and its phenomena, which is so necessary and so obvious in discussing the subject. Secondly, Butler's doctrine that Probability is the guide of life, led me, at least under the teaching to which a few years later I was introduced, to the question of the logical cogency of Faith, on which I have written so much. Thus to Butler I trace those two principles of my teaching, which have led to a charge against me both of fancifulness and of scepticism.

The analogy between this world and the next, a sound system of probability leading to religious faith—we shall see how equally essential both these principles were to Newman, intellectually and spiritually. The one brought about a second flowering of those spiritual intuitions of his childhood, the other provided him at last with a clear perception of the path that led between the rationalism of the intellectuals on the one hand and the fanatical emotionalism of the *illuminati* on the other, the path, in a word, which he had so long been seeking.

We shall not, however, fully realise his regard for Butler, its depth or its intensity, until we have gained a clear idea of the nature of the bond between them, a bond which Newman himself immediately recognised. Church, in his work on Butler, makes two very illuminating observations. The young Oxford don, finding himself unable completely to jettison his Evangelicalism, and equally unable satisfactorily to subsist upon it, now encountered in this venerable Bishop of Durham a perfect example of that religious high-seriousness, that dutiful submission to the will of God, the God who speaks in Revelation, which offers so striking a contrast to a religion inspired by the emotions. So much, then, for Butler in his purely religious aspect. But he also had his practical, his realistic side. Mistrustful though he was of abstractions as being misleading fancies, he held, nevertheless, that the complete reality of a thing is not to be grasped at a first external view of it. Relentlessly intolerant of "unreal words", to borrow Newman's phrase, he displayed an attitude as characteristic of Newman as it was of himself.

On both of these matters—that is to say, on religion as our seventeenth century understood the word; and on scientific realism, understanding by that, Science looked full in the face—Newman was at once in complete agreement. This time, there was no question of any youthful misinterpretation. In this instance, it may be said that it was the most precious part of his own possessions that his mature understanding adopted from Butler.

At the point of intersection of these two propositions, the idea which was the starting-point of Butler's whole philosophy, so clearly conveyed in a passage from Origen quoted by way of epigraph to the *Analogy* (and from which it derived its name), imparts to his view of the world, and of life, the unity which it was seeking. The passage in question runs thus, "He who believes the Scripture to have proceeded from him who is the Author of Nature may well expect to find the same sort of difficulties in it as are found in the constitution of Nature." The primary meaning of that excerpt gives the key to an apologetic whose very boldness is perhaps its surest wisdom. It amounts to saying that it is useless to try to deprive Revelation of its mystery. Rather should we recognise the presence of mystery everywhere. The visible world itself, properly considered, is a mystery so great and of such a nature that it should teach us not to be troubled by mysteries, and in particular by the mystery we encounter in the very core of Revelation. This very mystery is perhaps the surest evidence that it does indeed proceed from the Author of Nature himself.

This idea was, and always remained, the cornerstone of Newman's religious philosophy. It explains and interprets that oft-quoted saying of his, "A thousand difficulties do not make one doubt." But most important, now that his mind and ideas were at their formative stage, were the implications involved in a conception of this nature. How came it that this so-called egocentric, this confirmed self-analyst, and that he certainly was, was to become a Churchman in the fullest sense of the word, a man in whose eyes God's work in the world was inseparable from the building of Christ's Body, a visible Body, a Body composed of human elements? The answer is that, for Newman, the fundamental truth is henceforth clear—which is not to say that it did not also have its shadowy depths—the truth, namely, that as the God of the Bible is the God of this world, the God who speaks to the soul does so, not by any purely subjective and individual means, but through the great collective consciousness of an historic community, present in the midst of the world we see, in order to make it once again the way to God, which, through sin it had ceased to be. Newman saw too clearly ever again to be in doubt about the matter, that it was by that way, and by that way alone, that we pass *ex umbris et imaginibus in veritatem.*

V

THE TUTOR

In the evening of the 13th June, 1824, the day on which he was ordained deacon, Newman made the following entry in his diary:

> It is over. I am Thine, O Lord. I seem quite dizzy, and cannot altogether believe and understand it. At first, after the hands were laid on me, my heart shuddered within me; the words "for ever" are so terrible. It was hardly a godly feeling which made me feel melancholy at the idea of giving up all for God. At times indeed my heart burnt within me, particularly during the singing of the *Veni Creator*. Yet, Lord, I ask not for comfort in comparison of sanctification. . . . I feel as a man thrown suddenly into deep water.

Properly to understand those words, we must bear in mind that there are no Minor Orders in the Anglican Church preceding the diaconate, and that as soon as a candidate has received deacon's Orders, he enters upon his duties forthwith. That being so, we can understand how, that night, Newman felt not only the emotion of the Catholic sub-deacon who realises that he has bound himself beyond recall, but also the overwhelming responsibility of the priest entrusted with the cure of souls.

How, it may be asked, did he propose to fulfil his vocation and in what particular field? We have seen how strongly the idea of missionary work abroad had appealed to him on the morrow of his conversion, and how the feeling that he was intended to live a celibate life was more or less connected with that idea. The possibility of embracing such a career had by no means deserted him. The idea was fortified, if not confirmed, by his reading the life of Henry Martyn, a Protestant missionary in Persia. It will be remembered that, after his failure to get an honours degree, his mother bought him a Persian grammar, which rather suggests that he had reiterated his intention about that time. We may also recollect that missionary work had been one of his favourite topics of conversation with Pusey. Finally, on the 3rd July, 1824, less than three months after his ordination, a note in his diary records a visit he had paid to the Church Missionary House. His purpose had been to obtain full and accurate information as to the qualifications a missionary would be required to possess. He also says how relieved he was to find that a weak voice, shortsightedness, and a want of fluency were no fatal drawbacks.

For the time being, however, it seemed that the project could not be proceeded with, if for no other reason than the embarrassed state of the family finances, and the obligation he had undertaken to see Francis through his studies. Thus it was that, at Pusey's suggestion, he came to take the curacy at St Clement's.

We have remarked on the important effect this early appointment of his had on the subsequent development of his religious ideas. It may not be amiss to point out that it gave him his first chance of displaying that vigorous practical common-sense which his shyness, his intellectual pre-occupations, and his personal disinterestedness never availed to impair.

One of the tasks left in abeyance owing to the infirmity of the octogenarian vicar, the Rev. Dr John Gutch, was the organising of a fund for building a new church. Newman put his shoulder to the wheel, and succeeded beyond the most sanguine expectations. The unlovely edifice that abuts on Magdalen Park stands as a memorial of his efforts; it must be added, however, in justice to him, that he had nothing to do with its design. It was built, after he had left, on lines laid down by a committee of which he was not a member, and we know, from his own testimony, that he never set foot inside it.

His energy, as we may imagine, was still more conspicuously displayed in the purely pastoral sphere. Whether it was a matter of catechising, or of Sunday School classes, that particularly Protestant institution, or of the choir practice, or the visits to the parishioners to which we have already alluded, Newman attended to it all with such fervour that in time people began to call him a "Methody".

His father disapproved of his paying all these visits to the humbler members of his flock. He saw in them something painfully at variance with the reserve expected of every decent Englishman and, to be quite frank, just one more of those regrettable displays to be ascribed to his son's Evangelical leanings. The son eloquently, but with great good humour, defended his course of conduct, quoting remarks of some of his parishioners which were by no means lacking in point. Though not bringing any pressure on people to get them to come to church, he did not hesitate to call on dissenters, not omitting even the most hidebound among them. A particularly piquant incident arising from this line of action was his coming into contact with a certain highly respectable elderly gentleman to whom he thought he might quite properly express his surprise at never seeing him in church. The venerable gentleman in question turned out to be none other than a Jesuit Father, who evidently went to the limits of discretion in the practice of his sacred calling. Half a century or so later, Newman may well have been reminded of this incident when, a Cardinal of the Roman Church, he was visited by an Anglican clergyman at Edgbaston, who explained that he had come to call on him as being the most distinguished of his parishioners.

There was another circumstance connected with his early clerical activities which had an important effect on his subsequent career, and that was his initiation into the art of preaching. We know how severely Hawkins criticised his first sermon, and how promptly he embraced the opportunity it offered him of making a destructive attack on the main Evangelical position; but the cream of the story is that the Rev. Walter Mayers, in whose parish at Warton the sermon was preached, found it a great deal too lukewarm for his liking. "What was that he said about the communion which exists among all who are baptised, just as if baptism was of any avail if we were not 'converted'." Francis, too, who heard the sermon, and who was another of Mayers' converts, shared the latter's dissatisfaction.[1]

It need not surprise us to find the feminine members of the family entertaining opinions equally remote from both these contradictory views. Mrs Newman had always been anxious to read the sermons which, to her great regret, she was prevented from hearing, and from the very beginning she had declared herself a whole-hearted disciple of the young preacher.[2] Her daughters were quick to follow suit. Little did he, or any of his kinswomen, foresee the pain this early adherence to his teaching was fated to bring them, his mother and his sisters alike.

However, in the following spring, in reply to another letter from his mother assuring him, this time in the name of his sisters as well, of all the profit she and they were deriving from these precious documents, he used words which today sound almost prophetic:

> I feel pleased you like my sermons. I am sure I need not caution you against taking anything I say on trust. Do not be run away with by any opinion of mine. I have seen cause to change my mind in some respects, and I may change again. I see I know very little about anything, though I often think I know a great deal.[3]

[1] This, his first sermon, was preached on the 23rd June, 1824.

[2] Cf. her letter of 30th August, 1824. In it she alludes to this very sermon, his first, which, between them, Hawkins and Mayers, from their different points of view, had torn to pieces.

[3] *Letters*, Vol. I, p. 114.

With regard to the subject-matter of his sermons, we may draw attention to a note he made for his own benefit, and to a remark he made in a letter to his mother. Both alike stress the need to preach and practise the sort of Christianity which demands and produces a godly life. In this connection, we may recall the profound impression that the words of Scott had made on him on the morrow of his conversion, "Holiness rather than peace." The reader may also have remarked how the recollection of those words coloured his thoughts that evening after he had been ordained deacon. This explains how the consciousness of the spiritual effort going on in him and around him, dispelled from his mind those doctrines of forensic justification which he had inherited from certain Protestant works on theology, such as Romaine's.[1]

On the 16th September, 1824, he jots down this:

> Those who make comfort the great subject of their preaching seem to mistake the end of their ministry. *Holiness* is the great end. There must be a struggle and a toil here. Comfort is a cordial, but no one drinks cordials from morning to night.[2]

Writing probably in reply to the letter from Mrs Newman already referred to, he says:

> I shall certainly *always* strive in every pulpit *so* to preach the Christian doctrines as at the same time to warn people that it is quite idle to pretend faith and holiness, unless they show forth their inward principles by a pure disinterested, upright line of conduct.[3]

Nevertheless, it was not in parochial work that Newman was to discover the true field for the exercise of his vocation. That, it was for his university duties to supply. The letter in which he tried to convince his father of the usefulness and propriety of his parochial visits, contains a particularly revealing paragraph. It shows us how seriously, taking the parish as his pattern, he regarded the question of Christian education.

> Nor do I visit the poor only; I mean to go all through the parish; and I have already visited the shopkeepers and principal people. These, it is obvious, have facilities for educating their children, which the poor have not; and on that ground it is that a clergyman is more concerned with the children of the latter, though our church certainly intended that, not only schoolmasters of the poorer children, but all schoolmasters high and low, should be under her jurisdiction.[4]

[1] We learn the ultimate issue of this line of thought from the *Lectures on Justification*.
[2] *Letters*, Vol. I, p. 76.
[3] *Ibid.*, Vol. I, p. 78.
[4] Letter dated 9th August, 1824 (*Letters*, Vol. I, p. 77).

It must here be pointed out that, at this time, opinion was sharply divided as to whether a clerical vocation was, or was not, consistent with a university office. The Rev. Walter Mayers, who now had a parish of his own, had long felt scruples about devoting himself to exclusively educational work. His views of the matter were shared by Evangelicals as a whole. They looked on the work of a schoolmaster and a college-tutor as purely secular in character, and in no way to be regarded as a branch of the sacred ministry.

Newman had never taken this view. From his earliest days, he had envisaged one or other of two alternative careers for himself: he would either become a missionary, or live out his life in the University. It never seems to have entered his head that the latter was any less God's service than the former. This view of the matter did but gain strength as the years went by. When he was about to be appointed tutor at his college, and was on the eve of taking up his duties, he wrote as follows:

> May I engage in them, remembering that I am a minister of Christ, and I have a commission to preach the Gospel, remembering the worth of souls, and that I shall have to answer for the opportunities given me of benefiting those who are under my care.[1]

However, the more insight he gained into university teaching, the more convinced he became that it needed a thorough transformation. For a clergyman to devote himself to educational work was assuredly in no way to derogate from his sacred calling; nevertheless, one had to make quite sure that it *was* educational in the real sense of the word. It was very soon borne in upon him that the college system, as it then existed, was far from coming up to this requirement, a conclusion which applied to his own college as much as to any other. So he set about reforming it in accordance with his own ideas, and this it was that, for the first time, brought him into collision with the college authorities.

These problems, however, were not presented to him then and there. He was to serve a sort of apprenticeship preliminary to his Oriel tutorship. For this, Newman was indebted to Whately's kindness and high opinion of him.

In March 1825 Whately was appointed Principal of St Alban Hall, whereupon he at once invited Newman to be his Vice-Principal. As Newman told his mother in a letter he wrote her on the 29th March, what that really meant was that he had to combine the duties of dean, tutor, and bursar, and, when Whately was away, as he not infrequently was, those of Principal into the bargain.

[1] This passage of his *Memoranda* is quoted in *Letters*, Vol. I, p. 132.

However, a Hall, like St Alban's, which was a sort of dependency of Merton, was far from having the status of a college. In accepting this appointment, Newman was not merely taking on a number of exacting duties, he was also rehearsing, on a minor stage, the part of tutor which he was shortly to be invited to undertake at Oriel.

A few months before he took up this last-mentioned appointment, there occurred in the Newman family an event of capital importance. It caused him to reflect anew on the kind of life which, it had been for some time dawning upon him, God intended him to follow. On the 25th September, 1824, Newman got news that his father's health, which had been giving anxiety for some weeks past, had suddenly taken a turn for the worse. He hastened back to London at once by the night mail. On the 29th, his father died.

> The dread event has happened. Is it possible? O my Father! I got to town on Sunday morning. He knew me; tried to put out his hand, and said "God bless you!" Towards the evening of Monday he said his last words. He seemed in great peace of mind. He could, however, only articulate "God bless you; thank my God, thank my God!" and, lastly, "My dear." Dr C. came on Wednesday and pronounced him dying. Towards evening we joined in prayer, commending his soul to God. . . . Of late he had thought his end approaching. One day on the river he told my Mother, "I shall never see another summer." On Thursday he looked beautiful. Such calmness, sweetness, composure, and majesty were in his countenance. Can a man be a materialist who sees a dead body? I had never seen one before. His last words to me, or all but his last, were to bid me read to him the 53rd chapter of Isaiah.[1]

On the 6th October, full of these thoughts and memories, he wrote again:

> Performed the last sad duties to my dear Father. When I die, shall I be followed to the grave by my children? My Mother said the other day, she hoped to live to see me married; but I think I shall either die within college walls, or as a missionary in a foreign land. No matter where, so that I die in Christ.[2]

The allusion in the penultimate sentence referred to his fellowship and to his tutorial post, neither of which could be held except by a bachelor. If you did take the post, you were free to marry if you wanted to, but it meant resigning the position and looking out for a living, or some other appointment. But it is clear that Newman, if he gave up the missionary idea, never dreamt of exercising his clerical functions anywhere outside the educational sphere.

[1] Quoted in *Letters,* Vol. I, p. 79. [2] *Letters,* Vol. I, p. 79.

As often happens in such cases, his early experiences as tutor taught him as much or more than he taught his pupils, and had no small effect on his character. His brilliant success at Oriel, the somewhat overpowering influence of his constant association with the Noëtics, the parochial and university responsibilities which at so early an age he had been called upon to undertake—it is not to be wondered at if all this filled him with a sort of complacent intellectual self-sufficiency. Nothing could have been better calculated to cure him of this state of mind than contact with young people, particularly of the sort he had to deal with at Alban Hall.

The Halls at Oxford were intended to house students whose means were inadequate to meet the expenses of life in college. This Hall in particular contained a large proportion of candidates for Orders who were of very restricted means, and more than one case of what we should call deferred vocation. It was from this source that he was to receive a humorously worded rebuke which went home and which he evidently had not forgotten when he came to write his *Apologia*. Among the unpublished passages in the manuscript is one which we are now about to quote. Its significance will be apparent. He had been saying that, influenced by the Noëtics and by some of the books Whately had recommended him to read in connection with his articles to the *Encyclopaedia Metropolitana*, a sense of intellectual superiority had come over him. We may regard that as an example of the sort of second "growing-up" which not uncommonly affects young men when they are approaching their twenty-fifth year. As usually happens in such cases, he arrived at a state of intellectual self-reliance similar to that which had preceded his conversion.

> In those same years this new spirit showed itself in a different way; in what is commonly called donnishness. On this account I got into disfavour with my pupils at Alban Hall, and one of them, of some age, long dead, gave me a lesson which I never forgot—I believe it did me permanent good. I had given as a subject of an Essay, "Know thyself", and he wrote about "stiff and stately distance, strict etiquette in the exterior forms of address, great punctiliousness in balancing the quantity and quality of discourse to be addressed to each relatively to his standing, and an immoderate share of vanity to gloss over the odium and contempt which all sensible persons entertain and might express for these seeming insults on their situation, and these encroachments on a privilege only tolerated in despotic princes". "If", he continues, "the 'know thyself' is profitable to all as a means of edification, let it be instilled on those who come under the force of the preceding remarks. Let it place a mirror before them to reflect their persons and characters such as they really are, and such as they are discerned to be by others.

By such observance those who have passed their time in closets may impart the fruit of their solitary inquiries at once to instruct and command esteem, and prove to those who have lived in the world that they are at least their equals in true good breeding."

Evidently, then, the rebuke went home, for if there is one man in the Victorian age who stands out above all the rest as being free from the pose, the pomposity, the smug self-satisfaction which are so markedly characteristic of the period, that man is Newman. Howbeit, it was not so much his students, as one of his colleagues-to-be who was destined to free him from any risk of getting contentedly bogged down in a state of humdrum self-satisfaction, intellectually or spiritually. It was at Oriel, yet again, that this colleague was presently encountered. For the moment, however, Whately squeezes the last few drops of juice, and possibly some of the dregs as well, out of what he had to offer in their almost daily contacts with each other. In setting him to work on the two papers for the *Encyclopaedia Metropolitana*, the one on miracles, the other on Apollonius of Tyana, he not only extended to the extreme limits the critical ideas he had implanted in him, but even made ready to exceed them. These two works, which were to occupy pretty well all his spare time for the next two years or so, were the means of bringing out whatever there was, if not of scepticism at least of latent rationalism, in his intellectual composition. But they also made him acquainted with the literature of the early Christian centuries. Rekindling, as they did, all his old enthusiasm for Milner's Church History as well as calling back to mind all that Lloyd had put before him, they had the effect of plunging him into the study of the Fathers which, from the end of 1827 onwards, engrossed him ever more and more.

However, we have not yet arrived at that point. The year 1825, the year he was ordained to the Anglican priesthood (29th May, at Christ Church), proved to be one of intense activity for him in all manner of directions. There was Alban Hall, his many duties at St Clement's, the scientific studies already alluded to, and, in addition to all this, his family preoccupations, for on him, as the eldest son, the paternal responsibilities now devolved. Staying on at Oxford during the Long Vacation, Whately being away, he accepted the latter's hospitable offer, should he want to invite his mother and sisters to come up and keep him company, to place his rooms at their disposal.

We must not fail to note the important influence which Newman's relations with his family had upon his life at this period. By them, and by them alone, one whole side of his character is revealed to us. To begin with his sisters; in his relations with them there was a mixture of something like boyish glee, combined with a tender warmth of affection not a little surprising in a Vice-Principal whose pupils were so quick to accuse him of "donnishness". No sooner was he ordained priest, than he dashed off a letter to his mother, saying:

> I need not say how glad I am you are coming. I intend to have a Sacrament August 7, at St Clement's, and it will be a great satisfaction to me, if two of my sisters for the first time partake of it the first time you hear me do duty.[1]

In point of fact, Jemima and Mary had just been confirmed, and, in the Anglican Church, Confirmation is a necessary preliminary to First Communion.

Taking them on the whole, Newman's letters to his sisters were a medley of sage advice about their studies, a little good-natured banter, with some expressions, it may be no more than a word or two, of very tender affection. Harriet's poems, Jemima's sums, and Mary's grammar were all duly dealt with by him, interspersed with a few nonsense rhymes which reveal in him an unsuspected talent, suggestive of a sort of Lewis Carroll, only, in this case, a more natural one. Some years afterwards he did read *Alice in Wonderland*, and with a good deal of appreciation. As for his gift for amusing children, that was one day to be the delight of the Pusey family.

With his brothers, his relations were not at all the same. He spared neither time nor money in seeing to it that Francis should be able to go on with his studies. A number of entries in his diary make it clear, however, that there were frequent clashes of temperament between them. The self-accusations of ill-temper or impatience he makes in his contacts with his pupils in the course of these early teaching years become increasingly numerous when his young brother is concerned. Francis, who was also a disciple of the Rev. Mr Mayers, but a closer and more obedient one than John had been, had found in the latter a convinced defender and a stout champion of his Evangelicalism. But it was precisely in these subsequent years, when Newman was coming more and more to realise that his conversion did not require him to embrace any particular sect, but just made a Christian of him—it was precisely then, that his brother became more and more deeply imbued with sectarian zeal. In 1826, all the trouble to which John Henry had put himself found its reward in a double-first gained by Francis. But it

[1] *Letters*, Vol. I, p. 86.

was at that same juncture that a present bestowed by John Henry on his younger brother to mark the latter's success was the cause of a clash between them. The present had taken the form of a picture of the Virgin and Child, and Francis had the gross ill-manners to send it back to the dealer of whom his brother had purchased it. In after years he was stupid enough to refer to this incident as evidence that his brother was even then a convinced Catholic, and that he was prepared to go to any lengths to force his views on other people.

As for Charles, his other brother, things were even more unsatisfactory. His indolence, his cynicism (not unillumined by wit), the impossibility of getting him to settle down, an incorrigible itch to belittle the very people to whom he was looking for advancement—things like these all went to make up the figure which he always presented to the world, the figure, that is to say, of the picturesque but pitiful failure. On the 30th November that year, Newman, heaving no doubt a prodigious sigh of relief, notes that they have managed to get him a post of some sort in the Bank of England. This was one of the stages in the career of a sort of semi-lunatic, whose craziness none the less was varied with flashes of unusual intelligence.

It is worthy of note that, in the years we are reviewing, we may observe, on their respective levels, the same preoccupations, the same sense of responsibility in educational matters which governed not only Newman's relations with his family, but his entire university and clerical life. At home, as at Alban Hall, he was the one to whom the younger folk looked for guidance, to help them in this life, and to show them the path to the next; to find themselves, and to find God.

Alban Hall, however, was not a permanency. We learn from Thomas Mozley that, early in 1826, an unexpected opportunity presented itself to Newman. One day he received a message, a very laconic one, from Lloyd. It ran, "Dear Newman, just pop round here a minute, if you will!" Newman hurried round to Christ Church, and had just got his head inside the door when Lloyd holloaed out, "Newman, how old are you?" "Twenty-five," answered Newman. "Be off with you, child, I've no need of you!" Lloyd had just been asked to look about for a tutor for the future King of Hanover; but one proviso was that the candidates should be not less than twenty-seven years of age. Mozley used to amuse himself speculating how different Newman's future might have been had he become the Goethe of another Weimar. In point of fact, the probability is that he would have considered the appointment anything but attractive, and have declined it there and then. In the event, it was an Oriel tutor that got the post, and on the 20th January Newman was appointed tutor in his place.

With this appointment, which meant resigning his work at St Clement's and Alban Hall, Newman would appear to have got what he desired. He was now firmly established at his new college in an official teaching capacity. The work which he had early had in mind, which he had longed for, and prepared himself to undertake—that is to say, a clerical post in which he would devote himself to the intellectual and spiritual training of the young men committed to his charge—that post he had now obtained. It might well have seemed, and indeed it did seem, that he was now setting his hand to his life's real work. In his autobiographical memoir, he wrote, speaking of himself:

> He had accepted this task as if for an indefinite term of years, or rather for life. He did not look beyond; he desired nothing better than such a life-long residence at Oxford; nothing higher than such an influential position as was thus given him.[1]

A little farther on, he makes himself still clearer:

> It must be understood that, in his view, the tutorial office was but another way, though not so heroic a way as a mission to idolaters, of carrying out his vow.[2]

Taking up his duties at Easter 1826, he soon came to realise how urgently reforms were needed, if his ideals were to be translated into action. He had hardly got through his first month of office, when he wrote in his private journal:

> There is much in the system which I think wrong; I think the tutors see too little of the men, and there is not enough of direct religious instruction. It is my wish to consider myself as a minister of Christ. Unless I find that opportunities occur of doing spiritual good to those over whom I am placed, it will become a grave question whether I ought to continue in the tuition.[3]

Newman himself applied the term "pastoral" to his tutorial work, as he conceived it, and in contradistinction to purely secular instruction. He also expressly declared that he was setting up nothing new, but was merely returning to the letter and spirit of Laud's statutes, in which the tutor was defined as, *vir probitate et eruditione perspecta, religione sincerus . . . scholares tutelae suae commissos probis moribus instruat, et in probatis auctoribus instituat et maxime in rudimentis religionis et doctrinae articulis.*

[1] *Letters,* Vol. I, p. 129. [2] *Ibid.,* p. 131. [3] *Ibid.,* p. 133.

With such ideas as these in his head, his primary aim was to do away with anything there might be of outward formalism and concealed impiety in the conduct of the students. It will be remembered that it was that sort of thing that had shocked him very soon after he first came up to Trinity. Corporate Communion every term, followed by whole days of intoxication, were in his view sure signs of a system that was fundamentally unsound. On this matter he found himself, to begin with, in splendid isolation. As to compulsory termly Communion, and the problems it might have for the students' conscience, Hawkins said, "That question never, I believe, enters their heads, and I beg you will not put it into them." As for the drinking bouts which followed Communion within an hour or two, Tyler, who was senior fellow and Dean of the College, said, with a touch of cynicism, "I don't believe it, and, if it is true, I don't want to know it."

On the more strictly educational plane, Newman met with a greater measure of sympathy and support. In his attempt to tighten up discipline, he was, if not backed up, at least not hindered. In one thing, in particular, he was successful; he put the gentlemen-commoners in their place. These gentlemen-commoners, young men of birth, wealth, or rich prospects, had a status of their own, and enjoyed certain privileges which they were given to abusing by riotous behaviour and neglect of their studies. Speaking generally, the industrious, hard-working men, thanks to him, received help and encouragement, while the slowcoaches and the triflers were progressively eliminated.

Nevertheless, it was not long before he directed his efforts, not so much to reforming existing organisation and discipline, as to something that was exclusively his own idea, and that was a radical change in the relations hitherto subsisting between tutor and pupils.

In theory, every public tutor in a college (at Oriel there were four) was supposed to be responsible for the training, in the fullest sense of the word, of the pupils entrusted to him by the college Head. In practice, this charge, owing to the indifference of the tutors on the one hand, and the indiscipline of students on the other, amounted to nothing very much. As regards instruction, in its narrowest sense, seeing that the University Professors contented themselves with delivering a few courses of more or less perfunctory lectures, it was on the tutors that the main burden devolved. But in every college they arranged between themselves, as best suited their convenience, for each one in turn to deliver a set of lectures on one of the prescribed subjects to the students as whole. As regards his own particular pupils, therefore, it followed that the tutor exercised but little control over their work, or even over their conduct, and that control, such as it was, was less religious than moral, and less moral than purely disciplinary. Add to that the aloofness rigidly maintained by the dons, to which, however, the majority of the undergraduates took no objection, since it meant that they were left pretty well entirely to themselves.

Only the really conscientious students, such as Newman himself had been, suffered at all from this state of affairs. If they wanted to meet their own individual requirements, they had either to teach themselves, with all the handicaps that entails, or to engage a private tutor, and that meant money; and the expense of an Oxford course already called for resources which the more meritorious of the undergraduates seldom commanded.

Newman, enlightened by his own experience as an undergraduate at Trinity, and as Vice-Principal of Alban Hall, felt conscientiously impelled to adopt a different course. He considered that, over and above the strictly official routine work which the college demanded of him, he was in duty bound to devote his time and energies to his own particular pupils, so far as they were able, or willing, to profit by them. That they should ever be compelled to have recourse to a private tutor was a thing he regarded as completely out of the question.

But more than that, it is abundantly clear that he was far from thinking he had fulfilled all his responsibilities when he had discharged his purely instructional responsibilities. He had learnt from his recent experience at Alban Hall that to have any spiritual influence over his pupils, over and above the mere mundane teaching of them, it was necessary to discard the authoritarian attitude, and still more any suggestion of the high-and-mighty manner. To begin with, he merely comported himself as the other dons did, though perhaps with a little additional stiffness not unnatural in a young man of a shy and retiring disposition who was entering on the exercise of his new authority. But he was too much of a Christian, and had too much good sense, not to throw off this attitude as soon as he came into closer contact with his young pupils. A single lesson, such as that which he has so movingly recorded, had sufficed. He therefore started working with his pupils on a system which, novel and startling enough to begin with, gained him before very long, as he himself puts it, first their respect, and finally their affection. He began by putting himself wholly at their disposal so far as their work was concerned. As he got to know them better, he strove, by discerning and persuasive sympathy, to draw out from each whatever he was able to offer. With regard to those who looked on their studies as kind of obstacle that had to be got over somehow or other, he confined himself to doing just as much as his official duties demanded of him, and no more, letting them see, however, clearly enough what he thought of them. On the other hand, there was no limit to what he would do for the more promising ones among them, or even for those who, without being specially gifted in any way, showed signs of a genuine desire to get on. With regard to these latter, "he cultivated"—to use his own words—"relations, not only of intimacy, but of friendship, and almost of equality, putting off, as much as might be, the martinet manner then in fashion with College tutors, and seeking their society in outdoor exercise, on evenings, and in Vacation."[1]

Seeing the man Newman was, it is not surprising that this line of action should have won him, not only their trust, but their downright devotion. It was very natural, seeing how he linked up Christian training with academic studies, that men who recognised in him a first-rate tutor should also have come to look to him for spiritual inspiration and religious guidance.

However, it must be confessed that, from the very beginning, this experiment of his had no lack of critics. But, before many months were over, Newman was to receive unexpected support, just when an unlooked-for explosion of antagonism put him most in need of it.

A few days after Newman had entered on his duties, two new fellows had been elected at Oriel, both of them former pupils of Keble's. One was Robert Isaac Wilberforce, the other Richard Hurrell Froude. Little did Newman foresee what a tower of strength they were to be to him in his attempted reform—the forerunner of many more—still less the influence which the second of the two was to exert upon him in after years.

We have already seen how deeply Newman—in common with all who knew him—revered the character of Keble. But Keble had given up his rooms at Oriel before he, Newman, had properly settled in there, so that he did not really know him. He was doubtless a little uneasy in his mind about Keble's profound respect for ecclesiastical tradition, just as we may take it, with no less certainty, that Keble, for his part, had his misgivings about Newman's Evangelical antecedents. He does not seem to have suspected that Keble, quite quietly, and without any idea of bringing about any sweeping reform in

[1] *Autobiographical Memoir*, IV, in *Autobiographical Writings*, p. 90.

college habits, had already exemplified in his own person his ideal of what a tutor should be. Froude and Wilberforce were well aware of this; moreover, both were themselves shining examples of what that method of teaching was capable of producing. When, therefore, towards the end of 1827, Copleston was appointed Bishop of Llandaff and it became necessary to elect a new Provost, Froude and Wilberforce, precisely because they approved so warmly of what Newman had been doing, supported the candidature of Keble. To Newman, however, Keble was a name, representing a person of great intellectual delicacy, indeed, and of great elevation of character, but without having anything conspicuously in common with Oriel as it then was. His choice, naturally enough, lighted on Hawkins, to whom he was indebted for so much, and who seemed to him to be eminently endowed with the sort of practical abilities that would enable him to give effect to the aims and aspirations of his one-time disciple.

Thanks to those powers of persuasion that were, even now, one of his salient characteristics, Newman prevailed. It might well have seemed to him at first that his wishes and aims had been abundantly fulfilled. Two tutorships had fallen vacant while the election was pending, and one of Hawkins's first acts in his official capacity was to appoint Froude and Wilberforce to fill them. And both, as everybody knew, were in complete agreement with Newman, at least in principle, as to what the duties of a tutor really were.

Froude's arrival in the Senior Common Room at Oriel, though he could hardly have been called a stranger in the house where he had once lived as an undergraduate, came like a breath of fresh air, or, perhaps we should say, like the gust of a hurricane. Two years Newman's junior, this tall, fair-haired young man, so radiant in his good looks, a strange compound of merriment and dignity, of *hauteur* and warm-heartedness, seemed to present a living challenge to the commonly accepted notion of the typical don. The son of an Anglican archdeacon, belonging to an old family of well-to-do landowners, he was out-and-out Tory and High Church. All the same, we must not omit to add that he trampled on conventions with cool *insouciance* as only a young aristocrat knows how

Fond of sport but simple, even austere, in his habits; of brilliant intellectual endowments but wholly free from self-conceit, his tenderness of heart was equalled only by his dislike of any visible display of the emotions.

To Keble, who was as shy and reserved as he himself was outspoken and self-confident, it is impossible to say how much he owed. After studying under him at Oxford, he subsequently became one of his private pupils at the parsonage, Hursley, whither he, Keble, had so early retired.

We must not be misled by the appearance Froude presented to the world. Radiant, independent, self-reliant as he seemed to be, this outward show concealed a secret sorrow. Doubtless, Samuel Wilberforce was not far from the truth when he declared, incongruous as it sounds, that he always found something of the Hamlet about Hurrell Froude. His spirited nature, his contempt for display of feeling, all this concealed a secret wound, the brooding sorrow of a child bereft too soon of a charming mother's care and affection, a nature fiercely introspective. The wound which the child had so grievously suffered was reopened when, as a youth, he came to pore over a diary in which he discerned in his mother's soul, not only the disquietude which her religious future had aroused in her, but the same spiritual conflicts of which he himself was conscious in his own too-complex soul. He had come to Keble's parsonage with another very remarkable young man. Isaac Williams, too, nourished the bitter feelings of a frustrated youth, and looked with a jaundiced eye on himself and the world in general. But in their new surroundings, both were to find a strange and welcome relief, a sensation of well-being that put new life into them. They had been there no more than a few days when they confessed themselves astonished at the unaffectedness, the brotherly friendliness, the comradeship with which Keble treated them. Seeing him as they did from day to day, his saintliness was no less evident to them than his intellectual gifts and attainments, but what chiefly impressed them was that in his behaviour towards them there was not a trace of any sort of superiority, implied or expressed. On the contrary, they were treated with a quiet but most understanding affection, and a gaiety of as youthful a quality as would have become one of their own age. " 'Tis Master is as much of a boy as any of 'em," said the old manservant. The effect of this contact on two such morbidly introspective natures was to put a prompt and welcome end to their troubles. In Keble's society they found the happiness to be derived from a religion at once deep and serene and, be it added, most strict. At a stroke, this man, so simple and so candid, won to himself for ever those two spirits so untamed and, each in his own way, so complex.

We therefore readily understand how warmly Froude seconded the aims of Newman. In spite of all apparent differences between the two men, he discovered in Newman precisely the same desire, the same endeavour to understand and gain the affections of young people, to be as a father to them, that he had found in Keble. Together with Newman, he, too, might hope to pass on to others some portion of the priceless treasure he himself had received.

After Froude's election to his fellowship, Newman wrote home to his people saying:

> Froude is one of the acutest and clearest and deepest men in the memory of man. I hope our election will be *in honorem Dei et Sponsae suae Ecclesiae salutem*, as Edward II has it in our statutes.[1]

Two years later, Froude gave his view of Newman in a somewhat different style:

> Newman is a Fellow that I like more, the more I think of him; only, I would give a few odd pence if he were not a heretic.[2]

Newman, whom Froude looked on as more or less spoiled by his Evangelicalism and his liberalism, looked on Froude as a red-hot Tory High Churchman, and that, coming from him, was no mild criticism. The similarity of their views on university education was certainly what brought them together, although that may have been the occasion rather than the cause of the original mutual attraction. And then there was always this difference between them that, whereas what in Froude's case was a matter of spontaneous impulse and natural intuition, was with Newman far rather the fruit of calm and deliberate reflection. This is doubtless why Newman could not understand how it was that Froude was so anxious for Keble to be elected Provost rather than Hawkins, whose candidature he himself supported. Froude, moreover, imparted a touch of the provocative, one might almost say the outrageous, to Newman's innovations which, if Newman alone had been concerned, they would not have had. With Froude, however, you could rely on having plenty of things to shock you, if you wanted to be shocked. He would justify himself with a wealth of protestations, and enunciate the most startling propositions couched in students' slang uttered in the lordliest of tones, just as readily as he would help men to climb the wall when they got back late after being with him at some boating or skating party. What Newman did not realise was that when the methods adopted by Froude, Wilberforce, and himself came to be called in question, all these little matters would be carefully borne in mind and brought up against him by the very man to whom

[1] *Letters*, Vol. I, p. 115. [2] *Remains*, Vol. I, p. 233.

he had looked for his main support. If Froude gave him a backing he had little expected, Hawkins met him with an opposition, and finally with a downright veto, equally unlooked for.

The whole affair affected Newman to an extent, and with a psychological intensity, out of all proportion to the incidents themselves. To realise that, we have but to note how large a place it occupies in his autobiographical memoir, not taking into account the passages which he himself deleted and which Mlle Tardivel has recently made public. Numerous subsequent allusions, very long after the event, make it abundantly clear that Newman could not get the affair out of his mind, and that it was always haunting his recollection. Be it noted that this was but one, and the first, of many disappointments that the future had in store for him. That same authority who owed his position to his support, was the very one that was to exercise the power of his office to crush him. True, later on, that same authority bestowed compliments and expressions of esteem upon him as abundant as they were belated. However, it must be confessed that this regrettable collision with Hawkins is not fully explained by the somewhat bald account we have given of it. It is, we may point out to begin with, by no means uncommon in colleges and similar communities for men to vote a colleague into a position of authority in the belief that they will be able to count on his good offices to help them bring about certain reforms which they have at heart, and then to find him, when well in the saddle, exhibiting a narrow-minded conservatism as uncompromising as unexpected. But this, though true enough, does not wholly account for the Hawkins-Newman antagonism. There was another element, another circumstance, which Newman did not recognise to begin with, but which was to be made clear to him under conditions of a different nature. Newman had a marked gift for drawing out from people all sorts of germinating ideas, of inchoate notions, which he then proceeded to develop and expand in a manner he supposed to be agreeable to their wishes. In so doing, however, he brought to bear such a wealth of power and lucidity of expression as completely to take the wind out of the sails of his so-called teachers, though he still quite sincerely regarded himself as their disciple. The breach which occurred in the course of the Oxford Movement with those who had preceded him in the campaign is another instance of a similar nature, and thus it was always fated to be with him. But even so, these various explanations leave the inner core of the conflict still unrevealed. The more Newman pondered on the matter as time went on, the more convinced he became that the whole thing was an example of the inevitable clash between two opposing mentalities, two antagonistic types of educationist. Later on he himself, in his writings concerning *The Rise and Progress of Universities*, set the matter down in terms to which little or nothing need be added. The distinction is drawn between those who rely first and foremost on personal influence as a means of propagating truth, and those others who prefer to put their trust in stereotyped and regular institutional methods. Hawkins was definitely one of the latter school. As yet Newman did not realise to what extent he himself possessed the gifts which place one in the former category, just as the lack of them excludes one from it. As Newman himself subsequently declared, Hawkins all along was constitutionally unable to see anything but favouritism and capriciousness in that human approach which had been such a success for the young tutor and for his like-thinking colleagues. On the top of all this, Froude's mischievous pranks and—less flagrant perhaps, but in reality no less of a red rag—Wilberforce's thoroughgoing but very youthful radicalism, helped to exacerbate an instinctive antipathy and render it past curing. As for Hawkins, his obvious stiffness, the visible token of his dour and unimaginative gravity, helped not a little to dry up the springs. Nor must we forget that there was something of the *parvenu* about him, something of an intellectual of the second rank who had somehow found his way into the first. A certain feeling of jealousy, a morbidly sensitive susceptibility, are not uncommon in the man who, finding himself foremost in rank, realises that he is anything but foremost in ability. To put the cap on it all, a political disagreement which occurred in the early part of 1829 hurried on the final breach. As regards this last-mentioned circumstance, it was the first time Newman had had occasion to occupy himself with any public matter, and his way of dealing with the affair revealed in him the possession of abilities of a kind quite unsuspected by his friends. Sir Robert Peel was the representative of the University in the House of Commons. Those who had elected him had done so in the firm belief that he was the embodiment of those conservative traditions of which Oxford might be regarded as the ultimate stronghold. Later on, however, his policy underwent a change, as was shown by his support of the Catholic Emancipation Bill. Newman protested at the time that he had formed no definite views as regards this particular question, though in principle he favoured putting an end to what was obviously a detestable state of affairs. However, he was by this time sufficiently imbued with the

High Church spirit to detect in this measure some hint of a menace in the liberalism and indifferentism which were leading Peel to go back on his convictions. Not only that but, like most of the University folk, he felt there was something uncomfortably suggestive of the *fait accompli* way of going to work in the manner in which Peel, after taking a line directly contrary to that which his electors had a right to expect, resigned his seat and calmly asked them to re-elect him as a sign of their approval of what he had done.

All these motives led him, not only to vote against Peel, as did the other fellows of Oriel, but to take an active part in the agitation against him. Even so, it was not at the moment the treatment of the Catholics that interested him; what he was anxious to ensure was the independence of the University and the Church, of which she was, as it were, the home, in regard to a political measure that was wholly secular in its character and design.

Here, again, he and his colleagues found themselves in collision with the Provost who, with all the Noëtics, Whately at their head, was wholly committed to Peel. It must have been at this point that the dichotomy which marked the Oriel of the 1820s occurred, though there was no sign of it when Newman became a member of that society.

A more immediate result of this latest divergence was that it alienated the Provost for good and all from his tutors, and rendered the atmosphere of their official exchanges exceedingly uncomfortable. Newman, as we have already remarked, recurred again and again to these events. He always maintained that his position was, in principle, a perfectly sound one, but, as the years went on, he blamed himself more and more for the attitude which he had taken up. It was Hawkins, after all, who had brought him out, Hawkins who had given him his post as tutor and, finally, it was Hawkins who had appointed him to St Mary's in succession to himself. When he came to look back on these things, it seemed to him that his response to all these benefits had been singularly thankless.

There are a number of self-accusations, in his memoranda for the years which follow, which are completely enigmatic in the truncated version which Anne Mozley has given us. If, however, we refer to the original entries we shall see quite clearly that they relate to the incidents just recorded. This accounts for his thinking for a long time that he had profaned the Sacrament by receiving it when his heart was filled with resentment towards the Provost. As for their outward relations, he reproached himself for having displayed a disrespect almost amounting to insolence, and generally for betraying a dislike quite unjustified by the circumstances. We must, of course, in all this, make allowance for a conscience that was sensitive almost to the point of morbidity, particularly in matters touching the gratitude due to his superiors and to his seniors in office. However this may be, the truth of the matter seems to be that he *did* display at this juncture, more or less intentionally, redoubtable powers of controversy, rich in irony and satire. Like all natures susceptible of deep affection and devotion to a high ideal, Newman, as the counterpart to these qualities, possessed powers of invective greater than he fully realised.

Be that as it may, matters came to a climax owing, it would appear, to the intervention of a third party whose interest in the point at issue was probably no more than lukewarm. Hawkins supported his tutors so long as they were content to confine themselves to matters of coaching and discipline. When, however, they took measures to extend their personal influence over the men themselves, he regarded their efforts with disapproval. At last the crash came—and it was irremediable—when, in 1829, they proposed to adopt an entirely new scheme for their lectures. Instead of each tutor confining himself as heretofore to lectures on subjects which he considered best suited to himself, and delivering them to all the students in the college, it was now decided that, in addition to these general lectures, each tutor should give a series for the exclusive benefit of his own particular pupils. It may be noted that this system, far from curtailing the existing duties of the tutors, did but add to them.

Whenever even the most trifling occasions of disagreement had occurred, Newman had always made it clear to Hawkins, beyond all possibility of misunderstanding, that a tutor, though he owed his appointment to the head of his college, was the holder of a University office, for the due discharge of which he was responsible solely to the Vice-Chancellor. However, in the present instance, this latest reform was so important that for his part he would have liked to talk it over with Hawkins before actually putting it into operation. It was the senior tutor, Dornford, who dissuaded him.

The latter, however, looked on passively, perhaps even a little sceptically, at what his three junior colleagues were attempting. Nevertheless, it was he, as the *doyen* of the party so to speak, who had always had to bear the brunt of the Provost's displeasure, and the abrupt and haughty manner in which he had lately come to display it. And so, mischievously enough, he went out of his way to provoke him. Whereupon Hawkins, in a mighty rage, said they could use their time as they pleased, that was *their* affair, but from now onwards, and this was *his* affair, he would see to it that they got no more pupils.

The situation was too strained to admit of conciliation. As the students already allotted to them came to the end of their studies, Newman and his friends had to realise that, for all practical purposes, they had been relieved of their duties. Neither side having yielded an inch, Froude and he, by 1832, found themselves with no one to teach. They relinquished their functions, little dreaming that the freedom that was now theirs was but the prelude, and a brief one, to a new order of activity destined to influence, not Oxford alone, but the entire Church of England.

VI

ILLNESS AND BEREAVEMENT

THE two preceding chapters will have thrown some light on the growth and ripening of Newman's intellectual powers; they will also have afforded us some insight into the circumstances in which he came to translate into actual practice the theories and ideas at which he had now arrived, showing how the ideal and the practical acted and reacted, one upon the other.

Many and multifarious as were the tasks and preoccupations which now beset him in his daily life, there were factors of a more personal character to which due weight must be given. With him, as with all richly gifted natures, ideas and practical activities, though they may stimulate and nourish the inward life, are always submerged and outdistanced by it. Ideas and practice, what he thinks and what he does, are insensibly influenced and transfigured by what he is, or is coming to be, in his inmost being. In the course of these same years, if not a complete remoulding, at all events a very decided modification, was in process of coming about. Beneath the surface *ego*, progressively formed by the more overt intellectual influences, and by the work which absorbed his time and energies, another *ego*, more complex and in many ways very different from the first, was imperceptibly coming into being in the penumbra of his inner self. A time was to come, about the end of 1827, when a half-repressed assertion of his outward personality would herald the emergence of an inner spirit which was far more in accord with his earlier leanings, and with all the enduring elements of his character.

There is in the *Apologia* a seemingly isolated passage which conveys in a few words what we have been endeavouring to bring out. "The truth is, I was beginning to prefer intellectual excellence to moral; I was drifting in the direction of the Liberalism of the day. I was rudely awakened from my dream at the end of 1827 by two great blows—illness and bereavement." The illness to which he refers was the serious breakdown which overtook him on the 26th November, in the very middle of the examinations for which he had been preparing his pupils. The bereavement was a blow that fell upon him almost without warning, the death of his youngest sister, Mary, which occurred on the 5th of the following January.

If we would rightly understand the hidden elements of his personality which were now about to reveal themselves, we must first devote a little time to the consideration of his friendships and of his ties of affection.

His friendly feelings for Bowden had in no way been affected by physical separation. In the autumn of 1825, the year of his ordination to the priesthood and also of his spell of very hard work at St Clement's, Bowden managed to induce him to snatch a few days' holiday. So, at the end of September, he went for a brief stay to Peartree, which was the name of his friend's family estate. By the seashore, in wonderful country, this visit was taken up with yachting or country drives in the day time, and, in the evenings, with music interspersed with conversation with his beloved friend. All this was to him as if he had filled his lungs with a great draught of fresh air. Above all, he seems to have carried away with him the impression, either a fresh one or an old one revived, of the beauty of the visible world. No doubt the Isle of Wight, explored in a succession of lovely autumn days, presented a scene particularly favourable to such impressions. However, it was not until some years later, on a visit to the Froudes, that he became fully aware of the power that such an experience could have on him, how deeply it could stir his inmost being; and that was prior to his discovery, his wellnigh overwhelming discovery, of the Mediterranean.

The following year, he again spent some time with the Bowdens, on this occasion at Worthing, where they also had an estate. But before that he had struck up another friendship. It merits some consideration, as it was fraught with a good deal of importance for Newman and his family.

After a brief stay with his people in London—Mrs Newman and her daughters had taken up their abode at Strand-on-the-Green—he put in one month in the summer at the parsonage at Ulcombe, doing duty for the Vicar of the place, the Rev. Samuel Rickards, sometime fellow of Oriel. Harriet went, too, to keep house for her brother. When the Rickards family came back, Harriet found herself so quickly and so thoroughly at home with them that she stayed on for some time after John had left, and at once became Mrs Rickards' close friend and her husband's keen disciple. Newman, too, became on most cordial terms with both of them. So quickly, in fact, did the friendship grow that the following year the whole family went, one after another, to make a brief stay at the hospitable parsonage.

The Rickards seem to have been anything but an ordinary couple. Seriousness and fun seem to have played a pretty equal part in the affection they so naturally inspired. This piquant blend comes out clearly enough in two of Mary's letters, notwithstanding the helter-skelter way she rattled on in everything she wrote. These letters were sent off a few weeks before her untimely death, the first while she was still at Ulcombe, the second soon after her return home (home this time being Brighton, whither yet another move had taken them):

> Is it not odd that Jemima and I should be here alone? Yet I feel quite at home. It is enough to make one feel glad only to look at Mr Rickards, and Mrs Rickards makes me laugh so.

And then:

> I must tell you about Mr Rickards. You know, as Harriet would say, he cannot let anyone alone; so he has given me a great deal of good advice.

The fact is he had plunged this slip of a girl—she was but seventeen—into the deep waters of theology and philosophy, even getting her to read the *Logic* of Port Royal. Worse than that, he had encouraged her to try her hand at a verse translation of *Télémaque!*

> What a nice creature Mrs Rickards is! I always think of the word, I believe you applied to her, "fascinating", for I think that is exactly what she is; and it is so amusing to hear Mr Rickards and her talk to each other.[1]

A sort of humorous pedantry seems to have been one of the chief characteristics of this ex-don of a parson, and, bound up with it all, a desire to teach and improve the minds of the younger generation. And he was so kindly and good humoured in the way he went to work that his victims seem to have been only too pleased to resign themselves to his persecution. His great hobby, however, was playing the psychologist on the people about him. He was equally keen on graphology, and some of his deductions filled his friends with astonishment. Taking him on the whole, he was typically English and typically Anglican. The elderly rector that Morgan portrays for us in *Sparkenbroke*, whose apostolic zeal people did not know whether to ascribe to his charity or his curiosity regarding human nature, corresponds pretty closely to our idea of Mr Rickards. It must, however, be added that he had an unusually profound knowledge of the great seventeenth-century

[1] *Letters*. Vol I, p 150.

theologians, commonly called the Caroline Divines, and he it was that kindled Newman's interest in them. In return for that, the young don, whom he had asked to suggest a subject for him to work on, advised him to write something about their school of thought. The way Rickards got out of adopting this suggestion is a little gem of humour. His answer gives us such a vivid idea of those learned gentlemen whose delicate scruples will never allow them to write about what they think they would *like* to write about, that we must be permitted to quote at least a few lines of it:

> You entertained me by the magnificent work with which you design that I should ennoble myself; and by your so quietly taking for granted two such very debatable points as that I could write it and that other people would read it.

What he says later impresses us (as it was to impress Newman too, when he came to look back on it) as being more suitable to the times. That was that he should absorb the substance of the Caroline Divines and then re-express it in terms better suited to the age. But then Rickards adds, with a touch of something like cynicism: "We shall employ them to the most purpose by keeping them constantly in our sight and out of other people's."

As for the "fascinating" Mrs Rickards, here is a trifling detail that will throw a light on her charm, her typically Victorian charm. She had an album in which she used to ask her friends to write a few lines of poetry, of their own composition, on their favourite flower. It was for that album that Newman wrote the little poem dated Ulcombe, 2nd October, 1827, and alluded to in a passage omitted from the *Apologia*. It came immediately after the words relating to his dedication to a celibate life, which we have already quoted:

> And in 1827, in some verses I wrote for a friend's Album, after comparing myself to the "snapdragon" fringing the walls opposite the rooms in which I spent my first solitary three weeks at College in June 1817, and I express a hope that I may "in college live and die".[1]

Mr and Mrs Rickards were not the only occupants of the parsonage to love, and be loved by, Newman. There were two small children who quickly made friends with him and whom he treated with the ease and charm that never forsook him, even in extreme old age, in his dealings with children, as any of his young nephews and, for the matter of that, many an Oratory schoolboy would have borne eloquent

[1] *Verses on Various Occasions*, p. 17.

witness. A few days before putting him through the album ordeal, Mrs Rickards wrote to Harriet, saying:

> And now here is John come to keep me company, or rather to be plagued by the children. I wish you only could see him with both on his lap in the great armchair, pulling off and then putting on his glasses. They are quite overjoyed to see him.

Farther on, in the same letter, she makes an amusing reference to her husband. Harriet, it seems, had warned her, in terms purposely obscure, that John and Robert Isaac Wilberforce, who had arrived with them, were preparing to make a combined assault on the treasures of knowledge locked up in Mr Rickards' brain. She wrote:

> I did not understand your warning respecting the designs afloat against Samuel. I have been asking him if he has discovered any. He says only that they seem determined to pump him well, and find out all he knows, enlightening him when he is deficient, etc. He says that such examinations are worth more than three times as many hours of study alone. I hope the rest find the same to be the case.[1]

Without leaving Oxford, Newman was to discover another hospitable household where he was to profit by the intellectual riches of a superabundantly learned father and the delights of his high-spirited little children. And that was the Pusey family. Rickards had made him interested in the Caroline Divines; Pusey was to revive his interest in the Fathers.

In 1827, the austere, the pensive, the grave, we had wellnigh said the ponderous, Pusey took to himself a wife. Strange as that event may seem when we think of his imposing presence, his weighty arguments, and his no less massive tomes, it is even more so when we come to realise that this marriage was the conclusion of a highly romantic courtship. To his dying day, the memory of those far-off times never failed to bring tears to his eyes. Pusey's father was a very wealthy, and very autocratic, country squire who, for some unknown reason, had put his foot down when his son proposed to wed a certain young girl with whom he had for some time been deeply in love. For seven years, father and son pulled different ways, the son unwavering in his devotion, the father unyielding in his opposition. It was not only in the interest of his Hebrew studies that Pusey made two long stays at Goettingen, first in 1825, and again in 1826–1827. These visits, which Lloyd had encouraged with the object of finding means to

[1] *Letters*, Vol. I, p. 146.

parry the attack which everyone felt the German scientists would soon be making on the inspiration of the Scriptures, were possibly welcomed by the young student, not only for the reason assigned, but as a means of warding off the nervous breakdown that might have overtaken him had he continued to remain at home. However, when he returned in 1827, his hitherto unbending parent at last gave way.

Regius Professor of Hebrew, and Canon of Christ Church as he soon became, Pusey took up his abode within the shadow of the Cathedral, the silent cloisters on the one side, the open prospect of Christ Church meadow on the other. These calm and stately quarters were soon to echo to the sound of childish laughter. Newman was the most familiar guest. He who had been the friend and confidant of the luckless suitor, became the even more intimate friend of the family and of the young folk, in that time of happiness, alas, too brief. In Mrs Pusey we seem to behold a vision of liveliness and charm. No wonder her warmth of feeling won the affection of the grave and studious Pusey, that her airs and graces wrought on him a charm, in those happy days, that he was fated never to recapture. All the fragrance of that love of theirs is summed up in an oft-repeated story. Many years later, long after his young wife's death, when Pusey had for years been living a life of the sternest asceticism, his daughter one day brought him a sprig of verbena which she had gathered in the garden where Mrs Pusey had spent her girlhood days. The old man, as his eyes lighted on the slender perfumed spray, could not restrain his tears. Then he said, "Your mother gave me a spray of that verbena when I asked her to marry me."

With unusual candour, Pusey, when he presented Newman to his young wife, bade her look to him, rather than to himself, for spiritual inspiration. "He is worthier than I," he added. And, indeed, it fell to Newman's lot to bring Mrs Pusey away from the almost deistical Christianity in which she had been brought up, to the Anglicanism that was all but Catholicism, which was now her husband's religion, and his own. There being some doubts as to the validity of her baptism, Newman baptised her again, an office he also performed for the first child of the marriage, Lucy, whose delicacy seemed to make her doubly precious. Pusey, poor man, felt quite unequal to educating his children, let alone amusing them, but Newman was the life and soul of the little family. His visits to Pusey's quarters in Christ Church were the signal for outbursts of boisterous merriment that sometimes astonished other visitors who might happen to be there. Alas, the day was soon to come when he was to find himself called upon to play the hardest of all parts, that of bringing consolation in bereavement. Mrs Pusey, after giving birth to a puny and ailing boy, and then to a girl, who was destined to become the foundress of an order of Anglican nuns, bade farewell to this world. A few years later, the fair but delicate Lucy was laid to rest beside her mother in the nave of Christ Church. When the time came for Mrs Pusey to bid a last farewell to her grief-stricken husband, she found consolation in the thought that, by his side, would always stand their incomparable friend. While the Puseys were enjoying those fleeting days of happiness, Newman himself was fated to endure the sorrow of a parting rendered all the bitterer from the unforeseeable suddenness of its coming.

That winter, 1827–1828, Newman, to use his own words, was rudely awakened from his intellectual dream by two blows, illness and bereavement. Appointed University examiner, he became, as we have already seen, the victim of a nervous breakdown due to overwork. This happened on the 26th November. An immediate spell of complete rest at the home of Robert Isaac Wilberforce sufficed quickly to dispel the grave apprehensions to which his alarming symptoms had given rise. He had had a heavy burden to bear, and to bear it for a period unduly prolonged. The result was that his marvellously delicate cerebral apparatus had been temporarily thrown out of working order, though there was at no time any fear that it would definitely collapse.

However, while Newman, now with his family at Brighton, was recovering his health and spirits amid the joys of Christmas, the death of his youngest sister confirmed a change that had for some time been impending in his views and sentiments. To his life's end, he carefully preserved an account of this tragic event, an account so restrained, yet so moving, that it must be given here. Maria Giberne, one of his most faithful friends, said, in a letter written fifty years afterwards:

> But I do not want to talk of myself. I want to tell you of my entire sympathy with you in what you say and feel about the anniversary of our dear Mary's death. This season never comes round without my repassing in my heart of hearts, all the circumstances of those few days—my first visit to your dear family. Who could ever behold that dear sweet face for any length of time and forget it again? And again, who could ever have been acquainted with the soul and heart that lent their expression to that face, and not love her?
>
> My sister Fanny and I arrived at your house on the 3rd of January, and sweet Mary, who had drawn figures under my advice when she was staying with us at Wanstead, leant over me at a table in the drawing-room, and in

that sweet voice said, "I am so glad you are come; I hope you will help me in my drawing." I forget about the dinner and evening on that day, for I was doubtless under considerable awe of you in those first days; but the next day Mr Woodgate and Mr Williams dined there, and dear Mary sat next you, and I was on the other side; and while eating a bit of turkey she turned her face towards me, her hand on her heart, so pale, and a dark ring round her eyes, and she said she felt ill, and should she go away? I asked you, and she went; I longed to accompany her, but dared not for fear of making a stir. It was the last time I saw her alive. Soon after, Jemima went after her; and then your Mother, looking so distressed: and she said, "John, I never saw Mary so ill before; I think we must send for a doctor." You answered as if to cheer her, "Ah, yes, Mother, and don't forget the fee." How little I thought what the end would be! Next morning Harriet came to walk with us about one o'clock—after the doctor had been, I think—but though she said Mary had had a very bad night, she did not seem to apprehend danger. We went to dine with a friend, and only returned to your house about nine. I felt a shock in entering the house, seeing no one but you so pale, and so calm, and yet so inwardly moved; and how, when I asked you to pray with us for her, you made a great effort to quiet your voice, sitting against the table, your eyes on the fire, and you answered, "I must tell you the truth; she is dead already."[1]

It would be impossible, without taking a glance backward over the past, fully to understand how great was the significance of this event in the spiritual development of Newman. Here, it may be for the first time, as we look at him among those whom he loved so dearly, he reveals himself, not only as loved and lovable, but as loving. The first wholly personal chord in his earthly relationships was now to be sounded, the first, and maybe the last. This human love, thus stricken to death, was to keep open for ever the wound of a love divine which, yet again, the intellect had come near to searing over.

Mary Sophia Newman, born on the 9th November, 1809, was some eight or nine years younger than her brother John Henry. What they were to each other, and what she was in herself, is best brought out in one of her letters :

May 5, 1826.

Dear John, how extremely kind you are. Oh, I wish I could write as fast as I think. I cannot tell why, but whatever I write to you I am always ashamed of. I think it must be vanity; and yet I do not feel so to most others. And *now* all I have written I should like to burn.

Thank you for your long letter, which I do not deserve. I wish I *could* see you in your rooms. Are they called generally by the titles you give them? I hope the 'brown room' is not quite so grave as the name would lead one to suppose. At least Harriet would not be in the number of its admirers. You

[1] *Letters*, Vol. I, p. 155.

know *brown* is not a great favourite of hers. I had no idea you lectured in your rooms.

Oh, how delightful if you can do as you say! It really will be quite astonishing to have you for so long—but poor Frank! I wish, oh, that he might be with us too! I did not imagine, John, that with all your tutoric gravity, and your brown room, you could be so absurd as your letter (I beg your pardon) seems to betray.

How very thoughtless I must be! I have proceeded so far without saying one word of your "unwellness", which ought to have come first; I hope it was worthy of no higher appellation. In the Long Vacation, you know, we shall be able to nurse you.

Well, I really think I have found out the secret of my difficulty in writing to you. It is because I never told you that difficulty. At least, I find I write much easier since my confession.[1]

In that letter, in which emotion dances about hither and thither, like the blushes that come and go on a maiden's cheek, we catch a glimpse of her as she was in all the lively artlessness of her daily life. We see clearly what they must have been to each other, this brother and sister. She was, of course, duly impressed by her brother's grave demeanour, yet her shyness did not chase away her smiles. But over and above this, was there not a consciousness, shared assuredly by both, of some wholly special bond between them? No doubt the impression he made on her was a strong one, but, allowing for this, would she not have been more free had there not been some profound bond of union between them?

Towards the end of the following year, hardly more than a month before she died, she wrote him a letter which is yet one more example of the power she unconsciously possessed of portraying herself to the life in a couple of words or so: "How I long to see you! . . . I can fancy your face—there, it is looking at me."[2] The last letter she ever wrote him—we have already quoted it—was dated a day or two later. It was almost wholly taken up, it will be remembered, with the names of the books she was going to read, and pretty stiff reading they were for a girl of seventeen. This big brother, with his "tutoric gravity", as Mary called it, had always taken an interest in what the girls were reading. When Mary was eleven, and he had just been elected fellow of Oriel, he sent her some grammar exercises to do.[3] Later on, he corrected her first attempts at verse-writing, and we find him writing to his mother early in 1827, "Tell Mary I was quite delighted with her lines; they showed great elegance, poetical feeling, and good religious feeling, which is better still."[4]

[1] *Letters,* Vol. I, p. 117.
[2] *Ibid.*, p. 150.
[3] *Ibid.*, p. 71.
[4] *Ibid.*, p. 103.

The interest soon became reciprocal; it was not all on the brother's side. A letter from Jemima, written in 1826, contains this quizzical message:

> Mary desires her love, and begs that the next time you write you will be so kind as to enlighten her on the uses of reading the Fathers.

But the catastrophe none could foresee was now to lay the chill of death upon those smiles, and to quench, for her brother, a light that nothing could replace. Who would not be moved at this vision of life and light so swifty and irrevocably quenched? But, perhaps, most moving of all, is the posthumous life she was now to live in her brother's mind, a life that knew no end. This affords us one of the most remarkable instances of what memory was to Newman, memory that nothing could dim.

The first letter which Newman wrote after Mary's death is wholly animated by the thought of a past which belongs to him, and to him alone. We have in it one of the first indications of the idea he held regarding the relation between present and future:

> Oriel College, March 9, 1828.
>
> I hope you have not thought my silence unkind, dear Jemima. I have all along been going to write to you, but somehow or other, though I have not much to do, I find it difficult to make time. I am going out of the Schools, and Dornford (I fancy) will supply my place for the ensuing examination.
>
> Dear Jemima, I know you love me much, though your disposition does not lead you to say much about it, and I love you too, and you (I trust) know it. Carefully take down, if you have not already, all you can recollect that dear Mary said on every subject, both during the time of her short illness and the days before; we shall else forget it. Would it not, too, be desirable to write down some memoranda generally concerning her?—her general character, and all the delightful things we now recollect concerning her. Alas! memory does not remain vivid; the more minute these circumstances the better. To talk of her thus in the third person, and in all the common business and conversation of life, to allude to her as now out of the way and insensible to what we are doing (as is indeed the case), is to me the most distressing circumstance, perhaps, attending our loss.[1] It draws tears into my eyes to think that all at once we can only converse *about* her, as about some inanimate object, wood or stone. But she "shall flourish from the tomb". And in the meantime, it being but a little time, I would try to talk to her in imagination, and in hope of the future, by setting down all I can think of about her.[2]

[1] Anne Mozley draws attention to a beautiful passage in the sermon entitled *The Lapse of Time* which resumes and develops this subject: *Parochial and Plain Sermons*, Vol. VII, p. 4.

[2] *Letters*, Vol. I, p. 158.

That concluding sentence is very revealing of what memory was to Newman. It explains his anxiety, so clearly expressed in this passage, to glean, and piously to preserve, the minutest details of the past. This anxiety remained all through his life a conspicuous, one may say a distinctively characteristic, feature of Newman's personality. But great as was the importance he attached to it, it never suggests the sort of embalmment of the past, as of something over and done with, which is inevitable in the case of those who, unlike him, cannot take the past as a starting point for the future. With Newman, we cannot fail to recognise that contemplation of the past is contemplation of the unseen. This fidelity to remembered details leads to fidelity to the person seen now no longer in its mutable and transitory aspect, but in its eternal and unchanging essence. By the light of the invisible power which bore away the past, it behoves us to discover the invisible into which the visible has passed, nevermore to be extinguished, but to flourish everlastingly.

Little more than a month after this letter was written, we find the same thoughts expressed in a poem sent, this time, to Harriet. Its title is *Comfort in Bereavement*, and it is wholly concerned with the suddenness of the visitation which carried Mary away. The underlying idea is that this very suddenness was a mark of Divine mercy. Thus it is clear that her death betokened not extinction, but consecration. It was not the victory of sickness and decay claiming its victim, but a glorious triumph over Time the Destroyer. If Mary died so quickly, it was because, in this mortal life, she had been so soon made ready for the life eternal. Such was the swiftness of her death that her memory is with us like a light guiding us on to an unending future, not as something buried in the unfathomable past:

Death came unheralded:—but it was well;
  For so thy Saviour bore
Kind witness, thou wast meet at once to dwell
  On His eternal shore;

Joy of sad hearts, and light of downcast eyes!
  Dearest thou art enshrined
In all thy fragrance in our memories;
  For we must ever find
    Bare thought of thee
Freshen this weary life, while weary life shall be.

Later on he re-wrote the last two lines, making them still more emphatic :

Bare thought of thee
Kindle our sluggish souls, from care and gloom set free.

A few weeks go by, and then, early in May, Jemima receives this letter:

On Thursday I rode over to Cuddesdon. . . . The country is beautiful, the fresh leaves, the scents, the varied landscape. Yet I never felt so intensely the transitory nature of this world as when most delighted with these country scenes. And in riding out today I have been impressed more powerfully than before I had an idea was possible with the two lines:

Chanting with a *solemn* voice
Minds us of our *better choice*.

I could hardly believe the lines were not my own, and Keble had not taken them from me. I wish it were possible for words to put down those indefinite, vague, and withal subtle feelings which quite pierce the soul and make it sick. Dear Mary seems embodied in every tree and hid behind every hill. What a veil and curtain this world of sense is! Beautiful, but still a veil.[1]

There we come upon a direct reference to that vision of the unseen world, a world not separated from the world we see, but visible through it and beyond it, which is the soul of all Newman's poetry. Be it noted, moreover, that it is no Platonic ideal world with which we are concerned, but with the eternal world which draws us on beyond this transitory world but which nevertheless is present in it, *embodied in every tree and hid behind every hill*. This is the very essence of the Christian faith. The Invisible is the Kingdom "which is coming" and "which has already come", which is "in the midst of you . . . though you know it not". And this invisible world is essentially a world of personal presences. Therefore it is by a linking of person with person that we come to it. Thus Mary is now a supernatural guide. Here on earth she was loved with a love that was stronger than death; therefore, now, when she has passed beyond the veil, she is not lost to the hearts that cherished her, but draws them on to follow her to the place where she abides. Thus is memory, quickening like a seed through which life has forced a mysterious passage, raised to the level of a mystical experience.

In June, writing to Harriet, Newman says, "Not one half-hour passes but dear Mary's face is before my eyes."[2] And in November, to the same correspondent, he writes:

My ride of a morning is generally solitary; but I almost prefer being alone. When the spirits are good, everything is delightful in the view of still nature which the country gives. I have learned to like dying trees and black

[1] *Letters*, Vol. I, p. 161. [2] *Ibid.*, p. 161.

meadows—swamps have their grace, and fogs their sweetness. A solemn voice seems to chant from everything. I know whose voice it is—her dear voice. Her form is almost nightly before me, when I have put out the light and lain down. Is not this a blessing?

This faithful clinging to personal memory seems to set death at defiance. The beloved one, found once more and never again to be lost, not now as she was, but as she will be evermore, with her all the invisible seems to have become real; the invisible which is not merely near us, beside us, but actually with us. From the already imminent future it comes to us, and calls us in our turn.

That summer, when the first agony of his grief was somewhat abated, Newman wrote another poem in which with a calm, sure hand he recalled every detail of his vanished beloved. Here we see her, alive for all time, with all her familiar traits, her girlish smile, her simple ways, and that look of deep affection which went straight to the heart. But above all we hear her voice:

The thrilling voice I ne'er could hear
But felt a joy and pain.

And here we have that fleeting light which played upon her features, when she had asked her brother some question and he looked thoughtful and inclined to raise a doubt. Here we have her with all her girlish ways, smiling yet thoughtful, all the boundless hopefulness, the unclouded serenity of her nature, and then that final moment when, answering so dutifully the sudden call, she took those few swift steps that led her to eternity.

From friend-lit hearth, from social board,
All duteously she rose;
For weal or suffering, on His word
Faith found assured repose . . .

Then waited for the solemn spell,
Her trancèd soul to steep
In blissful dreams of breaking well
That brief-enduring sleep.

Such was she then, and such she is
Shrined in each mourner's breast;
Such shall she be, and more than this
In promised glory blest;

When in due lines her Saviour dear
His scattered saints shall range,
And knit in love souls parted here,
Where cloud is none, nor change.[1]

The last, and perhaps the most beautiful, of the compositions devoted to Mary was yet another poem. It was written for the first anniversary of that day of sorrow. He gave it the symbolical title of Epiphany Eve, and at the head of it he quoted these lines from the Bible.

God said, Let there be light, and there was light.

Awake thou that sleepest and arise from the dead;
And Christ shall give thee light!

And at the end he added two classical references, one the *Manibus date lilia plenis* of Virgil, the other these lines from the Greek whose note of resignation is coloured here with a warm Christian glow.

Weep no more, children, weep no more;
If her earthly graces now be hid,
Nothing is here for tears; such is her destiny.

If the wound remains open, does it not become like the glorious *stigmata* on the body of the Risen Saviour?

Speechless we sat; and watched, to know
How it would be;—but time moved slow,
Along that day of sacred woe.
A pause . . . then faith in mystery viewed
Christ's Epiphany renewed.

Dearest, gentlest, purest, fairest!
Strange half-being now thou sharest;
Wrapt around in peaceful bed
Conscience-whispered hope hath spread,
Mid those other gems, that shine
Paradised in the inmost shrine.
There thou liest, and in thy slumber
Times and changes thou dost number
Deeds and joys of earth o'er summing,
Visioning forth the glories coming
When thy soul shall reawaken
Those soft looks and form forsaken.

Then there recurs the thought of the haste divine, which on a sudden hurried Mary from this earthly spring into that heavenly spring which

[1] The poem, entitled "A Picture", in *Memorials of the Past*, which has the epigraph, "The maiden is not dead, but sleepeth".

knows no fading. It is a call which summons those she has left behind to follow her rather than vainly to long for her return.

Loveliest, meekest, blithest, kindest!
Lead! we seek the home thou findest!
Tho' thy name to us most dear,
Go! we would not have thee here.
Lead, a guiding beacon bright
To travellers on the Eve of Light.
Welcome aye thy Star before us,
Bring it grief or gladness o'er us.

At last, in the autumn of the year 1829, comes the answer to the final uncertainty. Not only does the form that has disappeared shine like a star to beckon us onward thither where she has gone, but she herself, though she has gone before us, drawn upward into the luminous realms of eternity, she herself has us always with her. She cannot come back, but she has no need to do so, for in God to whom she has gone, and where we shall rejoin her, she still beholds us.

A sea before
The Throne is spread; its pure still glass
Pictures all earth-scenes as they pass.
We on its shore
Share, in the bosom of our rest,
God's knowledge, and are blest!

If we have lingered long over this episode it was not only on account of the fleeting gleam of this sweet *Stella Matutina* that glowed and disappeared in Newman's glorious dawn. We have seen, without there being any need to draw attention to it, all that it brought back of the Newman of the earlier years, all that it portended in the Newman to be. Had it not been for these events and their influence on a spiritual nature providentially rendered sensitive by illness, we should have had the brilliant and subtle dialectician, no doubt; but what of the seer of the World Invisible, what of him for whom the track of memory was the pathway to Eternity?

The shock of Mary's death, with all its after-effects, seems to have prepared the way for yet another friendship and for the operation of influences destined to touch deeper chords in Newman's being than any hitherto attained. We refer to his friendship with Keble and to his study of the Fathers. We do not mean to say that either brought him any great store of new things. Whately, Hawkins, and, later, Froude were, both then and afterwards, his chief purveyors of new ideas. It was no new thing that we had in mind, but rather a resurgence, a second quickening of his hidden being.

We have seen how, as he meditated on Mary's death, one of Keble's poems had furnished him with an expression which seemed to him like a thought of his own. That is worthy of note. We know that up to now his relations with Keble had been purely external. The cause of the great change that was now to come about must have been the publication of the *Christian Year*, which had appeared twelve months before. In an essay written long afterwards, we are given an account of all that Newman discovered in it:

> If poems can be found to enliven in dejection, and to comfort in anxiety; to cool the over-sanguine, to refresh the weary, and to awe the worldly; to instil resignation into the impatient, and calmness into the fearful and agitated—they are these.

Froude, in those days, was bent on bringing Newman and Keble together. When, however, Hawkins was elected Provost, the project might well have appeared hopeless, and he must have been surprised, and a little diverted, to find that Keble's own poems had done what he himself had desired to do. Had he not himself told Keble, with that *enfant terrible* outspokenness of his, that there was something rather Sternhold and Hopkinsey about his style? The gentle and unassuming Keble was not in the least affronted at this criticism. He rhymed solely for his own pleasure and edification, and had agreed to publish merely to please his father, who was now on the brink of the grave. He himself was too fastidious in his taste not to agree with Froude's unflattering judgment. Nevertheless, it must be admitted that countless people would have sided with Newman in this matter, rather than with the author and his pitiless disciple. In the *Christian Year* there is something far more than agreeable versification on the well-worn conventional pattern, heightened every now and again with some admirable but unpretentious adornment. Newman bore witness, in the passage we have quoted, to the pure serenity in which the whole work is bathed. And there is this to be added, it is poetry instinct with a devotional quality, that is quietly but very unmistakably Catholic. That quality Keble had derived from his family traditions, which were not merely High Church but Non-juring. For Newman, this was a discovery.

To put the thing more accurately, the kind of religion which Whately, Hawkins, and more especially his reading of Butler, had begun to instil into him, took on, in Keble's poem, the warmth and colour of life. Theory became prayer. Beneath the somewhat chilly, highly cultured, and very delicately rustic Anglicanism of the Vicar of Hursley, Newman came upon an unsuspected element that harmonised with his own earliest and most cherished aspirations. The world of the senses, the symbol of those loftier realities which it at once suggests and conceals, God, invisible yet present, who seeks us and is with us in the humblest circumstances of our daily life. The *Christian Year* it was that taught him that Sacramental life, life in the Church, was the fulfilment, here and now, of those hidden and, as he deemed, incommunicable desires.

Another line of reading, which he took up at the same time as the *Christian Year*, which the *Christian Year* illustrated, and we may almost say interpreted, came in the very nick of time to nourish those spiritual aspirations which the death of Mary had brought to life once more.

We have noted the succession of events which led him to undertake the study of the Fathers. In this formidable enterprise, first suggested to him by his reading of Milner, he was further encouraged by some advice given him by Lloyd, with whom he had been brought into contact by the reading he had had to do on Christian antiquities for his *Essay on Miracles* and his study of the *Life of Apollonius Tyanæus*. Newman now took advantage of Pusey's second Continental visit to ask him to buy and send him the best available editions. On the 18th October, 1827, he writes to his mother telling her of their arrival: "My Fathers are arrived all safe—huge fellows they are, but very cheap—one folio costs a shilling! and all in this extravagantly moderate way."

These volumes which invaded his modest quarters at Oriel were always kept together, and they remained all in a row at Birmingham, where he installed them after the foundation of the Oratory. They are for the most part splendid Benedictine editions of the seventeenth century. The collection, begun by Pusey, was added to little by little. It was completed in 1831 by a handsome gift from his friends and pupils. Thirty-six volumes in magnificent bindings reached him all at once, including a St Athanasius which had once belonged to Bossuet and contained some manuscript notes in the handwriting of the Bishop of Meaux. Between the first and last of these massive arrivals was a St Gregory the Great, a personal present from Pusey in 1830. This token of friendship was prompted by Mrs Pusey's conditional baptism which Newman, as we have already seen, had recently performed. With the book came this note from Pusey:

My dear Friend,

I know not how to thank you for all your gentle tender kindness to me and mine, especially for yesterday, which, also, perhaps, but for you, had never been to us what I think it will be. I can only say with S.Aug., Retribues illi, Domine, in resurrectione justorum.

The accompanying book, which is meant as a sort of outward memorial, was Bp Lloyd's and has been mine for nearly nine years, and been used by me during the latter part of the time....

The fly-leaf of the book bears the following inscription, in Pusey's minute handwriting:

J. H. N.
d
E. B. P.
in gratam memoriam
beneficiorum quam plurimorum
sibi collatorum
tum maxime
Sabbati sancti
A.S. 1830

As regards the state of mind in which Newman began his reading of the Fathers and on the important bearing it eventually had in bringing him from Protestant religiosity to Catholicism, it will be opportune to quote yet another passage deleted by Anne Mozley from the *Autobiographical Memoir*. It follows the reference, already cited, to his reflections on the warnings he had had from his father regarding the unfortunate article he had contributed to the *Christian Observer*.

One additional feature in Mr Newman's mind shall be noticed, which seemed to indicate from the first that the ethical character of Evangelical Religion could not lastingly be imprinted upon it. This was his great attraction to what may be called the Literature of Religion, whether the writings of Classics, or the works of the Fathers. As to the Greek and Latin authors, poets and philosophers, Aeschylus, Pindar, Herodotus, Virgil and Horace, or again Aristotle and Cicero, he had from the first made much of them, as the Holy Fathers did, as being in a certain sense inspired moralists and prophets of truths greater than they knew, that in the familiar lines, "These relics of a guilty race are forfeit to the friends; what seemed an idol hymn now breathes of Thee, tuned by Faith's ear to some celestial melody." As to those Fathers themselves, much more did he ever delight, and even from a date earlier than his ordination, to find himself brought into their company.

All that explains what the study of the Fathers was to mean to Newman. Just as, in them, he came to recognise the spirit of a genuinely Christian humanism, so did they in their turn shed a Christian light on, and impart a Christian elevation to, an otherwise purely human culture.

We can see from the entries in his diary how this view of things gradually dawned on him. Starting in the Long Vacation of 1828, he set to work to read them methodically, in chronological order. Thus, he began with Ignatius of Antioch and St Justin. About the same time the following year, he wrote Harriet saying, "I am so hungry for Irenaeus and Cyprian I long for the vacation."[1]

When Hawkins told him he was not going to send him any more pupils, he thought first of all what a lot of time he would have for reading. "The Fathers arise again full before me", he wrote to his mother on the 18th June, 1830.

But to get an idea of all they really meant to him, of their effect on his spiritual life as well as on his intellectual development, we must again come back to a certain well-known passage in the *Apologia*, a passage in which, in a book so moving yet withal so reserved, we are conscious of an enthusiasm that refused to be silenced or repressed. It runs:

> The broad philosophy of Clement and Origen carried me away; the philosophy, not the theological doctrine; and I have drawn out some features of it in my volume (on the Arians) with the zeal and freshness, but with the partiality, of a neophyte. Some portions of their teaching, magnificent in themselves, came like music to my inward ear, as if in response to ideas, which with little external to encourage them, I had cherished so long. These were based on the mystical or sacramental principle, and spoke of the various Economies or Dispensations of the Eternal. I understood these passages to mean that the exterior world, physical and historical, was but the manifestation to our senses of realities greater than itself. Nature was a parable: Scripture was an allegory: pagan literature, philosophy, and mythology, properly understood, were but a preparation for the Gospel. The Greek poets and sages were in a certain sense prophets; for "thoughts beyond their thought to those high bards were given". There had been a directly divine dispensation granted to the Jews; but there had been in some sense a dispensation carried on in favour of the Gentiles. He who had taken the seed of Jacob for His elect people had not therefore cast the rest of mankind out of His sight. In the fulness of time both Judaism and Paganism had come to nought; the outward framework, which concealed yet suggested the Living Truth, had never been intended to last, and it was dissolving under the beams of the Sun of Justice which shone behind and through it. The process of change had been slow; it had been done not rashly, but by rule and measure, "at sundry times and in divers manners", first one disclosure and then another, till the whole evangelical doctrine was brought into full manifestation. And thus room was made for the anticipation of further and

[1] *Letters*, Vol. I, p. 184.

deeper disclosures, of truths still under the veil of the letter, and in their season to be revealed. The visible world still remains without its divine interpretation; Holy Church in her sacraments and her hierarchical appointments will remain, even to the end of the world, after all but a symbol of those heavenly facts which fill eternity. Her mysteries are but the expression in human language of truths to which the human mind is unequal. It is evident how much there was in all this in correspondence with the thoughts which had attracted me when I was young, and with the doctrine which I have already associated with the *Analogy* and the *Christian Year*.[1]

All that indicates clearly enough how deeply the reading of the Fathers affected Newman, and shows us the various circumstances which had helped it to exert its full effect. But it had taken the upheaval of the winter of 1827–1828, and, in particular, the thoughts engendered by Mary's death, to bring into full view a vision which till then had been enshrouded in twilight. Newman was certainly well endowed with gifts that fitted him to be the Seer as well as the Poet of the Invisible. But he possessed in equal measure the gifts of the critic and the dialectician. If his patristic studies were destined to advance the former at the expense of the latter, the events of that sorrowful year played a large and providential part in contributing to that result. Now the die was cast; his path was chosen. His sermons—and this is supported by the passage in the *Apologia*—were soon to bear this out. The call to holiness rather than to peace becomes ever clearer and more insistent in them. Trusting in the vision of that invisible world which lies beyond the world we see, Newman exhorts us ever more and more to look beyond this latter, so that we may come at length, in the words he chose for his epitaph, *ex umbris et imaginibus in veritatem*.

[1] *Apologia*, pp. 27–28.

VII

THE VOYAGE IN THE MEDITERRANEAN

If the conversion of 1816 had little that was visibly catastrophic or abrupt about it, still less had the inward transformation that took place during the years 1827 and 1828. Nor had it any appreciable effect on Newman's outward mode of existence. And what a long time it was before Newman's discovery, so to call it, of Keble was reflected by any marked change in the character of their mutual relations! We must not forget that it was in the spring of 1828 that Newman did his utmost to get Hawkins elected to the Provostship, instead of Keble. True, he had justified his conduct in terms highly flattering to the defeated candidate, but the letter in which he did so was so full of misapprehensions that it is worth while quoting what he himself said on the matter some years later, after Keble's death. This, then, is what he wrote in a letter to Fr Coleridge, dated the 18th April, 1866:

> I voted for Hawkins. I wrote to Keble to say why I did so and ended by saying, "However, it was unnecessary, for I knew he did not wish to be Head." He wrote me back a kind letter, but said I had no right to take it for granted he did not wish to be Head. I recollect being very much surprised. I must have his letter somewhere. I think he meant partly to snub me, as if I had no right to conjecture in so serious a matter what I knew nothing about, and had no right, writing to him, to treat him in a cavalier way.

In a previous letter, dated the 9th, he recalled what he had said to Froude:

> If an Angel's place was vacant, he should look towards Keble, but they were only electing a Provost.

This incident, though it indicates the distance that had to be travelled before a complete understanding between the two men was brought about, did nothing to delay it. The ties between them grew steadily closer as time went on. In 1831, when Keble returned to the University to take up the Chair of Poetry, the ice was finally broken.

All through these years Newman was a greatly overworked man. After the controversy over the Peel affair, which may be assigned to the early part of 1829, his tutorial duties became less and less onerous.

Hawkins, as we have said, decided to allot him no more pupils. On the other hand, apart from his work as University examiner, which, as we have seen, brought about a disastrous breakdown at the end of 1827, Newman, on Hawkins's election to the Provostship, was appointed to succeed him as Vicar of St Mary's. He was formally inducted on the 14th March, 1828, and took up his duties two days later. Newman, when he accepted the post, little foresaw the important effect it was destined to have on events a year or two later. For the time being, however, his duties, though they brought him more into the public eye, were far less of a tie than his work at St Clement's had been. Situated in the very heart of the city, St Mary's is the official University Church. There the Vice-Chancellor has his permanent stall, and there it is that all the official religious ceremonies take place. But that is quite separate from the work of the parish. This latter devolves wholly on the Vicar. At the time of which we are speaking, the parishioners consisted of a few High Street shopkeepers. Later on, of course, as Newman's influence gained ground, undergraduates flocked to the services to listen to sermons which, to begin with at any rate, by no means had them in view. The day was to come when the pulpit of St Mary's was to be the Oxford Movement's most active centre; but that day was not yet.

Here it must be recorded that, ever since July 1826, Newman's name had figured on the list of University preachers. Ten times each year, the University as a body is supposed to listen to a sermon specially composed for the occasion. These sermons are usually, but not invariably, delivered at St Mary's, whither the Vice-Chancellor and the various college heads wend their way in solemn procession, filling the church with their many-coloured robes. Letters from Mrs Newman and Harriet bear eloquent testimony to the delight they felt when they first beheld the scene, which was when Newman was occupying the pulpit. On the evening of the 2nd July, after his first appearance in this important role, he made an entry in his diary which reveals anything but a satisfied state of mind. He describes himself, in fact, as lying on his sofa and "writhing at the thought of what a fool I had made of myself".

As a matter of fact, he had been honoured with an offer of the post even before he had taken priest's orders. However, for one reason or another, possibly from mortification at this first experience of his, he did not perform the duty again until 1830. Then, in less than two years, he delivered five more University sermons. These six discourses subsequently made up the first part of the volume entitled *University Sermons*, a work which sheds a revealing light on his views regarding the relationship between Faith and Reason, between intellectual culture and the Christian life. We shall have occasion to return to these sermons later on, when we come to deal with the Oxford Movement.

Meanwhile, it is to be noted that his progressive emancipation from his tutorial duties was to coincide with the composition of his first major theological work. His reading of the Fathers, news of which soon got abroad, resulted in his being asked to undertake a history of the General Councils. Of this, he was destined to produce but one volume. When he set to work on the Council of Nice, he found that the deeper he delved into his subject, the more were the problems that confronted him. So many, indeed, were they, that they sufficed to fill the whole of the bulky volume to which he gave the title, *History of the Arians of the Fourth Century*.

An interesting outcome of this first work of his was that, through it, he became acquainted with a man who, a few years later, was to be the means of setting the Oxford Movement on its course. The man in question, however, was not a son of Oxford, but of Cambridge. Hugh James Rose, Chaplain to the Archbishop of Canterbury, was a particularly prominent representative of the High Church school of thought, though it would be hard to imagine a man more remote from the "*Two Bottle Orthodox*", then supposed to be its typical representatives. There is probably no one of whom Newman spoke in terms of greater respect than he did of Rose, who was undoubtedly a man of the highest character and the loftiest aspirations; altogether a man of very exceptional distinction. He was also the born Church dignitary, free, indeed, from arrogance and conceit, but just the sort of person to be scandalised by the behaviour and talk of such a man as Froude; whereas Newman's quiet tone, and what Mary mockingly called his "tutoric gravity", were well calculated to commend him; equally well, maybe, as some of his higher qualities.

The idea occurred to Rose to bring out a series of *Lives of the Fathers* with Rivingtons, who were henceforth Newman's regular publishers. The conference they had together about this matter was the occasion of Newman's first visit to Cambridge. The letter he wrote to his mother about this event merits quotation. It gives an attractive picture of the *sister-University*, as seen for the first time by a son of Oxford, little disposed, one may take it, *a priori*, to have much sympathy with this ancient nursery of latitudinarian and secularist ideas.

Cambridge: July 16, 1832.

Having come to this place with no anticipations, I am quite taken by surprise and overcome with delight. This, doubtless, you will think premature in me, inasmuch as I have seen yet scarcely anything, and have been writing letters of business to Mr Rose, and Rivingtons. But really, when I saw at the distance of four miles, on an extended plain, wider than the Oxford, amid thicker and greener groves, the Alma Mater Cantabrigiensis lying before me, I thought I should not be able to contain myself, and, in spite of my regret at her present defects and past history, and all that is wrong about her, I seemed almost to cry "*Floreat aeternum*". Surely there is a *genius loci* here, as in my own dear home; and the nearer I came to it the more I felt its power. I do really think the place finer than Oxford, though I suppose it isn't, for everyone says so. I like the narrow streets; they have a character, and they make the University buildings look larger by contrast. I cannot believe that King's College is not far grander than anything with us; the stone, too, is richer, and the foliage more thick and encompassing. I found my way from the town to Trinity College like old Oedipus, without guide, by instinct; how, I know not. I never studied the plan of Cambridge.

Mr Rose is away; he is very ill, which accounts for his silence. Should you see Froude, tell him he *is* married.[1]

That last sentence is amusing. It shows how impossible it was for Froude to picture to himself a worthy ecclesiastic without taking it for granted that he was a celibate.

This, his first visit to Cambridge, immediately preceded a summer holiday with the Rickards family. And here we may mention that there is extant a highly entertaining letter from Rickards concerning Rose. The Oxford man's disparaging idea of Cambridge comes out in it with a sort of genial brutality, as does the disdain of the scholar for the dignitary.

Thus every year, a few weeks' holiday, scrupulously measured, took Newman for a while away from Oxford. In 1827, he again took duty for a clergyman. This was a Mr Walsh of Hampstead, with whom, however, he does not appear to have been on the same sort of intimate terms as those which had established themselves so readily between himself and the Rickards family the year before.

In 1828, he spent a few days with his people at Brighton before taking them on to Nuneham, where they were to finish out the summer in a cottage belonging to his friend Dornford. In 1829, he did better still, and settled his mother and his two sisters at Horsepath. They were thus quite close to Oxford and he was able to ride over to them every day and stop the night. The ladies went back to Nuneham for the winter, but even so, he managed to ride out and see them every day.

[1] *Letters*, Vol. I, p. 234.

These expeditions on horseback were then his chief, and virtually his sole, distraction, and a distraction of some sort he felt he sorely needed. At this time, he had on his hands his tutorship, St Mary's, and the college bursarship, and, as if all that was not enough, he was acting as secretary to a missionary society, which, however, soon severed the connection, on account of Newman's increasingly High Church leanings. For the same reason he himself shortly before had withdrawn his subscription to the Bible Society. The death of the Rev. Walter Mayers occurred suddenly in 1828. Newman preached the funeral sermon, little realising, at the time, that he was pronouncing his own farewell to the Evangelicals.

However, while he was parting company with them, his brother Francis was moving in the opposite direction, and more and more throwing in his lot with them. He went out on a mission to Persia which, however, seems to have been a very ill-organised affair. As regards Charles, he was getting more out of hand than ever, and increasingly difficult to manage. Bereavement, separation, and the troubles brought on them by the irresponsible vagaries of its youngest member, led the Newman family to rely more and more on the eldest son. In the Long Vacation of 1830, Mrs Newman and her daughters bade a final adieu to Brighton. For a time, they stayed at Rose Hill, in the parish of Iffley, and were thus on the very threshold of Oxford. Soon afterwards, they moved to Rose Bank, a pleasant house in the same village, and there, close to her beloved son, Mrs Newman was to remain until her death in 1836.

It must be borne in mind that these breaks of his were by no means periods of complete repose. Apart from his reading and personal studies, which went on continuously, he always brought some of his pupils back with him whenever he could manage to get away from Oxford for a few weeks. The result was that these so-called holidays became what are called reading-parties. Thus it was that Henry Wilberforce, who was to become so deeply attached to him as time went on, the astounding Golightly, and a number of others became, as it were, members of the family. Their names, their facial peculiarities, and their fads find frequent quizzical mention in the young ladies' letters.

Fate was to ordain that some future day Harriet would wed one of John Henry's pupils, Thomas Mozley, and Jemima his brother John Mozley. Thomas, after cutting a brilliant figure among the younger Oriel fellows, proved a sad disappointment to his tutor, on account of his taste for the *dolce far niente*. With an indifference bordering on the cynical, he subsequently put into print a letter containing one of the sternest rebukes he had ever received from his mentor and brother-in-law in regard to this failing. The letter is to be found in those sparkling volumes of University gossip and notes on the Oxford Movement, of which Newman remarked that, when a story had only two legs to stand on, Tom was always ready to supply it with a third.

Another matter relating to this period we must not omit to mention, and that is Newman's brief, but not very profound, friendship with a somewhat strange personage, a Spanish ex-priest called Blanco. He was a man of great learning, but of a highly sceptical nature, who had recently become an Anglican. At Oxford, where he assumed the name of Blanco-White, he had been warmly received by the Oriel fellows, who welcomed him, and made him at home, as one of themselves. He soon associated himself with the Noëtics, but, as he was continually hounded along by some sort of inferiority complex, Oxford and Anglicanism proved for him but stages in a journey, and he ultimately found a home with the Unitarians, yet even their tenets seemed hardly vague enough for his brand of deism, which became more and more indeterminate. A Platonist, a poet (his sonnet "Night" is one of the jewels of English poetry), and a musician (he used to play duets with Newman, and people were wont to remark on the calm serenity of the one and the almost frenzied excitement of the other), and he brought to the discussions of the Oriel Common Room a host of fresh ideas and novel topics.

Bitter as were his feelings towards the Church, he furnished Newman with a great deal of elementary information about Catholicism. It is, by the way, curious to note that Blanco-White was the first to talk to him, and it seems in pretty sympathetic terms, about St Philip Neri and the Oratory. And Blanco-White it was who succeeded in getting from Newman, hard-driven though he was, an article on Aristotle's *Poetics* for a short-lived periodical, known as the *London Review*, in which he was interested.

However, amid all these varied currents of activity, we may get a clue as to the trend of his inner spirit from some words which appear in the manuscript draft of the *Apologia*, but never found their way into print.

Afterwards, what had been a mere anticipation, became a preference. Hitherto, up to February 1829 the idea had been obscured in my mind, for a month now, and a month then; but from that date I have had the continuous will and resolution, with divine aid, to live and die single. I determined to be "a pilgrim pale with Paul's stern girdle bound". I will add that in looking out these details of past years, I accidentally have found under date of September 1829 (and written the same year): "(I wrote this) in my rooms at Oriel, slowly advancing etc. and led on by God's hand blindly, not knowing whither he is leading me. Even so."

We have carefully examined all the extant memoranda relating to the month of February, in the hope of discovering something that would help to explain his reasons for suppressing this passage, but all we found was a number of particulars about the Peel affair. Are we to take it from that, that there was a strong line of demarcation dividing his inward life from his ordinary day-to-day existence? Or did his decision to throw in his lot with the High Church party mean that he was prepared to do anything, to go to any lengths, in order to preserve the Anglican Church from the doom that threatened her? In the absence of any definite documentary evidence, it would be idle to conjecture. All we can say is that we shall catch an unmistakable echo of the sacrifice to which he thus consented when, two years later, he was on a visit to the Froudes at Dartington.

Froude had a remarkable and very natural charm for all who were not scared, or offended, by the sort of *enfant terrible* ways he adopted. Newman was one of those who saw through all that. The startling agreement of their views about education was one link between them, and then, although Froude adopted a tone and mode of behaviour admirably calculated to scare and alienate an Evangelical, Newman discerned through it all the fundamental saintliness of his character, and this recognition soon brought him very close to Froude. Nor, for his part, was Froude slow to recognise the deeply religious nature and, it is not too soon to say, the grandeur of Newman's character. On the one side was an affectionate disposition entirely free from sentimentality; on the other, a quietness, a reserve wholly without guile or pretence. The two soon came together in a harmony destined never to be marred. These holidays of the year 1831 served to deepen and expand a friendship that was already far beyond its apprentice stage.

Froude and Newman embarked at Southampton early in July. Newman was horrified at the idea of spending the night among the miscellaneous crowd below deck, so he suggested that they should sleep in the open. Newman sadly recalled this later on, for there is no doubt that Froude caught a chill that night, from the effects of which he never completely recovered, and to that may be traced the beginning of the illness which so prematurely carried him away. When, in the morning light, they arrived at Torbay, Newman was filled with an enchantment that seems never to have left him all through his stay. Writing to his mother, he says:

> Limestone and sandstone rocks of Torbay are very brilliant in their colours, and sharp in their forms; strange to say, I believe I never saw real rocks before in my life. This consciousness keeps me very silent, for I feel I am admiring what everyone knows, and it is foolish to observe upon.

He goes on to add that what possessed Sir Walter Raleigh to leave such a beautiful spot for the court at Greenwich, he cannot understand. The Froudes' ancestral house at Dartington seems, if that were possible, to have added to his enthusiasm.

> What strikes me most is the strange richness of everything. The rocks blush into every variety of colour, the trees and fields are emeralds, and the cottages are rubies. A beetle I picked up at Torquay was as green and gold as the stone it lay upon, and a squirrel which ran up a tree here just now was not the pale reddish-brown to which I am accustomed, but a bright brown-red. Nay, my very hands and fingers look rosy, like Homer's Aurora, and I have been gazing on them with astonishment. All this wonder I know is simple, and therefore, of course, do not you repeat it. The exuberance of the grass and the foliage is oppressive, as if one had not room to breathe, though this is a fancy—the depth of the valleys and the steepness of the slopes increase the illusion—and the Duke of Wellington would be in a fidget to get some commanding point to see the country from. The scents are extremely fine, so very delicate yet so powerful, and the colours of the flowers as if they were all shot with white. The sweet peas especially have the complexion of a beautiful face. They trail up the wall mixed with myrtles as creepers. As to the sunset, the Dartmoor heights look purple, and the sky close upon them a clear orange. When I turn back and think of Southampton Water and the Isle of Wight, they seem by contrast to be drawn in Indian ink or pencil. Now I cannot make out that this is fancy; for why should I fancy? I am not especially in a poetic mood. I have heard of the brilliancy of Cintra, and still more of the East, and I suppose that this region would pale beside them; yet I am content to marvel at what I see, and think of Virgil's description of the purple meads of Elysium. Let me enjoy what I feel, even though I may unconsciously exaggerate.[1]

No doubt this letter expresses with *naïveté*, but a *naïveté* quite aware of itself, the wonderment of the town-dweller, of the over-taxed brain-worker, who is suddenly transported into the very heart of Nature. But it also reveals a temperament of unusual delicacy and

[1] *Letters*, Vol. I, pp. 213–214.

sensitivity. The English, in this connection, would use the words "sensuous" and "sensuousness", of which there is no precise equivalent in French. It signifies not just ordinary sensibility, still less does it denote sensuality, with the implications that usually attend that word. It means rather an activity of the senses at once extremely keen and extremely delicate and discerning. In this instance, we have a direct consciousness of the external world awakening, or reawakening, with a vigour all the greater for being unalloyed with any sensual attraction. At Dartington at that time there were, besides the three sons and their father, the Squire-Archdeacon, a whole bevy of young folk, cousins, male and female, and a number of friends. There survives, amid those faded pages which faintly portray for us that happy company in their Eden-like surroundings, something of the atmosphere of Jane Austen's novels, novels in which Newman continued to find pleasure, even in advanced old age—that atmosphere, with an added touch of animation. There seems no doubt that this society, so well-bred and youthful, appealed to him no less than the setting in which he discovered it. Very expressive is the poem he sent a week later to Harriet. It speaks, it is true, of trees and meadows, but how obvious it is that he had other beings more fully endowed with life in mind. If his previous letter spoke only of the attraction things had for him, it is notable, yet not surprising, that this attraction is now resisted by him with a quiet but inexorable "no". Under a form whose seductiveness, we say again, was the more potent for being radiant and pure, he detected, even as he admired it most, the danger it involved for him, the danger, in a word, that he would rest content with it, making an abiding-place of that which he himself had called, in words already quoted, but a curtain and a veil; the danger of making one's home in this world, whereas it is for that other unseen world that our hearts should ever yearn.

> There stray'd awhile, amid the woods of Dart,
> One who could love them, but who durst not love.
> A vow had bound him, ne'er to give his heart
> To streamlet bright, or soft secluded grove.
> 'Twas a hard humbling task, onwards to move
> His easy-captured eyes from each fair spot,
> With unattach'd and lonely step to rove
> O'er happy meads, which soon its print forgot;—
> Yet kept he safe his pledge, prizing his pilgrim-lot.

Bremond quotes these lines by way of epigraph to his book, and repeats them, with an added significance, at the beginning of his opening chapter, which he entitles *L'isolé volontaire*, the voluntary recluse. The outcome of all those flowing phrases of his, from which it is difficult to disenmesh oneself, is that from this moment Newman stands revealed as himself incapable of loving, yet having a passionate longing for the love of others; in other words, as an unconscious and incurable egocentric. It would be difficult to find an instance of so much art being employed to erect so frail and tottering a structure. This subtle psychologist, with his taste for the pathetic and the mysterious, has been led into the grossest of misconceptions; for what clumsier error could there be than that of mistaking, "I will not" for "I cannot"?

As to Newman's capacity for love, did not Mary's death reveal how delicate yet how deep it was? The man who, at the end of his life, broke down and wept like a child when he beheld the bier of a friend like Henry Wilberforce or Ambrose St John, was far from being incapable of loving. If he did not show it, the reason was that he feared to love too well. He had vowed to belong solely to God, and it was because he grew but too well aware of the power of this world, and of those who dwell in it, that he came to make that calm yet agonising renunciation. If Newman resolves with such inflexible determination to belong solely to his Creator, it is not that he shows indifference or disdain for the rest of his fellow-creatures, but because he knows his own heart so well, knows that it is capable of no divided allegiance, but must needs give itself wholly and all in all. But now it is no longer his own to give; it belongs to another. Henceforth his refusal to yield to a love which brings as much pleasure as it bestows is but the measure of his loyalty to a love which claims all, because it has given all.

We are not left to vague conjecture as to what was innermost in Newman's mind when he was at Dartington. One of his earliest printed sermons was composed and delivered there. It is the sermon numbered XXV in the first volume of the *Parochial and Plain Sermons*, and is entitled, "Scripture a Record of Human Sorrow". All the youthful members of his audience, we learn from Froude's *Remains*, found the sermon intolerably gloomy. Newman, however, protests that it was far from his intention to create such an impression. Nevertheless, when we consider the sermon in the context of the poems and letters we have quoted, when we put it back into the general framework, as we may more or less vaguely picture it, then its personal application becomes clear beyond all doubt. Newman, while addressing his words to these young people, is, in fact, speaking to himself. The smiling, seductive face of the world which, naturally enough, is the world as they saw it, is not the world as it really is. He does not mean that there are no clear vestiges of the Lost Paradise here below; but what folly to try to find in it a lasting home, to try to rebuild, with what remnants were left, a world which could have no reality about it, which could never be an abiding resting-place! The real world is the world of the Scriptures, not the fleeting beauty of a fine summer's day. Sorrow is the warp of all our earthly existence, for sin is inwoven in it. That lucky, that seemingly lucky providence, which spares some people from sorrow here below, is really sparing them the sight of things as they truly are. We need not envy them a privilege which prepares them so ill for the dread awakening of the Day of Judgment. If we have neglected to hearken to God's word, we shall hear it then, when it tells us, too late, that the world deceives us when it bids us delight in the joys it offers. The pleasures of a world cut off from God benefit that man alone who, passing through them uninfluenced by their paralysing charm, comes, the trial over, to his God at last.

It is interesting to note that in these days Newman betrayed a sort of timidity in regard both to asceticism and to indulgence in pleasure, an attitude of mind which is typically Protestant. He does not preach the renunciation of the world, and of its sanest and most harmless pleasures. On the other hand, it is not only contentment with things earthly that he fears from these latter. One sees the wavering confusion between temptation and sin. There is in all this something of the state of mind of the very young man whose reactions overshoot their target. There is also the undeniable influence of a pessimistic morality very alien to the Catholic tradition.

Nothing is more revealing than to compare this sermon with what Newman wrote later on about St Philip and St Benedict. The justification—indeed, one may say, the necessity—for asceticism, and a ruthless asceticism at that, rouses no more doubts in Newman's mind. But then he will speak of human joys as one who regards their innocence, their intrinsic healthiness as no less undeniable. A paradox, but only in appearance. The realising of this was to be one of the great spiritual conquests of the conversion of 1845.

The conflict between love of this world and all that it contains and the love of One greater than the world, was now, with Froude still at his side, to begin again for Newman more mightily than ever. It seems that it was then that the decisive victory was won. We refer to the long voyage in the Mediterranean which the two friends were to undertake the following year.

But before we come to that, we must try to ascertain as nearly as we can the real significance this friendship had for Newman, and the bearing it had on the problem to which we have just referred. It certainly affected Newman more markedly than any other. But this was due not so much to his words, to anything he may have said, as to what he was.

The charm, including the physical charm, of the young man whom Harriet called "the bright and beautiful Froude" was felt by all who came in contact with him. Radiance, beauty—these still cast a glow over those literary *Remains* of his, those stories and anecdotes that have come down to us undimmed by time. Yet, despite his warm-heartedness, his childlike playfulness which inwove themselves with a certain aristocratic pride, one is conscious of a certain independence, remoteness, isolation, which must have been still more evident to his contemporaries.

Endowed with every human charm, young, handsome, marvellously intelligent and sensitive, he nevertheless seemed to Newman like the angel of severance, of renunciation, of farewell. He convinced Newman, sometimes in words of scorching irony, that Christianity, although it was the religion of love, indeed, *because* it was the religion of love, of such a love, requires all that is involved in those words—severance, renunciation, farewell—with their fullest implications. All that youthful radiance, fated to burn itself out in the space of a few years, leaves with us the impression of a star flashing across the deep night sky, but leaving behind it a fiery cicatrice that never fades.

It was, indeed, that illness of Froude's, that illness from which he was never to recover, that was the occasion of the Mediterranean voyage. In 1832, Newman finds himself without pupils and, almost at the same time, free from the burden imposed upon him by his work on the Arians. One last spell of excessive labour had enabled him to complete it. He was now in some doubt as to what his next move was to be. Whately had been appointed Archbishop of Dublin, and he quite thought he would invite him to join him there, an invitation that he was prepared to accept. This idea of Newman's shows more clearly than anything else how little conscious he was of the distance he had travelled, how far he had separated from that quondam master of his, to whom, with something very like *naïveté*, he believed himself to be still attached. But Whately, after what had happened over the Peel affair, was under no such illusion. His sometime pupil was clearly lost for ever to the liberalism to which the Noëtics were more and more deeply committing themselves. Newman had failed to grasp what Whately had in mind when he placed him at dinner between two High Churchman of the most fossilised type and then asked him if he was proud of his new friends. In 1826, when his book *Logic* appeared, Whately expressed his gratitude to Newman for his help in terms whose warmly affectionate tone had surprised him. He was not less surprised to discover, six years later, that Whately, whatever his feelings about the past, looked for nothing fruitful from any future collaboration between them. The truth was that his present was much farther removed than he imagined from a past that was still comparatively recent. Is it not typical of his psychology that, in this as in other spheres, the present and what it signified did not reveal itself until it had ceased to be the present? But Whately, though far less poetically and religiously minded, reveals here, it must be confessed, a clear-sighted view of things that gave him a much prompter grasp of the state of affairs at any given time.

So the invitation to Dublin never came, and was never destined to come. Meanwhile events took a very different turn. Froude, compelled to give up work of every kind and ordered away to the south, asked Newman to go with him.

The need to get away for a time, to get a little change of scene after a baffling conflict that had ended in deadlock, and then again the longing awakened in the mind of a man who had been brought up on the Humanities, the classics of Greece and Rome—all these things combined to render the invitation of his friend irresistible. On the 8th December, Newman embarked with Froude and his father on the *Hermes*, bound for Malta.

This voyage was intended to be in the nature of a retreat before entering upon a fresh task incomparably more important than any that had so far fallen to his lot. It was with this idea in mind that Newman agreed to undertake it. But we must not interpret the word "retreat" as signifying a period of relaxation, of rest and recuperation in preparation for the toil and stress that lay ahead. We should rather speak of it, as Newman later on described the flight of the anchorites to the desert. It was anything rather than quitting the battle-field in search of a refuge of peace and tranquillity. Far from that, it was a flight from a delusive peace, a peace that was no peace. Looked at in one way, it was like Jacob's wrestling with the angel. It was also—but perhaps they were but two sides of the same thing—Christ, or St Antony and the anchorites, fighting the Evil One.

Properly to understand the matter, we must first of all remind ourselves of the things that were weighing on the minds of Froude and Newman at the time of their departure. For a year past, the revolutionary movement prevailing on the Continent had been having its effect in England. The Reform Bill had been brought in and debated, and was shortly to become law. The whole social and political structure of England was being overhauled, though the changes involved were of no fundamental character. In the midst of the ferment, the Church of England, which, officially at least, had been held to represent the nation on its religious side, was now being made the object of attack by the forces of Liberalism.

If it had been a question of separating Church and State, of Disestablishment, the ideas which Newman had derived from Whately, and Froude's own High Church convictions, might have accommodated themselves to such a measure. But, in point of fact, it was the very reverse that was the case. The State, which was giving up describing itself as Christian, was, for mainly political motives, hacking and hewing at the Church's constitution, the Church itself being looked on as its servant. Arnold's proposal which had recently been made public, the proposal that the Established Church should include every form of Christian creed and practice adopted by Englishmen except Roman Catholicism, was now very much in men's minds. And even if that were not to be, who could tell what abject denial of her principles might any day be, not merely demanded, but exacted from her?

In the face of a menace like this, both Newman and Froude saw quite clearly that a purely political agitation such as that which they themselves had encouraged *à propos* of Peel's re-election would be hopelessly inadequate to the situation. The Church itself must see to her own salvation. Small hope of her gaining the respect of the State, if she continued to take no higher view of herself than she did at present; if she failed to live up to her own ideals.

We may take it as certain that Froude had got Newman to share these convictions by the time they came to leave England. He, Froude, held Christianity to be wholly supernatural and indissolubly bound up with the idea of a Visible Church. These convictions he passed on to his friend, whose mind was fully prepared to accept them. Perhaps it would be nearer the mark to say that Froude, with characteristic boldness and lucidity, had given definite form and outline to ideas towards which Newman's spiritual and intellectual development, as well as his experience of practical Anglicanism, had already predisposed him.

Not only then were they full of these preoccupations when they started, but they promised to collaborate with those friends of theirs whom they were leaving behind them in the thick of the fight, by sending them poems calculated to kindle enthusiasm for the sacred cause. These poems were collected later on and published in the volume entitled *Lyra Apostolica*.

Newman's letters to his mother and sisters, and his contributions to the volume in question, provide us with a sort of dual travel commentary. On the one plane, we have an account of the various incidents and sights which attracted his attention and fired his imagination; on the other, we are made aware of those inward workings of the spirit which, dwelling on these things, sometimes transfigures them in a manner undreamt of. In the latter part of his voyage, when he was all alone, the two planes merge into one, and become the remarkable record entitled *My Illness in Sicily*.

While waiting at Whitchurch for the coach that was to take him on to Falmouth, where he was to embark with his friends, Newman wrote one of the happiest of the many poems composed during these weeks of leisure. It is entitled "Angelic Guidance":

Are these the tracks of some unearthly Friend?
His footprints, and his vesture skirts of light,
Who, as I talk with men, conforms aright
Their sympathetic words, or deeds that blend
With my hid thought;—or stoops him to attend
My doubtful-pleading grief;—or blunts the might
Of ill I see not;—or in dreams of night
Figures the scope in which what is will end?
Were I Christ's own, then fitly might I call
That vision real; for to the thoughtful mind
That walks with Him, He half unveils His face;
But when on common men such shadows fall,
They dare not make their own the gifts they find,
Yet, not all hopeless, eye His boundless grace.

We may almost take it that we have the echo of some kind of presentiment of what the end of his voyage was to bring, in these lines where so many recollections unite and blend so harmoniously together. Once more we meet with that idea of Providence, so peculiarly his that it seems to arise from some actual experience. And it is in the consciousness of the invisible, as something hidden by the visible—

which so closely resembled what he believed as a child, and which he had rediscovered not only in Keble, but in the Fathers, and which Mary's death had brought back to him with such startling vividness—that the idea took shape. Furthermore, it is very remarkable that his notion of Providence should be seen in an angelic vision which is itself enveloped by terrestrial ones. We shall see before long how vividly these ideas about angels which he had held, however vaguely, as a child, had remained fixed and active in his mind ever since.

But perhaps what it is most important of all to note is the intuitive consciousness he appears to have had of some providential correspondence between the incidents and circumstances of our daily lives, whereto, all unknown to ourselves, we are led by the hand of God, and our own innermost impressions and beliefs. Thus it comes to be borne in on us that our fate may be mysteriously bound up with events apparently the most fortuitous. It was in nothing less than the confirmation of this idea, at first sight so fantastic, that the voyage on which Newman was now embarking was to culminate. The innermost depths of his soul, the grace that had been seeking for him and was henceforth to be his guide, was revealed to him through some of the strangest and most incongruous events of his whole existence: his lonely sojourn in Sicily and his illness there.

The *Hermes*, on which the Froudes and Newman were the sole passengers, took them as far as Malta, calling at Gibraltar, Cadiz, and Algiers, but turning aside from the direct route to take in Zante, Patras, and Corfu. Held up for a long time in the Lazaret at Malta on account of quarantine restrictions (England had hardly got over the cholera epidemic), they eventually left there to pay a rapid visit to Sicily. At Egesta, Palermo, Messina, Naples, and the places near by, including, of course, Herculaneum and Pompeii, they stayed a few days, before going on to Rome, which they found so wonderful as virtually to eclipse all they had seen till then.

To begin with, Newman's letters home dwell mainly on his feelings of solitude, with the sky above him and the waters below. Then there is the vessel, picturesque it may be, but decidedly uncomfortable, and he is amused at the breezy geniality of the officers. However, there was the same sort of ingenuous wonderment about what he now wrote as marked his letters from Dartington. Here we have the untravelled man, the student, revealing himself, much to his own astonishment, as the possessor of a highly sensitive artistic temperament.

Gibraltar calls forth a poem on England, whom he hails as "Tyre of the West", which is certainly the most anti-Victorian ever written by an eminent Victorian about his native land. Far from seeing in all her expansion of wealth and her attainment of world-wide power a token of divine favour, he declares that it is only the despised remnant of the Church still there that causes God to withhold His chastising hand.

Throughout the whole of the voyage, a sort of wide-eyed wonder at the marvels of Nature he beheld, coupled with a resolutely good-natured curiosity regarding the people and their ways (despite some typically British and highly amusing reactions), were all given a Biblical setting of this nature. The general theme, selected by them before they left in view of the crisis in Church affairs, was derived from the great prophets of the Old Testament. A constant solicitude for God's people runs through the whole—a solicitude, that is to say, for their vocation, incurring as it did more dangers from earthly ambitions within itself than those which threatened it from pagan influences without.

In his contact with the world, a world till then so novel, so unfamiliar to him, the traveller felt himself an exile, and the more there was to excite his wonder and admiration, the deeper grew his sense of isolation. But at the same time he becomes conscious of some power drawing him ever nearer and nearer to God, his only home, wherefrom he learns more and more clearly that He is preparing him, in all that he is going through, first to realise, and then to make known, the Word that He is waiting to declare to him.

The poem written on his arrival at Corfu on the 5th January, 1833 (the anniversary of Mary's death), expresses this latter sentiment in terms so compelling that it must be quoted in full:

Thrice bless'd are they, who feel their loneliness;
    To whom nor voice of friends nor pleasant scene
    Brings that on which the sadden'd heart can lean;
Yea, the rich earth, garb'd in her daintiest dress
Of light and joy, doth but the more oppress,
    Claiming responsive smiles and rapture high;
    Till, sick at heart, beyond the veil they fly,
Seeking His Presence, who alone can bless.
Such, in strange days, the weapons of Heaven's grace;
    When, passing o'er the high-born Hebrew line,
    He forms the vessel of His vast design;
Fatherless, homeless, reft of age and place,
Sever'd from earth, and careless of its wreck,
Born through long woe His rare Melchizedek.

[1] *Letters*, Vol. I, p. 288.

Many people who read these poems, so characteristically British in their Biblical tone, so reminiscent of Milton and the Puritans, have been rather taken aback by the harshness, not to say the fanaticism, of their tone. It cannot be denied that the note they sound is indeed a call to repentance, when it is not a call to battle, and that both alike are inexorable. Newman tears away the mask of pseudo-Evangelicalism which would give the name of Christian peace and charity to consciences self-lulled to slumber, or to a brotherhood of selfish aims:

And would'st thou reach, rash scholar mine,
  Love's high unruffled state?
Awake! thy easy dreams resign,
  First learn thee how to hate:—

Hatred of sin, and Zeal and Fear,
  Lead up the Holy Hill;
Track them, till Charity appear
  A self-denial still.

Dim is the philosophic flame,
  By thoughts severe unfed:
Book-lore ne'er served, when trial came,
  Nor gifts, when faith was dead.

True, the tone is not soothing, and it cannot be denied that in those lines, as in many others, there is something of the same over-rigidity of the youthful moralist as displayed itself in the sermon at Dartington. But we should be shutting our eyes to the truth if we failed to recognise the sound and solid basis on which his religious faith reposed. Beyond everything, he abhorred those sentimental dreams which easy-going folk fondly mistook for the Beatific Vision. What did those dreams do for such a man but conceal from him the evil of today, instead of preparing him for the blessedness that the morrow might have brought, if only his faith had had courage; if only his zeal had been pure?

There was something a little too rigid about the austerity of the thirty-year-old Newman. It had to be toned down a little. All the same he never deviated from his fundamental principles. We imagine that if it is ever permitted to speak of Newman as a saint—and that the future will decide—to this persistence it will be mainly due. This severity in no way arose from lack of feeling, still less of ordinary human kindness. Of that, there is no better proof than the way he was affected by the memories of the Classics that came flooding in upon him as he entered the Mediterranean.

True, he makes no surrender to that doctrine of the all-sufficiency of man which marks the humanism of the Renaissance. When the vessel began to approach the isles of the Sirens, the captain took his guitar and drew from it strains most agonizingly romantic. And now Newman, yet again, seems to be speaking to another, when it is really to himself that his words are addressed:

Cease, Stranger, cease those piercing notes,
  The craft of Siren choirs;
Hush the seductive voice, that floats
  Upon the languid wires.

Music's ethereal fire was given,
  Not to dissolve our clay,
But draw Promethean beams from heaven,
  And purge the dross away.

Weak self! with thee the mischief lies,
  Those throbs a tale disclose;
Nor age nor trial has made wise
  The Man of many woes.

It is clear that it is no unconscious insensibility that we have here, but rather a sensibility that knows itself too well to respond to any idle stimulus. Meantime his memories of the Humanities (and indeed of Humanity) grow warm at the sight of that historic sea, the setting of Greek and Roman Epic Song. It is true that these memories are extended to times and places not their own. From the heroes of Classical Antiquity, we pass on to the Saints of Christendom; from the sages of Greece and Rome to the Fathers of the Church. Does this imply some lack of understanding, or love for ever calling into view, beyond the human dream of some distant Golden Age, the one and only Vision of Peace, a peace that cannot fade? It is much rather due to an understanding, sovereign and all-embracing, a loving charity from which nothing human is deemed to be excluded. But now the ancient phrase means not alone a community in sorrow and suffering, it betokens, far beyond all that, a sharing in the gifts of grace, and the soul's salvation.

When his vessel draws near to the Ionian sea, he takes up his *Odyssey*. At the sight of Ithaca, "charming little island", all the dreams awakened by the studies of his childhood come crowding back to him again, bringing with them once more the joys of those far-off days. Later on, taking up the *Iliad*, while he was sailing up from Grecian shores to Latium, he was astonished to find how deeply he was thrilled.

If this human sympathy is not too human, if it declines to stay and content itself with a happiness befitting its creature state, it is not only his ascetic scruples that forbid it, it is its completeness, its truth. Too superficial by far is the humanism which does not recognise the rift, the fatal flaw in the ideas and spiritual outlook of the ancients. The Christian saint who refuses to stop at the human level, satisfies better and beyond the hopes it dared to formulate, that ancient spirit of whose greatness the neo-pagan philosopher, completely involved in this world, and its ideas, can form no conception.

Such again is the meaning of those telling lines written off the shores of Messina:

> Why, wedded to the Lord, still yearns my heart
> Towards those scenes of ancient heathen fame?
> Yet legend hoar, and voice of bard that came
> Fixing my restless youth with its sweet art,
> And shades of power, and those who bore a part
> In the mad deeds that set the world in flame,
> So fret my memory here,—ah! is it blame?—
> That from my eyes the tear is fain to start.
> Nay, from no fount impure these drops arise;
> 'Tis but that sympathy with Adam's race
> Which in each brother's history reads his own.
> So let the cliffs and seas of this fair place
> Be named man's tomb and splendid record stone,
> High hope, pride stain'd, the course without the prize.[1]

If we now turn to consider the impressions Newman, as well, we may add, as Froude, took away with him regarding the peoples of the Mediterranean today—Greeks of the Isles, Sicilians, Maltese, Italians—especially of their Christianity, we shall find that, though their ideas may have been less sweeping than those of most other British folk, they were certainly unfavourable. Revolting filth, beggars pushing their way everywhere, sloth, dishonesty—all these things shocked them as they were calculated to shock any average Anglo-Saxon tourist. Nevertheless, they did not fail to detect innumerable evidences of kindliness and humanity. But the basis of their religion seemed on the whole to be a form of idolatry that had virtually no connection whatever with righteous living.

It will not surprise us to learn that it was Naples that made the worst impression on them—such things, for example, as priests in the confessional roaring with laughter at the sins they were about to absolve.

Newman's endeavours to draw a comparison between these things

[1] *Letters*, Vol. I, p. 305.

and the state of affairs in England are not so "provincial" in character as they might at first appear. When he compares the clergy of the Greek islands with what the Anglican Clergy might become if their Church were suddenly and brutally disestablished, or what aspect the cult of the Madonna might assume in an atmosphere of Baptist sentimentalism, it is not so much on the seemingly narrow insularity of his remarks that we should dwell as on the attempt they betoken to arrive at a genuinely sympathetic understanding of whatever there was in common between religious practices so novel to him and those with which he was familiarly acquainted.

As touching Rome, he was the first to remark on the complexity of his own feelings. He finds it impossible to separate what has to do with the City from that which belongs to the Church. The impression of grandeur, and of beauty in that grandeur, dominates everything else. But a sort of puzzling ambiguity seems to hang over this grandeur, which he can in no wise dispel. The sight of the ruins of old Rome side by side with the untarnished memorials of the Church of the Fathers, nay, of the Apostles themselves, and, over the whole, the blossoming of the fairylike city of the Renaissance, appeals to the Romantic in him, allures him with its incomparable beauty, but at the same time gives him a feeling of uneasiness for some cause or causes which he cannot fathom. To Rogers, one of his former pupils, and soon to become a fellow of Oriel, to whom he was united by ever-increasing ties of friendship, he writes as follows:

> We arrived at this wonderful place only Saturday last (March 2) from Naples. It is the first city which I have been able to admire, and it has swallowed up, like Aaron's rod, all the admiration which, in the case of others, is often distributed among Naples, Valletta, and other places. It is scarcely with patience I hear people talking of Naples in comparison – nor will I degrade Rome by dwelling on the notion. Of course, I have seen very little of it; but the effect of every part is so vast and overpowering – there is so much of greatness and repose cast over the whole, and, independent of what one knows from history, there are such traces of long sorrow and humiliation, suffering, punishment and decay, that one has a mixture of feelings, partly such as those with which one would approach a corpse, and partly those which would be excited by the sight of the spirit which had left it. It brings to my mind Jeremiah's word in the Lamentations, when Jerusalem, or (sometimes) the prophet, speaks as the smitten of God.[1]

Somewhat contrary to expectation, perhaps, the great Renaissance basilicas, though a little disquieting by reason of some faint pagan

[1] *Letters*, Vol. I, p. 318.

traces he discerned in their splendour, carried him away with the triumphant exaltation he saw in that same splendour. The impression was a lasting one. The Gothic style never regained its ascendancy over him. He was very far from regarding the classical style as profane, as did most of his contemporaries. Henceforth, it symbolised for him the glorious promise of the Resurrection and the path that would lead men back to the Paradise they had lost.

But what naturally held his heart in thrall were the reminders of the Apostles and the wellnigh intact memorials of the Church of the Fathers. Just before leaving Rome, he revisited Santa Maria in Cosmedin, and his thoughts turned to Pope Dionysius who founded it and to St Augustine of Canterbury who studied there. We cannot help wondering how amazed he would have been—he who always thought so much of providential signs and premonitions—could it have been revealed to him, in a momentary vision of things to come, that one day, in the still distant future, he would be Cardinal titular of the neighbouring church of San Giorgio in Velabro. He mounts the Janicular once more and pays a farewell visit to the tomb of St Peter.

There are two things he wrote which, when considered together, seem to present in due focus the sort of impression which Roman Catholicism left on Newman's mind, a vision subdued in tone yet strangely attractive. This is what he wrote from Malta to his mother on the 26th January, just after coming away from the Church of the Knights Templar:

> It is fearful to have before one's eyes the perversion of all the best, the holiest, the most exalted feelings of human nature. Everything in St John's Church is admirable, if it did not go too far; it is a beautiful flower run to seed. I am impressed with a sad presentiment, as if the gift of truth, when once lost, was lost for ever. And so the Christian world is gradually becoming barren and effete, as land which has been worked out and has become sand. We have lasted longer than the South, but we too are going, as it would seem.[1]

This idea of a Christianity devitalised within itself by an excessive external and too worldly exuberance is curiously expanded in a long and interesting letter to Mr Rickards.[2] He wrote it from Naples, whither he returned alone on leaving Rome. It is dominated all through by the apocalyptic view of history interpreted in a definitely Protestant sense, and that, be it remembered, he got from Milner. Rome, then, appears to him as the destined throne of Antichrist, the present abode of the

[1] *Letters*, Vol. I, p. 295. [2] *Ibid.*, pp. 340 et sqq.

Evil One. However, he brings in a distinction. It is the City as such, and not the Church that is "possessed". However, the conjunction, in the Pontifical State, of City and Church puts the Church in a position of thraldom to the Evil One. Nevertheless, this thraldom is not so close that the Church of the Apostles ceases to be the Church.

A strange view to take of the matter, no doubt. To start with, it shows how inextricably complex were the impressions he got from Rome. Then again, it reflects the underlying dualism which, as we have seen, had characterised Newman's ideas for so long a time. It was not only now that he saw the world, and the life of every individual in it, as the prize for which the Powers of Light and Darkness were perpetually striving. Little did he think how soon such a contest was to be joined; a contest in which his own soul was to be the prize at stake.

VIII

ILLNESS IN SICILY—THE OXFORD MOVEMENT

FROM the all-important document to which Newman gave the title, "My Illness in Sicily," Anne Mozley deleted, not only the physiological details—they offended her sense of decorum—but also every explicit reference to the Devil. If only Newman could have read that record of his after she had done with it, he would certainly have protested that it was "*Hamlet* without the Prince of Denmark".

Now, let us say at once that if certain data are to be withheld from our purview, we might as well abandon the attempt to plumb the depths of Newman's psychology altogether. Something instinctive there was, something that dated back to his earliest childhood days, something that always kept alive in his consciousness, and was ultimately confirmed by his Biblical and patristic studies, that came to be one of the permanent elements governing his view of life. It was this: the world in which we live is infinitely vaster than we take it to be. It is far deeper than we are wont to imagine, and it has one more dimension over and above those we are accustomed to assign to it. To a mind disposed to heed God's word, and its own presentiments, the material world is revealed as a spiritual creation. What we call the material world is but the fringe, the riddling hieroglyph of the spiritual. It is something that conceals from the careless what it suggests, or half-reveals, to the thoughtful. But this spiritual world is divided, disunited. Evil is not something that is wholly within ourselves. It is not merely a revolt of the senses, a rebellion of the wayward mind. It is the reflux, or backward ebbing, of the spiritual creation which in its withdrawal takes from the Creator perhaps the greatest part of what is His. It is a power that attracts and allures, that essays to arrest and reverse the spontaneous motion of men's souls towards the Love which created them and which would fain draw them home to Itself. Lastly, it—Evil—is Someone; this world's god, as St Paul says, who, within us and around us, everywhere, sets himself up to oppose the God of original Creation, the God of Jesus Christ.

Bremond has entitled one of his chapters, "The Fear of Hell". He piles quotation on quotation, all selected with the object of arousing the startled interest of the sort of reader he desires to attract. If only he had had a little more patience, he might have found still more quotations, and those even more revealing. But once more he has gone completely astray in his interpretation of Newman's mentality. For Bremond, the fear of Hell connotes the purely egoistic, or at any rate the excessively individualistic, fear of divine punishment in the world to come. For Newman, the fear of Hell meant the falling into sin here below, and of being deservedly left in thrall to that Power of Evil which everywhere confronts, though seldom in its true colours, the Power of God.

How much was at stake in this life, the importance of every decision we take, of every passing instant, was something native to Newman's inmost being. It was not just a matter of adding beauty or richness to our lives; what we had to be quite certain about was whether we were working with Christ or against Him. There was no neutral zone, or No Man's Land. The whole Universe, the whole witness of History, testifies to a confused but tremendous battle that is being waged between two opposing wills—the will of God and the will of the Devil. We obey the one, or we obey the other. Merely to turn away from the One is *pro tanto* to take service with the Other.

If, in spite of Newman's generous large-heartedness, the word *Liberalism* had come to denote something so completely abhorrent to him, the reason was that this "liberty" on which poor fallen man was fain to pride himself in his attitude towards God, was really the sign, the token of his servitude to Satan.

Throughout the whole of his Sicilian expedition he had two opposing ideas in mind. On the one hand, he saw in his determination to have his own way the sign that Satan had established dominion over him. On the other, in his encounter with God, who strikes him down even as Jacob or Moses was stricken down by the Angel in the darkness, he recognises the signal of the victory which brings us our release.

Just before leaving Oxford, he preached his ninth University Sermon, and he took for his text: Wilfulness the Sin of Saul.

When in Rome, he had gone with the Froudes to call on the Superior of the *Collegio Inglese* (the future Cardinal Wiseman). They had talked about the relations between Rome and the Anglicans. Wiseman had been greatly impressed by the gravity with which he repeated more than once, "We have a work awaiting us in England."

There we have the two themes clearly brought out. But now, regardless of the Froudes, regardless, too, of all the other friends he encountered in the Eternal City, he abandoned his companions, who were going home through France, and went back alone to Sicily. "I had two objects in coming," he says, "to see the antiquities, and to see the country."

But, faintly to begin with, intensely when he felt his illness coming on, the dread lest he had committed the sin of Saul never ceased to haunt him. He had been bent on pleasing himself, regardless of everything else; he had brushed aside all advice to the contrary; his waywardness had disconcerted not only his own arrangements, but his friends'. What he wanted to do was to trace once more the signs and vestiges of the Paradise that once had been, to linger and meditate upon the scene.

> Well, in an unlooked-for way I come to Sicily, and the Devil thinks his hour has come. I was delivered into his hands. From that time everything went wrong.

Nevertheless, if he is conscious of his transgression, if he realises the measureless gravity of a single deliberate choosing of his own will to the neglect of the will of God, it is borne in upon him, with a feeling of certitude he cannot explain, that God's will is his safeguard, his shield.

> However, I have got into the narrative here, without meaning it. What I wanted first to speak of was the providence and strange meaning of it. I could almost fancy that the Devil saw I was to be a useful instrument and that he endeavoured to destroy me. The fever was most dangerous; for a week my attendants gave me up, and people were dying of it on all sides; yet all through I had a confident feeling I should recover. I told my servant so, and gave as a reason (even when semi-delirious and engaged in giving him my friends' direction at home, and so preparing externally for death) that "I thought God had some work for me". These, I believe, were exactly my words, and when, after the fever, I was on the road to Palermo, so weak I could not walk by myself, I sat on the bed on the morning of May 26 or May 27 profusely weeping, and only able to say that I could not help thinking God had something for me to do at home. This I repeated to my servant, to whom the words were unintelligible of course.[1]

"Self-will. . . . I was delivered into his hands!" And then, "God had some work for me". We must note how closely point and counterpoint answered each other. The means by which the Devil lures us, are they not, we repeat, those authentic traces of the lost Paradise? Newman's dualism bears no relationship to the dualism of the Gnostics.

[1] *My Illness in Sicily*, in *Autobiographical Writings*, p. 122.

His is the purely Christian dualism of St Paul and St John. The attraction of a world which remains good in itself, because it is God's own handiwork, is what is set up in opposition to God. The Devil has nothing to serve him in his strife against God, but the gifts of God Himself. Nevertheless, it is to reject the Creator, even as the Devil rejected Him, to prefer the most exquisite of God's gifts, to God and the doing of His will.

On the other hand, the hour which Satan believes to be his own, is still—and herein is the great mystery—God's hour. It is in vain that the Devil rebels, for, if in his revolt he is a servant no longer, he is none the less a slave. He is still God's bondsman, do what he will. His revolt is still part of God's design for his overthrow. There is the strife with Satan; there is also the strife with the Angel. When the morning comes and the soul at last tears itself away from the deadly embrace, it catches a glimpse of the Angel of Light, and the Angel does not depart until he has bestowed his blessing upon him. "All things make for good for those who love God", says the Apostle; *omnia*, repeats St Augustine, *etiam peccata*. Is not this the topmost peak—the flash-point, so to speak—of that revelation of Providence, which grows clearer with the passing years, as Newman himself grows in spiritual stature.

After spending a few days in Naples, where he made the ascent of Vesuvius, Newman set sail for Sicily. From Catania, after an excursion in the direction of Taormina, he starts by boat for Syracuse, and it was during this expedition that he had his attack of fever. Meanwhile, on the 27th April, he writes to Harriet from Syracuse:

> The two last miles we diverged from the road up a steep path, and soon came to the ancient stone ascent leading to Taurominium. I never saw anything more enchanting than this spot. It realised all one had read of in books about scenery—a deep valley, brawling streams, beautiful trees, the sea (heard) in the distance. But when, after breakfast, on a bright day, we mounted to the theatre, and saw the famous view, what shall I say? I never knew that Nature could be so beautiful; and to see that view was the nearest approach to seeing Eden. O happy I! It was worth coming all the way, to endure sadness, loneliness, weariness to see it. I felt, for the first time in my life, that I should be a better, and more religious man if I lived there. . . .
>
> And so I went off to Giarre. There first I went through the river-beds. The hills receded—Etna was magnificent. The scene was sombre with clouds, when suddenly, as the sun descended upon the cone, its rays shot out between the clouds and the snow, turning the clouds into royal curtains, while on one side there was a sort of Jacob's ladder. I understood why the poets made the abode of the gods on Mount Olympus.[1]

[1] *Letters*, Vol. I, p. 349.

But the poem entitled "Taormina", which he posted off the same day to Jemima, strikes a different note; a hint of some sort of presentiment which, a few days later, was fulfilled:

Say, hast thou tracked a traveller's round,
Nor visions met thee there,
Thou could'st but marvel to have found
This blighted world so fair?

And feel an awe within thee rise,
That sinful man should see
Glories far worthier Seraphs' eyes
Than to be shared by thee?

Store them in heart! thou shalt not faint
'Mid coming pains and fears;
As the third heaven once nerved a Saint
For fourteen trial years.[1]

After these two letters, he wrote no more for over a month. His next letter was dated the 5th June, and it was written to Rogers to congratulate him on his fellowship, of which he had just learned at Palermo, and to give him a brief account of some of the disagreeable things that had been happening to himself.

Although he was unwell when he got back from Syracuse to Catania, he starts off, nevertheless, with his servant Gennaro, both riding mules, in the direction of Aderno. The date was the 1st May. They had great difficulty in getting along. However, they set out again next day. It was terribly hard going, but they managed to reach Leonforte by nightfall. After a sleepless night, Newman found himself too weak to get up. The only remedy the little town could produce was camomile tea.

As I lay in bed the first day, many thoughts came over me. I felt that God was fighting against me—and felt at last I knew *why*—it was for self-will. I felt I had been very self-willed, that the Froudes had been against my coming; so also at Naples the Wilberforces, perhaps the Neales and Andersons. . . Yet I felt and kept saying to myself, "I have not sinned against the light", and at one time I had a most consoling, overpowering thought of God's electing love, and seemed to feel I was His. But I believe all my feelings, painful and pleasant, were heightened by somewhat of delirium, though they still are from God in the way of Providence. Next day the self-reproaching feelings increased. I seemed to see more and more my utter hollowness. I began to think of all my professed principles, and felt they were

[1] *Letters*, Vol. I, p. 353.

mere intellectual deductions from one or two admitted truths. I compared myself with Keble, and felt that I was merely developing his, not my, convictions. I know I had *very* clear thoughts about this then, and I believe in the main true ones. Indeed, this is how I look on myself; very much (as the illustration goes) as a pane of glass, which transmits heat, being cold itself. I have a vivid perception of the consequences of certain admitted principles, have a considerable intellectual capacity of drawing them out, have the refinement to admire them and a rhetorical or histrionic power to represent them; and having no great (i.e. no vivid) love of this world, whether riches, honours, or anything else, and some firmness and natural dignity of character, take the profession of them upon me, as I might sing a tune which I liked—loving the Truth, but not possessing it, for I believe myself at heart to be nearly hollow—i.e. with little love, little self-denial. I believe I have some faith, that is all; and, as to my sins, they need my possessing no little amount of faith to set against them and gain their remission.[1]

That is the most pitiless piece of self-analysis yet penned by Newman. However, a few years later on, we shall meet with one more revealing still. Of course, we have to bear in mind that this one reflects the impressions made on a mind that had been rendered morbidly sensitive by an attack of fever. The view he then took of himself was something like the feeling that comes over us on a sleepless night when life seems full of gloom, and when we try to comfort ourselves by saying that all these terrifying ideas will vanish with the darkness, that we shall forget all about them when daylight comes. But is it not the night that gives us the truer vision, a vision that the daylight dilutes and tinges with the hues of our everyday existence, its habits and its longings? That is assuredly the view Newman took of the matter when, looking back over bygone years, he recalled in such minute detail what had been his state of mind at Leonforte and, calling it back from the past, made it live again in a timeless present. Nevertheless, what we can plead in his behalf against himself, is that such impressions, tearing away from our subliminal tendencies all that covers them, represent, not our moral being, but the bases of our psychology. Now, we are not, before God and our conscience, what those deeply hidden promptings would have us be, we are rather the lofty crest of our being, athrill with our determination to overcome, or to leave behind us, all such upsurges or contractions of our subliminal *ego*, and the first thing we have to do, in order to gain the mastery over that vague and confusedly complex *ego*, which belongs to the devil quite as much as to us, is to have the courage to look it fairly and squarely in the face, as Newman does here, with that calm honesty of purpose which scorns all mock-

[1] *My Illness in Sicily*, in *Autobiographical Writings*, pp. 124-125.

modesty and tears away every mask. This said, it would be difficult to exhaust the riches which this passage contains for us.

What we must note first of all is the clearness of vision, the luminous insight which here becomes so conscious of itself. The power to detect in principles, even when derived from outside, all the developments which flow from them, developments to which others, not excepting those to whom we owe them, are blind, is unquestionably one of Newman's most salient characteristics. It explains both the boldness of steps which, on the face of them, seemed to make havoc of his destiny, but which, in reality, could alone fulfil it, as well as the long succession of misunderstandings and tragic separations which were the price he had to pay for that fulfilment.

Next, we are enabled to perceive how the play of an intellect that worked almost too efficiently was always ready, but for his own efforts to counteract, to dominate his feelings, and override his will. It is not, be it said again, that he lacked sensibility, but rather, perhaps, that he had too much of it. It is not that he lacked the capacity to love; his difficulty was to find something, or someone, here below, that he could love on this side idolatry. But with him, as with many kindred spirits, intellectual activity always tends to leave the heart cold, either because the intellect outshines in clarity the confused impressions of the senses, or because it brings the critical faculty to bear on the object on which the heart is set, and draws it away therefrom.

What, then, were these faults, these sins, the weight of which now comes back upon him so crushingly? We must quote a few of the lines which follow on the passage we have cited, reinstating in their proper place the all-important particulars which fell victims to the scissors of Anne Mozley:

> Still more serious thoughts came over me. I thought I had been very self-willed about the tutorship affair, and now I viewed my whole course as one of presumption. It struck me that the 5th of May was just at hand, which was a memorable day as being that on which (what we called) my Ultimatum was sent into the Provost. On the third anniversary I should be lying on a sick bed in a strange country. Then I bitterly blamed myself, as disrespectful and insulting to the Provost, my superior. So keenly did I feel this, that I dictated to myself (as it were) a letter which I was to send to (I fixed upon) James, the late Fellow, on my getting to England, stating in strong terms my self-reproach, and I was not to preach at St Mary's or anywhere for a length of time as a penitent unworthy to show himself. I recollected, too, that my last act on leaving Oxford was to preach a University sermon against self-will. Yet still I said to myself "I have not sinned against the light".[1]

[1] *Ibid.*, pp. 125-126

The penultimate sentence echoes a statement which never got beyond the manuscript stage, a statement which Newman placed at the very beginning of the memorandum:

> I seem to see, and I saw, a strange providence in it. At the time I was deeply impressed with a feeling that it was a judgment for profaning the Lord's Supper in having cherished some resentment against the Provost for putting me out of the Tutorship; though this impression has now faded away.

The "now" refers to the 31st August, 1834, when, as we know, Newman began to write his memoir.

Those entries, those charges which he brings against himself at the time when he was going through his greatest inward struggle, or at least when he was the most keenly aware of the forces that were at grips within him, are of the utmost importance. They very possibly supply the key to one of the most delicate problems that confront his biographer. We refer to the vehement, but often vague, self-accusations to be found in so many entries in his diaries and personal memoranda.

The problem, of course, is of a kind that presents itself in the case of most spiritual natures. One hesitates between regarding them as the sort of trifling thing that a highly delicate soul might make much of and searching for more definite falls from grace such as might justify, in the eyes of ordinary humanity, the pursuance of further investigations. This hesitation is noticeable in several writers on Newman. When they don't make a clean jump over the whole thing, as Bremond does, contenting himself with a few wholly imaginary solutions, the other conjectures vary, according to the disposition of the writer, between the alarming suppositions of a Fernande Tardivel and the unflattering insinuations of a Geoffrey Faber. But on foundations so frail it is impossible to build any solid hypothesis. Some of the blame must rest on Newman himself who, towards the end of his life, destroyed a large number of his papers, leaving too many fragments to which, sundered from their context, it was difficult to assign a meaning. But the great culprit was Anne Mozley. Most of these hypothetical solutions completely collapse when, disregarding her petty attempts to throw dust in our eyes, we go back to the originals.

The example here given is peculiarly instructive. Newman certainly had in his nature passionate potentialities for love or hate, ranging from the most fleshly sensibilities of his being to the loftiest of its spiritual heights. We can have no doubt that this laid him open to all the temptations to which the normal man is exposed, particularly when we bear in mind the richness of his nature. But it appears from the notes we are now examining that his faults seemed to him, when his insight was at its very clearest, to be mainly a matter of self-will. That is what he accuses himself of in regard to Hawkins; it also forms the *gravamen* of his wrong-doing as a boy of fifteen, which wrung from him some bitter exclamations of regret. That, the poem "Lead, kindly Light", which marks the conclusion of the crisis, tells us in plain terms.

The crisis seems to have reached its height during the early days of his illness at Leonforte. However, Newman's tribulations were not to end there, alone as he was, and at death's door, far down in the heart of Sicily.

After a few days of mental exaltation caused by his semi-delirious condition, it was borne in upon him that he would have to get away from Leonforte at all costs, and, remembering the hopelessly inadequate treatment he received there, it is ten chances to one that he would never have survived if he had stayed on. With his Neapolitan servant Gennaro, who hinted that he might formally bequeath him his slender stock of baggage, since one could never tell what might happen, he set out on the 6th May for Palermo. Hardly, however, had they covered seven miles when, amid scenery of fantastic beauty, just below Etna, his strength completely gave out. As good luck would have it, a doctor happened to be on the spot. He insisted on his being taken at all costs to Castro Giovanni, and there, clinging as best he could to his mule, he arrived just as night was falling. There, he obtained fairly decent lodgings and better nursing than he had had at Leonforte. The doctor was a worthy but middling sort of person. Newman tried to communicate with him in Latin, but the doctor could not make much of that. He interpreted the ceremonious phrases employed by his patient as the incoherent utterances of a disordered imagination.

The landlord was most attentive. He even went the length of getting a party of musicians to play to him in an adjoining room. But Newman was far too exhausted to endure more than a few moments of that entertainment. The noise from a fair that was being held hard by, and the bells of a neighbouring church, nearly drove him to desperation.

After a time, Gennaro managed to get him downstairs and out into the open a little. He sat in a chair a little way from the house enjoying the wonderful spring weather. He could not help weeping, partly from weakness, partly from delight, "The sight of the sky was so piercing".[1] A crowd of beggars beset him, though he had already given a sum for distribution among them as a thank-offering. Then the bell began to toll for the funeral of the Lady Bountiful of the place, who had died from the very malady from which he was at last beginning to recover. A few days later, with Gennaro's assistance, he managed to get as far as the Cathedral. The coolness and silence of the place were refreshing alike to mind and body. The stillness and solitude of these churches, which he visited when no public service was going on—he did the same thing at Palermo—inspired one of the last of his contributions to the *Lyra Apostolica*, the only one which breathes any sort of tenderness towards a church in which he was still far from finding a home.

> Oh that thy creed were sound!
> For thou dost soothe the heart, thou Church of Rome. . . .
>
> I cannot walk the city's sultry streets,
> But the wide porch invites to still retreats,
> Where passion's thirst is calm'd, and care's unthankful gloom.

The faithful Gennaro, unwearying in the motherly care he took of this very out-of-the-ordinary Englishman, who kept saying, "God has a work for me to do," or, "I have not sinned against the light," had conceived a very real affection for him; we do not say it was wholly disinterested. He did everything he could think of to hasten his convalescence, thinking out little delicacies to give him, things suited to the English taste; eggs baked in wood ashes, tea, and those exquisite Sicilian cakes for which Newman remembered he kept on pestering him, just like a spoilt child.

> How I longed for it! And when I took the tea, I could not help crying out from delight. I used to say, "It is life from the dead!" I never had such feelings. All through my illness I had depended on Gennaro so much I could not bear him from the room five minutes. I used always to be crying out, for I don't know how long together, "Gen-na-ro-o-o-o-o-o!" They fed me on chicken broth. I did not take beef broth or beef tea till I got to Palermo, and that gave me something of the ecstatic feelings which the tea had given.[2]

At length, on the 25th, he set out for Palermo. It so turned out that he had to stop there for three weeks, waiting for a boat to take him back to his own country, for which he was longing so ardently. At last he embarked, after rewarding Gennaro on a liberal scale, but

[1] *My Illness in Sicily*, in *op. cit.*, p. 133. [2] *Ibid.*, p. 136.

drawing the line at parting with his old blue cloak, which he dearly cherished but which Gennaro coveted.

> A little thing for him to set his services at—at the same time a great thing for me to give, for I had an affection for it. It had nursed me all through my illness; had ever been put on my bed, put on me when I rose to have my bed made, etc. I had nearly lost it at Corfu—it was stolen by a soldier but recovered. I have it still. I have brought it up here to Littlemore, and on some cold nights I have had it on my bed. I have so few things to sympathise with me that I take to clokes.[1]

His vessel was a sailing-ship, and she was becalmed for a whole week in the Straits of Bonifacio. Then it was that he composed three stanzas which were to become the most famous of all his works. No hymn, it has been said, has been so often sung wherever the English language is spoken, in Protestant churches or in Catholic. We may read in the conclusion of all the trials he had been through, an ordeal so testing yet so revealing, and catch therein a prophetic glimpse of what the future had in store. And how many experiences are gathered up therein, merged in that mysterious protestation, "I have not sinned against the light."

Lead, kindly Light, amid the encircling gloom,
    Lead Thou me on!
The night is dark, and I am far from home—
    Lead Thou me on!
Keep Thou my feet; I do not ask to see
The distant scene; one step enough for me.

I was not ever thus, nor pray'd that Thou
    Shouldst lead me on;
I loved to choose and see my path; but now
    Lead Thou me on!
I loved the garish day, and, spite of fears,
Pride ruled my will: remember not past years.

So long Thy power hath blest me, sure it still
    Will lead me on,
O'er moor and fen, o'er crag and torrent, till
    The night is gone;
And with the morn those Angel faces smile,
Which I have loved long since, and lost awhile.[2]

To this story, to this long soliloquy we had perhaps better call it, to this most deeply significant of Newman's reminiscences, there is an

[1] *Ibid.*, p. 138.

[2] This poem, many times set to music, has been sung wherever English hymns are sung—except at the Birmingham Oratory. Newman, knowing as he did its intensely personal character, shuddered when he heard it sung.

epilogue. Newman, as we have said, appended it to his manuscript on the 25th March, 1840, when he was at Littlemore. Any conclusion other than that which he wrote himself would be out of place. We give it therefore, re-inserting in their proper places the more personal passages which Anne Mozley deleted, as she always did in such cases.

> The thought keeps pressing on me while I write this, what am I writing it for? For myself I may look at it once or twice in my life, and what sympathy is there in *my* looking at it? Whom have I, whom can I have, who would take interest in it? I was going to say, I only have found one who even took that sort of affectionate interest in me as to be pleased with such details—and that is H. Wilberforce and what shall I ever see of him? This is the sort of interest a wife takes and none but she—it is a woman's interest—and that interest, so be it, shall never be taken in me. Never, so be it, will I be other than God has found me. All my habits for years, my tendencies, are towards celibacy. I could not take that interest in this world which marriage requires. I am too disgusted with this world—And, above all, call it what one will, I have a repugnance to a clergyman's marrying. I do not say it is not lawful—I cannot deny the right—but, whether a prejudice or not, it shocks me. And therefore I willingly give up the possession of that sympathy, which I feel is not, cannot be, granted to me. Yet not the less do I feel the need of it. Who will care to be told such details as I have put down above? Shall I ever have in my old age spiritual children who will take an interest? How time is getting on! I seem to be reconciling myself to the idea of being old. It seems but yesterday that the Whigs came into power—another such tomorrow will make me almost fifty, an elderly man. What a dream is life! I used to regret festival days going so quick. They are come and they are gone; but so it is, time is nothing except as the seed of eternity.[1]

Coming up to the surface of everyday social life, after this plunge into the profoundest depths of his being, Newman found himself in the midst of a tempest that was then at its very height. With all the new strength that victory had given him, he flung himself forthwith into this latest conflict.

Hastening across France with what speed he might (he did not even visit Paris, so disgusted was he with the revolution and so greatly did the sight of the tricolour incense him), he arrived at his mother's house at Iffley on the 9th July. It so happened that his brother Frank got back about the same time, after his unfortunate experience as a missionary in Persia. But he did not stay long in the bosom of the family. Work, work of a public character, as he had foreseen, was calling him away; the great, the outstanding, task of his life demanded his presence elsewhere.

The Reform Bill had just gone through. The Government looked

[1] *My Illness in Sicily*, in *Autobiographical Writings*, pp. 137-138.

as though it intended to hack and hew at the Church of England with no more compunction than if it had been no more than one of the several departments of State. Had it not just suppressed ten of the Irish sees? There were all sorts of rumours going about. All sorts of plans and projects were in the air, Arnold's proposal, to which we have already referred, being one of the most moderate. Doing away with the creeds, drastic liturgical reforms, and a host of other ideas were mooted, and it was expected that the secular power would give effect to them as a matter of course.

For Newman and his friends, the question that transcended all others in importance was whether the Church had a livelier sense of the nature of her mission and of all that she owed to herself, than had those who were ready to treat her with such a conspicuous lack of respect. That was the question at issue, and they felt that some practical step was urgently demanded of them. Newman always took the view that the beginning of the Movement dated from the sermon preached by Keble the Sunday after his return from abroad.

The occasion of the sermon in question was the opening of the Assizes, which was then, and still is, preceded by a solemn service, and a sermon delivered by a select preacher in the presence of the judges. Those two important personages, arrayed in their judicial robes, must have had a good many surprises as they sat listening to that sermon, and given many a nervous clutch at their rose bouquets. The fact was that the gentle Keble, with the childlike smile, was hurling, over their bewigged pates, a crushing indictment of the powers they represented. Like a man who has made up his mind, at all events for once in his lifetime, to speak out, Keble drew on all the weapons in his armoury, sticking at nothing, either in the things he said, or in his manner of saying them. This sermon, laconically entitled *National Apostasy*, he sent forthwith to the printer.

A good deal of scorn was vented in some quarters about so much fuss being made over the suppression of dioceses which were dioceses only in name, having no churchfolk to people them. But those who took that view merely showed how completely they lacked the insight of which Newman and his associates gave such signal proof. Neither they nor the others were under any misapprehension regarding the real status of the Anglican Church in Ireland. What, however, they did see, and the others did not, was that this attack on the Church in her most vulnerable point was but the opening move in a battle whose duration and extent they were perhaps the only ones to foretell.

And so the conflict began, between a nation now wholly secularised by its complete surrender to religious indifferentism, and a Church which, up to now, had always buttressed it with the support of her historic tradition. What had now to be decided was whether or no the Church was going to put up with being thus secularised. It had to be admitted that she had gone far, too far, towards acquiescing in the process. Now was the time, now or never, for her to reascend the slope down which some people were anxious to hurry her. What lent Keble's sermon its great importance was that it was not only a call to resist the despoiler, but an appeal to the Church to remember her real nature and that of the mission she had been ordained to fulfil. Its purpose was, not to stir up the faithful against Caesar, but to revive her allegiance to the Apostolic ideal.

Notwithstanding all this, there are not a few who would minimise the importance of Keble's sermon in regard to its practical effect on the Oxford Movement. They point out that Rose's articles in the *British Magazine*, and the verses in the *Lyra Apostolica*, were the earliest signs of the Movement, earlier by weeks, by months, than Keble's Assize Sermon. That is true enough. Nevertheless, the fact remains that the sermon in question was the first complete and coherent expression of the tendencies and reactions which were to give unity to the Movement, and to the ideas and convictions that inspired it.

Moreover, insisting as he did on the need for a return to the Apostolical conception of the Church, Keble, at the very outset, indicated the difference between the Tractarians and the High Churchmen, the "High and Drys", called by Froude the "Z's"; while to the men after his own heart he gave the name "Apostolics".

Keble preached his sermon on the 14th July. On the 25th, Rose held a meeting at his parsonage at Hadleigh. The idea was to draw up a plan of campaign for the defence of the Church. Those present included William Palmer of Worcester College,[1] who had come to Oxford from Dublin; Perceval, a fellow of All Souls and a former pupil of Froude's and Keble's. Palmer, the learned author of *Origines Liturgicae*, was a sound theologian, but first and foremost a Churchman, abundantly furnished with connections among the higher dignitaries; perhaps a little encumbered by them. No less learned, but a great deal less assertive than Palmer, was Perceval, whose main assets were that he was the son of a peer, and had been chaplain to two kings. The

[1] Not to be confused with Palmer of Magdalen who ultimately became a Catholic and has left a very interesting *Memoir*, which Newman published.

choice of such men is a sufficient indication of Rose's conservatism. That he invited Froude as well, justifies Newman's description of him as a man of truly supernatural views.

The meeting came to little, as it was bound to do. Froude scandalised Palmer, and Palmer made Froude's blood run cold. Rose could not help feeling a little shocked at some of Froude's more extravagant utterances, and felt decidedly uneasy about the sort of policy into which he saw he was being drawn. Nevertheless, it was agreed that something would have to be done, though what form that "something" was to take, no one quite knew.

What finally emerged was a twofold plan. Palmer's idea was to form an association which, under influential patronage, was to bring in all clergy of the right way of thinking. Rose, on the other hand, favoured the idea of a letter to the Archbishop of Canterbury, with as many signatures to it as they could obtain. While assuring him of the loyalty of the clergy, the letter would indicate their principles, and the policy to which they would desire to render obedience. (We can imagine Froude giving expression to that, in words that would make Palmer explode, and the estimable Rose turn pale.)

Froude came away from Hadleigh with the desperate feeling that he had behaved like a great child; that no one had taken him seriously. Rose and Palmer had great hopes of the plans they respectively advocated. Newman, though he had little faith in either, was prepared to support their efforts, or at least to do nothing to hinder them. But he himself had something else in mind. As he observes in his *Apologia*, he had felt for some time that the ideas by which Froude and he were actuated were far removed from the vague conservatism of men like Rose and Palmer. No doubt, to start with, the Movement, in the form he was about to give it, would look like a rallying cry to the defence of the dignitaries whose position and emoluments were threatened. The protest about the Irish sees would lend colour to such an imputation. But, in point of fact, what he and his sympathisers felt to be the real crux of the matter was something totally different. Was the Church merely a department of State, entrusted with the performance of functions more or less loosely defined, or was she the successor of the Apostles? If the latter, though such a revival of her true character might seem designed to strengthen and buttress the position of her dignitaries, it was not impossible that it might ultimately lead to her disestablishment. In these circumstances, it is understandable that Newman, though too fair minded to do anything to discourage the efforts put forth in all sincerity by Rose, and too prudent to come into open collision with the well-meaning but vague proposals of Palmer, to say nothing of the still vaguer velleities of Perceval, had no intention of getting involved in any such measure as those put forward at Hadleigh. He said himself, in so many words, that living movements do not come of committees, and he did not think that committees could be depended upon to secure the safety of the Church. For that, he looked rather to personal influences, supported and unified by the living tradition of a home of culture, such as Oxford. It was with this idea in mind that he conceived and resolved to launch the daring experiment of the *Tracts for the Times*. From Rose and his group he looked for nothing more than a benevolent acquiescence. All he asked of them, in the event, was that they should not disapprove or disavow a Movement begun on his own sole responsibility, and continued with the help of others who, of their own free will, had since joined in the work.

And so it happened that, about the middle of September, there began to arrive at countless country parsonages, as well as at many deaneries and collegiate establishments, not to mention a few bishops' palaces, a strange four-paged document which aroused not a little curiosity. It had been printed and published by Rivingtons, and its price was one penny. But an energetic propaganda campaign saw to it that it found its way into hands that would have been little likely to order it. Such procedure was startling, but not more startling than the success which attended it. Not that there was anything new about tracts. Indeed, they were already too common for any great expectations of success to be founded on them. The Evangelicals had used them *ad nauseam*, and there was not a deaconess or district visitor who did not go about with armfuls of them. Distributed among all and sundry for the good of their souls, they had come by this time to be greeted with a derisive smile. But now, with the arrival of this latest specimen of the *genus*, the tracts came in for a new lease of life. The opening words struck a note so out of the ordinary that few readers could help reading on. Some put them down with astonishment, a few with indignation, and most people without knowing what to make of them. But no one was tempted to mock. Newman wrote the first tract, but he did not put his name to it. The reason for this anonymity he explained at the outset:

> I am but one of yourselves, —a Presbyter; and therefore I conceal my name, lest I should take too much on myself by speaking in my own person. Yet speak I must; for the times are very evil, yet no one speaks against them.

The tract displayed the Church as threatened in its very foundations —nay, in its very nature—by the political measures which the Government was beginning to put into operation, and which the Liberal Party hoped to push still farther. It appealed to the clergy to rally to a man round the Bishops, insisting that they should be recognised as the successors of the Apostles. That this might by no means involve their rehabilitation in the quasi-seigneurial privileges now somewhat in jeopardy, he was careful to make clear:

> We could not wish them a more blessed termination of their course than the spoiling of their goods, and martyrdom.

That, it must be confessed, was a very new note to strike in the Anglican Church. It might please Froude, but it was certainly calculated to awaken grave uneasiness in the minds of the average sort, who certainly did not expect to have their case defended on such original lines.

But Newman was not the man to stand still. No sooner had his new readers begun to recover a little from Tract Number One, than two more followed in quick succession, both of them written with a pen dipped in the same ink as the first. The first had invited them to reflect on their vocation and on the nature of the mission entrusted to them by Christ. The second dealt with the whole idea of the Catholic Church, as the Body of Christ, and not as an organ of government. The third was concerned with the proposed alterations in the Prayer-Book. Keble came to the rescue with the fourth tract. This went farther into the doctrine of the Apostolical Succession, which had been touched upon in Tract 1. The fifth, anonymous like its predecessors, was given out as representing the thoughts of a layman (Bowden was the layman). The stream had begun to flow, and it was to go on flowing for a long time yet.

It was clear at once that the Tracts were causing a considerable sensation. In all the Oxford Common Rooms they were the one topic of conversation. So, too, in parsonages and deaneries. But Newman and his party were going to see to it that they were talked about still more.

An inspirer of men—one might almost use the term agitator—he had always been, despite his retiring nature. He was now to display this gift on a scale beyond anything the campaign against Peel had led people to expect. Not content himself with writing, correcting, and dispatching the Tracts, he pressed his friends into the service, and put himself to endless trouble to ensure the circulation and diffusion of the ideas they conveyed. He went about calling on his former pupils in their various parsonages, in town or country. Not content with that, he set off on horseback with a bundle of Tracts on his saddle, making every village church a landmark. He left a Tract or two at every parsonage that he passed on his route, whether the parson was known to him or not. High Church or Low Church, it mattered little. At the same time, for all his native reserve, he expounded and argued, and drove his points home, tersely but firmly, in cases where paper and printer's ink failed to make things clear.

People were astonished, amazed, at this flood of new ideas bursting forth so suddenly, in a form so full of life, from Oxford, from this Alma Mater. One cleric, when Newman came to him with his papers, enquired, with a twinkle in his eye, whether Whately was not at the bottom of it all. We can tell from the accounts he himself has given, what amusing things were sometimes mingled with all this propagandist ardour. The important thing for him had been to stir men's minds and to move their hearts. The first objective had been attained, there was no doubt about that. The second soon would be.

IX

THE "VIA MEDIA"

It will have been observed how little Newman had seen of the world, how circumscribed had been his existence, until he went on that voyage to the Mediterranean. Save for the various places round London or Oxford, where his family had taken up their quarters at one time or another, he had, as late as his thirtieth year, seen little or nothing of England. Similarly with his church experiences. Certainly, before he went up to Oxford he had known Mayers, and through Mayers he had made acquaintance with a number of Evangelicals of the more or less moderate type. Of the High Church party, his glimpses had been few and far between, and those he got from books. It required a long time at Oriel, and considerable experience of parochial work to get him out of this narrow setting, however unsatisfying he may have found it. It took him a long time to get on really friendly terms with Keble. It took him just as long to acquaint himself with the High Church party in general. As for the Church of England as a whole, it may be said that he did not arrive at any thorough knowledge of it until the Tractarian Movement began. Hence the paradox that the Church of England did not become a reality to him till he felt it reacting to the influence he himself was exerting upon it.

And now it is time for us, too, to bid farewell to Oxford, to Oxford, where life is so pleasant yet so cloistered, time to ask ourselves what manner of institution the Church of England really was in the thirties of the nineteenth century. The question, we may as well at once admit, is by no means an easy one to answer. Indeed, take it at any period you will, from the sixteenth century down to our own times, it would be difficult in a few words to give an intelligible description of it. For it is in its very nature a compromise between Protestantism in its various manifestations on the one hand, and Catholic tradition on the other; a compromise, too, between regarding itself as a department of State, and as claiming to be a spiritual power wholly free and independent.

However, at the beginning of the nineteenth century, the Church of England, while finding herself in the position common to all Christian communities at the end of the Age of Enlightenment, was confronted with a state of affairs that tended to aggravate, rather than to attenuate, the perplexities of the situation, and that was the astounding ease with which the two extremes ran side by side together. We may shrink with horror when we are told that there were but six communicants at St Paul's Cathedral, London, on Easter Sunday, in the year 1800. Yet we must not forget that at the same date Notre Dame, Paris, was priestless, the last archbishop who had officiated there having publicly renounced his episcopate. It may appear a thing beyond belief for an Anglican Bishop like Hoadly calmly to declare that, though the Church of England was then Trinitarian in its belief, it might become Unitarian any day by virtue of an Act of Parliament. Nevertheless, we must not forget the sort of theology that Moehler and his like encountered, somewhere about the same period, in German Catholic schools.

However, what was certainly a monstrous anomaly might, so far as the Anglican Church was concerned, be looked on merely as the normal outcome of a system. On the Continent, the Catholic Church, after a tremendous struggle, had repelled the servitude which the Empire endeavoured to impose on the priesthood. In sixteenth-century England a struggle of a similar character had resulted in a complete victory for the Crown. Not only that, but a Protestantism, first Presbyterian, next Puritan, and finally Deistic in character, had become diffused throughout an already half-secularised ecclesiastical body. The pietistic reactions of the Methodists and the Evangelicals did but add to the chaos. And so, as a result of all this, we have, in the first place, Bishops who were imposing Officers of State, much more concerned with their seat in the House of Lords than with the affairs of their Bishopric. With some honourable but extremely rare exceptions, they paid only the scantiest and most intermittent attention to episcopal matters. No doubt in France the Catholic Church had its Talleyrands and its Loménies, whose religious faith and moral behaviour compared unfavourably with the faith and morals of the most ordinary Anglican Bishop; but then Loménie and Talleyrand had a much clearer idea of what they ought to have done, and of the institution they represented, than the best of the Bishops. Newman himself has a revealing story to tell about one good Bishop who, having read Tract 1, which was about Apostolical Succession, could not make up his mind whether he held the doctrine or not.

The successive changes which the Church of England went through from the sixteenth century to the Restoration had left it in a more or less ambiguous position. That ambiguity the eighteenth century had done nothing to resolve.

The Thirty-nine Articles, which the Clergy were obliged to subscribe, as well as University entrants, constituted a declaration of faith distinctly Protestant in character. However, they were so drawn up that anyone who still had any sort of leaning towards Catholic tradition, could, at a pinch, manage to get along with them. By contrast, the Liturgy, broadly speaking, was plainly based on Catholic lines. Its presentation, however, was added to here, or whittled away there, in a manner unmistakably Protestant. The most perplexed of all its sections was that of the Eucharist. A succession of inchoate but uncompleted rearrangements had made it very difficult to form any clear idea of what its final revisers really intended.

Add to all this, first the oncoming tide of latitudinarianism which drowned in natural religion all definite and clear-cut Christian doctrine; secondly, the sporadic influence of Wesleyanism, very sincere in its beliefs, but sentimental, individualistic, theologically loose, and we shall get an idea how vague and incoherent was the Anglicanism of the time. If we would contemplate it in action, Goldsmith's *Vicar of Wakefield* and the novels of Jane Austen portray pretty clearly what manner of men were the Rectors and Vicars of those days. Goldsmith said that one great merit of the Church of England was to ensure that there was a gentleman in every parish. We are sometimes tempted to wonder whether that was not its only merit.

Into a church, in which the altar was looked upon as just an ordinary piece of furniture at which the Lord's Supper was celebrated four times a year, often in a manner hardly decent, strode the "gentleman" on Sundays to read Morning and Evening Prayer, and to deliver an address, usually literary and humanistic in tone and substance, seldom religious, and hardly ever doctrinal. For the remainder of the week he confined his parochial work, assuming that he lived in the parish, to such benevolent deeds as might be expected of an incumbent who was himself in easy circumstances. For the rest—seeing that he was one of the gentry—he went hunting or shooting, superintended the cultivation of his glebe, and busied himself with whatever might be his own particular hobby, possibly an intellectual one, possibly not.

There were, of course, some exceptions. To begin with, there were the Evangelicals. They preached conversion, and did their utmost to convert their flock. On the other hand, they had scant respect for, and usually neglected, all that was traditional in the constitution of the Church.

Then, again, there were a few—a very few—High Churchmen whose religious views were something other than a mere corollary of their political Toryism. They held that the Church of England, though reformed in the sixteenth century, and therefore in one sense Protestant, still remained a part of the Church Catholic. Their attitude towards the sacraments was faithful to tradition, at least so far as Baptism and the Eucharist were concerned, and we may even include Penance. In some cases they fasted. But the churches where they could find a service to suit them were few and far between, apart from some college chapels, like that of Magdalen at Oxford. As for the great majority of those who called themselves High Churchmen, practically their only right to the title was based on a respect for the Hierarchy, indissolubly associated in their minds with the Crown—that, and a cordial detestation of Dissent in all its forms, Dissent which they considered the highway to Democracy.

Newman, for his part, had undoubtedly undergone a profound and lasting conversion under Evangelical influence. But in spite of its origin, this conversion exhibited none of the customary Evangelical characteristics. It was rather a rediscovery on his part of certain fundamental elements of Biblical teaching presented in the traditional setting which was still preserved, at least substantially, in the liturgy of the Church of England.

All, then, that he exhibited of essentially Protestant in his composition was a religion derived from the Bible and at the same time one personal to himself. But Protestantism as a general system, and more especially the attempted systematisation, in the light of Calvinistic conceptions, of Wesleyan mystical transports, had never brought him satisfaction. His parochial experiences and his own reflections on the matter, had convinced him that such a system had no foundation either in Holy Writ or in the realities of our existence. On the other hand, in certain great Catholic truths, truths which the Noëtics themselves had helped him to discover, he had found, between the teaching of the Bible and experience of life, the consonancy for which he had been seeking. His growing familiarity with members of the High Church group had led him to recognise in the great Anglican theological writers—the Caroline Divines and Butler—the same harmonious blending of complementary elements which his own experience as a plain straightforward Christian had enabled him to discern.

On the other hand, the Roman Catholic Church, viewing her as he did through the eyes of the Protestant historians, seemed to him to have marred and disturbed this perfect equilibrium by the introduction of idolatry and superstition: worship of the saints, prayers for the dead regarded as possessing some magical effect, divine honours rendered to the Pope, etc. What he had been able to see of the Roman Church in the course of his Mediterranean voyage (how well or ill interpreted, this is not the place to discuss) seemed to confirm this unfavourable impression. It must further be observed that the attitude of the English and Irish Catholics, who were making common cause with O'Connell in support of the Liberal policy, looked to him as though they were throwing in their lot with the current infidelity of the day, aggravated by the scandalous dishonesty of a Machiavellian policy. In the light of the unanimous statements of her leading theologians, it seemed to him that the sole aim of the Anglican reformers had been to restore to the Church, Catholic and Apostolic, its pristine purity.

We must, however, draw attention to two special features which were to distinguish the neo-Anglicanism of which he was the promoter, from the traditional High Church party. To Whately he owed a clear conception of the Church as an institution wholly independent of the State. The most "Catholic" of the Caroline Divines had never reached that point. Froude had given an additional stimulus to this idea, which he too held without, it would seem, owing it in any way to the Noëtics, when he linked it up with an essentially supernatural and ascetic view of Christianity. How could the Church be of this world, if Christianity was not?

To that Froude added a second element, scarcely less important though he owed it to influences that were incontestably romantic, and that was a veneration for the Middle Ages. All the "Cavalier" High Church and Tory elements in Froude predisposed him to a feeling of enthusiasm for mediaeval life and religion as depicted in the romances of Sir Walter Scott. His almost innate asceticism combined with his ideas of chivalry to inspire him with a passionate admiration for an ideal like that of St Bernard: a strict austerity in sentiment as in life, yet, withal, a romantic cult of the Virgin and of virginity.

It is very remarkable that Newman, for his part, was never in complete agreement with Froude on this point. Great as was his admiration for him, he could never bring himself, even after he became a Catholic, to look on the Middle Ages as an ideal phase in the annals of Christianity. Still, Froude's idea did have this effect, it sufficed to cure him of the notion that, after the patristic period, the Church's record had been one of progressive deterioration. It brought him to see in developments which, on the face of them, seemed to be bearing her away from antiquity, something very different from an incontrovertible proof of decay or corruption.

So now we have pretty well the whole *corpus* of ideas and sentiments which were to be the dominant inspiration of the earlier Tracts.

But Newman was the first to realise that the ideas disseminated by the Tracts required, if they were to take root, an intellectual campaign covering a far wider field than was practicable within the limits of the Tracts themselves. No sooner, then, was the Movement well under way, than he addressed himself to this constructive task. Only calm and mature reflection could restore vigour to the mind of a Church awakened at last from so long a slumber. The task which, not so long ago, he had designed for Rickards, circumstances now required him to undertake himself.

What had to be done was to bring out clearly the body of religious ideas needed to furnish a theological basis to the Anglican theory. But great and ever growing as was his admiration for the Caroline Divines, he was never content merely to repeat them, when comparing and systematising their principles.

Aware, like Rickards, that most of their writings and ideas were of the nature of improvisations; aware, too, of the gaps and contradictions they displayed, what he sought in them was an orientation and an inspiration. But, rather than to the Caroline Divines themselves, he would have recourse to those whom they had always acknowledged as their authorities—in other words, to the Fathers, with whose writings he was by this time well acquainted.

The publication of his *Arians of the Fourth Century* coincided with the start of the Movement. This work, for which he had relied on his own unaided resources, and which is somewhat suggestive of the prentice hand, is crammed with facts and citations from the ancient writers, all of them carefully digested and deeply pondered. But, more than that, there shines out, through the vision of the past which illumines it, his faith in a living Church. It is this belief in the existence of an ever-living Catholic Church, reflected in the writings of Athanasius, Basil, Gregory, and the like, that it was now Newman's aim to define, so that he might reinfuse it into the Anglicanism of his day. This was the theme on which he mainly descanted in a series of lectures which later on were condensed and printed in two volumes. They were a first step in the direction of establishing Anglicanism on a sound theoretic basis. However, they remain, amid the general body of his work, as sketches, tentative outlines, often marked with a touch of genius, no doubt, but still sketches, of a purely Catholic theology renewed by a return to its sources, and as a view of the problem as he personally understood it. The first of these volumes is the *Lectures on the Prophetical Office of the Church*, published in 1837; the second, *Lectures on Justification*, which appeared the following year.

Newman arranged to deliver these lectures in a chapel which formed part of St Mary's, known as Adam de Brome's chapel, so called after the founder of Oriel who was buried there. Hitherto, the place had been used as a sort of vestry. On special occasions, when University services were held in the church, the Vice-Chancellor and the various Heads of Houses assembled there to form up for their processional entry. There was a small pulpit in the place and Newman directed that some benches should be placed on either side of the tomb, which was in the centre.[1]

An audience, which was constantly increasing in numbers and which included the cream of intellectual Oxford, wedged their way into this dingy chamber to listen to theological disquisitions, the like of which had never fallen from the lips of any Regius Professor. It was about this time that Newman first came in contact with a person who, among the younger adherents of the Movement, was destined to exercise an influence comparable to his own. This was William George Ward. A thoroughgoing Liberal, a former pupil of Arnold's at Rugby, this youthful fellow of Balliol was persuaded to attend these lectures by another Old Rugbeian, Arthur Stanley. There was a touch of irony about all this. Stanley, then at the peak of his enthusiasm for Newman, was later to become the leading representative of the Broad Church Movement and its cultured scepticism; while Ward was not only to give the Movement a powerful impetus in the direction of Rome, but became himself one of the most vociferous advocates of reunion.

At this time, however, Ward, still loyal to Arnold and Whately, recoiled with horror from what he regarded as Newman's obscurantism. Nevertheless, from the very start of these lectures, to which Stanley had had so much ado to drag him, Ward fell under the speaker's spell, the spell of his intellectual power and the perfection of the language in which he clothed it. Ward, who was extraordinarily corpulent, and more remarkable in appearance than the most notorious of Oxford's eccentrics, now became possessed of a variety of sentiments to which his energetic and impulsive nature gave the most arresting and entertaining expression. In that little chapel, where the delicate modulations

[1] There is now no wall on the nave side, so it is no longer a separate chapel.

of Newman's voice scarcely awoke an echo, Ward kept turning and twisting about like a demon in the grip of an exorcist, delivering himself of loud stage-whispers to Stanley, with facial contortions which may have amused the audience but greatly worried the lecturer. So effective were these performances that at last, having put up with them for two or three lectures, Newman instructed the sacristan, instead of putting the seats facing the pulpit as he had done hitherto, to place them sideways like the stalls of a choir. That did not trouble Ward. To the end of his days Newman was fated to have this very singular disciple following at his heels. Ward was for ever amusing, pestering, or disheartening him. For the moment admiration was in the ascendant; disapprobation in the background. Impulsive as always, Ward compressed his new-found cult into the famous formula, *Credo in Newmannum*. On no one could this sort of thing have grated more harshly than on Newman. Yet it was many more years before he came to realise that no worse calamity could befall a party or a cause than to have a man like Ward to support it.

What, then, was the idea, or body of ideas, to which Newman's lectures were to win the assent of Ward, and of many others hardly better calculated than he to absorb them? The first series, *The Prophetical Office of the Church*, was designed to bring out in what sense the Anglican Church was to be regarded as a reformed Church. Thus, what he had to account for was the existence of a Church apart, a separate entity, rejecting Roman Catholicism on the one hand, and Protestant Dissent on the other.

The Reformation, so far as the Anglican Church was concerned, seemed to him, in the light of the concordant witness of her leading theologians, to have had no other object than that of reviving the Catholic and Apostolic Church, the Church of Tradition, in all its original purity. The Anglican Church did not break with the Roman in order to adopt a number of novelties put forward by the Protestants, novelties with no root in Antiquity, no foundation in the Scriptures as the Church in which the Gospel was written understands them. The sole reason for the renunciation by the Anglican Church of her communion with Rome was to rid herself of the various accretions, all of them more or less idolatrous, which Rome had added, or had suffered to be added, to the beliefs and traditions of the primitive Church. So far, in fact, was the Anglican Church from abandoning traditional Catholicism that its sole reason for breaking with Rome was the desire to restore that tradition in all its primitive integrity.

No doubt that is what all the Protestant reformers claimed to be doing. But the truth was that the vast majority, thinking they were merely scraping away some dead skin from the body of the Church, dismembered the body itself in the process. However, they had no compunction, for their part, in adding, to the superfetations of Rome, new inventions of their own, just as remote from primitive purity, and just as far from conforming to the traditional interpretation of the Scriptures.

Hence the *Via Media*, the steering of a middle course between the errors of Rome on the one hand, and the errors of Protestantism on the other, and that was what the Anglicanism of the seventeenth century had claimed to do. Thus considered, the *Via Media* is no mere rough-and-ready adjustment, no typically British compromise between Catholicism and Protestantism. It is Catholicism in its pristine purity, disencumbered of the parasitic accretions of Rome, rescued from the so-called purification, but in reality the ruinous ravages, of Protestantism.

In developing this theory along the lines taken by the Caroline theologians, Newman was perfectly alive to an objection that was bound to present itself and which he himself proceeded to formulate. Catholicism exists; it is a real and objective entity. Protestantism, substantially the same beneath all its various guises, also exists; it, too, is a living entity. But up to now, this pure Catholicism which the Anglican reformers were to present to the world had never got beyond the theoretic stage; it existed only on paper. There had been the initial wave of Protestantism to begin with; then the return to Rome under Mary Tudor; then the second wave of Protestantism. After these vicissitudes, the theologians of the two Charleses never found it possible to establish their system on a firm basis. Laud tried to do so, but then came Cromwell and brought his work to naught. Under the Restoration, matters fared no better, either on the political or the religious plane. Hardly had the Anglican Church risen once more from its ashes, than it went once more to its death, in company with the Non-Jurors. After that, only traces of it survived in some of the loftier spirits of the High Church party. But now, seeing that it was the existence of the Anglican Church that was at stake, what was needed, what had to be done, was to prove the validity of the theory by making it incarnate in a visible and stable body. That was what was needed, that had never been done, and that was to be the work of the present generation. There was no other means of overcoming the liberal spirit in religion—that is to say, the spirit of indifferentism which spelt death—than a return to the Christian life in all its original plenitude. Such, then, was the aim, such was the high emprise, that stirred the enthusiasm, that fired the hearts of all the young and ardent spirits in the Oxford of those days. Even in the ears of some of the Liberals themselves, men like Ward or Stanley, Newman made ring the imperious summons of God and His Word. But if he succeeded in so doing, it was precisely because he did not present that Word as something fixed in a system already cold in death. He told them of its creative, its regenerative powers, for ever inexhaustible. Nay more; he called on them to play their part, too, in the work of re-creation.

Nothing could have been better calculated to kindle the fires of enthusiasm in breasts that were gasping for breath in the antiquated fabric of a crumbling society and the impoverished atmosphere of an eighteenth-century rationalism that had outlived its destined day.

But how, in practice, was this true Catholicism, disfigured as it had been by Rome's errors, so-called, on the one hand; lopped and hacked about by the Protestants on the other—how was this true Catholicism to be recovered? This was a point concerning which Newman had nothing to offer save his own experience; but this he conveys in a formula of singular felicity. It is perhaps as near the truth as any theory ever advanced regarding the nature and meaning of Tradition.

In this view of the matter, there are two forms, distinct yet inseparable, in which Tradition may be manifested. One of these forms he calls "episcopal Tradition"; the other "prophetical Tradition". The former consists of the official formularies of the hierarchy, such as the several creeds. It is an addition to, and an interpretation of, the Scriptures, but it is itself something committed to writing and therefore fixed, bounded and stereotyped. Its purpose is to conserve and to safeguard.

But prophetical Tradition is both living and life-giving. Not confined to any particular period of time, it is, like life itself, both one and manifold. It suffuses the writings of the doctors, the formularies and ritual of the liturgies, the continuous teaching of the Church, and the soul of Christians as it expresses itself throughout the whole of their existence. Sometimes it is almost identical with episcopal Tradition; sometimes it overflows all limits and tends to fade and disappear in fable and legend. Therefore, if episcopal Tradition were not at hand to clarify and define it, prophetical Tradition would always be in danger of being overlaid by corruption; whereas it is the living truth that dwells for ever in Christian souls and in the Church. Rather than any catalogue of dogmas and definitions, it is "what St Paul calls 'the mind of the Spirit', the thought and principle which breathed in the Church, her accustomed and unconscious mode of viewing things".[1]

The spirit, the soul of the Church is not handed on by formal teaching; it is only by dwelling in the *milieu* which is permeated by it, by adopting what is called its ἦδος, its ideal of life, that we may make it ours.

Thus the Anglican Church will live again as Catholic if it renews once more its knowledge of the Fathers and recaptures their spirit. Nor is that a mere matter of study, of the reading of books, but rather of rekindling the spirit of our lives at the fire of their example. Hence the importance attached by Newman to those choice and telling extracts from the patristic writings which the Tracts were to make current—those and a *Library of the Fathers* in an English translation, publication of which was due to begin in 1836. Most of the younger recruits to the Movement were pressed into the service, and Thomas Mozley, in his usual picturesque style, tells us what it meant for him, and a good many others, in the way of hard work.

Newman was particularly attached to a work admirably representative of all the ancient spirit and fervour which the *pietas anglicana* had for a time succeeded in reviving. Not content with using them in his own private orisons, he translated into his incomparable English the devotions which a Bishop of Elizabeth's day—Lancelot Andrewes—had composed for his own use in Greek and Hebrew, afterwards bequeathing the manuscript of them to Archbishop Laud.

Andrewes and his *Preces* conjured up a living picture of what for a time was Newman's ideal of a churchman. A humanist as cultured as one could possibly be in that blossoming time of the English Renaissance, but deeply absorbed in the Scriptures, the Greek Fathers, and ancient liturgical works, Andrewes, though carrying on a hard-hitting controversy with Bellarmine, will always be known as the principal author of the English Bible and one of the first promoters in the Church of England of a liturgical revival and a renewal of the spirit of prayer and penance. This university dignitary, this great prelate, whose finely chiselled features and expressive countenance shown in the portrait at Jesus College against the shadowy background of an English cloister, was, above all, a man of prayer. And those prayers

[1] *Via Media*, Vol. I, pp. 249–251.

of his, in those *Preces privatae* which Newman translated with such loving care (the Greek text of them he always kept by him, even on his *prie-Dieu*, after he became a Cardinal) were all cast in the mould of the Scriptures, the Fathers, and the most venerable liturgical formularies. That is not to say that some memories of Greek Tragedy, some echoes of Virgil, or even Erasmus did not find a place there; even so, they afford the most moving testimony of the intense personal fervour that may dwell in that deliberate reserve which Newman rated so highly, always ready to give ear to the voice of the Church speaking through the Bible and Tradition.

The day is gone,
and I give Thee thanks, O Lord.
Evening is at hand,
make it bright unto us.
As day has its evening
So also has life;
the even of life is age,
age has overtaken me,
make it bright unto us.
Cast me not away in the time of age;
forsake me not when my strength faileth me.
Even to my old age be Thou He,
and even to hoar hairs carry me;
do Thou make, do Thou bear,
do Thou carry and deliver me.

Abide with me, Lord,
for it is toward evening
and the day is far spent
of this fretful life.
Let Thy strength be made perfect
in my weakness.

Day is fled and gone,
life too is going,
this lifeless life.
Night cometh,
and cometh death,
the deathless death.
Near as is the end of day,
so too the end of life.
We then, also remembering it,
beseech of Thee
for the close of our life,
that Thou wouldést direct it in peace,

Christian, acceptable,
sinless, shameless,
and if it please Thee, painless,
Lord, O Lord,
gathering us together
under the feet of Thine Elect,
when Thou wilt, and as Thou wilt,
only without shame and sins.
Remember we the days of darkness,
for they shall be many,
lest we be cast into outer darkness.
Remember we to outstrip the night
doing some good thing.
Near is judgment;—
a good and acceptable answer
at the dreadful and fearful judgment-seat
of Jesus Christ
vouchsafe to us, O Lord.

That long passage, with its measured, softly rhythmic phrases, its serenity, its gravity, bathed in an indescribable golden light, calls up to us, as in a vision, a Christian humanism that might have been, a humanism in which Renaissance and Reformation should have agreed together in a common loyalty to Catholic Tradition. We may well understand how dear it was to Newman, and that, long after his conversion, it still continued to represent for him an admirable Christian ideal.

However, in the course of these years, he discovered in the Roman Catholicism of Andrewes' day a very similar ideal. It caused us no little surprise to come across, among the publications of the Movement that were prepared and sponsored by Newman, two little Latin books bearing the title *Hymni Ecclesiae*. One merely contains the hymns of St Ambrose and St Hilary and others to be found in the Roman breviary. The other, however, is an anthology of the compositions of Santeuil and Coffin. As Bremond to his credit does not hesitate to declare, the choicest products of the French religious spirit are to be found in these —perhaps the last—jewels of Christian Latinity.

Midway between Andrewes and Keble, along the road to a Catholicism wholly positive in character, and rejecting nothing truly Christian, it is good, indeed, to hear the strains of *Labente jam solis rota* or of *O luce qui mortalibus* falling suddenly on the ear.

The second series of lectures delivered in Adam de Brome's chapel gives utterance on the theological plane to this longing for a religion that was not to be a mere system of ideas, but a way of life, a life dedicated to God. However, it must be admitted that the *Lectures on Justification* far exceed the range and plan of the *Via Media.* And that is so true that they were not understood by those who heard them at the time, whether friends or foes, Catholic or Protestant. That very sympathetic and clear-sighted critic, Richard Hutton, frankly avowed that he failed to see the drift or bearing of such a book, or of the problems with which it was concerned. One eminent theologian and historian, Döllinger, did see in it the masterpiece of a great Christian thinker; but this judgment found no echo.

But perhaps it is this very failure on the part of his contemporaries to understand the book that explains how it is that people today are inclined to regard as a mark of genius its anticipation of the problems which are our concern today, and of the treatment they call for. To bear that out we will content ourselves with quoting the opinion of one of the leading Anglican theologians of the present day. He declared to us that the book seemed to him one which transcended in interest all Newman's other works.

When he came to address himself to the problem of Justification, it was the interpretation of his own conversion that Newman had at the back of his mind, the very crux of the conflict between Catholicism and Protestantism.

The Oxford Movement, it must be pointed out, had now taken the direction of an ever-closer identification of Catholicism with anti-Protestantism. Newman did not long retain any very lively sympathy with the Reformers of the sixteenth century. He soon became aware of the excessive preponderance of the negative element in their measures of reform, while his dispassionate scrutiny enabled him to dissect the strangely assorted mixture of ideas on which their protest was based. It is thus the more remarkable that he always succeeded in looking on Catholicism as something other than the mere negation of a negation. Indeed, the deeper and clearer grew his vision of the Catholic Tradition in all its plenitude and purity, the more alive he became to the existence of the Christian values inherent in some forms of Protestantism, even the least satisfactory, and to the importance of preserving them.

His study of the Fathers, his devout meditations on their writings, enabled him to form a conception of Catholic doctrine which, it is no exaggeration to say, was whole worlds in advance of any attained by the foremost thinkers of his day. But in his case, endowed as he was with a penetrating insight altogether remarkable, this conception was accompanied by a psychological appreciation, no less remarkable, of what it was that had set Protestantism in motion.

The inestimable importance of the *Lectures on Justification* may be defined in a word or two. They show forth, and give expression to, the genuinely Christian elements underlying the Protestant religious movement, describing what it was, deep down in Protestantism, which explains its endurance and which might have made it, not a sectarian religion but a power, a regenerative power, beneficial to Catholicism itself. At the same time, soaring above the unsatisfying aridities of text-book theology, these lectures discover in the wealth of Catholic Tradition the spirit that might have given those original Protestants complete satisfaction, fulfilling their aspirations and removing all risk of their falling into heresy or schism.

Newman begins by putting side by side, first the ultra-Protestant statements of Luther, in which Justification is held to be something wholly external to the person justified; and then the modern Catholic declarations in which the inward reality of the change wrought by the action of grace is re-established. Is the justified man a sinner still? Is he simply indued with the justice of Christ without being in any way changed by it? Or is he inwardly renewed by Jesus Christ? It was easy for him to sustain the truth of the latter proposition, easy to show that it conformed to the requirements of the Gospel; but that he does with a flexibility and a breadth of view rarely met with in Catholic controversialists.

But having done thus much, he was a long way from considering his task at an end. Is there, then, no substance in the Lutheran argument? Most certainly there is. What the Protestants were then upholding, and are upholding still with their unhappy formularies, is the absolute and sovereign power of divine grace in our salvation; or to put it more precisely, it is the fullness and perfection of God's gift which is given us in Jesus Christ, and to which nothing can be added by man. In saying that, the Protestants were but restating with additional emphasis something that had always formed a part of Catholic Tradition, something that had been included by St Augustine in his condemnation of the Pelagians and the semi-Pelagians. Man does not work his own salvation. It is God who saves him. It is not a case of man doing something, however small it may be, in the work, and God doing the rest, however much. God does all, absolutely all, since, as St Paul says, it is He who creates in us the will and the fulfilment thereof. There were some Catholic theologians who had recognised all that from the very outset of the controversy. Some of them, like Seripando and Contarini, did their best to do justice to the element of truth in the Protestant argument. But their doctrine of a dual justification weakens the force of the Catholic teaching on the matter as laid down by the Council of Trent, and takes insufficient account of the difficulties of the Protestants. It admits in the Christian the presence of some merits, but insufficient to work his salvation. Only the merits of Christ can make up the difference between what God requires of us and what we are able to supply. Ideas like that have this in common with those of the semi-Pelagians, they please nobody. The Protestants find matter for objection in them because they imply that man can have merits in some way apart from Christ. The Catholics, on the other hand, fail to find in them what they have a right to demand, and that is a justification full and real that creates humanity anew, a salvation that truly saves.

But now Newman goes on to show how the Catholic doctrine, formulated at the Council of Trent, if properly interpreted, suffices to dispel all the Protestant misgivings. The merits of the good man are real merits; he is not merely called good by a sort of fiction. The Word of God which declares him righteous is the creative Word which gives effect with invincible infallibility to what it pronounces. But these merits, this righteousness, are, and can be, in no way an addition to the merits, the righteousness of Jesus Christ.

The Word of God, in truth, only declares and makes us righteous by merging us in Jesus Christ, so that henceforth we have no life but in Him. "It is not I who live," says St Paul; "it is Christ who liveth in me." Which is like saying that our merits, our righteousness, are wholly His, without being, on that account, any the less our own. We are only what we are as being wholly in Him. But we can be all that He is gathered up into the Only-Begotten One, participators in His Resurrection, sharers in His own Divine Life.

We cannot do more here than give a bare outline of this idea, an idea so notable for its fairness and its rigour. It is as though it were an advance pattern, or model, of a whole "oecumenical" theology, a theology which brings all Christians together, not by a compromise satisfactory to none, but by an acceptance, made possible by a clearer understanding, of the whole, in all its plenitude.

Be it added that these lectures, if they did not actually bring them out, paved the way for all the most fruitful developments that were to proceed from the twentieth-century theology of the Mystical Body.

And further, let us remark how far we are, with all this loftiness of vision, from the *Via Media*, and scarcely less so from the intellectual and spiritual routine to which, with a tacit but very common accord, Catholics and Protestants alike adhered. We need not be astonished that Newman's followers in this matter were few in number, and that he himself did not feel sufficiently encouraged ever to resume the theme.

X

ST MARY'S AND LITTLEMORE

It would not be easy to find at the starting-point of any religious movement men so little open to the imputation of anti-intellectualism as those who began the Oxford Movement. And among them, notwithstanding some misapprehensions which we shall make it our business to dispel, no one ran less risk of incurring such a reproach than Newman, the *quondam* disciple of the Noëtics. It is therefore the more remarkable that the Tractarian Movement, and the *Via Media* on which it proceeded, should have made the practical life of the Christian and all which it demanded its one and only concern.

Some time after the Hadleigh meeting, Froude gave a striking definition of the difference between the "Apostolicals" and the average Tory High Churchman. With his usual audacity and irreverence, he declared that what they had to do, and to persist in doing, was to see to it that the Church of their desire had nothing in common with "smug parsons", and "pampered aristocrats".

What was most powerfully compelling in the new Movement was the ever-increasing number of examples it afforded of a Christianity at once eager for, and creative of, righteousness. It was no mere abstraction that won over so many enthusiastic and valuable recruits to the Movement, but its direct and practical appeal. What lent the Movement its power and its greatness was that it was neither a merely intellectual revival on the one hand, nor, on the other hand, a religious revival, such as Methodism, without any doctrinal foundation to support it. Just as its theological researches led inevitably to a renewal of the spiritual life, so it was that the most real religious needs were the mainspring of its speculative investigations. This it is that invests the great Tractarians with such an aureole of splendour, making them an honour, not to England alone, but to the whole of nineteenth-century Christendom. They addressed themselves to their task actuated by one sole determination, and that was to do the will of God as it was made known to them by Jesus Christ. What specially redounds to their credit is that they perceived with admirable clearness of vision—and that in the very hey-day of the romantic era—that no Christian sanctity can rest on anything but the truth.

Thus they were enabled to bring to their search for truth not only transparent intellectual honesty combined with exceptional mental endowments, but their whole and undivided being, mind and spirit, spirit and mind, in one. If there was a time when Newman had been in danger of rating intellectual distinction higher than spiritual excellence, his crowning achievement was in the end to bring about so perfect an alliance between the two that what Fr Przywara says of him seems in no way an overstatement: What St Augustine was for the ancient world, that St Thomas Aquinas was for the Middle Ages, and that Newman must be held to be in relation to the world of today.

The same sort of harmony of mind and spirit prevailed to some extent among all his Oxford companions. Indeed, we must recognise in Keble, the eldest and the source of inspiration of them all, the signal merit of having been the first among them to make the perfect offering, the offering of his gifted mind in furtherance of the behests of the loftiest of spirits. Judged from this standpoint, he has a better title than anyone to be called, as some have called him, the Saint of Anglicanism. That may require some reservations; these we shall consider in due time. Meanwhile, it is only right that we should acknowledge the light that shone so brightly from that radiant figure at the Movement's early dawn. But taking them as a whole, what was it these men possessed that proved so attractive an influence? As touching Newman, and Keble, Pusey, and Froude, and all those many others who shine with a smaller but, it may be, just as pure a light, does not the answer lie in the incomparable unity we perceive in them of mind and spirit, spirit and mind? If ever there was a thing that deserved the name of Christian humanism, it is to be found in those ten years of the Oxford Movement that saw it bud and blossom. But, we do not hesitate to repeat, all this was due to the fact that the Tractarians, far from indulging in any sort of complacency, went on to draw the richest and purest of natures to consent to the dearest of sacrifices.

No factor in the Movement was better calculated to give it this stamp of supernatural humanity, and, in consequence, its rare effulgence, than Newman's pastoral work at St Mary's and Littlemore.

No sooner did he succeed Hawkins as Vicar, than he threw himself into the work of his parish with all the zeal he had formerly displayed at St Clement's. The energy and conscientiousness with which he undertook the humblest of parish work never abated, even in the most critical days of the Movement, or when his own work imposed its heaviest burden upon him. During the cholera epidemic, a worthy

Oxford ecclesiastic, firmly resolved to expose himself to no unnecessary risk, drew up, before making for the country, a list of fellow-clergymen to whom his parishoners might apply for help in case of need. Newman headed the list.

Nevertheless, despite his best endeavours, the activities of the new Vicar were not attended by the success that had rewarded his labours at St Clement's. The reason was not far to seek. It arose from the artificial nature of the parish. Except for the colleges, and they were not properly a part of it, the parish consisted almost entirely of shopkeepers. This being so, it was hardly to be expected that he would obtain the same sort of response he got from the good folk on the other side of Magdalen Bridge. Newman was not slow to perceive that what most of his parishioners hoped for from their Vicar was to be let alone.

For this disillusionment, if such it was, two compensations presented themselves; the first, the more startling of the two, he had neither sought nor expected. The other, less conspicuous, was the fruit of some carefully matured plans of his own. The first, then, was the constantly increasing number of people who came to St Mary's from outside the parish, drawn thither by the personality of the new incumbent. The second was the successful development of the outlying parish at Littlemore, and the building of the church there. Little was it then foreseen that thither, in 1841, Newman was to come to spend the last few years of his life as an Anglican.

We have already stated that St Mary's, besides being a church with a parish of its own, was also the official University Church. On Sunday and Saints' Day mornings, services would be held at which one of the Select Preachers would occupy the pulpit, each in due rotation. It was therefore only natural that the Vicar should reserve his own discourse for the evening service, which, in theory, is always strictly parochial. Sunday by Sunday, having nothing in view but the spiritual welfare of a few shopkeepers, charwomen, and college servants, Newman was accustomed at the close of day to mount the pulpit and to expound in the simplest language some text from the Bible.

Never, in his own view, or in other peoples', was there less of an orator, at least as we in France understand the word. Almost entirely without gesture, in a voice which, though clear as crystal, was entirely innocent of inflection, as one rapt in inward contemplation, a mood which he quickly communicated to his hearers, he would speak for a quarter of an hour, or perhaps a little less. In order to spare his eyes, worn with much reading and nocturnal study, the lights round about him were turned low. His lineaments were dimly discernible, his tall, slender figure was a little bowed. Were sermons ever preached, we may surely ask, in circumstances better calculated to keep success at bay?

Every Sunday saw newcomers to St Mary's. In the porch, with its twisted pillars surmounted by Laud's statue of the Virgin, one noticed few but youthful faces. First came undergraduates from Oriel, soon followed by men from other colleges. The congregation continued to grow, till at last all the most brilliant people in Oxford began to make a point of attending Evensong at St Mary's, rubbing shoulders there with pious shoeblacks, devout housemaids, and a few High Street shopkeepers, who did not think it right to let Sunday go by without a spot of church-going. Nothing in the preacher's tone or bearing, and little in the subjects treated, indicated that he had become aware of the change that had taken place in the character of his audience.

All the same he *had* noted it, and noted it immediately. At first, he had been a little mystified, not less by the comparative absence of his parishioners proper, than by the formidable invasion of eager listeners from elsewhere. Quite simply and plainly he made up his mind about the matter. Without deeming it necessary to make any drastic change in the subject-matter of his sermons, he took upon himself, as a duty laid upon him by God, the responsibility for these alien souls now coming to him in the place of his regular flock, who cared for little outside their business.

In view of the fact that they were mainly young people who kept coming to him in impressively increasing numbers, he did his best to touch on subjects appropriate to his audience, taking great care, however, never to go so far in this direction as to risk saying anything over the heads of his parishioners proper. Never did his sermons deviate from that perfect simplicity which had been their outstanding characteristic from the beginning. When great controversies came to be debated, people went to St Mary's curious to hear what the Vicar would have to say. As a rule they were disappointed to find that the preacher seemed to be quite uninformed about them. Never was there the most distant allusion to matters of topical concern. Never did Newman champion from the pulpit the cause of any particular party. He preached the Gospel; that and that alone. But the manner of his preaching, the way he brought the listener to the heart of the sacred Word, and the sacred Word to the heart of the listener, did more to win disciples to the Movement than any amount of discussion and argument could have done. More clearly than anything else, these sermons brought out what it was that the Tractarians were aiming to do, and that was, not to found a school, but to revive a religion. Whosoever came to hear him, in friendly or in hostile mood, realised, when the time came to depart, that what the preacher had above all things at heart, was not to label people, but to help them to recognise God's will, and then, in due course, to fulfil it. Of all Newman's many writings, the *Parochial and Plain Sermons* will probably always be assigned the highest place. Judged merely as literature, they merit this pre-eminence. Nowhere does Newman's famous prose surpass the crystalline purity of these sermons; the perfection of music, sinuous, nervous, unerring balance of form and imagery, all blended into one miraculous whole—such is the style of Newman. But what saves that style from the things that "date" so disastrously in the works of the vast majority of the Great Victorians, is the sober directness of his vocabulary and diction. One of these sermons has for its title, *Unreal Words*. If any pulpit oratory, if any written compositions can claim never to force the note, never to exaggerate, never to incur the faintest suspicion of insincerity, that claim must be allowed to the works of Newman. So measured, so temperate are his words, never overlaying the sense, which is always present, always clear, that their quiet power seems immune from decay. Not a trace of rhetoric in his composition, which we can only compare to Racine's, the Racine of *l'Abrégé de l'histoire de Port-Royal*. But what a depth of emotion—of emotion that never loses its bloom for all the restraint that is put upon it—these words convey to readers who will no more grow tired of reading than did their listeners of hearing them.

But this art, perhaps unparalleled in its delicacy and restraint, is only the least recommendation of these sermons at St Mary's. Nowhere else are Newman's religious character and—shall we say, his saintliness?—so clearly revealed. Nothing could be farther removed from any kind of personal display. If what he says carries with it the convincing force of reality, it is because he, the witness, believes heart and soul in the truth of his testimony.

In his *Grammar of Assent*, Newman develops at length what he regards as the all-important distinction between notional and real assent. Notional assent is that which we give to a statement as the result of a process of abstract reasoning. Real assent, on the other hand, involves what the schoolmen would call a deep underlying similarity of nature between subject and object, brought out by process of assimilation.

Thus it may be said of these sermons, that they had no other object, and no more striking effect, than to bring their readers to accord to the truths of Christianity a real, instead of a notional, assent.

All Christian doctrine is contained in them, all the moral teaching of the Gospels, but put in a way that calls on us, that compels us, to stand and deliver our "yes" or "no"; not the assent or dissent of the intellect alone, but of our whole being. Never discussing, never arguing, they commit the hearer, or the reader, to a definite pledge which he feels he can never evade without leaving an indelible stain on his conscience. Whence do these sermons derive their power? In the first place, Christian dogma is the living thing it is in Newman's exposition of it, because he takes it directly from the Word of God. Newman's knowledge of the Bible is remarkable, even in a country which prides itself on having for its religion, the Bible, the whole Bible, and nothing but the Bible. But it is far from being merely by way of illustration that these innumerable Scriptural allusions are woven into his discourse. The Scriptures were, and always remained, the vital source on which he draws. He sees the Christian faith, and transmits it, in the direct, living form with which the Prophets and the Apostles had invested it.

It was not merely a matter of being faithful to the letter of the Scriptures. How many are the Protestant pulpiteers whose homilies are made up of a whole string of Bible texts, and who only leave behind them a savour of the most narrow-minded sectarianism, worlds away from that fidelity to God's Word—from that walking side by side with it, may we say?—which strikes us so forcibly in Newman. Such fidelity is by no means to be mistaken for a lifeless adherence to the mere letter. What it implies, what it *is*, is the discovering of the great underlying ideas, the permanent trends, the life-currents which run through the Bible from end to end, giving it a unity at once so living, so flexible, and yet so firm. It is now that, after the Anglican liturgy, the study of the Fathers reveals its invaluable contribution to the mind and the religious life of Newman. As he himself said in one of his University sermons, where the Fathers help us to understand the Scriptures, is not in their detailed explanations of this or that passage, but in the fact that they lived in familiar contact with all that the Bible speaks of. Their ideas express themselves in the setting, in the very terms, of Revelation. Their attitude to revealed truth is such as the latter calls for and suggests. So, thanks to them, to the contagion of their example, he was wholly convinced of Christian truth, as though by events taking place before his eyes, a drama of world-history in which God appears, giving it form and direction awhile, and at last, in the person of Jesus Christ, becoming its principal actor. There is doubtless no other way of grasping and conveying to others this idea of the living, personal reality of the dogmatic truths of religion. But the story of God's people, which is what the Bible is, is likewise our own story, for it tells how God came to man to enlighten him about himself and to bring him that aid without which he cannot be himself, cannot be what God who made him intended him to be.

No wonder, then, that nothing moves us more than Newman's knowledge of God's Word, unless it be, indeed, his knowledge of the human heart.

It would be an endless task to quote what was said by people who dropped in more or less casually at St Mary's to hear what was going on and were suddenly overwhelmed by the feeling that that slight and dimly seen figure in the pulpit was talking to *them*, quietly telling them about themselves, telling them things which they had thought unknown to any but themselves. With that calm but inexorable scrutiny which we have seen him bring to bear when probing his own conscience, Newman penetrates the hidden recesses of every human heart. Masks are dropped, make-believe, pretence are thrown aside. The uneasy conscience, burdened with something, it scarce knows what, so difficult to probe, knows peace no more, so potent is the effect of that glance, so searching yet so calm.

Here we doubtless have the fruit of psychological gifts applied in the first place to himself who never knew timidity or faint-heartedness. Only those who can truly say, "I have not sinned against the light," can direct into others, as into themselves, the ray which illumines without vacillating the unplumbed deeps of the soul. But, more than that, meditation on the Scriptures and a strangely docile and willing absorption of their message had of itself lent clearness to his inward vision.

On the other hand, this insight, so strangely penetrating, opened the way to hidden depths in the Word of God beyond the range of ordinary vision. Only he who has given ear to One who reads our hearts more clearly than we ourselves can read them, because it was He who made them—only such an one can read his heart henceforth and the hearts of other men. And only he who, in his own case, has known "what is in man" can understand so clearly the Word that God speaks to man. Here, then, in this give and take, this mutual interchange, we draw near to the deepest implications of the motto which Newman chose for his Cardinal's shield, and which perhaps provides the master key to the power, the influence, of these his sermons: *Cor ad cor loquitur*.

True, this gift was seconded by another of which we have but to open a book of his to become profoundly aware, though it is nowhere more conspicuous than in his *Parochial and Plain Sermons*. Bremond calls it "poetical", and that is perhaps the most fitting epithet to apply to it, provided we make quite clear what we mean when we so denote it.

Poetical, then, these sermons are, in a way seldom exhibited by religious compositions, always excepting the Holy Scriptures themselves. This it is that accounts for the enduring charm that haunts these volumes, a charm whose magic we have only to read again a page or two immediately to recall.

But now what, precisely, does this imply? To begin with, Newman was endowed with a sort of second-sight which enabled him to see the invisible in and beyond the visible, things the most transcendental as well as those most deeply immanent in the human heart. Moreover, this visionary power was accompanied by a gift for acting on the minds of others which, though partly to be explained by his consummate command of language, derived also from some mysterious power he possessed of entering into their hearts and reading their sentiments. This latter trait, we must understand, was not merely passive, but active. Newman understands our experiences as well as—nay, better than—we do ourselves. He deciphers them for us, so to speak and, so doing, reveals to us the most intimate secrets of his own. We recognise ourselves in what he tells us and discover what he alone had been able to discern. But, let us hasten to add, how strict was the control Newman exercised over this faculty, so that it might always remain subservient to the message which it was his mission to deliver. Sermons such as that entitled *The Invisible World*, or that other, no less remarkable, on *The Individuality of the Soul*, bring a new universe to our vision, only to leave us in the immediate presence of Him who fills it, and who seemed to have been absent from the world we knew. In the exercise of this, perhaps his greatest gift, there is no trace of self-satisfaction. Newman continually brings before us celestial scenes, just as constantly forbidding us to linger over them. He reveals them to us only to guide us to the Cross, to which they point the way, and to which it is his purpose to bring us.

In the constraining, the inexorably compelling, tone of these sermons lies, in the last analysis, the secret of his sovereign greatness. Though they are among the most perfect literary creations that ever fell from a Christian pulpit, these sermons never for a moment suffer us to enjoy them as mere works of art. The non-religious person may read and admire the funeral oration of the Great Condé without any serious disturbance of his equanimity. But one cannot read any sermons of Newman for the mere pleasure of the thing. That sort of detached attitude is simply out of the question for anyone hearing or reading them. Whether we will or no, we must needs regard them as things addressed directly to ourselves. They put us on our trial, they arraign us, they challenge us in a way that precludes all possibility of slipping away on some side-issue, aesthetic or other. As someone has said, you could not come away from St Mary's without feeling the need of giving up something, of making some sort of sacrifice, of shaking off the benumbing influence of habit, and of ceasing to settle down contentedly with one's own mediocrity.

Something there is that remains with the reader of these words, something that touches him very closely, something that forbids him to return to his old easy-going ways, to his comfortable ideas of morality and religion. It calls on him for a decision, to make up his mind, and that decision, once made, calls inevitably for sacrifice. "The Ventures of Faith", the title of one of these sermons, sums up what is really the underlying message of them all, and that is, that our Christianity, the Christianity we profess, is but an empty thing unless it compels us to stake our all, to venture everything, for its sake. Let us bear in mind the words which made so deep an impression on him at the time of his conversion: *Holiness rather than peace*. It is noteworthy that his first printed sermon bears the title, "Holiness necessary for Future Blessedness". It is no soothing religion that Newman sets out to preach, but one which at the very outset awakens our apprehensions. To use his own words, *To be at ease is to be unsafe*. Man is a sinner; that means it is a fearful thing for him to fall into the hands of the living God. To gloss over that truth would but make the realisation of it still more fearful later on. Nor is the change-over from a state of sin to a state of righteousness an easy and an instantaneous matter, as the revivalists would have us believe, but rather a long and laborious task which, so soon as we set our hand thereto, demands of us new and ever greater sacrifices. Here we may quote another saying of Scott's, *Growth the only evidence of Life*. In the blessed self-complacency which reigned in the England of those Victorian days, those sermons at St Mary's awoke some disturbing echoes. Peremptorily they warned us to beware of being content with ourselves, and with settling down comfortably with things as they were. They called on us to make ever sterner and sterner trial of ourselves, to make ever greater and greater sacrifices, till at last our self-renunciation was complete. Abraham, and the call "Go, leave thy country and the house and family of thy father"; the words of Jesus to the rich young man, "Sell all that thou hast, give it to the poor and follow Me." Such was Newman's final exhortation to the cream of England's aristocracy, to the flower of Oxford culture. So persistent was this theme that it evidently embarrassed those who felt no inclination to act upon it. There is, in this wonderfully human Christianity of the *Parochial Sermons*, something that is distinctly disquieting. Protestants regarded it as a hint of asceticism, of monasticism, and saw in it a symptom of Newman's subsequent conversion to Catholicism. But, more remarkable still, Catholics, particularly Anglo-Saxon Catholics, who were more familiar with "muscular Christianity" than with the Fathers of the Desert, contended that these sermons were Protestant, and are there not traces of Puritanism in them, traces of those dualistic ideas which, we never denied, are to be found in some of his earlier sermons, particularly in the one he preached at Dartington? But that is too specious an argument by far. That there are to be found here and there traces of the Protestant attitude of mind no one would think of denying, though they grow less and less pronounced with each successive volume. But to say that the great current that bears him along towards a Christianity beyond the present to greet the age to come, to say that this onward sweep, this great upsoaring, was but the *residuum*, the dregs of Protestantism, is surely too preposterous. On the contrary, it is beyond question that this current, this spiritual flood, gained in force and amplitude in proportion as the narrow sectarianism which marked the earlier sermons was eliminated. Nay, more, it is perfectly certain—and this is the crux of the whole matter—that it was this aspiring towards a holiness born of a perfect responsiveness to the promptings of grace, of an unwavering fidelity to "the Light", whatever renunciations, whatever separations all this might involve, that at length brought Newman and his followers from Protestantism, from the *Via Media*, into the narrow way of the One True Church.

If there still lingers on here and there a turn of phrase which suggests the belated Evangelical, we must not allow it to lead us into turning a deaf ear to the Word of God conveyed to us through the voice of Newman. What was new about these sermons was that they inculcated a Christianity supernatural, ascetic, calling for wholehearted obedience to the voice of God. In contrast to the worldly, "business man" sort of Christianity, a Christianity toned down to suit the average man, which was what the Anglo-Saxon Protestantism of the day had become, it brought back the living spirit of a real Catholicism that had been lost sight of for centuries. Ward, at any rate, deserves credit for recognising that this was the essence of Newman's teaching: the true Church is the Church which calls for holiness of life, and which produces it.

Still more forcibly do these remarks apply to another characteristic of Newman's sermons, one which brings out with peculiar vividness what is perhaps the most profoundly significant element in the Oxford Movement. I refer to what I will not hesitate to call their apocalyptic character.

All the participants in the Oxford Movement, and Newman more than any of them, had the feeling that they were living at a turning-point in the world's history. The conflict on which they were engaging seemed in their eyes to involve issues far vaster and more important than those immediately at stake. Nor did it suffice to say that, over and above the suppression of the Irish bishoprics, they beheld the far graver problem—that of the nature of the Church and of the rights and duties devolving therefrom on its members and ministers. It seemed to them that their epoch was to mark that awakening of the powers of evil which had been clearly prophesied in the Scriptures. In that bourgeois liberalism, against which they had to contend, they recognised what Newman to his dying day never ceased to denounce, and that was perhaps the last, supreme effort of the spirit of evil to banish from the world the saving power of the Cross.

While not absolutely condemning the constituted authorities, while not pronouncing a wholesale denunciation of the modern man and all his works, the Tractarians firmly believed that these people, whether consciously or not, were doing the work of Satan, and that those accomplishments of theirs were but a snare laid by the spirit of Pride to entrap the man whose faith was failing him. Thus they came to hold that the world was a place of waiting, of expectation, that its destruction might be sudden, that at any moment Christ might come to judge and to condemn. All human effort therefore seemed to them to be vain, unless it amounted to taking sides with Christ against the world.

To say that such is the view of things conveyed by the Oxford sermons is to stop somewhat short of the truth. It is, indeed, the framework into which everything they say is integrated. That the machinations of Antichrist were already manifest, that they were the prelude to a revelation of the Kingdom of Christ, was not just one link in the chain, it was the very basis of Newman's whole belief.

Here again we have a hint, a suspicion, of the Protestant sectary. Nothing was more characteristic of revivalist religiosity than the urgency with which such ideas were canvassed.

It is perfectly true, and Newman himself did not conceal it, that he owed these apocalyptic convictions to a view of history such as that propounded by Thomas Newton in his work on the Prophecies. The identifying of Rome with Babylon, of the Pope with Antichrist in one of his manifestations—all this derives from that source, and the day was not far off when it was to fall to the ground—the day, that is to say, when Newman would be called on to make his choice between Protestantism and Catholicism. It is remarkable, however, that he persisted in regarding as Christian and Catholic this dualistic view of human history and, in particular, this pessimistic outlook on contemporary events, with its background of eschatological expectancy deepened by the sense of a crucial testing-time. However critical he may have become of the apocalyptic exegetists of his young days, and of their conclusions in matters of detail, he continued to see in their basic principle a sound basis for any truly Christian representation of things. As a matter of fact, this sort of dissociation is a thing of all time. In every age, the Saints have lived in imminent expectation of the coming of Christ, in the wake of Satan's kingdom, even when this latter seemed to be carrying all before it. And in every age, too, man is over-prone to supplement the realities of the world of faith with the baseless fabric of the world he sees. But never must the vagaries of the human imagination be permitted to dull a consciousness of the world to come. A Christianity comfortably installed in this world, on good terms with this world, and as little anxious to rise above it as to fall out with it, has never been other than a decadent Christianity. That the Christianity preached at St Mary's was a lively and perpetual protest against this swearing a peace where peace could never be, is perhaps the surest guarantee of its primitive soundness and vigour. It also explains, better than anything else, how it was that a style of preaching so quiet and restrained, a style so little "popular" in the ordinary sense of the word, should have had such an overmastering effect. At all events, far from our having here a transient and, so to speak, uncharacteristic element in Newman's spiritual make-up, it provides us with what is perhaps the most constant and continuous of them all.

Despite some differences, more apparent than real, that may seem to divide them, the *Parochial Sermons* should always be studied in conjunction with the *University Sermons* on Faith and Reason. There could be no more fatal error, no graver source of misunderstanding, than to regard these latter as a mere academic exercise, a sort of abstract appraisal of the relationship between the two.

As Newman himself makes clear, the "reason" here involved denotes the concrete exercise of the reason which had come in with the eighteenth century and was characterised by an arrogant independence and lawless freedom in its attitude to God and the Word of God. On the other hand, the word Faith is not limited to the supernatural gift in its strictest sense, but must be taken to include any activity of the mind which disposes it to an attitude of docility and reverential obedience to the Word of God. Thus the *University Sermons*, taken as a whole, are concentrated on the conflict whose significance and interpretation also define and explain the apocalyptic atmosphere of the *Parochial Sermons*.

Thus the first of these sermons develops the idea that Christian belief, and still more the practice of the Christian religion, disposes the thinker to exercise his reason along lines that will effectually lead him to the truth. The second goes into the question of Natural religion, not as it has sometimes been conceived in the abstract, but as the history of actual practical religions shows it to be, and makes us see therein a corroboration of the mysteries of man's fall and corruption, of which revealed religion makes us aware.

On personal influence as a means of propagating truth, the fifth sermon anticipates one of the basic themes of *The Idea of a University*. At the same time, it illustrates some of the educational ideas which had involved him in his early collision with Hawkins. The great religious truths which govern men's lives are not to be brought out by a mere process of abstract reasoning. The human heart would always be cunning enough to twist reason any way it wanted. There must be some personal and convincing experience of something to which the propounder of truth can himself bear first-hand testimony.

The thirteenth, dealing with reason implicit or explicit, staked out the ground for what was afterwards to become the *Grammar of Assent*. There is an implicit logic in the major decisions which govern our lives, and this, though we may not be able to give an explicit account of it, has a far deeper rational value than many a conclusion arrived at as the result of a formal process of reasoning. This implicit reason it is which justifies the believer in his belief, despite all the professors of worldly wisdom, and which gives the lie to the pseudo-intellectual superiority on which they pride themselves.

The fourteenth, contrasting Christian knowledge with the bigotry of a belief incapable of answering for itself, defines true faith as the marriage of the *intellectus quaerens fidem* and the *fides quaerens intellectum* in a common fidelity to grace and truth.

Lastly, the fifteenth is, in the first place, a sketch, an outline of the theses which were later on to be so strikingly brought out in the *Essay on Development*, arguing as it does that religious truth is a living reality whose nature, far from closing the door to renewal and change, is maintained and enriched by them. But it includes many things besides. What is perhaps the most valuable of them is the intuitive recognition that the object of religious faith is not merely a series of propositions put side by side but, as he shows it to be, the reality, the one living reality of the mystery of God revealed in Jesus Christ which these propositions enclose on every side, without ever being able to exhaust it, still less to rend it into fragments.

For one possessed of so vital a sense of the verities of faith, one so insistent on their practical application to the life of the believer, it goes without saying that something more than preaching was necessary in order to explain and communicate its significance. At St Mary's, moreover, Newman had always been careful to make his sermons an act of worship, for that must always be an indispensable element in a service making known the Word of God, a service of praise and prayer.

We must bear in mind that he habitually preached at Evensong. This is the evening service in the Anglican liturgy and is made up of a combination of Vespers, Compline, and passages from some of the old Vigils. After the singing of the Psalms comes a lengthy lesson from the Old Testament. Then comes the *Magnificat*. Another equally long lesson, this time from the New Testament, precedes the singing of the *Nunc Dimittis*, after which some night prayers bring the service to a close.

Newman always preached from a text taken from one of the lessons appointed for the day. Usually he read at least one of the lessons himself. These lengthy extracts from the Bible are assuredly one of the most impressive parts of the English liturgy, and most closely in harmony with the spirit of ancient Christendom. It takes the incurable frivolity of a Bremond to see anything tedious in such readings from the Word of God. We may be sure that Newman, by the scrupulous simplicity and deep sincerity of his reading, must have kindled a new understanding of its meaning. So, too, the clearness, the simple gravity with which he recited the prayers, brought out anew the power of liturgical prayer, its richness, its traditional continuity, its age-old appeal, not to the emotions, but to the very heart of the religious consciousness.

Newman had not been long at St Mary's when he restored the practice—which, though prescribed by the Prayer Book, had fallen into desuetude—of daily celebrating Matins and Evensong. A little later, he introduced the celebration, at first weekly, afterwards more frequently, of Holy Communion.

In after years, the Tractarians were conspicuous for their efforts to reintroduce Catholic ceremonial into the Anglican services, sometimes by restoring the ritual of mediaeval English Catholicism, sometimes by adopting the modern Roman ceremonial, and applying it to the Anglican formularies. Newman, on the other hand, and the majority of his friends, never made any such attempt. To no set of men would the epithet "ritualists" have been more inappropriately applied than to the pioneers of the Oxford Movement.

But while carefully abstaining from introducing anything new, even though it claimed to be "traditional", contenting himself with the simple observances to which Oxford was accustomed, Newman imparted to these services an atmosphere of deep religious feeling and of joyfulness in the spirit of adoration created by the sacred words and the mysteries they constantly evoke. Many were the Oxford men of those days who, in after years, recalled their unforgettable experience of things divine, of things visible to the eyes of faith alone, at those early morning Communion services in the choir of St Mary's, when Newman was the celebrant. Those unearthly things whereof he himself had told in one of the most moving passages in all his sermons, those he made real to them also.

> A thick black veil is spread between this world and the next. We mortal men range up and down it, to and fro, and see nothing. There is no access through it into the next world. In the Gospel this veil is not removed; it remains, but every now and then marvellous disclosures are made to us of what is behind it. At times we seem to catch a glimpse of a Form which we shall hereafter see face to face. We approach, and in spite of the darkness, our hands, or our head, or our brow, or our lips become, as it were, sensible of the contact of something more than earthly. We know not where we are, but we have been bathing in water, and a voice tells us that it is blood. We have a mark signed upon our foreheads, and it spake of Calvary. Or we

recollect a hand laid upon our heads, and surely it had the print of the nails in it, and resembled His who with a touch gave sight to the blind and raised the dead. Or we have been eating and drinking; and it was not a dream surely, that One fed us from His wounded side, and renewed our nature by the heavenly meat He gave.[1]

But it was not St Mary's that was destined to become the centre, the home of that living religion which Newman wished his church to be. What we have already said about the sort of people who attended there of a Sunday will explain why that was. However, included in the parish there was a hamlet, Littlemore, some way out of Oxford, that had never had a church of its own. This raised a problem which Newman, almost as soon as he had been appointed, took seriously in hand. The inhabitants of the place were all people of the same class, all peasants, workers on the land, worthy folk, but woefully lacking in opportunities for the regular practice of religion. What gave him an added interest in the place was that Oxford itself, the main part of his cure, had so many of these opportunities and profited by them so little. He got his mother and sisters to help him in his parish work as soon as they moved into a house at Iffley, which is about midway between Littlemore and Oxford. He organised a regular round of visits to the parish folk, particularly to the sick. Then, not content with ministering to their spiritual needs in their own houses, he started to think about building a church. Very soon, thanks to a substantial contribution from Mrs Newman and help from a number of friends, a little country church, the more attractive for being so unpretentious, rose up with its quiet churchyard around it, quite close to a school.

Bloxam, Newman's curate, entered with great zest into all this, and Newman himself, smilingly sharing his enthusiasm, interested himself in every detail, no matter how minute, concerning the furnishing of the chancel. The altar, backed by the eastern wall, had a cross upon it (not a crucifix), and was covered with a cloth worked by the Newman ladies. This was a very cautious, very discreet return to Tradition.

For the service of Dedication, all the good folk in their Sunday best, the children in new clothes, which the parson had paid for, as well as some of the most eminent people in Oxford, came crowding into the church. As he breathed in the cool scents of the flowers and verdure which were the sole adornment of this little House of God, Newman, amid the weighty preoccupations with which he was oppressed, must have caught the fleeting vision of a springtime of faith and prayer.

[1] *Parochial and Plain Sermons,* Vol. V, pp. 10–11.

Littlemore, where the common life of the parish was so full of vigour, where the great Christian verities came to life beneath his hand, in such purity and strength, was to prove for him a sort of spiritual oasis. Thither he would betake himself, more and more often, to refresh himself at the springs of a piety fervent but manifested with the deepest humility, without a trace of formalism, or dubious sanctimoniousness.

Thither he came little by little to withdraw, to dwell on the agonising issues of a Movement which had begun with such high-soaring hopes. There he was one day to preach his last Anglican sermon, the sermon entitled, *The Parting of Friends*. And there, long years after, he was to return, unheralded, unknown. One fine evening an elderly parishioner, seized with a kind of fear and filled with respectful emotion, recognised in an old man clad in black who was silently weeping as he leaned over the fence of the little graveyard, the master, the pastor, the father of old times—of old times and always, as it seemed to these good, simple-hearted folk. "Parson has come back again!" was the simple announcement proclaimed by the witness of this scene.

XI

CRISIS

THE first few years of the Oxford Movement were perhaps the happiest in Newman's life. He tells us that he felt, after his illness in Sicily, once more in the full flush of strength and vigour. The task which he had gradually come to regard as his life's work was engrossing all his energies. In the sphere of thought as in that of action, in the inward as in the practical life, we see an efflorescence of all the resources he had in him ready to meet the needs of the hour.

In all this vitality of his, he seemed to detect later on a touch of hardness, a certain disdainful impatience in his attitude to the many mediocrities, friends or foes, whom he met on his way. These heart-searchings arose from two accusations—they were contradictory accusations—that were brought against him. One charged him with Jesuitry, the other with fanaticism. Fanaticism, because of the rigour with which he expressed himself (sometimes implying criticism of many who had till lately been his friends) regarding the conflict between God and the World, between Christ and Satan; Jesuitry, because his intellectual skill sometimes tempted him to take a sly pleasure in sowing seeds of truth in the minds of people who could not foresee where they would ultimately lead them.

In point of fact, the only possible ground for the charges, the one or the other, lay in a sort of youthful impulsiveness which was to remain with him till after he had turned forty. He found it no easy matter to keep these astonishing powers of his under proper control until the trials and tribulations of life taught him their lesson. However great our admiration of those powers, there was undoubtedly this fly in the amber. Alas, experience of life was soon to cure it, and only too completely.

This is not to say that everything was rosy during these early years of the Movement. It had only just been started, when the man who had given it so vigorous a send-off, the man to whom Newman was indebted for so many inspiring ideas, Richard Hurrell Froude, was compelled to drop out. The voyage in the Mediterranean had failed to work a cure. In the ensuing autumn it became clear that he would have to go and live in a warmer climate. So he went to Barbados, where he was appointed professor of theology in the Anglican seminary. In 1836 he came home. He was hardly recognisable, so wasted and so worn did he appear. A few weeks later, at Dartington, he died.

Some weeks after that, as though by way of compensation, one who had expressed a certain amount of sympathy with the Movement when it began, but had rather hesitated to join it outright, now made up his mind to do so. Henceforth Pusey, whom Hugh James Rose had at first been rather inclined to regard as a dangerous liberal because of the interest he took in German Biblical criticism, was definitely one of the Tractarians.

We are compelled to say, however, that he had got involved in it quite unintentionally, as a result of one of those abortive schemes of his, for which he was becoming rather noted. Having written a tract for the series, it occurred to him to make it clear that, because he had written this particular one, it was not to be inferred that he countenanced the whole series. Up to then, the tracts had all been anonymous, and now he thought he could best display his independence by putting his initials to this one, which he did, "E.B.P.". As might have been foreseen, the effect of this manoeuvre was the exact opposite to what he had intended. Since he was the first to sign, people took it that he was willing to answer for all that had so far appeared. Thus, willy-nilly, the worthy Pusey was to find himself regarded as the leader of a party to which he had barely professed his allegiance. In the end, however, he threw in his whole weight. Not only that, he completely changed the character of the tracts. He wrote one, on Baptism, and it was a volume in itself. But, more than that, the gravity of his bearing, the dignities he bore, Regius Professor and Canon of Christ Church, gave the Movement the prestige of a party, and no inconsiderable party at that. Newman was perhaps exaggerating when he said that he and Froude "were nobodies" in the University, or in the Church. Anyhow, it was certain that Pusey *was* someone, and someone of weight. After the death of Froude and Rose, and when Newman too, had departed, he remained where he was, stolid and unchanged. It is not surprising, therefore, that the Movement came to be called the Puseyite Movement.

It goes without saying that a Movement so broad in its scope and so rapid in its development, and that along lines so little familiar to the English mentality, was bound to encounter increasing opposition. As long as it bore the appearance of a measure designed to preserve the Church, it gained the approval of a large section of the clergy, but it was bound to excite, and it did excite, growing suspicion among the Evangelicals, who were already numerous, and the Liberals, whose numbers were increasing. Little affected by the anti-Roman sentiments of the *Via Media*, which they took as a matter of course, they were very keenly sensible on the other hand to its aim—its very obvious aim—of bringing about a Catholic revival. That was quite apparent when the Tractarians succeeded in securing the condemnation by Convocation of the newly appointed Regius Professor of Divinity, Dr Hampden. The Evangelicals, who voted with the Tractarians against this first attempted incursion by the Broad Church party, as it came to be called, made no secret of their hope that, next time, they would be voting against the Puseyites.

We must bear in mind that for a long time Newman had only a distant acquaintance with the attitude of mind of most of the average clergy. Perhaps he hardly realised how shocked these worthy folk must have been at what, to him, was merely the practical application of principles associated with the greatest names in the tradition of Anglicanism. On the other hand, it is possible that his naturally moderate and objective mind, which only wanted to be quite sure where it was going before taking any fresh step, may have failed to realise the enthusiasm excited, especially among the younger minds, by those principles and ideas which he was calling so abruptly back to life. "He is not afraid of inferences," Rose had once said with quiet humour, speaking about Froude. More and more numerous grew the new recruits of whom the same thing might have been said. But then again, there were reactions in the opposite direction, reactions that rather disconcerted Newman, so sudden were they, and so fierce. He and Keble were soon to have their first experience of this sort of thing when, shortly after Froude's death, they concerted together to publish his *Remains*. Of these there were four volumes. The first two, which came out in 1838, were amply sufficient to provoke an extraordinary uproar, which the two that followed did nothing to mitigate. It must, of course, be borne in mind that they had known Froude for a long time and had learned to make allowance for a number of things that were bound to jar on the ordinary Englishman, particularly on the moderate, middle-of-the-road churchman. All the same, it is a little difficult to understand how they could have failed so completely to foresee the sort of indignant amazement their contemporaries were bound to exhibit at the revelation of Froude's monastic austerities, to say nothing of his startling outspokenness. The Diary, which is the most notable part of these *Remains*, is primarily the record of perpetual mortification of the flesh and endless searchings of conscience. The fastings, the penances of every kind which Froude imposed on himself, were bound to be very disturbing to easy-going Victorian ideas of religion, and no less so his references to his own faults, however slight; references which, though hard on himself, could not have been very agreeable reading for others. For a religion which has made its peace with the world the best way to counter such a disturbing revelation of Christian austerity, and to conceal its own uneasiness, is to condemn it out of hand. A less immediate but more durable effect of the publication of these *Remains* was the spirit of emulation excited among some of the younger disciples by religious ideas so definitely Catholic in tone. It helped in no small measure to carry a number of them to a destination for which it was a long time before Newman could bring himself to set out.

All this troubling of the waters, however, was not in itself so very disturbing. Some years were to pass before the ideas of the adverse party took shape, and not until then did the real difficulties begin.

But for Newman himself a crisis was at hand, or at all events brewing, before that major conflict developed. This was an inward misgiving, something that haunted his mind, something that seemed to him to cast a doubt on the validity of his theological position. To begin with, it was but a fleeting sensation, like a shadow that passes over the mind and then departs again without our being perceptibly affected by it. But in this case, to use his own words, the ghost came back, and a few months later still, it was a ghost no more, but a dogged, determined foe, that disputed every inch of the ground.

What, then, had happened? During the summer of 1839, Newman had come across, in the *Dublin Review*, an article on the Donatists, schismatics of St Augustine's day, who had caused a grievous division in the Church while claiming to purify its doctrine. The author of the article in question was no unknown person. He was, in fact, none other than the Mgr Wiseman, Superior of the Collegio Inglese at Rome, on whom he and Froude had called during their visit to that city, in order to ascertain from him the real Catholic position, and how they stood in regard to it. In those *Remains* of his, which the British public were now reading with such horrified feelings, Froude's way of putting the matter was that they went to ask on what terms they might be allowed to surrender. Now, in spite of Froude's sympathetic attitude towards Catholicism, both mediaeval and modern, which at that time was far more pronounced than Newman's, it was sufficiently clear from the context that he was speaking ironically. Not for a moment did Froude, still less Newman, contemplate individual or corporate union with Rome.

Little, however, did the two young English churchmen dream what a commotion their visit and their conversation were going to arouse in the bosom of the genial and somewhat hot-headed British Monsignor Wiseman, who, with that mixture of prophetic insight and complacent wishful thinking which was so characteristic of him, was marvellously excited at meeting two clergymen so deeply interested in the ancient Catholic tradition and so clearly dominated by the thought of the work that was waiting for them to do at home.

This article of his was but one of a numerous series which he continued to turn out, in season and out of season. So ardent was his longing to bring them into the fold that when at length Newman and a number of others did come over, he almost convinced himself that it was all owing to his efforts.

The immediate aim of the article, however, was to emphasise as strongly as possible the analogy between the position of the Anglicans in regard to Rome, and that of the Donatists in regard to the Church of their day. It was written with the *brio*, the not very convincing massiveness, of all Wiseman's writings. To Newman, with his delicate and discerning critical faculty, the whole thing seemed to lack point; the analogies struck him as vague and far-fetched. On him, the article in itself had little effect.

It so happened, however, that when it came into his hands he had just been delving deeply into the Fathers of the Fifth Century, in pursuance of his enquiries into the history of the Monophysites. All at once it had occurred to him how striking was the resemblance between that conflict of the fifth century and the dispute between Rome and Anglicanism today. As he puts it in the *Apologia*, in reference to the *Via Media*:

> My stronghold was Antiquity; now here, in the middle of the fifth century, I found, as it seemed, to me, Christendom of the sixteenth and the nineteenth centuries reflected. I saw my face in that mirror and I was a Monophysite.[1]

He brings this out a little farther on:

> It was difficult to make out how the Eutychians or Monophysites were heretics, unless Protestants and Anglicans were heretics also; difficult to find arguments against the Tridentine Fathers, which did not tell against the Fathers of Chalcedon; difficult to condemn the Popes of the sixteenth century, without condemning the Popes of the fifth.[2]

[1] *Apologia*, p. 114. [2] *Ibid.*, p. 115.

The case of the Donatists, however, bore no resemblance to that of the Anglicans. The Donatist schism was a matter of setting up Altar against Altar in a land where the Catholic Church was still established. What, however, did strike him in Wiseman's article was a phrase quoted from St Augustine, to which a friend who had shown him the article in the first place had drawn his particular attention. It ran, *Securus judicat orbis terrarum*. Immediately, those words revived all the apprehensions to which his own reflections had given rise. Today, even as when St Leo confronted Dioscorus, the Monophysite Patriarch, the great bulk of the Church was on the side of Rome. Canterbury was simply a branch lopped off from the main trunk.

It is of great importance to realise as accurately as possible the exact nature of the doubts that were for the first time beginning to assail Newman regarding the tenableness of his position. We shall then be able to note, in this second conversion of his, which we may call his conversion to the Church, an even greater independence of view, an even completer intellectual autonomy than characterised his first conversion, his conversion to God. Extraneous circumstances did but furnish the occasion, apparently a purely fortuitous one, which set in motion the inner workings of his mind, and outside personalities only came in later on, when he had already arrived at his conclusion, to supply a formula and to express a truth which he had already discovered for himself, and of which he had perhaps a greater grasp than those who brought him what he knew all along had been coming.

Now, for the first time, when the summer of 1839 was drawing to an end, the thought crossed his mind, "Perhaps the Church of Rome will be found right after all". But, we must hasten to add, suddenly as this notion came, it disappeared as suddenly. That in no way signifies that Newman had, or could have, become insensible to the force of the analogies he had so recently come to recognise, or to the arguments to be deduced from them. Nevertheless, in a matter at once so grave and so complex as the quest for religious truth, he could not allow himself to be carried away by a single *ex parte* argument, however cogent it might seem.

In his *University Sermons* on Faith and Reason he himself, following the lines laid down by Butler, had clearly shown that the rationalistic critics of the eighteenth century derived their apparent force from the very narrowness and superficial nature of the ground on which they based their arguments. Such arguments are wholly illusory, based as they are on a criticism so frail and partial of a rich and living reality.

Seeing this, he was not going to let himself be carried away in the opposite direction by similarly defective reasoning, and to base a sweeping judgment on coincidences of so special and limited a character.

None the less, the coincidences remained and, do what he might, he could not explain them away. It almost looked as if they had been thrust in like a metal wedge, with the mischievous purpose of disrupting that fine piece of timber-work, the *Via Media*. Though they were hardly enough to bring a man over to Catholicism there and then, they did in the long run, effect an irreparable breach in the structure Newman had just erected as a home of refuge for Anglicanism. The more he contemplated that crack, the more formidable it seemed to grow. More effectively than all the arguments of his opponents, Catholic or Protestant, his own reflections convinced him that the *Via Media* was not a workable theory. As we have seen, he said himself that, so far, it had only existed on paper. It would be a bold undertaking to try to make it a living reality, but that is what would have to be done if Anglicanism was to be kept alive. To this end, he had devoted all his energies. To achieve this, at all events at this particular juncture, might seem to be an augury of success, if only a partial success. But now, lo and behold, before the main onslaught on the building was made or even threatened, the first man to discern a flaw in its structure was the architect himself.

It is of first-rate importance that we should make this perfectly clear. Some have seen in Newman's final resolve to abandon Anglicanism for Rome the outcome of disappointment, the hidden workings of a "resentment complex", the sort of mental condition which Max Scheler and his like have so skilfully analysed for us. Newman, astonished and painfully disappointed at the stolid incomprehension of his co-religionists in general, and of the English episcopacy to start with, a state of mind which persisted from 1841 to 1845, had—this is the theory—at last come to despair of Anglicanism. In other words, what he really did was to blame the system, Anglicanism, for his own special grievances, for injustices inflicted on himself personally. Such is the explanation elaborated by that distinguished, discerning, and deferential interpreter of character, Canon F. L. Cross.[1]

But how is such a theory to be reconciled with the fact that Newman's misgivings with regard to the Anglican position began to haunt him before, and not after, the personal rebuffs of which he was later on the object? It was not until much later that he became convinced of

[1] F. L. Cross, *John Henry Newman*, Philip Allan, pp. 46–55 and 130–144.

the truth of Catholicism. The fact of the matter is that his hopes of proving the soundness of Anglicanism, as he had come to conceive it, and as the Puseyites were to go on conceiving it, received their death-blow, so far as he was concerned, at the very moment when everything seemed to be going well. When he had become a universally respected theologian and the most moving preacher of his times, when his influence was at its zenith, and when the Movement he had inspired was going from success to success, then it was that the seeds of doubt and uncertainty about what he had so brilliantly put forward began to germinate.

Of course, at that time he had no serious idea of going over to Rome. So far the whole matter was problematic, theoretic. On one point, however, he soon came to a definite conclusion, and that was the intrinsic impossibility of upholding the *Via Media*. The longer he dwelt upon the matter, the more deeply he reflected upon it, the more convinced he became that that sudden and transient misgiving of his had been well founded. The *Via Media* represented itself as a revival of the Church of the Fathers, of the Primitive Church; yet the Fathers would have condemned it as severely in their day as Rome condemned it now. Whatever was to be said for or against the claims of Rome today, we find nothing in the Fathers to support the *Via Media*, but, on the contrary, a good deal to condemn it.

They explicitly reject the idea that some local church might possess the truth, while the Church as a whole, the Church Universal, was in error. This is what St Augustine meant when he said, *Securus judicat orbis terrarum*. In such a case, and Newman was far too alert to make a mistake in the matter (he knew too much about the Arian controversy for that), the principle of majority rule had no relevancy. Of course, in any particular Council, considered by itself, a preponderating majority of Bishops may be wrong, as against a few who continue to proclaim the truth to all men; the events of the fourth century prove that clearly enough. But it is a very different thing if the Episcopate as a whole and the Church as a whole, in firm and stable agreement, find themselves opposed by a few dissentients, Bishops and faithful. In such circumstances, it is no case of a majority ruling in connection with a matter that may be explained and perhaps modified as circumstances may suggest; it is the conflict between whole and part; between the body living in unity, and limbs that have voluntarily condemned themselves to severance and to death.

Thus Christian truth is not a matter of compromise, not a matter of give-and-take, as so many Monophysites, and most Anglicans seem to imagine; nor is it a matter of unilateral pronouncements or one-sided declarations, as the Protestants like Eutyches and the extreme anti-Nestorians believe. But it is a plenitude, a completeness which, admitting no impoverishment, no half-measures, reconciles all extremes, even as St Leo proclaimed, and the whole Council of Chalcedon after him.

The more impartially Newman brought his mind to bear on Antiquity, with the expectation still keen, and the conviction still unshaken that, in spite of all, he would find some support for his views, the more obstinately these truths took possession of him. They indicated the impossibility of ever discovering the true faith in what—following on the lines of Hammond, Jewel, Stillingfleet, Barrow, and the rest—Newman himself had taught, in what, for the benefit of his own disciples, he had busied himself in erecting into a system. That same Authority which the fathers of Anglicanism had taught him to revere, namely, Christian Antiquity—that same Authority now bade him forsake them, those same fathers, seeing the difference that had been made manifest between Antiquity and them.

For a long time yet he might go on doubting whether or not the Church of Rome was the true Church today. What he could no longer have any doubts about was that in the true Church, St Athanasius, St Leo, and St Augustine were in their real home. That being so,

> What was the use of continuing the controversy, or defending my position, if, after all, I was forging arguments for Arius or Eutyches, and turning devil's advocate against the much-enduring Athanasius and the majestic Leo? Be my soul with the Saints! and shall I lift up my hand against them? Sooner may my right hand forget her cunning, and wither outright, as his who once stretched it out against a prophet of God![1]

Here, an objection readily suggests itself. These latter arguments would seem to imply something that Newman, in his *Prophetical Office* appeared to dismiss as a baseless prejudice, and that was the idea that Anglicanism was a mere compromise between Catholicism and Protestantism without any organic life of its own. Had not Newman himself demonstrated in brilliant fashion that it was something quite different from that, that it was Catholicism restored to its original purity, equally remote, it is true, from Rome and Geneva, but only because it was untainted by the errors of either. The *Via Media*, as he

[1] *Apologia*, pp. 115–116.

had envisaged it, was no compromise, but stood for that unsullied plenitude in which extremes are reconciled in a higher synthesis. Was not that the very idea which the *Lectures on Justification* had developed and applied in the clearest fashion?

The answer is that, in broad outline, the basic principles of the *Via Media* and, more particularly, of the *Lectures on Justification*, were never abandoned by Newman, either now, or later on, when he became a Catholic. Such a thing never entered his head. The preface he wrote, at the very end of his life, for the reprint of the *Via Media*, proves that, beyond all question. He may in the meantime have discovered some complementary truths, but his conception of the Church and of the perpetual renovations which are an essential condition of its life, remained unchanged. It simply comes to this, that what he then thought the Anglican Church provided or might come to provide, he came, as time went on—and despite his rooted prejudices—to find in the Church of Rome and in that Church alone.

However, before this new faith came to birth, the old one had to die. And die it did, because the hope of seeing the Anglican Church fulfil the role designed for it proved a pure illusion. The Church of England, as it was in fact and not as he had dreamed it, as history portrayed it, and in its present aspect, was not, and never had been, imbued with the Catholicism he aspired to, a Catholicism drawing from the pure treasure of Tradition, now won back once more, the wherewithal to satisfy those lawful aspirations which the preachers of Protestantism had traduced rather than interpreted. It was what the hazards of history had made it, struggling to preserve its traditional framework, a framework void of most of its treasure but encompassing a sheaf composed of anarchical Protestantism and political opportunism. His views in 1839 had not as yet attained that degree of clarity and conviction, but such were the lines on which they finally developed.

But, it will be asked, why this change of outlook just now? If his basic principles did not, and never were to, change, why, at this particular moment, should he despair of seeing them embodied in the Church of his baptism, particularly as none of the others had had any inkling of the problem he had encountered?

He himself pointed out that the germ of his doubts had, if the truth be told, been in him from the very beginning of the Movement. From the very start, he had been firmly convinced that the grounds on which the Church of England could base its claims to be considered a part of the Church of Christ were that in the sixteenth century its one and only aim had been to restore, in all its pristine purity (changing nothing, suppressing nothing), the Church of the Fathers, the Catholicism of Antiquity. In choosing this ground, there can be no doubt on this point, he was but reoccupying the position on which the Caroline Divines had sought to take their stand. But then, as we have said, he at once realised that they had not been able to achieve their ideal. Nay, though they had formulated certain abstract principles, and deduced certain conclusions therefrom, they had never succeeded, even in theory, in presenting a coherent entity. Hence his misgivings as to the soundness of the case. Did, he asked himself, did this ideal correspond in any way with the concrete facts of history and with what Anglicanism in practice really was? Was it in any way possible to find a place for this ideal in the Church of England? Or was it not rather an attempt to justify *a posteriori* an institution which had in it nothing, or nothing essential, in common with the character now claimed for it? Was this theoretic idea of the Church in any way reconcilable with what Anglicanism really was?

An impartial view of the Church of England and its history since the days of Henry VIII provided little to encourage this sort of theorising. The motley character of that institution, embracing at random whatever it could, in its efforts to form a compromise—here a bit of Protestantism, there some shreds of Catholicism, combined with what were merely national interests—was patent to the eye. Whether this outward aspect reflected its inner spirit, only a practical experiment could show; show, that is to say, whether the Establishment was the sort of institution to give life and being to the Catholicism of the Fathers. That experiment was now in operation, and the difficulties attending it were beginning to appear. Perhaps for the clear-sighted they had been visible from the beginning. How effective an obstacle mere inertia could prove was as yet far from manifest. What, then, was it that led Newman, as far back as 1839, to forebode that in the end, that obstacle would prove to be invincible? That answer is that it was the immemorial link which had now been so strikingly brought home to him between the plenitude of Catholic truth, which he had had from the beginning, and the concrete reality of world-wide Catholic communion of which the words *Securus judicat orbis terrarum* had suddenly dawned on him as the symbol. Hitherto, narrowed in as he had been by the insular character of his early upbringing, it may be assumed that he had never really been impressed by the universality, actual and concrete, of the Church, which is inherent in the very word *Catholic*. The truly Christian character of the Anglican Church would, he thought, be unassailable if that Church conformed, or could be brought again to conform, to an ecclesiastical pattern of which Antiquity furnished the model. But now, behold, that model, on closer examination, was found to possess an all-important characteristic in which the Church of England did not, and could not, claim to share; and that was a real and effective union in the faith, in the sacramental life, in the government of each and every local church, with the Church Universal. Hitherto, he had regarded the diocese as the essential ecclesiastical unit. Faithful to the primitive ideal of St Ignatius of Antioch, he had seen the bond which held the church together in the Bishop, Pastor, Pontiff, Doctor guaranteeing in the name of Christ, by virtue of the Apostolic Succession, the union of his flock in the faith. But he had failed to recognise a factor no less important, no less decisive, in the eyes of Antiquity, and that was the communion of the several Bishops, one with another, throughout the world, the binding together of the various local churches to form one sole Church Universal. Now, however, the history of the Monophysites, viewed in the light of the criterion formulated by St Augustine with regard to the Donatists, clearly brought home to him that the possibility of a Church, at once Catholic and, so to speak, atomised, had never been sanctioned by the Fathers. A unit consisting of an individual Bishop and his flock had no *locus standi*, unless that same Bishop was in communion with his brother Bishops. If the Bishops were the successors of the Apostles, the Apostles had never been a number of isolated individuals, but an indissoluble *collegium*. There could be no Catholic *Churches*, unless they came, one and all, within the orbit of the One Church Universal.

That the Church of England lacked this essential attribute was beyond all question. And that was why the idea of the *Via Media* fell to pieces, not, that is to say, because the elements that made up its ideal of the Church were unsound, but because to imagine it possible to apply that ideal to the Anglican system looked uncommonly like a contradiction in terms. How was one to regard a separated Church as an authentic revival of the Primitive Church, if that same Primitive Church regarded such separation as a crime against itself.

Where, then, did Newman stand? Whatever flattering unction he might from time to time have laid to his soul, he was compelled at last to abandon the hope of finding in Anglicanism the stable position, the coherent whole, the living unity, with which he had once thought to invest it.

Nevertheless, three landmarks from which he had started to develop his *Via Media* idea remained firm and intact, though the idea itself came to grief. The first was the dogmatic principle in Christianity, which he had held to be essential ever since his conversion. Any form of Christianity not founded on a basis of dogmatic truth, of truth revealed by God Himself, he always regarded as quite untenable. The second was the sacramental character of the Christian economy; of the Church. His own reflections, his own meditations on Scripture and Antiquity, the influence of Hawkins and, later, of High Churchmen of the Keble school, had implanted it in him as the one concrete presentation of Christianity which was in conformity alike with Revelation and with the experience of life itself. The third principle, buttressed and bastioned by his Protestant upbringing, was the conviction that there could be no linking up with Rome without incurring the guilt of idolatry and superstition.

The aim of the *Via Media* had been to co-ordinate these three convictions of his and to display them as existing in the Anglican Church. However, the *Via Media* had come to naught; but, in spite of that, these three convictions held their ground. What, then, was to be done, union with Rome being out of the question? Newman, however, was beginning to perceive that some of his younger and more ardent followers were gazing wistfully in that direction. How was it then, if he himself was beginning to feel a little disturbed by the same idea, how was it that he so long and absolutely persisted in shunning it, as though it were a sort of evil temptation? It might seem strange to us that he should have taken so long to convince himself, we do not say that Roman Catholicism was the real and true Catholicism, but that the matter was at all events one that merited serious enquiry. If so, our astonishment would be misplaced. It would imply a misunderstanding of the circumstances of the case. We should, in fact, be underestimating the virtually decisive effect of three other factors, and these are, first, a traditionally Protestant upbringing, and an English one at that; then, what he had seen of Catholicism in action during his Mediterranean cruise, and thirdly, the political behaviour of the English and Irish Catholics, especially in regard to O'Connell.

Newman himself pointed out that Froude, who had been brought up, and passed all his days, in a High Church atmosphere, could never understand how it was that he, Newman, would persist in looking upon Rome, if not as Antichrist, at all events as the seat of Antichrist. If, however, there was a Protestant conviction implanted in his mind more deeply than any other, that was undoubtedly the one. We have but to remind ourselves that the idea occurred on page after page of Milner's *Church History*, though that was the book from which he derived his esteem and admiration for the Fathers.

As to the second reason, explain it how we will, what he saw of Christianity as practised in Malta, Sicily, and Italy seemed to demonstrate all too throughly how well founded were his prejudices against Catholic idolatry and superstition. Nor must we fail to observe that Froude, though far less steeped in anti-Catholic prejudice than Newman, had returned from his travels with precisely similar impressions. A grossly self-seeking worship of the Madonna, the cult of the Virgin and Child displacing the worship of the one true God, religion nothing but selfish superstition, entirely divorced from any sort of moral code—such was the picture of Catholicism which both these islanders brought home with them from their travels. However strange it may seem to us, we must perforce accept it as a fact that this was the idea of Catholicism produced on the most religiously-minded Protestants by what they saw of it in those countries. Astounded and saddened we may be at such an idea; but so general is it that we must needs accept it as a fact.

As for the third point, the line of action followed by the Catholics in England at the beginning of the nineteenth century, we must here pause to consider the difficulties of the situation. The whole basis of the Oxford Movement, what actually brought it into being, was that the Whigs dissembled their real policy in religious matters, which was a repudiation of the God of Jesus Christ and the rejection of Divine Revelation, behind a screen of measures of the most seemingly liberal character. That being so, let us next bear in mind that the Catholics, both English and Irish, had entered into close political alliance with the Whigs for the sole purpose of securing their civil emancipation. That being so, it is easy to imagine what Newman and his friends must have thought about the matter. It seemed to them that the English Catholics were virtually denying, and deliberately betraying, their religion for the sake of a purely material advantage. The whole thing looked to them like a piece of cynical and barefaced Machiavellianism. What better proof, then, that Rome, if she herself was not Antichrist, was at all events doing the work of Antichrist? This being the apparent position of affairs, what alternative was left them but to try, at all costs, to erect and maintain, where they already stood, a dogmatic and sacramental

Christianity derived from sources of unimpeachable authenticity?

The idea that the Church of England was the shrine of such a Christianity, the collapse of the *Via Media* rendered no longer tenable. All that now remained to them, the last and only spar they had to cling to, was the hope that their Church would not oppose it, and that she might help, however, imperfectly, to give it a home.

She was not, and could not be regarded as, a revival pure and simple of the Church of the Fathers. Where, then, was that Church? If it was not Rome, still less was it the Eastern Church which, they considered, combined all the objections against Rome, with none of Rome's logical advantages. Where, then, was it? There lay the great mystery, a mystery at once so baffling and so burdensome to the religious conscience. It was a mystery to which, for the moment, Newman could find no certain clue.

He was led to fall back on the conclusion that the Church in her plenitude, if she had not already disappeared from the earth, had obscured the full light of her countenance, secreting a portion here and a portion there; one facet of the truth here, another there. What had to be done, therefore, was to preserve as much of it as possible, no matter where it was to be found.

In view of all this, Newman began to feel more and more that he could not, and ought not, to remain in the Church of England as one of her formal teachers and directors. The Church of England might have retained some of the Church's essential elements, but he doubted whether she could call herself *the* Church. From now onwards he began to feel ever more keenly that he ought to give up St Mary's and divest himself of all responsibility, till he could see his own way clear. He clung tenaciously to the idea that, although the *Via Media* had failed him, some other view of things might be discovered to support the Anglican position; but, for the time being, he was completely in the dark. Nevertheless, he had no intention of departing from the Anglican fold. At the moment, he saw nowhere to betake himself that would not be a change for the worse.

Though he was momentarily tempted, now and again, to stay on in the Anglican Church in lay communion, resigning any right to speak in her name, there were other considerations which kept him for a long time where he was, and hindered him from fulfilling what seems to have been his deepest desire. Although his humility—always, it seems, rather disconcerting to his friends—prevented him from fully realising how many were the souls now looking to him for guidance, he could not shirk responsibility for a Movement which clearly owed its origin to him, its real inspirer.

Yet, here again, his fundamental conviction, the conviction that Christianity in the true sense must be founded on dogma and the sacraments, was never in question. What *was* in question was whether, and, if so, how, it was possible to enshrine it abidingly in Anglicanism, since he saw no better home for it elsewhere. But, while they had not yet arrived at that point, and he, in his present state of uncertainty doubted whether he ought to lead them to it, there were numberless souls in the Anglican fold who always unhesitatingly believed what he believed. His first, his most pressing obligation, therefore, was not to leave them to their fate.

Among the Anglicans who were not Tractarians, the violent reaction which Froude's *Remains* had stirred up against these latter led them to regard opposition to traditional Catholicism as one and the same thing as opposition to Rome. The louder, then, grew the outcry against the Tractarians, the charges of treason and breach of trust because they had restored some remnants of early Christianity, the louder the accusation that they were the dupes, or the secret agents, of Rome, the more the parties so accused were tempted to go and seek in Rome for that which was denied them in Anglicanism. For Newman, who persistently refused to take this view of the matter, holding that Rome had corrupted primitive Christianity far more vitally than Anglicanism had departed from it, there was no possibility of passive acquiescence in a climax only too easy to foresee.

His duty was to demonstrate to his disciples that they could and should find in Anglicanism, if not the Church in all its plenitude, at least those fundamentally vital elements without which there could be no genuine Christianity. This view of the matter it was that led Newman, while preparing for his ultimate withdrawal from the forefront of the stage, to stay on at St Mary's for some time longer, and to keep the Movement where it was, to consolidate the ground already won, if not to advance still farther. It was precisely in order to cope with these responsibilities, with the immediate needs of the situation, that he addressed himself to the composition of Tract 90. It was fated to be the last of the series. It resulted in Newman's withdrawal from the scene of action, a thing which he had so long desired, but which he had not thought it right to bring about of his own volition.[1]

[1] The whole of the concluding part of this chapter is based so closely on the latter part of chapter III of the *Apologia* that we have thought it unnecessary to give detailed references.

XII

FROM TRACT 90 TO ROME

WE must now suspend for a while our consideration of Newman and his personal problems and preoccupations to take one last general glance at the Church which was still his, though it was not much longer to remain so.

The Tractarian Movement, as we have seen, was not concerned with politics, not even with church politics; nor was it purely or primarily intellectual; not a matter of ideas, even theological ideas. What it was, and what it had been from its very beginning, was a profoundly religious movement; religious in the fullest and deepest sense of the word, embracing as it did all the truths of revelation and all the ordinances, rites, and ceremonies of the visible Church, without which there is no real Christianity, or at best a thing maimed and stricken, like a branch lopped off from the living trunk. It was this spiritual character of the Movement, so compelling in the demands that it made, yet in no sense narrow, that won it so many ardent supporters, particularly among the younger generation.

Religious men, indeed, they were, these Tractarians, but they were also students, men of secluded habits and none of them, not even Newman, none of them, with perhaps the one exception of Froude, fated so soon to be withdrawn from it, gauged the emotional power, the soul-stirring influence with which their message was endowed. In a world perilously encompassed by an all-pervading atmosphere of rationalism and incredulity, their teaching and ideas marked the sudden resurgence of a religion to which, with its richness and fervour, England had for three centuries been a stranger. To the younger folk, so full of zest and eagerness, it came like an invigorating and inspiring draught of oxygen. The Christianity of which the St Mary's sermons spoke to them, of which they read in Froude's *Remains*, gave wings to many an echo already faintly stirred by the poetry of the *Christian Year*. It was not the staid and sober religion of the "scholar and gentleman", nor did it bear any resemblance to the sentimental effusions, sincere and generous if you will, but alas! how precariously founded, which Methodism stood for. It was a religion which embraced the whole man, which gave a religious significance to the entire world, and which flooded the annals of the past. The infinitely varied treasures of doctrine, of ritual and devotional practice, of Catholic tradition translated into action, were now again unsealed. And while this religion enlarged the moral and spiritual stature of man, it sent forth an appeal to his generosity, to his spirit of self-sacrifice, such as had not been heard since the days of the sixteenth-century martyrs. It was a religion that set no limit to what it gave, or to what it asked in return, a religion that gave all and demanded all; nor is it easy to say which of these two aspects was the more potent attraction. A religion so rich, so all-sufficing, must of necessity display itself with a brilliance, a majesty, with which England had been too long unfamiliar. Such mild Antiquarian revivals as the Caroline Divines had permitted themselves were scarcely adequate to the needs of the hour. For such youthful enthusiasts as Ward and Faber, something far more than that was demanded. It was therefore only to be expected that they would look about them for what was within reach and, in the process, discover in continental Catholicism all that they lacked at home.

Up to the very last, Newman looked askance at these foreign importations. He saw in them something that to many people might look like sham, like play-acting. Anyhow, was it not the sort of patching of old clothes with new cloth which the Gospel expressly warns us to avoid? If the Catholic element was legitimately to be infused into the Anglican Church, it should be by means proper to that Church, and along her own traditional lines. It must on no account be artificially applied, like a sort of foreign veneer.

However, to persuade young men dazzled by their own discoveries to take this view was no easy matter. The actual practices—the manners and customs, so to call them—of Catholicism had nowhere really been preserved save by churches in the Roman communion. This at last became so overwhelmingly clear that even Rome's doughtiest opponents were forced to acknowledge that it was so. So that we find even such a man as Pusey eagerly availing himself, in his later years, of the devotional manuals of modern Catholicism.

Nowadays, Anglo-Catholics often cause astonishment to Catholics proper by adopting with such zeal everything that is most characteristically post-Tridentine. Often enough in England it is people who dub themselves Catholics, carefully suppressing the "Roman", who are the most conspicuously Italian in their devotional deportment.

Needless to say, these innovations were more than enough to stir the

Protestant susceptibilities of Anglicans, even among those of traditionally High Church leanings. That inveterate hostility to the Papacy which is almost instinctive in the average Englishman, almost bred in his bones, wanted no more inviting stimulus to action. Newman had been expecting from the very beginning to be taxed with paving the way to Rome. He, on the contrary, had at once made up his mind that the most effective way of keeping men back *from* Rome was to re-Catholicise the Church of England. This view of the matter he steadily retained to the very eve of his conversion. He was convinced that real, integral Christianity must be imbued with the pure Catholic tradition, but he was equally convinced of what he then regarded as the "corruptions" of Rome. It was therefore perfectly natural for him to see no more effective means of resisting the Roman lure than to revive the Catholic tradition in the Anglican Church quite independently of Rome.

Notwithstanding his own personal misgivings, and his now incurable dissatisfaction with the *Via Media*, nothing, in his view, was of more urgent importance than to demonstrate to friends and foes alike, the genuine possibility of bringing about such a Catholic revival. He abandoned the idea that it was the mainspring of Anglicanism, nor could he be sure that the Anglican Church as it then was would be in a position to make such a revival possible, at least for the time being. But it would be impossible for him to remain within her fold and carry out his pastoral duties if she formally and in set terms rejected the principle of a Catholic revival.

The big gun in his adversaries' armoury, the ever-increasing stumbling-block for his disciples, was the official declaration of faith which all candidates for Holy Orders and all candidates for admission to a University (in Oxford they subscribed to the 39 Articles, in Cambridge there was an equivalent test) were called on to subscribe. Were not these Articles definitely Protestant, and no less definitely anti-Catholic in tone and content? That question cried out for an answer. To shirk it any longer was impossible; it would have been tantamount to a complete surrender. Moreover, it would mean, whatever his efforts to restrain them, sending the more impulsive of his followers straight to Rome.

When, during the winter of 1840-1841, he set to work on the problem, it appeared to him one of singular complexity. It never entered his head for a moment to deny that the Articles in their general tendency were favourable to Protestantism. Their framers, at least the majority of them, were clearly Protestant sympathisers. But the fact that the Articles were to be read in conjunction with the Prayer-Book, which undoubtedly teaches the major elements of Catholic doctrine, and, still more significant, that they expressly encourage the study of the Book of Homilies, of which the same is to be said, made it clear that the Protestant interpretation of them was by no means the only legitimate one. In a word, the Articles seemed to him—and no historian would contest the view today—to be a typical example of those compromises in which the Church of England abounds. Certainly, that dissipated any hopes he may once have entertained of beholding in her the Church of the Fathers restored once more to life, but it confirmed him in the project to which he had all along tenaciously clung, that of pursuing a line of teaching and practice consonant with a truly patristic and Apostolic Christianity. In fact, Protestants as most of them were, or at any rate Protestant sympathisers, the compilers of the Articles had framed them with the evident intention of retaining in the Anglican fold as many as they possibly could of those who remained Catholics at heart. It was only fair to insist on this when endeavouring to maintain and even to augment the patristic and Apostolic element in the Church of England. Hence the threefold distinction which Newman laid down. People say that the Articles are anti-Catholic. But what precisely are we to understand by that? Does it mean that they reject the great truths laid down by the early Councils and embodied in the early liturgies? By no means, since the Homilies, which we are exhorted to study, as well as the Book of Common Prayer, expressly inculcate them. Are we then to take it that they condemn the official Roman doctrines as defined by the Council of Trent? This could hardly be, seeing that the Council of Trent was not over when the Articles were drawn up. If we compare in detail the teaching of the one side and the other, we see how few are the points on which they differ, and even then it is not certain that the differences are not merely a matter of words. For example, the Council of Trent conferred canonical authority on the word Transubstantiation. The Articles condemn a doctrine set forth under this name, but what they understand by it is apparently something very different from the doctrine formulated by the Council of Trent. What, then, it comes to is, that we may say that the Articles condemn neither Catholic doctrine, nor, for that matter, Roman doctrine, but only the things which English people call "Romish"; that is to say, not the formal doctrines, but the popular corruptions of them, such as idolatrous worship of the Saints, superstitious properties ascribed to Indulgences, or Prayers for the Dead.

It follows that the obligation to sign the Thirty-nine Articles did not preclude Anglicans from preaching and practising traditional Catholicism. Nay more, it was not incompatible with some degree of sympathy with modern Roman Catholicism. What it did rule out was what Newman at this time still regarded as Roman "corruptions". All this would not be seriously contested by present-day historians of the Church of England. Certain it is that in Newman's mind it was one thing to Romanise, quite another to aim at restoring integral Christianity in all its primitive plenitude and purity. Far from being part of a cunning plot to Romanise the Anglican Church, Tract 90 was a supreme effort to dissuade the Tractarians from taking what he had always regarded as an inadmissible step, the step to Rome.

While not entirely disclaiming all sympathy with Rome, for Rome had preserved, if only in a material sense, certain treasures from the great upheaval, and even though, not so much for himself as for the sake of his disciples, he had stressed these sympathies, Tract 90 was none the less, in Newman's view, an additional bulwark against Rome, now that the *Via Media* was no longer a valid defence.

When he had finished it and sent it to the printer, he was conscious of a great sense of relief. No doubt it lacked the confident and decisive tone of the former, and now discarded, theory. Now, for his "Anglican Catholicism", he had had to fall back on material that was decidedly "second-best", however sound it seemed to him at the time. The new theory, it is true, did not settle everything, as its predecessor had seemed to do, but it did give a much-needed answer to the questions of the hour, and that was what chiefly mattered.

We shall not be exaggerating when we say that Newman, during the first few months of 1841, felt the sort of relief a mortally sick person might derive from an unlooked-for, but temporary, rally.

Tract 90 made its appearance in February 1841. People could barely have had time to read it, when an outcry was raised whose violence took Newman more by surprise than did the uproar that greeted the publication of Froude's *Remains*. He had, it seemed, given the adversaries of the Movement just the sort of opportunity they had been waiting for to open the flood-gates of their hatred and suspicion. Everywhere the Tract was denounced as thoroughly dishonest. What it came to was that a man might be a Roman Catholic and yet stay on in the Church of England, a traitor within the gates. Some even went the length of saying that, while it meant a base surrender to Rome, it provided a specious excuse for traitors to retain their benefices in the

Establishment and enjoy their emoluments. Some of the more moderate critics, like Dr Bagot, Newman's own Bishop, thought it permissible to remark that, according to this Tract, the Articles might mean anything or nothing.

It must be confessed that Newman was not the only one to be taken aback at the violence of the reaction. Many more moderate men than he in the Movement were taken by surprise, men such as William Palmer of Worcester College, who, however, defended the Tract with commendable spirit.

It must, however, be remarked that this outburst of indignation was not quite so spontaneous as it seemed. Many ultra-Protestants within the Anglican ranks pounced on the Tract as a heaven-sent pretext for dealing a shrewd blow at a man and a party against whom, up to now, they had found nothing serious to allege. But this is not the whole of the matter. In Oxford, and far beyond it, the agitation was vigorously fomented by an individual whose name has already been mentioned in these pages. We refer to Golightly, one of Newman's former pupils, who for a time had been his curate, but with whom he had severed relations in view of the young man's definitely anti-Catholic pulpit-pronouncements. Apparently they had parted without any ill-feeling on either side. But Golightly, an odd, unbalanced sort of person, seems to have taken the thing very much to heart, and now displayed his resentment in this somewhat incongruous manner. So successful were his manoeuvres that the Hebdomadal Board, made up of the several Heads of Houses under the chairmanship of the Vice-Chancellor, formally condemned the Tract. Against this action Dr Routh, the President of Magdalen, had protested with all his might. Hawkins had urged them at least to wait a little. In point of fact, the condemnation was of no great importance. It was at least doubtful whether the body in question had any jurisdiction in such matters. Newman, with rather grim humour, has described the feelings with which he saw himself placarded up on posters, like some pastrycook of ill-repute with whom the undergraduates were forbidden to have any dealings. As for the measure itself, there was no need to take it too tragically. Nevertheless, the commotion which had attended its adoption led him to decide on a step which he had long contemplated, and that was to leave St Mary's more or less entirely in charge of a curate, and himself to retire to Littlemore.

The idea of throwing up his living altogether, and what led up to it, we have already recorded; but Keble, to whom, in those perplexing times, be betook himself as to a counsellor, even a spiritual director, strongly dissuaded him from doing anything of the kind. This was how it came about that Newman, while still retaining his living, went to live at Littlemore from the summer of 1841 onwards. He had already stayed there during Lent in 1840, and the experiment had more or less decided him to arrange something more permanent. The fuss that was now being made about Tract 90 confirmed him in this resolve.

Though he had never had a strictly monastic institution in mind, he had long wished that there had been in the Church of England some sort of haven for silence and meditation such as the cloister had always provided in the Catholic Church. His thoughts ran on some such retreat as that of his beloved Cappadocians, Basil and Gregory Nazianzen, in the valley of the Iris. Littlemore, when he became used to it, seemed just the sort of place he had dreamed of. Without having any definite purpose in view, he had bought a plot of land there, and had it planted with trees.

Now he definitely made up his mind to get away from the University environment. He felt somehow that he had lost credit there by reason of this unlooked-for blow, though the pain this caused him was more than counterbalanced by a great sense of relief. Now, alone in the presence of God, he would ponder in peace and quiet on all the problems that were besetting him, and try to find a way out.

Though he had no idea or intention of starting any kind of permanent community at Littlemore, he did not go there alone. There were a number of men who were puzzled about the course they ought to take. Some were men who had gone farther than he in the Romeward direction, but who wanted to see their way quite clear before taking the final step; others were men who, involved in the growing suspicion—and it seemed likely to go on growing—that attached to all who had in any way been mixed up with the Tracts, found themselves the object of all manner of pin-pricks at the hands of the University people and the clergy. More than one such sufferer found a temporary refuge at Littlemore. Newman's task was not to urge these people towards Rome, but, quite the contrary, to prevent them doing anything in a hurry; to help them, and, if necessary, to compel them, to look at things calmly and as in God's presence, to avoid any sort of action that might seem, however remotely, to come of wounded feelings or romantic dreaming.

The mean-looking little cottages near the church—the "monastery" as Newman's fanatical opponents called them—still stand, they and the surrounding village being pretty much as they were in Newman's day. A few rooms had been furnished with Spartan-like severity. The dining-room and the library, the latter serving on occasion as a chapel, were the only "monastic" apartments. There was nothing in the way of ornament or decoration but the handsomely bound set of the Fathers transported thither from Newman's rooms at Oriel. The frugality of the meals matched the austerity of the rooms in which they were eaten. In Lent, the plainness of the fare was positively Cistercian. The inmates of the house went to the village church for Matins and Evensong. Newman, who had kept Froude's Breviary as a personal memento of its late owner, recited the Hours with his guests in the Library *cum* Chapel. To the last, however, he omitted the invocations to the Virgin and the Saints, saying that one could not have two religions at a time.

Long hours devoted to prayer, sometimes silent, sometimes recited from Catholic books of devotion (it was about this time that Newman discovered the *Exercises* of St Ignatius), were added to an already crowded time-table. The rule of silence was observed until tea-time, when Newman would end it with some light and easy conversation from which, at any rate when there were a number of them present, all discussion of difficult problems was as far as possible excluded. Tea-time over, he would frequently take his companions for a long walk across country.

As for himself, such times as he was not helping them with their own particular perplexities and trying to bring ease and comfort to their harassed minds, such time, too, as he could spare from an exacting correspondence on the same sort of theme, was devoted by him to study, to study and prayer and meditation, when he would resume unwearyingly once more the multiple threads of his own besetting problems.

Hardly had he settled down at Littlemore, when, in the midst of these meditations of his, he sustained a shock that disturbed him far more gravely than the affair of the Tracts. Here again it was a case of an inward doubt preceding, but only by a hair's breadth, another, or rather two other, shocks from without.

In connection with the contemplated publication of selections from the works of St Athanasius, he had begun his enquiries into the Arian controversy all over again; and now, suddenly, something that had failed to strike him when he was writing his lengthy *History of the Arians*, became clearly apparent to his now more highly sensitised perception. In the complex story of the Arians and their views, he beheld once more, as in a mirror, the reflected image of his own times. The Arians were the Protestants, Rome stood where she had always stood, while the Anglicans were the semi-Arians. The likeness was even more striking than that presented by the moderate Monophysites, for in this case there was a definite plea for a *Via Media* and an appeal—on the face of it legitimate—to Antiquity, to Tradition, interpreted from a more or less archaeological point of view, in contrast with, and in opposition to, the developments of the Catholicism of the day.

Hardly had these new ideas on the matter begun to take shape in his mind when, one after another, the Anglican Bishops began to fulminate against Tract 90, his own Bishop amongst them, though in noticeably milder terms than the others. This was a very unexpected blow, and one which Newman believed he had been assured would never happen. After the storm aroused by Tract 90, Newman, at the request of the Bishop of Oxford, had agreed to suspend the series, though not to stop the sale of those already issued. In return, he had received a promise, whose diplomatic wording seemed to provide a loophole for its withdrawal, that no episcopal condemnation would be directed against the Tractarian Movement in general. But feelings were running high, and there was no holding them in check.

Spurred into action by their own convictions—or by the reasons which often actuate leaders when their followers take the bit between their teeth: "I am their leader; that means I must go where they go!" —the Bishops, to a man, all condemned Tract 90. At the same time they declared, not merely as an *ipso facto*, but in more or less formal terms, that the essential doctrines of traditional Catholicism could not be taught or tolerated in the Church of England.

Then, as if all this was not enough, something else, an almost grotesque affair, supervened to add to the turmoil. It had no direct connection with the Tractarian Movement, but it occurred just at the right time to convince Newman that Anglicanism had no more respect for Catholic sacramental practice than it had for Catholic doctrine. The incident in question was the affair of the Jerusalem Bishopric.

For some considerable time, the British Government had been looking about for a means to extend its control over the Holy Places. France had long held a position there as the traditional protectress of the Catholic institutions. More recently, Russia had put in her say, claiming to perform the same functions in connection with the

Russian Orthodox Church. But now, what seemed a heaven-sent opportunity to secure a footing, was offered to the British Government by the Prussian Minister, the Chevalier Bunsen. At this time, the King of Prussia was busily occupied in carrying out a high-handed reorganisation of the Protestant churches in his dominions. He was, in fact, attempting, in the light of Schleiermacher's liberal theology, to bring about a union between the Lutheran and Calvinist communities. The suggested common denominator on which the union was to be based was in reality a bit of pure window-dressing, designed to disguise a piece of ecclesiastical jack-booting very typical of the Hohenzollerns. What the King wanted, though he thought it imprudent to advertise his aims too openly, was to consolidate the work of fusion by the setting up of a Bishopric nominally independent, but actually under his control. He, too, would not be at all backward in cutting a figure at Jerusalem.

Bunsen accordingly proposed, on his sovereign's behalf, that a Bishop of Jerusalem should be consecrated at Canterbury, and that the said Bishop should include in his fold not Anglicans only, but all the Prussian subjects there residing, and in a general way—thus the proposal went on—all people who were willing to place themselves under his authority. This last rubric was designed to provide for the inclusion of such Nestorians and Monophysites as might be persuaded to seek protection in the Anglican fold—these, and a half-dozen or so converted Jews. Naturally, there was no question of asking the members of this very miscellaneous flock to subscribe any definite creed. Quite content if he was lucky enough to get hold of a few such nondescript sheep, the "Bishop of Jerusalem" would ask for nothing more.

If the condemnation of Tract 90 by the Bishops meant for Newman a denial on their part of the first of the three principles which the collapse of the *Via Media* theory had left intact, the Jerusalem Bishopric affair implied at least as flagrant a denial of the second. The Anglican Church, having made it impossible for him to preach traditional doctrine in her name, now made it equally impossible for him to recognise in her hierarchy and sacraments any connection with the rites and ordinances of Apostolic times.

To ease his conscience in the matter, he at once drew up a protest against the creation of this extraordinary Bishopric. Naturally, it had no effect. It therefore followed, as he himself declared, that he had now no weapon left him to withstand the lure of Rome, save the Protestant one—that is to say, a blunt denial of her claims. The Anglican Church might have suffered a serious, perhaps an irremediable, disaster, hierarchical as well as doctrinal, but that in no way invalidated the arguments against Rome, which he still considered to be as sound as ever.

Rome might preserve, in a material sense, articles of faith and sacramental observances which Anglicanism either neglected or disowned, but if she sullied them with corruptions that were superstitious, idolatrous, and immoral, then to abandon the one Church for the other would be to exchange one evil for another that was still worse.

As the winter of 1841 drew near, Newman must have felt himself in a position of the gravest perplexity. It looked as if all the notes of the true Church which, up to now, the Anglican Church had appeared to possess, though somewhat obscured, and which he had hoped to restore in all their pristine vigour, had now been extinguished for ever.

It was not merely that she could not claim to be the true Church, but that she had failed to preserve those fundamentals that may survive even in a schismatical body, and those were; doctrine and sacraments. But then, if the Church which *did* seem to have preserved them, and which in consequence was beginning to exert such a powerful attraction on the younger members of the Movement—if this Church had degraded them with all manner of corrupt beliefs and practices, what was he to do? To that question there was but one answer; he must bide his time, and wait for the light to guide him.

For the moment but one consolation was left him, a solitary star amid the ever-deepening gloom. It was not wholly true that the Anglican Church had lost all the notes of the true Church. The note most difficult to appreciate from without, but also the deepest, the most essential in the light of God's purposes, she had *not* lost. Of that he became more and more certain. And that note was the note of Sanctity. How many marvellous souls, fed and watered by that same unhappy Anglican Church, had he known who seemed to him to bear undeniable witness to her Sanctity! He had but to think of Keble, or of Pusey, or, better still, to call to mind the angel faces of Mary or of Froude. Could a Church that had moulded souls like those have been abandoned by God? How, then, could *he* desert her? The Tractarian Movement, particularly its younger members, who were all around him, who troubled him but whom he could not help admiring for their openheartedness, their eagerness, their unselfish fervour—the Tractarian Movement was revealing itself as an unlooked-for source of spiritual riches. All this, after the heavy blows he had sustained, he crystallised in a memorable utterance, "We could not be as if we had never been a Church; we were Samaria."

The *Sermons on Subjects of the Day* are largely a development of this theme. Samaria had incurred the guilt of schism; Samaria was in grave peril of losing the faith. Yet God did not desert her. To her, indeed, He sent His mightiest prophets, such as Elias and Eliseus. Never did He seem to expect, never did He demand, that her children, such as the widow of Sarepta and her kinsfolk, should quit her in her evil days. It seems, indeed, to have been far otherwise. God revealed to the prophet that among those people seemingly so lost to God, a faithful remnant, to the number of seven thousand, had never bowed the knee to Baal, and were still pleasing in His sight.

To outward appearance, Rome might present all the characteristics of original Catholicism, but what did that avail if it countenanced the political Machiavellianism of a Daniel O'Connell, or the setting up of the Madonna in the place of God, which, often enough, was pure image-worship?

These sermons clearly show how tragically Newman's feelings were rent asunder. If ever his inward sufferings found an echo in his preaching, it was in the sermons he delivered during those painful months. Then, again, he had to bear the burden of responsibility for the spiritual welfare of his congregation. They did not understand the matter as he did, they had not his range of vision, and he had to temper what he said to them so as to keep within their limits, but without committing himself to any statement in which he himself did not literally and explicitly believe. But of the agony of mind by which he himself was beset, which it was his lot to endure alone, he said no word. Nor of those gleams, those illuminations which had come to him, did he think he could properly make mention in the name of the Church which still left him with her authority to preach.

However, the remarkable thing is that these sermons, followed though they were with passionate eagerness, with a depth of emotion, an intensity of anxiety that grew daily more acute, satisfied no one; they satisfied neither his friends of long standing, like Keble or Pusey, who saw with alarm that he was destroying with his own hands the structure which he himself had erected in his *Prophetical Office*, and which to them seemed as sound as ever; nor did they find favour with his younger disciples for whom they were more expressly designed, and whom he was anxious to restrain from taking some hasty step which they might ever afterwards have reason to regret. The truth was that, say what he might, these younger men could no longer feel themselves to be the sons of a Mother who disowned them.

We can hardly imagine how painful must have been the isolation of Newman from the end of 1841 to the end of 1843. He was unable to sympathise—in fact, he never had wholly sympathised—with what he calls the new school inside the Movement—that is to say, with men like Ward or Oakeley who, each in his own way, were its leading representatives. Nor did he any longer feel himself in complete agreement with his companions of the early days. The worst of it was that both parties alike—the earlier and the later adherents—would persist in regarding him as their leader, and all of them looked to him for guidance. The younger ones strained at the leash; the others felt perplexed and disheartened, at a loss to understand an attitude they put down to some transient and, to them, wholly inexplicable state of mind.

We must try, as we take stock of the immense correspondence of those days, to gauge the ambiguity, the inevitable ambiguity, which the situation presented. We shall then see in the "voluntary" with which Bremond qualifies the word "recluse", a crowning and unconsciously humorous, if not malevolent, misinterpretation of the real state of affairs. It is but too clear that Newman longed with all his heart to remain on the same terms of close and intimate agreement with Pusey and Keble as had united them in the early stages of the Movement. He hoped and prayed that he would be able to shake off his doubts about the validity of a position he himself had been the first to expound and support. He could not bear to think that the day might come when he would be compelled to forsake the religion in which Mary and Hurrell Froude had died, and in which his dear friend Bowden was before long to follow them to the grave. The spiritual estrangement which was already beginning to show itself when, as far back as 1836, his mother was hurried away by sudden death, and which, ever since, had been alienating him more and more from his sisters, gave him intolerable pain, added, as it was, to his other completely incommunicable spiritual distresses.

Still, what was he to do? The others, Keble and Pusey, might be able to console themselves for the blows dealt at them and at their Movement by their adversaries from without, their confidence in the stability of its foundations being still unshaken, but he, he who had done more than anyone else to construct those foundations, he, before any visible defect had appeared in them, was beginning to have grave doubts about them. Though he fully realised how difficult it would be to make his friends see the position as he saw it, he did tell them about his misgivings as they came more and more to weigh upon his mind. But none of them had sufficient knowledge of Christian Antiquity, none of them had that independence of judgment, or that clearness of insight, which, for him, made his conclusions ineluctable, and before long he gave up discussing such matters with them.

Had he not said all there was to say? For the rest, it must depend on the light within, which they might or might not have, but without which it was vain to hope that they would follow. Besides, he himself was by no means clear whither he was tending. How could he have the heart to destroy the firm convictions of others, when he was not at all sure what to offer them in their place? All this involved other causes for anxiety which, as time was to show, were well founded. All those people whom he had snatched from Evangelical Protestantism, or from stark rationalism, to bring them to the *Via Media*, what would they think, what would they make of it all, when they heard that he had left them in the lurch? Was it not only too much to be feared that they would take refuge in scepticism pure and simple. One has but to remember what happened to such men as Stanley and, above all, Mark Pattison to see how well founded were these apprehensions.

It is when the testing time comes that the weak spot is shown up, even in the best of characters. Pusey's isolation, his utter inability to see things from any point of view but his own—all this was now becoming more and more evident. Not only did he fail to understand Newman's evolution, he could not be persuaded that there had been any evolution at all. While Newman did all in his power to convince him of the gravity of his problems, Pusey pledged his word that his friend had never wavered in any of his principles. He had the scholar's typical disinclination to be taken out of his own groove, the characteristic inability of the recluse to see things as they really are. He was less interested in actual people and concrete things than in his own abstract reasonings about them. Behind all that, Newman divined the wounded sensibility of the thwarted child and felt that he ought not to do anything to exacerbate it. After all, what would have been the good? What could he have done but inflict bitter pain on him, and all to no purpose? Pusey was, and would always remain, unable to contemplate the bare idea of abandoning the religion in which his beloved young wife had died, and in which, when the crisis was at its height, his little daughter Lucy was also to end her days.

As for Keble, the situation was not altogether dissimilar, but with him it was not a case of the abstract mind colliding with reality, but of a mind that was always dependent upon others. His sensitivity was invincible because it was unarmed. Of this, Newman had painful experience. If he applied to him for counsel or spiritual guidance, all he ever brought away with him was a fresh crop of uncertainties. One day, these dire words escaped him:

> Hence you could not get *his own* opinion. It was the opinion of his brother, his sister, or his wife.[1]

In spite of the denunciations of the episcopate, the beautiful conception of the Church of England which Newman had aided them to form was their consolation. The flaws, the gaping cracks in its foundations they saw not, they could not see, and in their heart of hearts they devoutly hoped they would never have to turn their gaze that way. This Church of theirs was an ideal, a dream, but it was a dream haunted by beloved presences, presences all the more deeply cherished when they were of those who had passed from human sight.

How could one have the heart to bid them compare with the Donatists, the Monophysites or the semi-Arians that Church which, for one of them, was symbolised in that little country parish of Fairford, where, beside his son and his successor, an aged father was wearing out the evening of his days; while, for another, it represented the stately nave of Christ Church, beneath whose stones rested all that was mortal of his beloved wife, too soon to be joined by their little daughter?

With Newman, it was far otherwise. When the Bishops continued to denounce Tract 90, when they accepted without demur the preposterous idea of the Jerusalem Bishopric, he saw, in what was taking place today, merely the fulfilment of yesterday's presage. The Anglican Church was not a Church. Of her own accord, she had barred her door against Christian faith and sacramental grace.

However, there were hotheads, like Ward, who could not understand how this Church, if such they were to call her, could still be referred to by Newman by the name of Mother. Liberals or Protestants who had been suddenly won over to the Catholic idea saw in the Establishment only an old and tottering structure, solemn and senile, barring the way to the one true Church. That Newman, sharing all the feelings of Keble and Pusey, should yet fail to realise that truth must not be sacrificed to personal feelings, however poignant or even heart-rending they might be, was something almost beyond their compre-

[1] Letter to Woodgate, 18th October, 1878.

hension. In their view there was no alternative but to introduce into Anglicanism what Rome possessed, or if Anglicanism would not consent, then to go to Rome.

About this time, and more especially during 1842, Newman began to feel aware of a certain inward sympathy between himself and these very positive and enthusiastic brethren and disciples of his. As far as Rome was concerned, he still maintained his detached and critical attitude and the unfavourable opinion of her which he still considered to be based on unassailable grounds. At the same time, he was bound by ties of affection to the one Church in which, hitherto, he had seen the flower of sanctity blossoming around him. But now it began to dawn on him that this note, difficult though it was to admit it, was also possessed by Rome, and by Rome perhaps more conspicuously than by England. The profound impression made on him by the Eternal City on his first visit, a mysterious impression which he could not account for at the time, taken in conjunction with all that he had subsequently accumulated regarding her, left him in no doubt that the Rome of today was the Rome of the martyrs and holy men, the living successor of the Rome of St Leo, of the Rome which was the very heart of the Church of the Fathers.

If he was mistaken to some extent in his view of the Roman—that is to say, the Catholic—devotion to Mary and the Saints, there was, deep down within him, an innate instinct of devotion to the ideal of immaculate purity which is incarnated in Mary's consecration to Christ to which he yielded unresisting allegiance. He had always looked on it as a dispensation of Providence that St Mary's was the title of his parish, and he never passed through the porch with its twisted pillars, without an obeisance to the beautiful statue of the Virgin, Laud's statue, which adorns it.

Nevertheless, he had striven, with all his might, both inwardly and with those about him, to resist this new, yet old, attraction, which grew and continued to grow ever brighter and brighter, so profoundly convinced was he that we ought not to allow ourselves to be swayed by sentiment, by the promptings of the heart, whether it were a matter of remaining in the Church of England, or of setting out for Rome. The will of God, obedience to God's Word, a determination to submit to the truth, these and these alone should order our deeds, and to these all else should be subordinated.

The Church of England still retained her hold on him in spite of everything. She did so by reason of the fruits of holiness which he considered she was continuously bringing forth. Still, he could not deny that Rome, too, was productive of the like fruits. Indeed, on this point, the strong point as he had come to deem it of the Anglican position, he was beginning now to wonder whether Rome did not bear away the palm. His study of the Fathers had taught him something which he had already had in mind, something which Froude had exemplified in his life, and that was that true Christianity was not of this world, that the true Church anticipated the Last Day by freely renouncing all worldly things. Where, then, should we look today for an Anthony, a Basil, or a Gregory? Should we be likely to discover the object of our search in some English parsonage with its glowing hearth, its comfortable appointments, or in the cell of some monk who had given up everything, all earthly ties and affections, all the charities of home, nay, even, maybe, the advantages of learning and culture, so as to be ready to follow the Master at His slightest bidding?

However, the old arguments against Rome still persisted. Newman had now reached a stage in his enquiries when the quest for points of resemblance between the Church of England and the Primitive Church could elicit nothing further. No solution of the matter was to be looked for in that quarter. Inevitably, therefore, the comparison had to be between Anglicanism and the Church which, to him, was still an alien church. Unless he was to take it that there was now no Church at all, that man's redemption had come to naught, or unless he was to continue in a state of doubt and uncertainty that could not go on for ever, he would have to settle down to making a first-hand study of the beliefs and practices of the Church of Rome. He had to find out for himself whether it was after all so certain that Rome had so gravely betrayed the Church of the Apostles and the Fathers. He had to make sure, beyond all manner of doubt, whether or not this lure of Rome was anything more than a deceptive mirage.

Apparently, this new line of investigation was one of the major tasks for 1842, yet another year spent in the seclusion of Littlemore. Such, then, was the task; but the question was, how to set about it.

Wiseman was not the only Catholic to take an interest in the Tractarian Movement from its very beginning, and to try to direct its course from outside. Though, as a matter of fact, the great majority of English-speaking Catholics saw nothing but make-believe and an absurd aping of their own Church in these Anglican efforts to restore the faith and practices of ancient tradition, there were some notable exceptions, and Dr Russell of Maynooth, the famous Irish seminary, was one of them. From the year 1841 he had been doing his best to establish contact. He visited Oxford, saw Newman and his friends, and earnestly exhorted them to pray that all might be brought together into one Church.

Newman, though he received him with reserve, had been taken with his attitude and impressed by his evident sincerity. It was to him, therefore, that he wrote the following year, requesting him to send him some popular books of devotion so that he might find out for himself exactly what Catholics meant, or did not mean, by honouring the Saints.

When he came to read St Alfonzo di Liguori, he was surprised to find none of the idolatry or superstition he had expected to encounter. Put back into their proper context, some of the expressions which formed the favourite quotations of the controversialists appeared devoid of offence. Others, not so readily explained, did not figure in the copies of the English translation which Russell had sent. Newman wrote to him about this. Russell told him quite frankly that they had been purposely omitted on the grounds that what suited the Italians might not suit the English. The answer was double-edged. It showed that certain forms of devotion which gave offence to Anglicans did exist in Catholicism, but it also showed that they might not be to the taste of some Catholics who were nevertheless perfectly orthodox, and that they were far from expressing the essentials of their religion. Moreover, he came to see that, when viewed against their national background, even the most seemingly extravagant of these popular devotional practices involved nothing that was necessarily incompatible with fundamental Christianity. A Catholic might find this sort of devotions to his taste, or he might not, but looked at objectively, it was difficult to see how they could be regarded as presenting a serious argument against the Church which tolerated them.

These very simple discoveries, coming, as they did, at the psychological moment, put a different face on the problem. Henceforth the ground was cleared, and the two Churches stood face to face, fairly and squarely. No more preconceptions now for either of them, favourable or unfavourable. Doubtless, Newman, always so keenly on the look-out for the signs of Providence, was not to quit the Church of his baptism till he had made quite sure that it was his duty to do so, but, at any rate, whether he was to go, or to remain where he was, was now a legitimately debatable question.

Time was when he believed that the Church of England was, or might prove to be, the Primitive Church restored to life. That belief he now discarded, nor was it long before he ceased to entertain the corresponding belief, namely that the Church of Rome had irremediably corrupted the faith and worship of the Church of the Fathers. Nevertheless, it was certain that neither in the Roman nor in the Anglican communion was the Church of Antiquity to be found. In the former, the Middle Ages, the Council of Trent and all that went with it had wrought changes no less striking, perhaps more so, than those which the latter had undergone. Thus the problem now hinged on the question of development. What developments are admissible, taking the Primitive Church as the starting-point, and what are not? On the answer to that question would depend whether the step which at one time had seemed to him so dim and far away, would have to be taken after all.

The Church is a living reality. It cannot be a mere abstraction. All the New Testament, all the testimony of Tradition, cries out against such an idea. His constant researches into the Scriptures, into Antiquity, convince him more and more of this primordial truth. The Church of England makes it impossible for men to regard her as that living reality. An impartial enquiry into her history, her permanent position in Christendom, make it evident that such she could not be, or be made to become. Could it be that Rome, notwithstanding the manifold changes of her outward form, was nevertheless the true embodiment of the living soul, the one and only Church?

That there were manifold and material differences between the Catholic Church of the nineteenth century and the Catholic Church of the Fathers could not be denied; but that need not have surprised one for whom Thomas Scott's dictum, "Growth the only evidence of life", had as much of the force of truth in it as that other saying of his, "Holiness rather than peace". But the question that had to be decided was, were the changes exhibited by the Church of Rome signs of healthy vitality and growth, or were they, as in the Church of England, indications of breaches, of disruptions that meant death? For Newman, as he had come to look at things at the beginning of 1843, everything depended on the answer to that question.

On the 2nd February that year, Newman, his young colleague Christie having resigned in his favour his turn to preach, delivered the fifteenth and last of his University Sermons, and this he entitled, *The Theory of Development in Religious Doctrine*. The Roman Church was not specifically referred to, but the whole purpose of the sermon was to lay down the principles in the light of which Faith and Reason, acting together, should be able to decide which Church was entitled to call itself, not only the lawful successor of the Apostles, but the true, the living, Apostolic Church. To apply these principles was the task to which Newman was patiently to address himself for two years to come, or maybe longer, in no way prejudging the issue. Implicitly participating in it were all those who had the discovery of the real, the whole truth at heart.

Newman would never have allowed himself to preach this sermon had he seen in it anything of a nature to compromise his loyalty to the Church of England, to which he considered himself wholly committed. If the Church of England was a Church in the full enjoyment of Christian truth, she would answer the tests which he was applying to her, just as he would apply them to any other Church aspiring to that title. These tests, framed in accordance with the principles laid down by the Caroline Divines themselves, left only one survivor among the claimants to title of the Church of Jesus Christ, and that one survivor was the Church of Rome. The Caroline Divines held that the Church of the Apostles and the Fathers was the one true Church, and claimed that theirs was that Church. But the Roman Church, and she alone, could show that, through all her developments, she had preserved unbroken her continuity with the Primitive Church, the Church set up by Christ, and founded on the Twelve.

Here we will pause for a moment to take stock of the rich contents of this, the last of his University Sermons. It is obvious, of course, to begin with, that it is an adumbration, a preliminary draft of a work of capital importance, and that is the work in which, in due time, he was to describe the final steps which brought him at long last into the Church of Rome. That book, however, deals only with the application to one isolated instance of the general principles which this sermon so luminously sets forth. We have here, as it were in little, the fruit of all Newman's meditations on Christian truth, on religious faith, on Revelation, and on the work of Christ.

Newman had now arrived at his full spiritual and intellectual maturity, and in the midst of a crisis which was at once a personal one and part of a general intellectual and religious movement, his intellectual genius and saintly spirit offer us in these pages the quintessance of his profoundest thought and the latest fruit of all his investigations. Not only does Newman sketch in this sermon the foundations of the *Essay on the Development of Christian Doctrine*, the book in which he records his decision to enter the one Church which he had at last recognised as the true one, but he anticipates some of the loftiest of those intuitive ideas which, towards the end of his life, he was to set down in his *Grammar of Assent*. One could hardly wish for a clearer illustration than that which this sermon presents, of the true, the vital character of the Christian faith. He shows us, behind the multiplicity of dogmatic formulas, the living unity of the religious truth presented to us, God revealed and made known to us in Jesus Christ. And in those same formulas he explains the analogy by which we express therein, in terms borrowed from the facts and circumstances of our own lives, that ineffable Reality which transcends all human experience.

It is by beginning with this profound Unity, this Oneness, as of Someone, of Someone who comes to us by bringing our lives into His own, by taking us into Himself, that we explain and account for this living principle of truth within the Church which is the mainspring, the soul of development. Religious truth is not something contained in a lifeless formula, something congealed, as it were, for all time in ice. It is the truth of the Creative Being communicated to all His human creatures in such wise as to bring their lives into His. Hence a line of development, determined indeed by the circumstances of their human existence, yet not in such wise as to lose sight of the Unity of the whole amid the multiplicity of its parts, but always rather to gather together and bring into the circle of the One Truth the minds of all humanity.

XIII

THE PARTING OF FRIENDS

WE should be making a great mistake if we assumed that Newman, alone, in the solitude and silence of Littlemore, was allowed to resolve the problems that beset him in an atmosphere of peace, penitence, and prayer. Visitors were constantly coming and going, his correspondents were numberless, and they were perpetually harassing him with their difficulties and anxious questionings. And, as if all that was not enough, hordes of inquisitive folk came to see what signs of Popery they could ferret out, and then went away spreading the most fantastic tales, the sort of thing which in any other circumstances would have been merely laughable. Coming back from a walk one day, Newman found the place swarming with undergraduates who had come to spy out the land, and to see for themselves what was really going on there. On another occasion, answering the door in person, he found himself face to face with a don who asked to be allowed to look over the "monastery". Things came to such a pass that the poor Bishop of Oxford, kindly disposed though he was, was so pestered by complaints and accusations that he was driven to write to Newman asking him to give the lie to these preposterous fables.

Years later, Newman was fired with indignation when he recalled the absurd and unseemly persecution to which he had been subjected.

> "What was I doing at Littlemore?" Doing there! have I not retreated from you? have I not given up my position and my place? am I alone of Englishmen, not to have the privilege to go where I will, no questions asked? am I alone to be followed about by jealous, prying eyes, which take note whether I go in at a back door or at the front, and who the men are who happen to call on me in the afternoon? Cowards! If I advanced one step, you would run away; it is not you that I fear: *Di me terrent, et Jupiter hostis*. It is because the Bishops still go on charging against me, though I have quite given up: it is that secret misgiving of heart which tells me that they do well, for I have neither lot nor part with them: this it is which weighs me down. I cannot walk into or out of my house but curious eyes are upon me. Why will you not let me die in peace? Wounded beasts creep into some hole to die in, and no one grudges them. Let me alone, I shall not trouble you long. This was the keen feeling which pierced me, and, I think, these are the very words in which I expressed it to myself.[1]

[1] *Apologia*, p. 172.

To soothe the agitated feelings of his many disciples who were upset at all these happenings, Newman had undertaken the publication of a new series: *The Lives of the English Saints*. Is not this to be interpreted as one last effort on his part to reawaken in the Church of England that note of holiness which, of all others, he was anxious to preserve? Unfortunately, it was soon borne in upon him that Anglicans in general had no great sympathy with the mortifications and austerities practised by such men as St Stephen Harding, and other great saints of mediaeval days.

In 1843, Newman took definite steps in preparation for his final departure. In February, being now convinced of the hollowness of the accusations he had brought against the doctrines and practices of the Church of Rome, these accusations (which he had repeated with confidence, seeing that they were based on the authority of the great Anglican divines) he now thought it his duty publicly to withdraw. This he did, with as little stir as possible, in a semi-private organ known as the *Conservative Review*. No one was in any doubt about the authorship of the article, and Golightly, in the *Oxford Herald*, promptly availed himself of it to sow confusion in the ranks of the Tractarians.

Needless to say, ignorant calumnies abounded. Newman did everything in his power to hold back the younger men, and all whom he thought insufficiently informed, from taking any irrevocable step without fully realising what they were doing. The result was that he was accused of persuading them to remain in the Church of England while, all along, they were the secret adherents of Rome. Moreover, people said the same thing about Newman himself.

However, there were some magnanimous spirits who condoled with him over these stupid accusations, men like Dr Routh, the aged President of Magdalen, who, immediately after his retractation, made a point of soliciting his aid as an examiner.

September was not many days old when Newman at last made up his mind to take the step about which he had hesitated so long. On the 18th of that month, he formally resigned St Mary's. The Bishops now almost to a man had pronounced their condemnation of Tract 90, and this was a hastening factor. His decision was further confirmed by the storm which followed the first instalment of the *Lives of the English Saints*. The sudden conversion of one of the younger men, in spite of all the efforts he had made to retain him in the Anglican fold, convinced him that he could not go on as he was. He was loath to give up

Littlemore, and would have been willing to stay on as his successor's curate, but this would never have answered.

For two more years he was to continue to put off the final step, but now, if an Anglican he still remained, it was to all intents and purposes as a layman. He preached for the last time at Littlemore on the 26th September. This sermon was the celebrated one which bears the title, *On the Parting of Friends*.

The dignified Pusey conducted the service, and the little church was a mass of flowers, as always on the anniversary of its dedication. All the prominent figures in the Oxford Movement were present, sitting among the parishioners and, like them, deeply moved. Tears rolled down their faces as Newman pronounced those words of final leave-taking, words that told of all he felt he was giving up in leaving the Anglican fold, of all those things that kept so many other generous hearts from following in his steps. To these emotions, mingled with sorrowing reproaches, he gave unforgettable expression.

> O my mother, whence is this unto thee that thou hast good things poured out upon thee and canst not keep them, and barest children, yet dare not own them? Why hast thou not the skill to use their services, nor the heart to rejoice in their love? How is it that whatever is generous in purpose, and tender or deep in devotion, thy flower and thy promise, falls from thy bosom and finds no home within thine arms? Who hath put this note upon thee, to have, "a miscarrying womb, and dry breasts", to be strange to thine own flesh, and thine eye cruel towards thy little ones? Thine own offspring, the fruit of thy womb, who love thee and would toil for thee, thou dost gaze upon with fear, as though a portent, or thou dost loathe as an offence;—or at best thou dost but endure, as if they had no claim but on thy patience, self-possession, and vigilance, to be rid of them as easily as they mayest. Thou makest them "stand all day idle", as the very condition of thy bearing with them; or thou biddest them be gone, where they will be more welcome; or thou sellest them for nought to the stranger that passes by. And what wilt thou do in the end thereof? . . .
>
> And, O my brethren, O kind and affectionate hearts, O loving friends, should you know any one whose lot it has been, by writing or by word of mouth, in some degree to help you thus to act; if he has ever told you what you knew about yourselves, or what you did not know; has read to you your wants or your feelings, and comforted you by the very reading; has made you feel that there was a higher life than this daily one, and a brighter world than that you see; or encouraged you, or sobered you, or opened a way to the inquiring, or soothed the perplexed; if what he has said or done has ever made you take an interest in him, and feel well inclined towards him; remember such a one in time to come, tho' you hear him not, and pray for him, that in all things he may know God's will, and at all times he may be ready to fulfil it.[1]

[1] *Sermons on Subjects of the Day*, pp. 406 et sqq.

When the preacher descended from the pulpit, while Pusey at the altar was reciting the offertory prayer in a voice choked with sobs, it was observed that Newman took off his hood and threw it across the altar-rails. No doubt he did this automatically, such being his custom whenever he was going to receive Holy Communion. But people knew that he had preached to them for the last time, and many of them interpreted this action as a sign that he was now renouncing all further right to address them as a minister of the Church of England. Nevertheless, even now he had not definitely made up his mind to go, and on several occasions thereafter, though he preached to them no more, he administered the Sacraments.

A few days before all this, and without any intervention on his part, one of his brothers-in-law had been very near becoming a convert before him. When, a little later, he did intervene, the result was that the intending convert gave up the idea, and never was converted, then or afterwards. The person in question was Thomas Mozley, Harriet's husband. He had been staying in France, in Normandy, and what he had seen there, though it left him still a little critical of some things in contemporary Catholicism, seems on the whole to have convinced him that the Church of Rome was the true Church, and that it was his duty to join it. Newman, who knew how impressionable and impulsive he was, and who was pretty sure that this holiday abroad would have had a completely opposite effect on Harriet, hurried away to the Cholderton parsonage. Harriet was still in France, and Thomas, left to his own devices, was on the point of putting his resolution into effect.

Newman arrived about seven in the morning, and spent the whole day doing his best to calm him down and imploring him to wait a little. As he said in a letter to Jemima, he thought he was excited and a bad judge of what he was doing. When the truth, or what one takes to be the truth, comes on one suddenly, it excites one.

Tom suffered himself to be talked over. When a little while later, he told his wife about it all, the disclosure had the unexpected effect of making her far more indignant with her brother than with her husband. The truth of the matter was that Newman, realising how far Mozley's ideas had taken him, had not hesitated to let him know what his own feelings were, his idea being that nothing would more effectively restrain him than making him understand that someone else, with convictions at least as strong as his, saw no need for precipitate action.

The epilogue to this strange incident is contained in a letter which

John Henry wrote to Harriet on the 29th September, in a last attempt to make her, the eldest of his sisters, understand how matters stood with him. Anne Mozley cut out all but what was purely impersonal in the letter. We here give it in its entirety.

Your distressing letter just read has equally surprised and perplexed me. I really do not think that any answer can soothe you at present, yet no answer to you seems worse still.

I am much pained at T.'s indiscretion—but I am sure that he meant everything that was kind, and he thought (most erroneously) that he gave the least pain by being frank and open. I think his abruptness arose from awkwardness how to tell you what he felt must be told.

Only see what a position we are in—how difficult to please you. T. you blame for telling you, me for not telling. T. is cruel and I am disingenuous.

However, I am only concerned with myself. First I will say that T. had no right to tell what he told you about me. Next J. has not understood me, certainly has not quoted my words.

I do so despair of the Church of England, and am so evidently cast off by her, and, on the other hand, I am so drawn to the Church of Rome, that I think it *safer*, as a matter of honesty, *not* to keep my living.

This is a very different thing from having any *intention* of joining the Church of Rome. However, to avow generally as much as I have said would be wrong for ten thousand reasons. People cannot understand a man being in a state of *doubt*, of *misgiving*, of being unequal to *responsibilities*, etc.; but they will conclude that he has clear views either one way or the other. All I know is, that I could not without hypocrisy profess myself any longer a *teacher* and a *champion* for our Church.

Very few persons know this—hardly one person, only one (I think) in Oxford, viz. James Mozley. I think it would be most cruel, most unkind, most unsettling to tell them. I could not help telling T. the other day at Cholderton.

As to T., he surprised me by writing word that he thought he must go over at once to the Church of Rome. I never had a dream that he was unsettled. I set off for Cholderton the next hour, and though I could not get any promise from him, I succeeded 1st in restraining him from any immediate step. 2nd from giving up Cholderton at once—but 3rd I acquiesced readily in his relinquishment of the British Critic. It is a step I had twice formally recommended to him in the last two years. As to his state of excitement, it is very great, but if you knew what the feeling is for it to break upon a man that he is out of the Church, and that in the Church only is salvation, you would excuse anything in him.

My dear H., you must learn patience—so must we all, and resignation to the will of God.

It may be said that all through the two ensuing years the conviction was growing upon Newman that the Church of Rome was the true Church, and that, if he was to do God's will, he must needs join it. If, however, he still did not make up his mind to take the step, it was because he was afraid of yielding to some illusory attraction that time might subsequently dispel. The contemplated step was of capital importance and never was he more mistrustful of paper logic than now. He deemed he could only make such a decision if, apart from all other considerations, he was perfectly certain that it was the will of God. He did not think he had as yet reached that stage.

> I felt altogether the force of the maxim of St Ambrose, *Non in dialectica complacuit Deo salvum facere populum suum*—I had a great dislike of paper logic. For myself, it was not logic that carried me on; as well might one say that the quicksilver in the barometer changes the weather. It is the concrete being that reasons; pass a number of years, and I find myself in a new place; how? the whole man moves; paper logic is but the record of it. All the logic in the world would not have made me move faster towards Rome than I did; as well might you say that I have arrived at the end of my journey, because I see the village church before me as venture to assert that the miles, over which my soul had to pass before it got to Rome, could be annihilated, even though I had been in possession of some far clearer view than I then had, that Rome was my ultimate destination. Great acts take time. At least this is what I felt in my own case; and therefore to come to me with methods of logic had in it the nature of a provocation, and, though I do not think I ever showed it, made me somewhat indifferent how I met them, and perhaps led me, as a means of relieving my impatience, to be mysterious or irrelevant, or to give in because I could not meet them to my satisfaction.[1]

In the year 1844, far from his receiving the hoped-for providential signs that were to dispel all his hesitations, it appeared that circumstances of an intimate, a personal character were still further to protract his delay. There came to him evidence, convincing evidence, of the existence in the Anglican Church of that note of holiness which he could not bring himself to believe it had ever lost.

Lucy Pusey, barely fifteen years old, was on her deathbed. Newman wrote to his friend in this hour of crushing sorrow:

> Dear Lucy has been made His in Baptism, she has been made His in suffering; and now she asks to be made His by love. Well may you find her sweet countenance pleasant to look upon, when here at a distance I have such pleasure in thinking of her. . . . tell her that she is constantly in my thoughts . . . as she who has gone first, is in my mind day by day, morning and evening, continually. . . .

A few days later, when it was all over, Pusey wrote:

> The struggle was so long and so severe that I could not but think it a realising, in a degree, of a wish that she had named to me (about two years

[1] *Apologia*, pp. 169–170.

ago, I think), that she might die a martyr. . . . All at once her eyes opened wide, and I never saw such a gaze as at what was invisible to us; after this had continued for some little while, she looked at me full in the face, and there came such an unearthly smile, so full of love also; all expression of pain disappeared and was swallowed up in joy; I never saw anything like that smile; there was no sound, else it seemed almost a laugh for joy, and I could hardly help laughing for joy in answer . . . and now I would not exchange that smile for worlds. . . . I cannot sorrow for one whom I have seen with the light of Heaven.[1]

At the end of the following summer, Bowden, the earliest friend of his Oxford days, died of consumption, in London. We may recall what he said to Keble in a letter previously quoted, "In losing him, I seem to lose Oxford". During the last weeks of his illness, Newman celebrated the Anglican Eucharist at his bedside, and administered Holy Communion. We may here note that, up to the time of his conversion, he had never had any doubts as to the validity of Anglican Orders.

When Bowden's eyes were closed in death, Newman wrote to Ambrose St John, a young disciple who, little as he guessed it at the time, was to be for him in his old age what Bowden had been for his youth.

When one sees so blessed an end, and that at the termination of so blameless a life, of one who really fed on our ordinances and got strength from them—and see the same continued in a whole family—the little children finding quite a solace for their pain in the Daily Prayer, it is impossible not to feel more at ease in our Church, as at least a sort of Zoar, a place of refuge and temporary rest because of the steepness of the way.[2]

The way was hard, but he still held on. A letter he wrote to E. Coleridge on the 16th November, 1844, throws a singularly revealing light on the position in which he then stood, notwithstanding the reflections to which these two deaths had given rise.

That our Lord is present in our Eucharist, if we have the Apostolical Succession, and the right form of consecration, is acknowledged even by Roman Catholics—and that the Gift is, not sealed up, but actually imparted, though our Church be in schism, to those who are in involuntary ignorance, this again is even acknowledged by them. And that it is in fact bountifully imparted I have proof on every side of me—but still, it is imparted to those who are in involuntary ignorance, not to those who are according to this mysterious Providence enlightened to discern what the true state of the Church is. If I am once absolutely convinced that our Church is in schism, there is, according to the doctrine (I believe) of every age, no safety in it.

[1] These two letters quoted by Maisie Ward, p. 428 of her *Young Mr Newman*.
[2] *Correspondence of J. H. Newman with Keble and others*, p. 334.

The same letter, a few lines above, expressed, in the clearest of terms, his general view of things, and, in particular, what he thought about the problem of the two Churches.

What possible reason of mere "preference" can I have for the Roman Church above our own? I hardly ever, even abroad, was at any of their services. I was scarcely ever, even for an hour, in the same room with a Roman Catholic in my life. I have had no correspondence with anyone. I know nothing of them except that external aspect that is so uninviting. In the "Tablet" and "Dublin Review" in radical combinations, and liberal meetings, this is how I know them. My habits, taste, feelings are as different as can well be conceived from theirs, as they show outwardly.

No—as far as I know myself the one single over-powering feeling is that our Church is in schism—and that there is no salvation in it *for one who is convinced of this*. It is now more than five years since a consideration of the Monophysite and Donatist controversies wrought in me a clear conviction that we were now, what those heretics were then. Two persons alone, whom I was with at the time, knew what had happened to me—and I instantly addressed myself to overcome the feeling. I think I was quite right in attempting it—I should have been wrong not to have done so. And I succeeded—for two years I was satisfied it was my duty to remain quiet, whatever change in actual opinion had taken place in me. I dwelt upon the Roman corruptions, as we consider them, and balanced them against our difficulties. But this time three years the conviction came on me again, and now for that long time it has been clear and unbroken under all change of circumstance, place, and spirits. Through this time my own question has been "Is it a delusion?" and I have waited, not because my conviction was not clear, but because I doubted whether it was a duty to trust it. I am still waiting on that consideration.[1]

If anyone was disconcerted and troubled by Newman's doubts, yet quite unable to share them, that man was Keble. In his opinion, the whole thing arose from the incomprehension, the ingratitude, and the injustice that Newman had met with. He did everything he could to collect and point out to him examples of the warm sympathy which so many Anglicans entertained for him, notwithstanding the disapproval with which the ecclesiastical authorities regarded him. In after years Keble bitterly reproached himself for failing to impress this upon him with sufficient force. As it was, he now wrote:

I can only speak for *one*, of certain knowledge. Your sermons put me in the way, and your healing ministration helped me beyond measure. This is *certain knowledge* of mine; and here is Wilson sitting opposite with just the same feelings; and Young next door, and Moberly at Winchester, and Ryder a few miles off, and Ellison whom I saw the other day; and in short, wherever

[1] *Correspondence of J. H. Newman with Keble and others*, pp. 345–346.

I go, there is someone to whom you have been a channel of untold blessing. You must not be angry, for I feel as if I could not help saying it, and I am sure the very air of England around you would say the same, if it could be made vocal. They have had unspeakable help from you, and it is now their turn to help you with their prayers and good wishes, now that you seem to be called for a while to be patient in comparative silence and inactivity.[1]

On the 21st November, Newman replied:

. . . What I feel most at present as to the attacks made on me, or rather the only thing which I *feel*, is the charge of dishonesty. Really no one but O'Connell is called so distinctly and so ordinarily a liar, as I am. I think nothing tends to hurt my spirits but this. I am not treated merely as a gentleman, and that by educated people. Now as far as any such expression as Sir J. C.'s went to protest against this, I should value it much—but then it strikes me I should be removing a cross from me, and I might have a heavier one put on me. If there is a cross which is blessed from those who have borne it from our Lord's own time, it is this—and it is safest to be content with it.

His letter went far beyond this, however—and such words as "veneration, love" etc . I really could not bear. I am not used to them. I never have heard them. I hope there is nothing wrong and ungrateful in shrinking from them. I am not sure that there is not something of pride. But I really could not bear them. And though I say this, yet, inconsistent as it is, while I should be pained at them, I really do think I could be elated too—and, please, do keep me from *this*.

And then I do think they would increase, not diminish, my greatest grief of all—which is the unsettlement of people's minds. For the more I realised that people sympathised in me, the more acutely I should feel the pain I was giving them. Is this selfish?

I am making too much of this, you will say—yet I will add one thing—I should fear that some persons at least, who took part in such an expression of kindness, would think that my present tendencies arose from the want of such expressions, and would hope to stop them by means of it. Now I have had extremely kind letters from Manning, Gladstone, Blowell [? Browell] and others, but they have not operated ever so little in shaking the deep confidence I have at present that Christianity and the Roman Catholic system are convertible terms, or in reviving more hopeful or comfortable feelings about our present state.

I hope you will not think I am writing a cold reasoning answer to your so very kind letter. I wrote one first of all thanking you etc.—and then it struck me that all this was unnecessary between us, so I have burnt it, and begun again.

While I am on the subject of myself, I will say one or two things more.

When I was first taught the doctrine of Baptismal Regeneration by Hawkins on my getting into Oriel, of "the Church" by Whately in 1825, and of Apostolic Succession by Hurrell seven years later in 1829 (after James on "Episcopacy" in 1823), I began to profess them and commit myself by defin-

[1] *Correspondence*, p. 349.

ite acts to the profession, with far less of intellectual conviction and feeling of certainty than I now have of Papal Supremacy and Catholic communion. I doubt whether I should ever have held those doctrines, if I had gone on in the shilly shally way in which I am going on (rightly or wrongly) about the last mentioned.

I doubt whether I *can* have clearer conviction than I have without a miracle, if then. And Bishop Butler warns us against expecting too clear evidence in moral questions.

For three full years I have been in a state of unbroken certainty. Against this certainty I have acted, under the notion that it might be a dream, and that I might break it as a dream by acting—but I cannot.

In that time I have had no ups and downs—no strong temptations to move, and relapses again—though of course at particular moments the (if so be) truth has often flashed upon me with unusual force.

I scarcely ever was present at a Roman service even abroad. I know no Roman Catholics. I have no sympathies towards them as an existing body. (I should observe, however, that I have certainly been touched by hearing some were praying for me.) I am setting my face absolutely towards the wilderness. . . .

My sole ascertainable reason for moving is a feeling of indefinite *risk* to my soul in staying. This, I seem to ascertain in the following manner. I don't think I could die in our Communion. Then the question comes upon one, is not death the test? shall one bear to live, where die one cannot?

I am kept first from deference to my friends—next by the fear of some dreadful delusion being over me.

A sorrowful and unthankful reply this to yours—which, I will but add, cheered me as far, as with such dreadful questions before me, I can be cheered.[1]

Not everyone, whichever side they were on, envisaged the problem, or attempted to solve it, at such a lofty spiritual level. If, on the Protestant side, the campaign of calumny and insult exceeded all bounds, it must be confessed that among the Romanising Anglicans moderation of tone and delicacy of feeling did not universally or conspicuously prevail. People have been surprised that, when referring to what we may call the hotheads among the Tractarians, Newman never so much as breathed the name of Ward, but mentioned, as their ringleader, Oakeley, who seems to have been a relatively colourless personality.

Some people have been disposed to see in this some indication of personal resentment. But surely, ordinary discretion would have been enough to prompt him to silence. Into what seemed like a sort of death-chamber atmosphere, Ward had had the merit—if that be the right name for it—of introducing a piece of irresistible buffoonery, and that

[1] *Correspondence*, pp. 349 et sqq.

was all there was to be said about him. That is not in any way to question his sincerity. That was as clear as Newman's. But it was so dazzling, too, that it was not always easy to determine where sincerity ended and cynicism began. Certainly, in this Anglican atmosphere of compromise after compromise, it may have been salutary to blurt out the blunt and brutal truth, but one can hardly imagine a line of behaviour better calculated to defeat the truth than that adopted by Ward. He laid down the arguments for the celibacy of the clergy in terms of exaggerated emphasis, and then went off and got married himself. He rated asceticism as high as holiness among the notes of the true Church—but he ate meat on Fridays. He reproached the Church of England for being wealthy and for despising the poor; and then, as soon as he was converted, he began to live in great style, apparently unvisited by any stings of conscience. Throughout his life, he venerated Newman as a saint. This did not prevent him from denouncing him as a heretic to the Roman authorities, having previously done him the disservice, in Anglican eyes, of referring to himself as his most devoted disciple.

Pestering Newman to give him some measure of approval of the *paper logic* of which he was so outstanding an exponent, thinking far more about his logic than about acting on the conclusions he drew from it, he composed, or rather rattled off, during the year 1843, a book in which the good went cheek by jowl with the bad. This formidable bundle of verbiage and vicious vituperation was entitled *The Ideal of a Christian Church*. The ideal in question was a Church in which the one thing needful was Sanctity. But by Sanctity we were to understand a sort of romantic ascesis and austerity, of mortification and self-denial, that being the only antidote he could think of, the only possible balm, to soothe the fury aroused in him by Arnold's proposals for a Church. That this ideal of his was fulfilled by the Roman Church in all respects, and by the Anglican in none, he did not merely infer, he shouted it aloud with all the violence and irony he had at his command. Someone has remarked that, whereas Newman approached the Church of England with infinite tenderness and respect, to try and remedy the shortcomings which his clarity of vision could not fail to detect in her, Ward strode up to her bludgeon in hand and shouted with glee as he brutally belaboured her.

It must be confessed that there is something almost exhilarating about this truculence, this insolence, this outspoken defiance, when we compare it with the pompous and deliberate indifference with which the Anglican authorities endeavoured to stifle the voice of the "Apostolical" party. That word reminds us of Froude, and suggests a comparison of his irony with Ward's. With Froude's irony, devastating though it was, with his deliberate attempts to shock, none but second-rate minds could have been seriously offended. The depth of feeling, the complete unworldliness which, as by a process of reaction, called forth these schoolboy pranks as a protest against sham and hollow humbug, were abundantly clear. In Ward's case, it was the lack of seriousness that was mainly evident, though his good faith, too, was undeniable.

There is certainly something distinctly entertaining, something that reminds us of the *Lutrin*, in the squabbles in which this Balliol don found himself involved with the Master. Dr Jenkyns was a typical example of the old-fashioned college dignitary, a man whose almost overpowering politeness breathed the very perfume of the eighteenth century. He was a worthy man, withal, and greatly attached to his young colleague, who, incidentally, took him off with a perfection that sent the whole Common Room into roars of laughter. Dr Jenkyns, then, plunged into the book, little dreaming what was in store for him. When he had got about half-way through—it was pretty hard doctrine for anyone to swallow, but bound to outrage the feelings of a man of his stamp—a visitor dropped in, and found the Master pacing up and down his study and giving vent to this sort of thing in tones of utter horror and amazement: "We are a corrupted Church. We are in a state of degradation. We must humbly ask pardon at the feet of Rome." And the master went on in more and more horrified tones: "Humbly!"

One might be justly reproached for wasting time over such ludicrous episodes were it not that later on they were to have a very distinct bearing on Newman's position. The book caused such a scandal that a special meeting of Convocation was summoned to go into the matter, and to decide how the author should be dealt with. He had provided the adversaries of the Movement with an undreamt-of opportunity for dealing it a crushing blow. It was proposed, not merely to censure the book, to deprive Ward of his degree, but also to pronounce the University's formal condemnation of Tract 90, of which, quite erroneously, the *Ideal* was represented as the logical outcome.

On the eve of St Valentine's Day, 1845—and a very cold day it was, the snowy weather having lasted a long time that year—the procession of dignitaries made its way to the Sheldonian Theatre, there to pronounce judgment on the man who already bore the nickname of "Ideal Ward".

The undergraduates, excluded from a meeting which promised to be a highly entertaining one, and being, of course, on Ward's side because he had snapped his fingers at the big-wigs, not content with greeting him with a volley of cheers, greeted the Vice-Chancellor and his train with a volley of snowballs.

After defending himself in a speech whose inordinate length would have aggravated the case against him, had that been possible, Ward heard his book condemned by 777 votes to 391. The majority on the motion to deprive him of his degree was much smaller, being 569 to 511. Then came the motion to condemn Tract 90. But now something happened, something so moving that the pathos of it was long remembered in the University. It was a long-standing privilege, though one that was rarely put into practice, for the two Proctors to impose their veto on any measure which seemed to them to be an infringement of the University traditions or rights. That year the Proctors were Church (one of Newman's most loyal disciples and one of the most loyal friends among those who remained behind in the Anglican Church), and Guillemarde, not so closely united, but still very far from including Newman in the wave of disapprobation which Ward had aroused.

When the motion had been read out and two Proctors were seen to rise from their seats, a tempest of applause broke out from a number of Masters of Arts and from practically all the undergraduates who were besieging the hall passionately eager to find out what was going on. The sensation was so great that after the brief period of total silence in which the voice of Guillemarde pronounced the solemn formula *Nobis Procuratoribus non placet*; the Vice-Chancellor, without so much as formally declaring the session closed, hurried down from his stall and hastened away with his attendants amid the triumphant shouts of the undergraduates.

Messages of congratulation arrived in a flood at Littlemore. But Newman had reached a point when sympathy could no more hold him back than antipathy had availed to hurry him forward. If an expression of sympathy and affection did touch him, it was surely that which he received from his beloved Jemima, the last of all his relations to maintain her trust in him, who now expressed her heartrending sorrow at what was to be the inevitable end of it all. This is what he wrote to her in a letter which really amounted to a last farewell:

Littlemore.
March 15, 1845.

My dear Jemima,

I have just received your very painful letter, and wish I saw any way of making things easier to you or to myself.

If I went by what I wished, I should complete my seven years of waiting. Surely more than this, or as much, cannot be expected of me—cannot be right in me to give at my age. How life is going! I see men dying who were boys, almost children, when I was born. Pass a very few years, and I am an old man. What means of judging can I have more than I have? What maturity of mind am I to expect? If I am right to move at all, surely it is high time not to delay about it longer. Let me give my strength to the work, not my weakness—years in which I can profit His cause who calls me, not the dregs of life. Is it not like a death-bed repentance to put off what one feels one ought to do?

As to my convictions, I can but say what I have told you already, that I cannot at all make out why I should determine on moving, except as thinking I should offend God by not doing so. I cannot make out what I am *at* except on this supposition. At my time of life men love ease. I love ease myself. I am giving up a maintenance involving no duties, and adequate to all my wants. What in the world am I doing this for (I ask *myself* this), except that I think I am called to do so? I am making a large income by my sermons. I am, to say the very least, risking this; the chance is that my sermons will have no further sale at all, I have a good name with many; I am deliberately sacrificing it. I have a bad name with more; I am fulfilling all their worst wishes, and giving them their most coveted triumph. I am distressing all I love, unsettling all I have instructed or aided. I am going to those whom I do not know, and of whom I expect very little. I am making myself an outcast, and that at my age. Oh, what can it be but a stern necessity which causes all this.

Pity me, my dear Jemima. What have I done thus to be deserted, thus to be left to take a wrong course, if it is wrong? I began by defending my own Church with all my might when others would not defend her. I went through obloquy in defending her. I in a fair measure succeed. At the very time of this success, before any reverse, in the course of my reading, it breaks upon me that I am in a schismatical Church. I oppose myself to the notion; I write against it—year after year, I write against it, and I do my utmost to keep others in the Church. From the time my doubts come upon me I begin to live more strictly; and really from that time to this I have done more towards my inward improvement, as far as I can judge, than in any time of my life. Of course I have had all through many imperfections, and might have done every single thing I have done much better than I have done it. Make all deductions on this score, still, after all, may I not humbly trust that I have not so acted as to forefeit God's gracious guidance? And how is it that I have improved in other points if in respect of this momentous matter I am so fearfully blinded? Suppose I were suddenly dying, one may deceive oneself as to what one should do—but I think I should directly send for a Priest. Is not this a test of one's state of mind? Ought I to live where I could not bear to die? Again, I assure you it makes me quite uncomfortable travelling, lest some accident should cut me off in my present state. Is this a right frame of mind to be in? Have I lived so many years, have I made such high profession, have I preached to others so peremptorily, to be myself now in fear of death? What is the difference between me and a poor profligate? We both feel we have a work to do which is undone.

Why should I distress your kind heart with my miseries? Yet you must know them, to avoid the greater misery of looking at me externally, and wondering and grieving over what seems incomprehensible. Shall I add that, distressing as is my state, it has not once come upon me to say, O that I had never begun to read theology! O that I had never written the Tracts &c! I lay no stress on this, but state it....

Of course the human heart is most mysterious. I may have some deep evil in me which I cannot fathom; I may have done some irreparable thing which demands punishment; but may not one humbly trust that the earnest prayers of many good people will be heard for me? May not one *resign* oneself to the event, whatever it turn out to be? May one not hope and believe, though one does not see it, that God's hand is in the deed, if a deed there is to be; that He has a purpose, and will bring it to good, and will show us that it is good in His own time? Let us not doubt, may we never have cause to doubt, that He is with us. Continually do I pray that He would discover to me if I am under a delusion: what can I do more? What hope have I but in Him? To whom should I go? Who can do me any good? Who can speak a word of comfort but He? Who is there but looks on me with sorrowful face?—but He can lift up the light of His countenance upon me. All is against me—may He not add Himself as an adversary! May He tell me, may I listen to Him, if His will is other than I think it to be.

Palm Sunday. So, my dear Jemima, if you can suggest any warning to me which I am not considering, well, and thank you; else do take comfort and think that perhaps you have a right to have faith in me, perhaps you have a right to believe that He who has led me hitherto will not suffer me to go wrong. I am somehow in better spirits this morning, and I say what it occurs to me to say at the time. Have I not a right to ask you not to say, as you have said in your letter, that I shall do *wrong*? What right have you to judge me? Have the multitude who will judge me any right to judge me? Who of my equals, who of the many who will talk flippantly about me, has a right? Who has a right to judge me but my Judge? Who has taken such pains to know my duty (poor as they have been) as myself? Who is more likely than I to know what I ought to do? I may be wrong, but He that judgeth me is the Lord, and judges nothing before the time.

His ways are not our ways, nor His thoughts as our thoughts. He may have purposes as merciful as they are beyond us. Let us do our best and leave the event to Him; He will give us strength to bear all that may come upon us—whatever others have to bear, surely I have to bear most; and if I do not shrink from bearing it, others must not shrink. May I do my best; am I not trying to do my best?—may we not trust it will turn to the best.

By the beginning of the summer, he came to an end of the considerable amount of work he had had to get through in connection with translating and annotating the selections from St Athanasius. Instead, however, of taking advantage of the spell of rest on which he had been counting, he now felt himself compelled to put down in black and white his ideas on the question of development, a subject that he had had on his mind for close on two years. Now, with strange clearness and rapidity, the "notes" which are the mark of true development—that is to say, development which preserves the substance and unity of the living truth—became clear to his mind. At the same time, it became evident that these notes of true development were possessed by the Catholic Church and by the Catholic Church alone.

Newman did not finish the work. So clearly and vividly did the evidence present itself to his mind, that, before he had completed his task, he felt that further delay was out of the question.

On the 8th October, an Italian Passionist, who from his childhood days had been strongly drawn to England and to the enterprise of winning her back to the Faith, was expected to arrive at Littlemore. He was Father Dominic Barberi. On the morning of that day, in a letter to Maria Giberne, the same to whom we owe the account of Mary's death, Newman wrote as follows,

> Father Dominic the Passionist comes here tonight. He does not know of my intention—he comes to see my friend Dalgairns whom he received into the Church about a week since—I shall ask him to do the same charitable work to me. This will not go till it is over.[1]

[1] *Letters*, Vol. II, pp. 410 et sqq.

XIV

EARLY CATHOLIC DAYS

THAT wet October evening, Ambrose St John and Dalgairns came back from Oxford, bringing with them Fr Dominic, who was tired out and drenched to the skin. As he sat by the fire drying his sodden garments, a slender, shadowy, slightly stooping figure glided quietly into the room. His face, worn with constant fasting and long and anxious study, was pale with emotion. Next day Newman, overcome by the suddenness with which events had hurried to their climax, came forth with faltering steps from the little oratory where Fr Dominic had been hearing his confession before receiving him into what he had at last come to recognise as the one true Church.

On the 10th, in company with his little band of friends, Dalgairns and St John, recent converts, Stanton and Bowles, who had been admitted at the same time as himself, he attended Mass, and received Holy Communion. And so, the event long hoped for by some, long dreaded by others, had come to pass. The Church of England had lost for ever the man who had done more than any other to inspire her with new life, while the Catholic Church at last welcomed to her bosom one who had long venerated her as a Mother, yet had taken so long to discern her true features beneath her unfamiliar veil.

And now, it seemed, the days of toil and struggle were over. The haven, which had so long been hidden in the mists, was reached at last. All that remained for him to do was to possess his soul in peace, and quietly enjoy the light that now was his. Or, if he must needs address himself to some new task, how different it all would be! No more now of those adventurous undertakings of the early Tractarian days. Still less would it resemble that laborious tunnelling by which he made his slow and difficult way beneath the wreckage of the *Via Media*, into the clear light of day. It would be a season of blossoming and auspicious increase in the bright pellucid air. Yet, if strife and battle there was still to be, was not the truth on his side now, his trusty shield against encroaching error! Alas! how sad and ironical all such images and similes were doomed to prove!

On the spiritual plane, Newman never suffered disappointment. Nor did the faintest shadow of such a thing ever enter his head. What he had longed for, what he had striven so sorely to attain, he at last had gained—Jerusalem, The Vision of Peace, God with us. In the letters he wrote following his conversion, there are repeated references to the ineffable joy and peace he felt in the knowledge that Christ is sacramentally present with His Church. That belief he held unwaveringly till his last hour. The Shekinah, the Blessed Presence, luminous and life-giving, which went with Israel hidden within the cloud, he had found again, though shrouded in the densest of clouds, and God knows how dense they can be—that Presence he had found, and never lost again.

As to the human, or, rather, the terrestrial plane, we have seen how little he was tempted to delude himself regarding the material consequences of his embracing Catholicism. During the period immediately following his conversion however, while he was in the full glow of supernatural truths embraced by a living faith, and not merely honoured from afar, some agreeable and unexpected incidents tended to modify his outlook. For some time it seemed that what he called the Second Spring of the Church was to be his own second spring. It was but a mirage—a merciful dispensation of Providence, shall we call it?—that thus vouchsafed him a little breathing space before starting him on a yet more arduous ascent. Or perhaps we may wonder whether these modest encouragements did anything more, or anything else, than deepen the hues of those seemingly inevitable frustrations and disappointments, the coming, or rather the return, of which was now so close at hand.

Everything in the Catholic mind rises in revolt against the treatment meted out to one who had gained his faith at the cost of so dear a sacrifice, and meted out by those to whom he came bringing with him all his gifts. It is well that we should feel thus, though it were also well that we should remind ourselves of these words of Christ: "Ye are raising up the tombs of the prophets which your forefathers laid low".

However belated, however free from hypocrisy we may hope it is—though of that we are not always so sure—the admiration we now express by way of making amends is all we can offer to one who has set us so shining an example of enduring steadfastness in the faith. Even so, that example would not exert the power it does had it not been an example of lowliness, of self-abnegation, of sorrow, even as was that of Christ Himself. On the last page of his *Essay on Development*, Newman wrote these words:

> Such were the thoughts concerning the "Blessed Vision of Peace", of one whose long-continued petition had been that the Most Merciful would not despise the work of His own Hands, nor leave him to himself; while yet his eyes were dim, and his breast laden, and he could but employ Reason in the things of Faith. And now, dear Reader, time is short, eternity is long. Put not from you what you have here found; regard it not as mere matter of present controversy; set not out resolved to refute it, and looking about for the best way of doing so; seduce not yourself with the imagination that it comes of disappointment, or disgust, or wounded feeling, or undue sensibility, or other weakness. Wrap not yourself round in the associations of years past, nor determine that to be truth which you wish to be so, nor make an idol of cherished anticipations. Time is short, eternity is long.
>
> Nunc dimittis servum tuum, Domine,
> secundum verbum tuum in pace
> quia viderunt oculi mei salutare tuum.

It is a fact that the only possible plea that could be advanced by those who accepted Newman's principles, but declined to act upon them, was that some feeling of frustration, of disappointment, of a purely personal nature, had sent him from Anglicanism into the arms of Rome. The one answer to this—and it is a sufficient one—is that, if not Rome, then the Catholics among whom his lot was cast had much greater disappointments in store for him than any he had suffered in the Church of England, and that neither his religion nor his practice of it, had ever been in the least disturbed by them. If the words "I have not sinned against the light" were appropriate to the first half of his life, still more so were they to the second. They echo so resoundingly in our ears because of the magnitude of the ordeal endured and overcome. Newman's witness to the truth of Catholicism would not have been so compelling had it not been so completely unalloyed. Nor would its purity impress us as it does if aught of a worldly nature had been mingled with the call divine.

All this being granted, it must be added that, though there were plenty of shortcomings on the part of the ecclesiastics to whom the Littlemore convert betook himself, these did not originate, but merely added to the incomprehension which the circumstances of the time already made inevitable.

We twentieth-century Catholics, prone though we sometimes are to self-criticism, fail to realise the extent of the transformation that has taken place in the circumstances of the Catholic community during the last hundred years, a change of which we are now enjoying the benefit. Without the efforts, unavailing though at first they were, of Newman and some others, that change for the better would never have come about. As late as the middle of the last century, Catholics in England were looked upon as a conquered people, whose sorry plight was made the sorrier by the rags and tatters of their former greatness, which they still dragged about with them. Think of what happened to the Papacy in the days of Napoleon, and even after the restoration how precarious was its position until 1870, and later even than that. Think still more of the utter extinction of the Catholic schools and universities at the time of the Revolution. After that, there was a religious revival—that is to say, a revival of religious sentiment—which we associate with such names as Chateaubriand and Lacordaire. Nor must we forget Lamennais, though bating in his case some of the enthusiasm. But these names sufficiently indicate how almost incredibly fragile was the structure of ideas and principles underlying this revival. Round about the year 1840, Catholic theology was, it must be admitted, non-existent. The faith of the man in the street, based on the most fantastic apologetics, the most extravagant philosophising, was practically all there was to be discovered under this name.

The Jesuit Perrone—he and his like—who had retained, or renewed, contact with a sorely decaying scholastic tradition, would have furnished the only, or almost the only, example of a Catholic thinker who was not a mere amateur. Now, apart from Tradition, there is no Catholic theology, for Catholic theology is but the voice of Tradition taking stock of itself in the minds of those whom it has fed and watered. But how was Tradition to be preserved in a world where all the schools that had ensured its continuity, at all events since the Middle Ages, had been expelled or abolished? It was necessary either to attempt no problem at all (unless it concerned something as harmless and trivial as a crossword puzzle), or else, hazarding some baseless solution, to find oneself hopelessly wide of the mark. From this dilemma there was no escape unless and until some outstanding geniuses came to the rescue. Of these, Newman was one, and probably the greatest. Apart from him, only a few names occur, and those German, such as Moehler and Scheeben. The circumstances of the time did not so much as afford them the satisfaction of making personal contact with one another.

Is that the whole of the matter? Not quite. Within this general framework, the position of the Catholic Church in England was peculiar. There it had suffered more grievously in the past than in any other land. In England, the most elementary civil rights had only just been restored to Catholics. Hitherto, they had lived the lives of a downtrodden, despised, and negligible minority, outside the pale of society. Small wonder, then, if they still continued to comport themselves like people perpetually on the defensive, as if, in short, they were handicapped by a chronic inferiority complex. Debarred from the Universities, unable to give their priests a worthy cultural education, they lived as it were on the fringe of the world, clinging like wild creatures to the protection of a sort of ghetto, which, even when the chance was given them, they showed no disposition to quit. Add to all this, the shock which Newman had felt at the alliances which Irishmen like O'Connell had been perfectly willing to enter into, merely to secure their political emancipation. Take all this into account and it will be quite clear why Newman entertained no merely human or practical expectations when he decided to become a Catholic.

For some little time after his conversion, Newman continued to make fresh personal contacts, from which, so modest were his expectations, he seemed at first to derive considerable satisfaction.

On the Feast of All Saints he visited the theological college at Oscott, near Birmingham, where Wiseman, now one of the Vicars-Apostolic in England, had taken up his residence. Everybody did his best to make himself agreeable. Wiseman was one of the few Catholics who, from the very beginning, had gauged the profound significance of the Oxford Movement, one of the few who had foreseen its eventual trend towards Rome. However, his first meeting with Newman and the other converts was strained in the extreme. They belonged to different worlds, and there was no common ground between them.

On the 1st November, the Littlemore contingent all received Confirmation at the hands of the first Archbishop of Westminster to be. Newman chose Mary for his Confirmation name.

And now fresh conversions followed almost every day. From the depths of despondency in which they had so long been plunged, many Catholics were now exalted to heights of optimism. If Pusey and Keble had both followed in Newman's steps within a week or two, they would have looked on that as something quite in the natural order of things.

For the time being, Newman was very much taken up with seeing his *Essay on Development* through the press. Wiseman was sufficiently tactful and broad-minded to exempt it from the censorship. The main value of the book lay in its being the work of an Anglican who, starting from principles which he himself had chosen to lay down, had been led step by step, in the light of his own reasoning, to find his destination in the Church of Rome. It was of the utmost importance, therefore, that it should be published exactly as it was.

To Wiseman also is due the credit, not only for leading Newman and his little group into the way of the priesthood, but also for inspiring them with the idea of undertaking some sort of intellectual apostolate. Strange that, to begin with, Newman had been doubtful even about taking Orders. Wiseman's enthusiastic ardour, which soon broke down any suspicion of stiffness or constraint there may have been between them, was the deciding factor. Certain it is, that after this visit to Oscott, the prospect of a new work, answering to his own aspirations and worthy of his incomparable gifts, seemed to be assuming practical shape.

All through November and December, he was travelling up and down the country, getting into touch with various Catholic centres. In the south, there was the college of St Edmund's at Ware, in Hertfordshire. Next, there was Prior Park, near Bath, at that time the residence of Dr Thomas Brindle. Here, in the place itself, in its atmosphere, and in his hosts, he was amused to find something that reminded him of the style of life, the "gentlemanlike" set-out which seemed to him specifically Anglican. The sort of Anglicanism we have in mind is not, indeed, conspicuously apostolic, but refined, dignified, well-bred; the kind of thing that might have been exemplified in the Magdalen College of those days.

Returning to Littlemore just before Christmas, he set out again on a still more congested itinerary it took him the whole of January to complete. He visited the other Vicars-Apostolic in their respective abodes, called on one or two of the Catholic aristocracy, among them Ambrose Lisle Phillipps; then on to the Trappists of Mount St Bernard; and, lastly, to Ushaw College in the far north of England, where the President, Dr Newsham, made a deeper impression on him than any other Catholic dignitary, with the possible exception of Wiseman.

Meanwhile projects were beginning to take shape. Wiseman, who was anxious not only to put heart into Newman and the converts in his orbit and to find work for them, was also anxious to manage them, to run their affairs for them. He now urged Newman to close down at Littlemore, and offered to place at his disposal an attractive old house known as Old Oscott, where, he said, he might remain with his little community until some definite plans for the future were decided upon. Readily, if not exactly cheerfully, Newman agreed. Thus most of February was taken up with those unenviable tasks that necessarily precede a removal. On the 22nd, he bade farewell to his lowly but beloved home and, at the same time, severed the last of his remaining links with Oxford.

During these latter weeks, he wrote a number of letters, and in them he gives utterance to all the different feelings which these upheavals excited in him. In January 1846, he wrote to Miss Maria Giberne, herself a convert, saying,

> As you say, "one step enough for me"—let us hope and believe that that Most Merciful Hand, which has guided us hitherto, will guide us still—and that we shall, one and all, you as well as I and my Littlemore infants, all find our vocation happily. We are called into God's Church for something, not for nothing surely. Let us wait and be cheerful, and be sure that good is destined for us, and that we are to be made useful.[1]

So there, as touching the future, we have something resembling an echo of what, we may remember, he said to Jemima, "May I give my strength to the task, not my weakness, the years in which I can be useful to the Cause of Him who calls me, not the lees of my existence." What was then a far-off hope now seemed a practical possibility. A letter to the same correspondent, written a week later, on the 28th January, gives us an account of the feelings with which the past and the present inspired him, the present, whence his hopes arise,

> . . . Divine Mercy wonderfully makes up my losses, as if "instead of thy fathers thou shalt have children" were fulfilled in individuals as well as to the Church. I am now engaged in looking over, sorting, burning my papers and letters, and have had pangs and uttered deep sighs, such as I have not at all yet (thought I used before) since my reception into the Church. So many dead, so many separated. My mother gone; my sisters nothing to me, or rather foreign to me; of my greatest friends, Froude, Wood, Bowden taken away, all of whom would now be, or be coming, on my side. Other dear friends who *are* preserved in life *not* moving with me; Pusey strongly bent on an opposite course; Williams protesting against my conduct as rationalistic, and dying; Rogers and J. Mozley viewing it with utter repugnance. Of my friends of a dozen years ago whom have I now? and what did I know of my present friends a dozen years ago? Why, they were at school, or they were freshmen looking up to me, if they knew my name, as some immense and unapproachable don; and now they know nothing, can know

[1] Wilfrid Ward, *Life of Cardinal Newman*, Vol. I, p. 112.

nothing of my earlier life; things which to me are as yesterday are to them as dreams of the past; they do not know the names, the state of things, the occurrences, they have not the associations, which are part of my own world, in which I live. And yet I am very happy with them, and can truly say with St Paul, "I have all and abound," and, moreover, I have with them, what I never can have had with others, Catholic hopes and beliefs—Catholic objects. And so in your own case, depend on it, God's Mercy will make up to you all you lose, and you will be blessed, not indeed in the same way but in a higher.[1]

However, he does not seem to have felt the full effect of all these partings, drawn out over so many months, till the time arrived for him to leave Littlemore. That was when the great wrench came. A letter he wrote to Mrs William Froude (Hurrell's sister-in-law) on the 15th February makes that clear enough,

... Part of us are gone—part going—I shall, I suppose, remain the last, as I came in first. A happy time indeed have I had here, happy to look back on though suspense and waiting are dreary in themselves;—happy, because it is the only place perhaps I ever lived in, which I can look back on, without an evil conscience, in Oxford, indeed, where I have been near thirty years from first to last, I trust I have all along served God from the day I went there—but in those many years, amid the waywardness and weakness of youth and the turmoil of business, of course many things must have occurred to leave sad thoughts on the memory. Nay even my responsibilities at St Mary's, as one who had the cure of souls, have always all along weighed most oppressively on me and do still. Alas, I will not speak against my circumstances, when my own personal fault is so great. Yet how dreadful is a cure of souls in the English Church, an engagement, with no *means* to carry it into effect—a Jewish yoke. Oxford then is not to me in the twenty or thirty years I have been there more or less, what Littlemore has been for five or six. Doubtless if my life here for these last years were placed in the light of God's countenance, it would be like a room when a sunbeam comes into it, full of hidden unknown impurities—but still I look back to it as a very soothing happy period. I came into this house by myself, and for nights was the sole person here, except God Almighty Himself, my Judge; and St Francis's *Deus meus et omnia*, was ever and spontaneously on my lips. And now, so be it, I shall go out of it by myself, having found rest.[2]

On the 21st February, the night of his forty-fifth birthday, on the eve of his departure from the little house, now empty, he wrote to Henry Wilberforce, the dearest, because the most affectionate of his disciples (whom he had passionately, but vainly, adjured to follow him, yet who, a few years later, though still hesitating, came away easily like a ripe peach):

[1] W. Ward, Vol. I, pp. 112–113. [2] *Ibid.*, p. 115.

I am here today by myself—all my friends gone—and the books. Tomorrow I leave here, for dinner at the Observatory, where I sleep. On Monday morning I go off for Oscott, Birmingham.

I have had a very trying time, parting with the people. I came into this bower by myself—I quit it by myself. Very happy times have I had here, (though in such doubt)—and I am loth to leave it. Perhaps I shall never have quiet again—Shall I ever see Littlemore again?[1]

Of the two following days, his diary gives us a brief account, more moving with its litany of familiar names than any poetical elegy could have been.

Feb. 22. Went to mass at St Clement's for the last time with C. Woodmason. Fly came for me and my luggage at four o'clock to take me to Johnson's, where I dined with Lewis, Buckle, Copeland and Bowles, who came from Hendred. Church and Pattison came in the evening. Called on Ogle. Pusey came up to Johnson's late at night to see me.

Feb 23. Went off by 8½ o'clock with Bowles for Maryvale via Leamington. Got there before 5 o'clock. St John missed us in Birmingham. Walker came. Thus we were six—St John, J. Morris, Stanton, I, Bowles, Walker.

But in a letter to Copeland, who had been his curate at Littlemore, his emotion will out:

I quite tore myself away, and could not help kissing my bed, and mantelpiece, and other parts of the house. I have been most happy there, though in a state of suspense. And there it has been that I have both been taught my way and received an answer to my prayers. Without having any plan or shadow of a view on the subject, I cannot help thinking I shall one day see Littlemore again, and see its dear inhabitants, including yourself, once again one with me in the bosom of the true fold of Christ.[2]

There was, it may be remembered, a passage in *Loss and Gain* which we thought gave expression to the delight he himself felt at the beginning of his own days in Oxford. Wilfrid Ward thinks it beyond doubt that on another page, the most beautiful of all, he describes his feelings on his last day there.

The morning was frosty, and there was a mist; the leaves flitted about; all was in unison with the state of his feelings. He re-entered the monastic buildings, meeting with nothing but scouts with boxes of cinders, and old women carrying off the remains of the kitchen. He crossed to the Meadow, and walked steadily down to the junction of the Cherwell with the Isis; he then turned back. What thoughts came upon him! for the last time! There was no one to see him; he threw his arms round the willows so dear to him, and kissed them; he tore off some of their black leaves and put them in his bosom. "I am like Undine," he said, "killing with a kiss."[3]

[1] W. Ward, Vol. I, p. 116. [2] *Ibid.*, p. 117. [3] *Ibid.*, p. 117

What did he find now to make up for these unforgettable ties? Certainly, Old Oscott, or Maryvale, as Newman himself rechristened it, seemed to offer itself like another Littlemore, just as peaceful and retired, and undoubtedly far more attractive, than the one he had parted from, to say nothing of the Presence, the ineffably consoling Presence, that dwelt within it.

Today, Oscott itself and the whole of the sequestered valley in which it lay have fallen victims to the tentacles of bricks and mortar which Birmingham, the insatiable, is spreading out across the land. But in those days it must have been one of the most engaging retreats that Merrie England had to offer. Enclosed within a narrow, richly wooded valley, it had been, during the later years of the persecution, an ideal retreat for the Vicars-Apostolic of the Midlands. Early in the nineteenth century Dr Milner had begun to build a college, which was transferred to the new premises at Sutton Coldfield as soon as it began to take shape. Enlarged, with an elegant portico that extended half-way round an umbrageous garden, the graceful and very simple eighteenth-century dwelling, its former solitude now restored, was an ideal setting for Newman and his friends to pursue their meditations. Surely their hearts were in the chapel there, where they could always find Him whom they had sought so long, to whom they now turned for inspiration that they might serve Him as and where He would.

Again it is to Henry Wilberforce that Newman writes to tell him of the feelings of thankfulness and peace which fill his heart to overflowing. The letter is dated the 26th February.

Carissime,—I write my first letter from my new home to you. Pusey is my oldest friend since dear J. W. B. was taken away—you come next. I am going to write to him, and had got out my paper, but somehow my fingers have slipt away with my purpose, and I write to you, who have been so faithful to me. No one can be truer or more faithful to me than Pusey himself—but Aristotle says something about our hearts going more with those younger than ourselves than with others; and of those who in any sense have been providentially placed under me you alone have been affectionate to me. And that is the reason perhaps I love St John so much because he comes from you and from your teaching. Oh that he might be a pledge to me that you are yourself to repair that breach which you sorrow over, by your doing what he has done—but I say the above whatever you resolve upon, Carissime, great indeed as must be my distress, as well as yours, while we are divided.

I am writing next room to the Chapel. It is such an incomprehensible blessing to have Christ's bodily presence in one's house, within one's walls, as swallows up all other privileges and destroys, or should destroy, every pain.

To know that He is close by—to be able again and again through the day to go in to Him; and be sure, my dearest W. when I am thus in His Presence you are not forgotten. It is *the* place for intercession surely where the Blessed Sacrament is. Thus Abraham, our father, pleaded before his hidden Lord and God in the valley.

My last morning at Littlemore, when I was by myself, the call of Abraham, as you know in the English service, was the subject of the lesson—and when I got here the first office was that of St Matthias, who took his place in the Apostolate later than his brethren.

I have brought here your little reading-desk which was Wood's. I had not the heart to let it remain behind. (You should not have lost it if it had.) It formed part of the altar on which Father Dominic offered Mass, and from which I received my first communion, last 11th of October.

Please come and fetch it—I can't help saying so—excuse this importunate letter, and believe me,

Ever yours most affectionately,

J. H. N.[1]

Again he adjures, albeit a little less urgently, Wilberforce to join him. That, and the reference to Pusey, touch on the most painful part of the whole matter. The worst was not this parting of friends, about which, before it had actually come to pass, he had spoken in such moving terms. The most painful thing of all was the incomprehension, the utter failure to understand that any separation had taken place at all.

We may recall how difficult it had been for Pusey to bring himself to believe that Newman really was contemplating the possibility of exchanging Anglicanism for Rome. However, now that it had actually happened, he consoled himself with a theory which he thought would meet the case. The theory was that Rome and Canterbury were two branches of the same vine. Some special, mysterious call had compelled Newman to make the change. Now that the change had been made, and since they could no longer work together, what they had to do was to work, on parallel lines indeed, but each in his own separate sphere, without any notion of proselytising. Taking this view of the matter, a view which he thought Newman was bound to share, it never occurred to him, as it did to so many who had remained behind with him, to have any compunction about meetings, which, most of them thought, were bound to be painful for both sides. On the contrary, he went out of his way, during Newman's last weeks at Littlemore, to bring about as many meetings as he could. Thus Newman was under the painful necessity of impressing on Pusey something

[1] W. Ward, Vol. I, pp. 117–118.

which he was extremely loath to admit, and that was that if he, his friend, had passed over to Rome, it was for the simple reason that now, for him, the Church, the One True Church, was the Church of Rome.

It cannot be gainsaid that, in these earlier days, Newman did manifest an eagerness to make converts which he afterwards came to see was more productive of heat than light. By that we are not suggesting that the rebuffs and set-backs he afterwards had to endure in any way diminished his longing to see all those dear friends of his gathered together into One Fold and under One Shepherd. How could that have been, seeing that those same rebuffs never tempted him to regret in the faintest degree the step which he himself had taken?

Nevertheless, from his own particular experience, he did deduce a general truth, and that was that for those who have the light, the best way to make it shine for others is themselves to be living witnesses to the truth, without bringing undue pressure to bear and, by so doing, to usurp the role of Providence. Of all other ways, experience was to show him, not merely the fruitlessness, but the perils.

However, as we have seen in the case of Henry Wilberforce, he not only welcomed with joy the ever-lengthening string of conversions, but did his best to hasten them. Mrs. Bowden's conversion the following year, as well as that of her children, was welcome news indeed. However, with regard to all these activities of his, he came later on to think he had not observed becoming discretion.

All this while, life was going on quietly and smoothly enough at Maryvale. Ambrose St John gives us an entertaining account of it in a letter which must be given in full.

> Day begins at five, Newman ringing the bell, which office the Bishop has given him together with seeing that all the rooms are in decent order by 10 o'clock. Mass at 7, Prime and Tierce at a quarter to eight. Breakfast quarter past eight. Sext and None quarter past twelve, a Latin Conference half past twelve to one; quarter past one dinner; silence ends with a visit to the Blessed Sacrament after dinner; and begins agains at 6, with Vespers and Compline—then tea. Rosary or Litany half past eight, Matins quarter to nine; bed. Moreover, Newman has formed a choir, consisting of Walker, Bowles, Stanton, Christie, C. Woodmason. The rest of us form the awkward squad. We have not been able to get Benediction yet. The library at last is in order except a few shelves; the great room and the small adjoining one hold all, but some of the books are awfully high. Newman grumbles uncommonly, but what was to be done? The floor would not bear projecting bookcases like the Bodleian; and there was no alternative without expensive alterations. The large bookcases from Littlemore have been heightened and the rest are new; altogether the house looks very much improved inside. It is strikingly

> like the Sandford paper mills without. So much for our habitation. It only remains to say that nothing can be kinder than the Bishop is towards us, and I think we all rejoice that Providence has put us in the way of such a director.[1]

Newman by this time had made up his mind to enter the priesthood, and in May that year he received minor Orders. The cordiality with which he had been welcomed in the various theological colleges, the high expectations which seemed to be entertained of these Oxford men, gave him an ever-growing confidence in Wiseman's plans. The high intellectual mission which that prelate had designed for the converts looked like taking shape. What was envisaged was nothing less than a school of Theological Science. Newman himself was becoming increasingly conscious of the lack of any positive science of dogmatic tradition in what he knew so far of the Catholic Church. As regards Christian Antiquity, the Scriptures, the Fathers of the Church, ideas seemed to him to be terribly vague. All this constituted a grave danger, in view of the rapid developments in historical science. It was natural and fitting that he should devote himself to a task involving a subject into which, for reasons of his own, he had gone more deeply than anyone else in England, whether Catholic or Protestant. But prior to all that, he felt the need for some preparatory labours of a very different order from the amateurish scholasticism which, at any rate for the time being, formed the staple occupation at Maryvale. Very early, it would seem, Newman had confided in Wiseman a wish to go to Rome, there to prepare himself for the priesthood, and to make ready to undertake whatever special work the Church might have in store for him. Wiseman, like a sportsman anxious to keep a watchful eye on his bag of game, had side-tracked the idea. Now, however, having pretty thoroughly convinced himself that these Oxford conversions were due to him, he had come to the conclusion that it would be no bad thing if Rome thought so too. Therefore he did everything in his power to ensure that Newman and his friends should get away as soon as possible. Dalgairns, a native of Guernsey, had friends in France, and had already set out for Langres with the intention of studying at the seminary there. Very soon after his arrival, he was smitten with a great enthusiasm for Lacordaire and the Dominican Order. He wrote a number of letters to the Maryvale community on the subject, but they did not seem to be carried away with the idea. A rule more flexible, more up to date, was thought desirable. What was it to be? That, too, that in particular, Rome would decide for them,

[1] W. Ward, Vol. I, p. 120.

and it was to be something they had never dreamed of, something about which, to tell the truth, they as yet knew nothing at all.

The new Pope, whose election had taken place in June, sent Newman his blessing, which seemed to augur well for the future. Early in September, Newman, with Ambrose St John who was to remain his bosom friend and support till an untimely death removed him, set out for Rome.

XV

ROME AND THE ORATORY

IN Paris, at Langres, where they met Dalgairns, at Bésançon, where they halted for a few days before going on to Italy by way of Switzerland, the two travellers were welcomed with unvarying cordiality. They were agreeably surprised at the warmth with which the Bishops everywhere received them, and they were the objects of all manner of attention from the clergy in general. They felt, however, what English people often do feel about French hospitality, and that is, that their hosts spend too much time in surfeiting them with food which they could have done without, especially when it was cooked *à l'anglaise*. After these interludes, some of them affecting, some of them comic, they went on their way, and had a very pleasant journey across Switzerland to Milan, where they tarried for about a month.

Breathing an atmosphere fragrant with the memories of St Ambrose and St Augustine, soothed and rested by the tranquillity of the house in which they had taken up their quarters, and the peaceful harmony of its surroundings, Newman was able to enjoy a brief spell of agreeable and beneficent repose. We know how deeply impressed he had been by the religious art of the Renaissance when he visited Rome for the first time. It is interesting to note how this admiration increases as he comes more and more to enter into the abounding riches of Catholic spiritual life. Speaking of the church of San Fidelio, which adjoined the house in which they were staying, he writes to his beloved Henry Wilberforce:

> It is like a Jesuit Church, Grecian and Palladian—and I cannot deny that, however my reason may go with Gothic, my heart has ever gone with Grecian. I loved Trinity Chapel at Oxford more than any other building. There is in the Italian style such a simplicity, purity, elegance, beauty, brightness, which I suppose the word "classical" implies, that it seems to befit the notion of an Angel or Saint. The Gothic style does not seem to me to typify the sanctity or innocence of the Blessed Virgin, or St Gabriel, or the lightness, grace and sweet cheerfulness of the elect as the Grecian does. I could go into this beautiful Church, with its polished tall pillars, and its smiling winning altar, all day long without tiring. And it is so calm . . . that it is always a rest to the mind to enter it. Nothing moves there but the distant glittering lamp

which betokens the Presence of Our Undying Life, hidden but ever working, though entered into His rest.[1]

Evidently he was deeply impressed by this idea, for, writing to another friend the same day, he expressed himself in similar terms:

> It is always a refreshment to the mind, and elevates it, to enter a Church such as San Fidelio. It has such a sweet, smiling, open countenance—and the altar is so gracious and winning, standing out for all to see, to approach. The tall polished marble columns, the marble rails, the marble floor, the bright pictures, all speak the same language. And a light dome crowns the whole. Perhaps I do but follow the way of elderly persons, who have seen enough that is sad in life to be able to dispense with officious sadness—and as the young prefer autumn and the old spring, the young tragedy and the old comedy, so in the ceremonial of religion, younger men may have my leave to prefer Gothic, if they will but tolerate me in my weakness which requires the Italian. It is so soothing and pleasant, after the hot streets, to go into these delicate yet rich interiors, which are like the bowers of paradise, or an angel's chamber.[2]

This feeling, as of one coming out into the sunlight, reflects his state of mind on emerging from the twilight greys of a semi-Protestant religion. It may be said that he recognised in Catholicism the continuance in perpetuity of the atmosphere which the Fathers breathed, and described not inaptly in the case of the basilicas at Jerusalem as being the Hellenism of Golgotha crowning the Hellenism of the Acropolis. For Newman, Christianity, true Christianity, austere and exacting though it might seem, was always illumined by the glory of the Resurrection. The Cross is always there, but it is the Cross Triumphant, drawing all to itself within an aureole of radiance that knows no wane. It may be well, before entering upon the sombre chronicle of the events that followed, to bear this in mind, and always to remember how deep and lasting that impression was to prove.

Having, in the course of their stay in Milan, picked up as much Italian as they thought they needed to get them along, Newman and St John resumed their journey. On Wednesday, the 28th October, about two o'clock in the morning, they arrived in Rome. Next day, they betook themselves to St Peter's. They were fortunate enough to get there just as the Pope arrived, practically without ceremony, to celebrate Mass at the Apostle's tomb.

They were quartered in the *Collegio di Propaganda*, which was founded by Urban VIII for the training of missionaries for service in non-Catholic countries. It was under the direction of the Company of

[1] W. Ward, Vol. I, p. 139. [2] *Ibid.*, p. 140.

Jesus. They had every reason to congratulate themselves on the kindness shown them by their hosts. Great care had been taken to assign them the most comfortable rooms. It was not expected that they would observe the strict rules of the house, and there was considerable surprise when it was learnt that they had no desire to be treated as a pair of pious tourists, but were anxious to attend the classes and to prepare themselves systematically for ordination.

The warmth of their reception, the politeness of the Italians, more easy, if less personal, than the cordiality of the French, the joy of finding themselves in Rome, and the deep satisfaction of living the Catholic life there—all this was not to prevent Newman from soon becoming conscious of a sense of profound disappointment.

On the 23rd November, Pius IX received them in audience. Newman, in coming to Rome, had been hoping, more than anything else, to give the Pope a plain, unvarnished account of the needs and possibilities, as he saw them, of the situation in England, perhaps, to indicate, in a more general way, the line that would have to be taken in order to counteract the incredulity of the day. Now that he was some distance away, he could see things more clearly than when he was in the thick of the fight, and was enabled to form a judgment as to the way the Christian Church, in its full Catholic plenitude, should be presented to the modern mind, if the modern mind was to be won over. Encouraged by Wiseman's enthusiastic attitude, what he desired above all things was to lay at the feet of the Sovereign Pontiff, as it were, his lifelong harvest of original research, an unrivalled store of religious experience, an influence of whose power and possibilities even he himself may not have been fully conscious. He was ready and eager to throw himself into any task that might be allotted to him. A revival of theological teaching was what Wiseman wished that task to be, though Newman thought this over-ambitious; or there was the preaching of an apologetic designed to cope with the circumstances of the day, or, again, a further exploration of the riches of patristic tradition, a subject that had been almost entirely neglected since the end of the eighteenth century—he was only waiting for the Pope to give the word, and he would do whatever he commanded and in whatever manner he commanded. This first interview, however, was disappointment number one. Not that the Pope was not kind; he was, indeed, most affable and truly paternal. Newman, however, was fatally handicapped by his lack of Italian and French, as well as by his constitutional shyness and his dislike of putting himself forward in any way. Like the worthy Ambrose St John, it was to these drawbacks that he put down the very superficial character of the interview. Doubtless these things had something to do with it, but the fact was that the Pope, while anxious to appear gracious and friendly, had evidently no notion of what Newman was trying to explain, and evinced but little interest in questions which to Newman were of urgent importance. He treated the two Englishmen like a couple of children and, having bestowed on St John a medal and on Newman a picture, sent them gently away.

True, he promised that he would see Newman again many times. Nor was that merely a piece of polite condescension; he meant what he said. But other preoccupations intervened, and he forgot all about it. Then, a few weeks later, a most untoward event occurred, something that gave him a totally false impression of Newman, but an impression he never completely got rid of. Early in December, a niece of Lady Shrewsbury's died suddenly, immediately after her arrival in Rome. Prince Borghese conceived the idea of getting Newman to preach at her funeral, which all the English society people in Rome would, of course, be sure to attend. What an admirable opportunity it would be for telling this herd of heretics that it was high time they were converted. It would have been difficult to imagine a proposal more utterly distasteful to Newman, or one in itself more impolitic. However, the Prince pressed his point with such insistence that Newman felt obliged to give way.

Pitchforked, willy-nilly, into a Roman pulpit while he was not as yet so much as a subdeacon, facing this array of Protestant aristocrats, Newman, with little relish for the task, preached his first Catholic sermon. St John and a few others, who caught echoes of some of the most touching of his sermons at St Mary's, were deeply moved. But the audience in general, little expecting such an address, saw in it nothing but a gratuitous insult, the preacher, himself, of course, coming in for a full measure of the odium his discourse had aroused.

Here, a very trying individual, an Englishman and a convert, and a Papal chamberlain, who was soon to become one of the Pope's chief confidants, makes his first appearance on the stage, and a very significant one it was to prove. We refer to Monsignor Talbot. At first, he praised the sermon up to the skies, and warmly congratulated the preacher. But when he came to realise which way the wind was blowing, and heard of the annoyance that the sermon had caused in the upper ranks of Roman society, some rumours of which had already reached the ears of the Pope, he swung round with all the alacrity of the accomplished courtier and promptly changed his tune, doing his best to get it fixed in the Holy Father's mind that Newman had displayed a lamentable want of tact. Having succeeded in that design, he proceeded to put it about as the idea of the Pope himself.

While Newman was thus becoming acquainted with some of the crooked ways of Court life, a still more formidable situation was soon to confront him.

The *Essay on Development* had been a success, from the material point of view, but it was not that, so much as the light it shed on the minds of his Protestant contemporaries, whether Conservatives, or Liberals who were smitten with the Higher Criticism—men like Stanley, for example—that confirmed him in the belief that the arguments he had set forth were well founded. At the same time, he was growing increasingly confident of the cogency of these general views on Faith and Reason which had gradually taken shape in his mind, and which were indeed the source from which the *Essay* itself had sprung. If he had anything to bring by way of offering to the Church, it was surely a presentation of the views by which he himself had been led into her fold, and many another with him. The more he devoted himself to the study of Catholic tradition, the Fathers, and the great Scholastics, the more convinced was he of the soundness of that chain of reasoning which had brought him at last to the One True Church. All that it needed to make it a suitable handbook for theologians teaching in the Church's name was to be corrected on a few points of detail. It was in order to get these corrections made and to secure authoritative approval of his work, as a whole, and then to get some definite mission assigned him, that he had come to Rome.

If he looked like being disappointed on this last-mentioned score, on the others he was to have such a shock as he had never even dreamt of. He had scarcely had a chance of getting into touch with the Roman theological teachers when some very disquieting news began to come in from America. Over there, a band of aggressive Unitarians had pounced on certain passages in Newman's book which, they averred, tended to show beyond all question that the process of development had been as operative in connection with the doctrine of the Trinity as it had been in respect of things which Protestants expressly condemned—the cult of the Virgin Mary, for example. This, they declared, was tantamount to an admission by Newman that the doctrine of the Trinity was not primitive. Nor did the matter end there. The

American ecclesiastical authorities, without troubling to read the book, let alone master it, issued a fierce denunciation of the work and its author. And so it happened that when, for the first time, Newman proceeded to bring up this question of Development with two professors of theology, one of them a Jesuit belonging to the Collegio Romano, he found them well enough disposed towards himself, personally, but invincibly hostile to his book. They knew nothing of it save what the American Catholics had given out about it, and all *they* knew was what the Boston Unitarians chose to deduce from it. However, the verdict had gone forth, and the verdict was final. Vainly did Newman protest and ask that he might be judged by what he had written, and by the whole of it. It was clear that neither his interlocutors nor any of their *confrères* had the smallest intention of reading a book written by an Anglican who was only half-converted when he wrote it. Besides, the matter had been settled, and that was all there was to be said about it. Why should they be bothered with this tiresome book?

Dalgairns had undertaken to translate various works of Newman's into French, and Newman now writes urging him to hurry on with the task, thinking that if they were cast into the customary language of the diplomats, people might condescend to read them. Meanwhile, the weeks slip by, and all he finds out is that the Roman professors, who carry on their activities within a stone's throw of him, are bringing him into their lectures. Still on the strength of those same American quotations, he was made to figure among those heresy-mongers, and fabricators of monstrous error whose works are systematically confuted and demolished. Nay, more than that, while all this was going on, Perrone, the most distinguished and most prominent theologian of the day, brought out a new edition of his lectures on dogma. Great was Newman's amazement to find himself quoted there, but in a sort of hotchpotch in which the *Essay on Development* was mentioned in the same breath with all the things he had said against Rome ten years before the book was written. So we come across such schoolbook sentences as, *Newman Romanum Pontificem vocat diabolum.* What added to the irony and absurdity of the situation, and made it all the more disheartening, was that Newman happened just then to be reading Perrone with considerable interest and finding in his views on Faith and Reason a great many ideas that squared with his own. What is more, in pressing for the definition of the Immaculate Conception, as a doctrine *de fide*, the learned Jesuit was himself giving a striking example of the Development theory in action.

But Newman and these theologians might have been living in two separate worlds. Linguistic difficulties no doubt had a good deal to do with these misunderstandings. Newman incurs much disapproval for making use of Butler's argument from Probability. But a translator could make no greater mistake than to confuse his idea of the certitude that derives from an accumulation of probabilities with the quite contrary notion that there is, and can be, no such thing as certitude in matters of religion.

All these things, however, may have seemed to him of secondary importance. What did make him open his eyes was what happened when he set out to show that renowned scholastic theologians, long before him, had laid down, on the latter point in particular, views essentially identical with those he was now expressing. Thus it was with Luzo, the outstanding representative of what is known as the Silver Age of Scholasticism. The neo-scholasticism of the hastily compiled manuals current in Rome since the schools had been reopened there knew nothing even of an authority so recent as that. Newman receives one shock after another. It is soon borne in upon him that so far from gaining credit with the teachers of the day by his references to St Thomas and Aristotle it was those very references that were mainly responsible for bringing him under suspicion. We must read what he said to Dalgairns in a letter dated the 22nd November. There we get a piping-hot account of a talk he had just been having on these matters with a Jesuit of Propaganda.

> It arose from our talking of the Greek studies of the Propaganda, and asking whether the youths learned Aristotle. "Oh no," he said, "Aristotle is in no favour here—no, not in Rome—nor St Thomas. I have read Aristotle and St Thomas and owe a great deal to them, but they are out of favour here and throughout Italy. St Thomas is a great saint—people don't care to speak against him; they profess to reverence him, but put him aside." I asked what philosophy they did adopt. He said, "*None*. Odds and ends—whatever seems to them best—like St Clement's Stromata. They have no philosophy. *Facts* are the great things, and nothing else. Exegesis, but not doctrine." He went on to say that many privately were sorry for this, many Jesuits, he said; but no one dared oppose the fashion. When I said I thought there was a latent power in Rome which would stop the evil, and that the Pope had introduced Aristotle and St Thomas into the Church, and the Pope was bound to maintain them, he shrugged his shoulders and said that the Pope could do nothing if people would not obey him, and that the Romans were a giddy people, not like the English.[1]

[1] W. Ward, Vol. I, p. 166.

In view of all that, it was abundantly evident that any idea of making such theologians as these understand the difficulties arising from a critical study of the Scriptures and of Tradition, and the consequent need for a philosophy of faith on the lines of the *Oxford University Sermons* and the *Essay on Development*, would have been the wildest of dreams. It was not only the solutions propounded by Newman that shocked them; the mere fact that he should ever have raised the questions which these solutions were supposed to satisfy, was in itself something quite beyond their comprehension.

And now here comes in Newman's marvellous—shall we call it, miraculous?—mental poise. Not for a moment did it occur to him to entertain any doubts about the Church he had joined; still less to rebel. For a moment, he had thought of raising the matter with the Pope, but that idea he had soon dismissed. He felt perfectly sure in his own mind that this state of affairs was purely transient, fortuitous, and in no sense permanent. The truths that Newman had acquired at so heavy a cost, the principles he had rediscovered or unearthed—these would of themselves prevail. Truth would win through in the long run.

Meanwhile, what it amounted to was that the school of theology which Wiseman had put into his head was clearly out of the question. And so he put aside, at any rate for the time being, all projects connected with the work that had so deeply engrossed him for the past few years. His one object now was to avoid any sort of sensational clash, to dispel obvious misapprehensions, to forestall serious misunderstandings, and, above all, to do nothing that would invite hasty condemnation. Such condemnation might attain other targets than himself, and be the means of keeping out of the Church many men of goodwill whose only fault would have been that they were aware, from their own experience, of problems which these easy-going theologians, shut up as they were in a little world of their own, had never so much as dreamt of. Therefore, however abundant the ideas within him, he would hold his peace. Before long he would be a priest, and in that capacity there would be plenty of tasks to keep him busy.

To get some idea of the simple-heartedness, as well as of the grandeur of this sacrifice, we must read another of his letters to Dalgairns. Newman, going through his *University Sermons*, in connection with a French translation that was being made of them, calmly, without the least trace of pique, or wounded pride, but with the utmost clarity of vision, again dwells on the gravity of the issues raised therein and on the manner in which he had dealt with them. Yet he decides, without a murmur, to put aside all consideration of them, since the hour for doing so is past, or else is not yet come.

> And now, after reading these Sermons, I must say I think they are as a whole the best things I have written, and I cannot believe that they are not Catholic, and will not be useful. Indeed, these are the times (I mean after reading them and the like) that feelings come upon me which do not often else, but then vividly—I mean the feeling that I have not yet been done justice to—but I must leave all this to Him who knows what to do with me. People do not know me—and sometimes they half pass me by. It has been the portion of Saints, even; and may well be my portion. He who gives gifts, is the best judge how to use His own. He has the sole right to do as He will, and He knows what He is doing. Yet sometimes it is marvellous to me how my life is going, and I have never been brought out prominently—and now I am likely less than ever—for there seems something of an iron form here, tho' I may be wrong; but I mean, people are at no trouble to deepen their views. It is natural.[1]

Together with the plans for a school of theology, the last vague ideas of joining the Order of St Dominic had flickered out. Lacordaire's Dominicans, according to what they told him in Italy, was an Order of its own; whereas the old, original Order was on the decline. However, he was told that the Florentine Dominicans were an exceptionally flourishing body. For a moment his interest revived as he visualised to himself a sound Thomist school, but he soon learnt that the "flourishing house at Florence" was a manufactory famous for its *eau de Cologne*.

On the other hand, one of the projects suggested by Wiseman in his voluble, but sometimes happily inspired, discourse, looked as if it might take practical shape, and that was the Oratory project. On the face of it, the idea of transporting St Philip, his work, his spiritual influence and aura from Rome to England, seemed rather like a jest, but, on reflection, now that the idea of a school of theology was fading out, it looked, after all, as if there might be something in it.

The Oratorians live in community, but they are not regulars. Their aim is to unite a deeply spiritual life with the performance of their sacerdotal duties; but they are bound by no vows. It is not so much a rule as a spirit which unites them. Bossuet has described all that in his incomparable way, and brought out all the positive element that lies hidden in these various negatives. "Their mind", he says, "is the mind of the Church herself. Her canons are their only rules. They have no superiors but her bishops, no bonds but her charity, no solemn vows

[1] W. Ward, Vol. I, p. 173.

but those of baptism and the priesthood. A saintly freedom is the bond which unites them, theirs is obedience without servitude, government without commands, authority melted into gentleness, respect without fear. Charity, which banishes fear, works a great miracle, and, imposing no yoke apart from her own spirit, she is able not only to take self-will captive, but to destroy it. That they may become true priests, they are led to the fountain-head of truth, to the Sacred Books, which are ever in their hands, that they may search unwearyingly the letter thereof through study, the spirit through prayer, the depth, by withdrawal from the world, the efficacy by practical works, the end through charity, in which all ends and aims are summed up."

What led Newman to turn his eyes in this direction, almost as soon as he arrived in Rome, was the similarity he saw in this ideal with what he had always conceived as the ideal of an Oxford college. Now, since it seemed to him to be his lot to develop and expand, as a Catholic, the truths that had come to him as an Anglican, truths which had led him to leave the Church of England, he considered that his work should continue on similar lines. For the sake of those who had been associated with him at Littlemore, and who wished to carry on community life with him in the Church; for the sake also of those who had been influenced by him, and whom he was loath to leave to themselves, it was important for him to avoid any unnecessary severance. He was now half-way through the normal span of life. To develop within the Church all those elements in his life which had led him to her fold was what seemed to him more and more to be the vocation he ought to follow. There were other influences, the sort of reactions usual in the case of neophytes, of which he had displayed some symptoms and which were to affect him in after years, and these told in an opposite direction, but true fidelity to the Light had nothing in common with such spectacular manifestations.

All these complex moods and ideas gradually crystallised into something clear and definite, as is evident from the letter he wrote to Dalgairns on the 31st December.

> We have seen the Chiesa Nuova and the Casa adjoining, with Theiner—who said Mass with and for us and communicated us in the small room where St Philip had his ecstasies. The "casa" is the most beautiful thing of the kind we have seen in Rome—rather too comfortable, i.e. fine galleries for walking in summer, splendid orange trees etc., etc. If I wished to follow my bent, I should join them (the Oratorians) if I joined any. They have a good library, and handsome sets of rooms apparently. It is like a college with hardly any rule. They keep their own property, and furnish their own rooms. It is

what Dr Wiseman actually wishes, and really I should not wonder, if at last I felt strongly inclined to it, for I must own I feel the notion of giving up property try my faith very much.

I have the greatest fear I am bamboozling myself when I talk of an order; and that, just as Anglicans talk of being Catholics but draw back when it comes to the point, so I, at my time of life, shall never feel able to give up property and take to new habits. Not that I should not do it, had I a *clear* call—but it is so difficult to know what a clear call is. I do not know enough of the rule of the different congregations to have any opinion yet—and again I do not think I could, religiously, do anything that Dr Wiseman disapproved. . . . But as much as this I think I do see—that I shall not be a Dominican. I shall be of a (so-called) lax school. Another great difficulty I have in thinking of a regular life, is my own previous history. When it comes upon me how late I am trying to serve the Church, the obvious answer is, Even Saints, such as St Augustine, St Ignatius, did not begin in earnest till a late age. "Yes, but I am much older than they." So then, I go on, to think and to trust that my past life may form a sort of *ἀφορμή* and a ground of future usefulness. Having lived so long in Oxford, my name and person are known to a very great many people I do not know—so are my books—and I may have begun a work which I am now to finish.[1]

Nevertheless, there were difficulties in the way. The Roman Oratory was modelled, as it were, on the pattern of a religious gathering, a meeting for prayer (the original Oratorio). It was far too specifically Italian to be transplanted, just as it was, into an Anglo-Saxon and Protestant country. Religious gatherings, where the members scourged themselves in public, and went about from church to church singing hymns or intoning compositions, partly sacred, partly secular—all this was the sort of thing that Newman and his Oxford companions would certainly fight shy of. All the same, it is worth noting that it was precisely this ultra-Italian character of the proceedings that took the fancy of some of the earlier recruits in England. But of that, more later. For the moment we may point out that an enthusiast such as Faber, looking at things from his point of view, may have been but little less justified in his attitude in these matters than Newman. What might horrify some people about all these exotic extravagances may have appeared in a very different light to others, within the Church, who may have thought they might quite properly seek sanctification in a "revival" on the Wesley pattern.

Be that as it may, contact with the Oratorians in Rome, and more particularly with that very original personage Theiner, soon made it clear to these English visitors that there was nothing rigid or stereotyped about St Philip and his school. If Oratorians can claim to be considered

[1] W. Ward, Vol. I, p. 169.

true followers of St Philip, one reason, and that the paramount reason, is that they refuse to be slaves to precedent or to be hampered by such traditional practices as have degenerated into mere routine.

This mention of the Roman saint leads us to draw attention to a matter of some little interest. It appears that the founder of the Oratory excited, first the interest, next the regard, and finally the love, of these his latter-day disciples. To start with, they liked the look of the building. Then, once they were inside it, they realised that their going thither was far more providential than they had at first imagined. If there was a Second Spring for Newman, now that he was a Catholic, he owed it, as we have said, to St Philip Neri. But that is to anticipate. Up to now it was no more than an instinctive attraction that was not yet fully conscious of itself. Veneration there was, but it was a veneration not altogether unmingled with surprise. On the 22nd January, in another letter to Dalgairns about the new project, he writes:

> If ever there was a Saint who set his face against humbug it was St Philip. Fancy his sending a smart spruce noble youth to a public house with an enormously large bottle and a piece of gold to buy a pen'orth of wine![1]

In his previous letter, written the week before, he alluded to something about the Oratory that especially appealed to him, in view of the circumstances in which he was placed, and that was that he might be able to go on with his own work, but quite privately and unobtrusively, and, as it were, on the margin of an ordinary ministry. Baronius had lived that sort of life, Theiner was apparently doing the same now, and that was the life he would choose for himself, seeing that the theological plan had had to go by the board. "I confess that, as far as I am concerned, *I* should prefer much a season given to active duties, before returning to my books."[2]

The Pope, on being told of the plan, expressed his warm approval. This attitude, which exceeded all his hopes, brought great comfort to Newman. However, the Pope's view of the matter was perfectly understandable. Nothing could be more typically Roman than the Oratory, however informal it might outwardly appear; and, notwithstanding this unconventional exterior, nothing more thoroughly *sui generis*, and, taking it on the whole, nothing less "intellectualist". Nothing, therefore, could have been better calculated to set his mind at rest than the proposal to form such a community of peaceable and harmless individuals. The idea was patently providential. Here, this

[1] W. Ward, Vol. I, p. 179. [2] *Ibid.*, pp. 176–177.

Englishman, who was something of a puzzle, a dreamer not easy to handle, who might become dangerous away from the atmosphere of collegiate life, would find himself amid surroundings ideally conducive to quietude of spirit. Even if he did nothing useful, he would at least be quite tranquil-minded, and have no occasion to go stirring up trouble. Pius IX's benevolence was by no means assumed, it supplied so perfect a cure for the anxieties he had been undergoing as Sovereign Pontiff, that he was only too glad to seize on such an eminently convenient solution of the problem. Delighted, too, that the plan should have suggested itself spontaneously, the Pope did everything he could think of to hasten its fulfilment.

St John, in one of his letters, alludes to the promptness of the Pope's reaction to the proposal. Hardly were the words out of Monsignor Brunelli's mouth than the Pope exclaimed, "Tell them to write off at once to their friends and arrange for them to come as soon as possible after Easter." The Pope, of his own accord, undertook that their noviciate should be a brief one (it was to last no more than three months), promised then a *bellissimo sito* for their quarters, a novice master specially suited to the post. At the same time, consideration would be given to the modifications necessary to adapt an Order so specifically Roman in character to make it suitable for a country like England. These would be set forth in the brief. For the *bel sito*, the Pope thought first of the old Oratorian house in Malta, but as the Bishop there did not appear very enthusiastic about the idea, he resolved to allot them a wing of the Bernardine monastery at Santa Croce. The novice master selected was Father Rossi, a Roman Oratorian, who was not only a very saintly man, but a very sociable one.

And so their lot was cast. A few days after his admission to the priesthood, Newman quitted Propaganda. Accompanied, not only by Ambrose St John, but by Dalgairns, fresh from France, as well as by Bowles, Stanton, Coffin, and Perry, who had just come from England, he took up his quarters beneath the shadow of Santa Croce in Gerusalemme, there to undergo, with his companions, initiation into the Order of St Philip.

While preparing for his ordination, and in the course of this noviciate, Newman committed to writing some notes regarding the self-analysis to which he had subjected himself, notes that throw an almost unbearably pitiless light on the workings of his inmost conscience. Still more valuable, perhaps, than the record of his illness in Sicily, this document, hitherto unpublished, must now be quoted in its entirety.

Never did Newman give us, or turn upon himself, a more revealing flashlight of his state of mind, at this, or at any other crisis in his career.

Psychologists like Jung and his school who have made the middle-age climacteric their special study, could not wish for a more revealing document. The conjunction in one and the same person of such a delicate sensibility and such exceptional powers of intellect, gives this piece of voluntary conscience-probing an illuminating power which no analyses of the sub-conscious through the medium of dreams have ever surpassed, and few have equalled. Never was the peril of apathy, of intellectual and spiritual sclerosis, speciously disguised as firmness and stability, discerned with insight more acute.

The fabric which he had built up in his earlier years had come tumbling down about his ears. He had had to tear up his roots at the very time when, in the ordinary way, men are thinking about planting them more firmly in the soil. All this, no doubt, prompted him to cling to his freedom. Yet it was precisely this insistent determination to retain his freedom that brought about these catastrophes, these salutary catastrophes. But what a premature drain on his sensibility, on the springs of affection, these catastrophes entailed! How great, therefore, was his consciousness of the opposite danger, the danger of relapsing into a state of torpor and inertia, of wrapping himself up in a cloak of indifference, of falling back on the selfish "What's the good?", which suffers itself to drift without aim or purpose.

And this, perhaps, is the point on which special emphasis should be laid. The piercing ray which Newman directs upon himself is his accuser, and an accuser such as no devil's advocate could have rivalled. But, then, that same piercing ray is the only physician with power to heal the wounds that it inflicts. How easily here such a spiritual experience as this overtakes and outstrips the results of modern psychology. In that calm and unwavering insistence on the truth by which Newman is actuated, and which he directs upon himself, lies his solace and his peace. It is its own cure. Suffering no hidden evil to lurk in the recesses of his being, he lances it calmly and with terrifying resolution, and cures it as by a miracle, or rather proclaims it triumphantly downtrodden. He who has the will and the courage to bring such a light to bear upon his conscience puts all his weaknesses to rout. Only to the Saints is it granted thus to bring the detecting ray to bear on all their soul's distress, all their sins and failings; but the very fact that they behold them so clearly is a sign that they have already got the better of them.

We shall carefully analyse this document, paragraph by paragraph, yet, having done so, we shall not presume to say that we have extracted all its riches. The original, which consists of notes set down during a retreat at St Eusebio, from the 8th to the 17th April, is written, not in English but in Latin.

> I have got in my mind a sort of wound or canker which prevents me from being a good Oratorian. Impossible to describe it in a few words for it is a complicated thing. I am in a state that enables me to do what I have to do satisfactorily along a fixed line, but I can't rise above it. I can crawl along on the ground, or, if you like, I can run, but I have not got it in me to rise any higher.

That opening paragraph brings out more clearly than ever Bremond contrived to do, what he thought might be regarded as a complete lack of mysticism. We shall not here discuss the aptness of that interpretation. We shall content ourselves with noting what we are told about a particular psychological state, and allow the sequel to tell its own story.

Be it noted, however, that Newman is troubled at this state of mind. In plain language, we see from his opening words that he considers it to be out of key with the Oratorian ideal. We understand what he feels. In St Philip we see a joyful, and so to speak inspired, alacrity in the service and, still more, in the love of God. That is an impression perceptible to the senses, but there is something deeper than that, something beyond the reach of sensibility, and that is a harmony with God's Will so deep that it seems to anticipate His mandates.

As for a religion of sentiment, of the Methodist type, we know how Newman regarded that; how he mistrusted it. What we are about to read will show us—indeed, we had already divined it—that Newman does not condemn a religion of the heart, of the emotions, as such, provided we do not stop there. On the contrary, one would say that what he is complaining of at the moment regarding himself is that he lacks even a touch of that sensibility without which the soul's spontaneity might seem to be in doubt. But we must look into this state of mind more closely before we ask ourselves whether it was innate or not, and how, if it was not innate, it came into being.

> As far as I can tell, I have no worldly ambitions; I don't hanker after wealth, power or a great name. On the other hand I don't like poverty, or worries, straightened circumstances or difficulties. I dread ill-health as one who knows what it is to be ill. I like to live with a certain measure of comfort, and that is one of my temptations. Nevertheless, I hope if God so ordained I should give up all I have without any great difficulty.

I don't like a rigid rule of life, although for eighteen years I have wanted to live on more or less regular lines. I am fond of tranquillity, security, living among friends, with my books, with no worries, in short an Epicurean sort of existence. That has always been my state of mind, and the passing years have but increased it.

Is not that which Newman here condemns in himself precisely that which forms the burden of nearly all his sermons at St Mary's? The very thing that lends them the definitely ascetic other-worldliness to which we have drawn attention? This sort of second-grade morality, this substituting for the spiritual life the typically Victorian determination to make the best of both worlds, was a temptation to which his humanism made him only too keenly alive. He was always acutely conscious of the danger to true religion that lay in such spiritual anchylosis, in spite of the specious veil of "respectability" which disguised it. But he does not delude himself with the idea that he has banished the danger once for all by virtue of the heroic sacrifice he has resolved to make.

Although it has always been my unfailing habit to refer all things to the will of God, and although I try to fulfil that will and observe this rule in all my principal deeds, I do not do so in matters of minor importance. And even in important matters, although I have earnestly prayed to know His will, what I have done has been the result of a sort of conscientiousness, a sense of what becomes me and of what I owe to myself so that my actions have proceeded rather from a feeling of self-respect than from the promptings of faith and charity.

Now, another probe of the scalpel and we are in a very different region. This time, what Newman refers to in his own spiritual make-up is what he was one day to describe with apparent approval in his portrayal of the "gentleman". In that word is conveyed the high standard of honour a man ought to set himself, the standard which Pericles praises the Athenians for adopting as their rule of life. Newman goes the length of saying that in a society acquainted with Christianity, self-respect seems to enable a man to perform Christian actions more worthily than Christians themselves, inasmuch as he performs them without regard to the praise or blame of any external judge. But, he adds, such a view of the matter is wholly misleading, since it is an essential property of the supernatural to take us out of ourselves, out of our self-complacency, and to merge us in the Divine. Whoso remains wrapped up in himself, were he to do all that charity demands of him, would possess no more than the shadow thereof.

> The growing years have also had this effect upon me that the vigour and vitality of mind which once I had I now have no longer. Just as the limbs of the body grow stiff, so my mind now lacks the youthful agility and versatility it once possessed. I am slow and unwilling now to address myself to good works, which causes me no little uneasiness now that I am a Catholic. In fact the Church's most hallowed customs, its sacred functions, works necessary for the gaining of indulgences, attending expositions of the Blessed Sacrament itself disturb my mind as though I were someone engaged in things to which he was unaccustomed. I love the Mass, visits to the Blessed Sacrament, the Litanies, the Breviary, but when I am called upon to do a number of things and they quite little such as prayers for obtaining an indulgence, or in fulfilment of a promise, or following a Novena—all these things tax my memory, burden my mind, distract and almost terrify me; and this the more so perhaps because I am usually liable to scruples; to give a timely example, I am very much afraid of making "resolutions".

This last passage is, one must admit, moving, because of the almost childlike simplicity it betrays; it is also not without its comical side. It would be hard to say how far Newman was conscious of this when he wrote it; but it would be harder still to suppose that he was not conscious of it at all. Be that as it may, what he had in mind was doubtless that liking of his for going along on an even keel, his dislike of being irked, or put out in any way. Of this he now became newly and keenly aware, not an uncommon occurrence in a man at his time of life. The curious thing is that these scruples are aroused in connection with Catholic practices which are, as he indicates, completely new to him, but which are also of secondary importance. The simplicity of the convert anxious to regard with equal reverence everything that is offered for his acceptance, is, though not always attended by success, at all events laudable. What he describes as an instinctive inclination was not for indolence, though indolence might accompany it. It was an instinct for what is real, for what is essential, an instinct which, in the case of Newman, expressed itself in an ever-growing opposition to the wholesale Italianising practices of some of his associates.

> In almost all things I like to follow my own bent. I don't like changing my surroundings or my work or busying myself with someone else's affairs, or going for a walk, or making a journey, or paying visits, when I would rather stay at home. Little things worry me and get on my mind. I am irritable and shy, lazy and suspicious; I trail along on the ground, dispirited, downcast, despondent.
>
> What is more, I have no longer the practical, lively and actual faith against the continual working of the evil spirit in my heart which I ought to have.

There we have a sort of reflection, or after-glow, of an element in Newman's personality which was noticeable from his earliest youth upwards, and that was his independence of spirit. He was now well into his forties, and that independence of his was further accentuated by a dislike of any changes in his customary mode of existence, a dislike natural enough in a man of his years. He shunned being taken out of his shell, so to speak, any break in his customary way of life. He was a man of extraordinary sensitivity, unquiet, and almost always prone to melancholy. As is usual with such people, when their feelings are repeatedly wounded, as his had been, by discouraging experiences, he was inclined to withdraw into himself. When a man has suffered so much that any new contact merely holds out the prospect of some further unwelcome experience, small wonder if he is tempted to keep to himself and to avoid striking out on any new line.

We should be doing a twofold injustice to Newman if we blamed him for what he here blames himself. No one can be held responsible for his own constitution; still less so for the slings and arrows that may assail him in life, and their inevitable psychological effects on his own particular nervous system. Sanctity is not a matter of having no nerves at all, or of avoiding anything calculated to jar them. But when the trial does come, sanctity will be revealed in the judgment a man passes on his instinctive reactions, and in the fullness of spirit with which he masters them. Under these two heads, we do not see what more could be demanded of Newman. The pain brought upon him by this necessary struggle against a temperament, and in circumstances peculiarly unfavourable, far from lowering him in our esteem, does but give us the measure of his worth.

That such an inward state of mind constitutes a lasting danger to religious faith, that it is one of the most effective weapons in the Devil's armoury, is, as he admits, beyond all question. Newman's glory, in the eyes of God, is that, fully aware as he was of the temptation, he fought so strenuously against it. Yet again we may detect, as we come to the inmost core of this confession, a feeling which never left him, a sense as of some demoniac presence which conceals itself from us in our wanderings, the better to lure us from the presence of God.

In my youth and early manhood, I put my hope and trust in God, I mean I trusted securely in His wisdom, and had the utmost faith in the efficacy of prayer, always telling myself in times of trouble to be easy in my mind for He would deliver me in His own good time. I gave encouragement to others and I was lively and cheerful—and I often experienced things which as I thought, and thought rightly as I believe, that the God of Mercy had heard my prayers. But when I came to apply my intellect to sacred things, to read and to write these twenty years or more ago, though what I wrote was on

> the whole true and useful, then it was that to begin with I lost the natural and spontaneous character of my faith so that now I greatly fear the sacred office dreading lest I should fail to comport myself with due reverence in regard to the most holy things. Then also I lost my simple faith in the word of God. Cheerfulness and gentleness I had not lost, so far. Among my friends and people in general, I was cheerful and lively, but little by little my former trust in God's immense charity towards me and in the efficacy of prayer faded away. Not indeed that I lost my inward sense of the Divine Presence everywhere, nor a good conscience and the peace of mind that flows therefrom, but I looked no more, or a great deal less than formerly, on the habit of prayer as a great gift and privilege whereby all became possible but rather a a duty to be got through. That subtle and delicate vigour of faith and hope has remained dimmed and weakened in me till this very day.

The opening statement of that passage is plainly incontestable and should be borne carefully in mind. There had been a time—and this is amply confirmed by what we know of Newman's early Oxford days—there had been a time when his spiritual nature radiated and blossomed freely, spontaneously. He had enjoyed, before all those trials from within and without came to bear so heavily upon him, a period of happiness and light which he diffused among all his companions. Religious faith and notably a lively trust in Providence, his guide, inspired him in prayer and supported him in action. In this stirring of the soul's depths the divine presence answering his prayers may have seemed as real to him as it is to the believer who discerns it with the eye of faith.

It is remarkable that Newman saw the primary cause of the change, not in his earlier trials, but in the systematic elaboration of a religious theory. A great many things have been said by various people about Newman's holding the intellect in small esteem. It would, however, be wholly erroneous to suppose that he mistrusted the conclusions arrived at by the intellect when operating in its proper sphere. Newman, indeed, is mistrustful of the intellect when it sets itself up in opposition to Grace, but he is firmly convinced of its ability to reach the truth so long as it observes, in whatever domain it operates, the laws which that domain imposes. Far from being in that sense an anti-intellectualist, he has as much respect for the intellect as any loyal disciple of Aristotle who had drawn his science from the fountain-head could possibly have had. What he condemns is not the intellect in general, but the intellect attempting to apply the rationalising process to matters of faith. It was not so much that he doubted the soundness of its conclusions, as that he saw something relatively inferior in the spirituality of a man who put himself on that level in considering matters of faith, as compared with one whose faith is displayed in religious contemplation and finds its expression in the exercise of charity.

In the latter case faith itself permeates the understanding; in the former, there is always the danger that the intellect, claiming, as of right, to treat of things supernatural, should obscure their deepest spiritual significance. On this, Newman, in his *Apologia*, emphatically insists. Quoting the words of St Ambrose, he says, *Non in dialectica complacuit Deo salvum facere populum suum.* The soul whose logic is derived from faith, from faith which expresses itself in adoration and humility, is necessarily opposed, in the sphere of faith and morals, to the critical faculty which would presume to judge instead of itself being judged.

Though the joyful serenity of spirit which blossomed forth so freely in the light of God's presence was not affected, the immediate, instinctive response of trust and gratitude, which was the token of that serenity, was sensibly diminished. Thus prayer, in these conditions, assumed the character of a duty, a self-imposed task. It was no longer the native climate of the soul. And thus faith and hope, though in their essence as strong as ever, lost something of their former plenitude of manifestation and expression. This lack was to make itself cruelly felt in the troubles and trials that lay ahead. Be it noted, however, that his sense of the divine presence never wavered. Nothing marred his inward peace. But now this place of peace was the soul's last stronghold, its final refuge. It was no longer a beacon sending forth its rays to illumine all around.

> What is more, for some years I fell into something like despair and into a dark and gloomy state of mind. This is not to say that I could not inwardly exclaim with all my heart *Deus meus et omnia*, for these words were constantly in my heart, but I had many things to weigh me down. In many ways I had given up hope. In the Anglican Church I had a number of detractors; I was the target for countless calumnies; what I was trying to do for the good of that Church was interpreted to my detriment by almost all who wielded authority in that body. I found myself in exile, in which I lived for some years with a few friends, and even here I was not free from people who pursued me and hunted me down out of curiosity. I hope and believe I was not angered, or indignant or anything of that sort at this sort of thing, for I am not very sensitive in such matters, but I was depressed and lost heart. And now that cheerfulness which once was mine, I have no longer. And I feel very keenly that I am not a young man, and I look back sadly on the years gone by, and it seems to me that I am no good for anything any more; just a useless log.

It only needed that passage to make us realise how grievously the long and trying time on which Newman entered as the summer of

1838 began, told, not only on his feelings, but on his physical strength. Cast aside by those to whom he came bearing all that he had found most precious in his quest for the Way, the Truth, and the Life; and even as he came bringing his offering, vilified and calumniated. Hounded down in the retreat to which he had betaken himself to seek the truth—truth that seemed as if it would always elude his grasp—we should never have known, but for this written record of his thoughts, how deep was the pain that the uncomprehending judgment of his fellows, the scornful rejection of the richest part of all his labours, inflicted on his spirit. Even the letter to Jemima does not reveal as do these notes, intended for God and himself alone, the anguish which a a soul like his can suffer at the frustration of its dearest hopes. Faith, Hope, in their supernatural aspect, may have emerged triumphantly from these trials, more shining than before; but their outward radiance was dimmed and chilled, perhaps for ever. For temperaments like his, sacrifices such as those he had had to make, though they may increase a man's spiritual stature, leave behind them scars which time is powerless to efface. There are injuries that nothing can repair. It is not (how could we doubt the truth of what he says in terms so simple and unadorned?) that he ever rebelled. But, wounded, as he had been, in some of the tenderest fibres of his being, he did lose beyond all question some of that spontaneity, that radiance, which mark the springtime of mind and spirit. His faith is deeper and purer than ever, but that depth, that purity, are acquired at the cost of his passing once for all into the autumn of the heart.

But is that the whole of the story? Could things be really so? After his entry into the City of Peace, might there not have been a revival of that eagerness of the heart which the cruellest of all the trials he had endured did not avail to subdue? So we are inclined to think, and to ask, whether a man who had lately told, and was soon to tell again, the incomparable joy he had found in his new life could really have considered himself to be, as he put it, a *lignum inutile*, a useless log.

Must we not take it that the strange recrudescence in the true Church of the trials and rebuffs that had fallen to his lot in the one he had quitted, had again reopened the closed wound? As always, the things that touch him most deeply reveal their full significance only after some time has elapsed. A few years later on, when his trials, far from being over, had reached an almost agonising limit, the *Journal* gave what we cannot doubt is the true and final answer to that question.

> Then, when I became a Catholic, I lost a number of friends, as I had previously many others and those most dear, by death. Moreover, when I was living in my place of retreat with a few others, seeking a way of life, we had been accustomed to observe certain rules proper to Catholics, fasting, meditations, spiritual exercises, the use of the Breviary and other observances of ecclesiastical or rather monastic life. And now I am undergoing what is called reaction and have no longer the zest in doing those things, which I had in plenty in the Church of England.

If what he had had to endure had hurried on a state of mind that is common to middle age, it left him, as it were, defenceless against the strokes of a mysterious providence. Natural separations dealt the final blow to what the most crushing sacrifices had already stricken to the quick. Meanwhile, the one-time novelty of spiritual treasures, gradually revealed, no longer availed to console him for the unbearable pain inflicted by these losses.

> Furthermore, and this is difficult to explain and surprises even myself, but I have this peculiarity that in the stirring of my affections whether sacred or human my physical energies seem unable to go beyond certain limits. In the contemplation of things divine I am always growing languid, like one walking with his feet tied together. It is as if a chair had been thrown over me so that I can no longer show vehemence in preaching or speaking, or fervour in meditation or prayer, as if this resulted from some physical law.
>
> And this in addition. I can never fix and concentrate my mind on the subject proposed for meditation, or on the words of the daily office. My mind strays away continually and my head seems racked if I try to concentrate my whole mind on one single matter.

It is the humbleness of spirit of that last confession that moves us to pause in the first place; yet, read in conjunction with what precedes, we are here surely at the very heart of things. Here perhaps we are at the very source and origin of the gravest of Bremond's errors. Trials, it is true, in a way only reveal congenital weaknesses. Are we, therefore, to take it that Newman, from the outset, was lacking to some extent in real generosity? Does it mean, in other words, that the word "heart", which falls so often from our pen, is not really the appropriate term to employ—for an extreme sensitivity can quite well accompany a considerable aridity of heart? Is that what Newman is avowing here? Not in the very least. On the contrary, it is in the very fact that the range of his emotions seems to him so narrowly confined that we may gauge the greatness of a love that mourns its inability to expand to its full measure in a delicate organism worn out by too rude a trial. It needs a heart of uncommon fervour to bewail its lack of feeling, which, in Newman's case, means that it suffers because it cannot suffer enough.

XVI

THE ORATORY IN ENGLAND: EARLY DAYS

CONCERNING his ordination, Newman left only a few brief notes:

> 22nd May, 1847. St John and I went for examination to the Vicariate. Began saying office.
>
> Ember Wednesday. Ordained (St John and I) subdeacon by Cardinal Fransoni in his private chapel—five others present.
>
> 29th May. St John and I ordained Deacons in St John Lateran.
>
> Trinity Sunday. Ordained (St John and I) priests by Cardinal Fransoni.
>
> 3rd June, 1847. Corpus Christi. My first mass in the small Jesuits' chapel. Clifford serving. St John's first mass the Community mass when he communicated the whole College and they kissed his hand. Went for the procession to St Peter's.

Apart from the fact that Newman after his ordination let some days go by before celebrating Mass—that being in accordance with the traditional practice of the great spiritual leaders of the seventeenth century, and those the least suspected of Jansenism, such as Père Condren, for example—we must here draw attention to a certain scruple by which he was visited when the time was drawing near for him to receive major Orders, and he spoke of it to the prelate who was about to ordain him. No formal ruling had so far been promulgated regarding the matter of Anglican Orders. For his own part, Newman was disposed to look on them as valid. The Cardinal replied that he had a very strong feeling that Newman and his friends were priests already and that he had consequently decided that he would ordain them *sub conditione:* and that was what he did.

Nothing is recorded of the few months devoted to the noviciate, which began almost immediately afterwards amid the beautiful surroundings of the Cistercian monastery at Santa Croce. Does that imply that they were happy? A note made in the *Journal* in 1863 seems to point to some sort of disenchantment:

> And then how dreary (after the happy months, thank God, at Propaganda), how dreary Fr Rossi and Sta Croce, 1847.

We are somewhat at a loss as to how to interpret that remark, which is echoed nowhere else. It looks as if Padre Rossi had something to do with it. We may take it that he had not the faintest idea of the sort of life these men, whom he was supposed to be training, would be called upon to lead when they were back in England. Perhaps he was just as hazy as to what sort of men they actually were in themselves. Maybe, too, Newman was now beginning to realise all the deficiencies that would have to be made good if this first community was to succeed in England. About all this, we must needs remain in doubt.

At the end of July, Wiseman, when passing through Rome, went out to Santa Croce. Newman had high expectations of this meeting, and hoped it would result in their coming to some understanding with the Cardinal regarding their future work. Unhappily, Wiseman had to curtail his visit and hurry away to England, and all they were able to accomplish was the drafting of the brief for setting up the English Oratory. This was submitted to the Holy See on the 4th August, and on the 9th the novices were honoured with a visit from the Pope himself. Two days later, Newman, writing to Henry Wilberforce, said,

> "Lead Thou me on" is quite as appropriate to my state as ever, for what I shall be called to do when I get back, or how I shall be used, is quite a mystery to me.[1]

The last few days of August and the beginning of September were spent in a visit to the Oratory at Naples. While there, they took the opportunity of making a pilgrimage to the reputed tomb of Virgil. They also went to Amalfi and Pompeii. On their way back, they took in Monte Cassino, the famous Benedictine abbey, which must have often been visited by St Philip.

The close of the year witnessed the ordination of those members of the group who were not already priests. Newman, meanwhile, devoted his leisure, which seems to have been pretty ample, to the composition of a novel dealing with Oxford life, which he called *Loss and Gain*. Such an occupation strikes one as a little odd in the case of a man like Newman, and not less so as a means of filling up the leisure moments of a noviciate. The idea had occurred to Newman as a means of helping an Anglican publisher, James Burns, who had become a convert to Catholicism, to get, financially speaking, on his feet again. The story has little but a documentary interest. It gives one a good idea of student life in Oxford during the later phases of the Tractarian

[1] W. Ward, Vol. I, p. 188.

Movement. To look on it as in any sense autobiographical would be a great mistake, although a recent translator has gone out of his way so to describe it. That is not to say that there are not, here and there, some references that have the unmistakable flavour of personal reminiscence.

On 3rd December, Newman, accompanied by Francis Knox, a new novice, and by Ambrose St John, went to take leave of the Holy Father at the Quirinal. On the 6th, he and St John set out for home, travelling by way of Loreto and Innsbruck, where they were warmly welcomed by Döllinger. Embarking at Ostend on the 23rd they duly arrived at Dover and were back in London by Christmas Eve. On New Year's Day, Newman said his first Mass at Maryvale.

Speaking of this pilgrimage of his to Loreto, and recalling how he had dedicated his new home to the Virgin, Newman, in a letter written to Henry Wilberforce on the 12th January, says:

> We went there [to Loreto] to get the Blessed Virgin's blessing on us. I have ever been under her shadow, if I may say it. My College was St Mary's and my Church; and when I went to Littlemore, there, by my own previous disposition, our Blessed Lady was waiting for me. Nor did she do nothing for me in that low habitation, of which I always think with pleasure.[1]

This fragrant effluence of devotion to Our Lady enables us to realise how trusting, how warmly radiating was the atmosphere of piety which had compassed Newman about since his conversion, and which waxed insensibly greater day by day. Nor must we forget the inward peace and joy which grew ever deeper and deeper within him, even when that part of the mind which is called on to deal with mundane affairs was unceasingly harassed by disquiet and anxiety.

There is no denying that, if the Roman noviciate had not been without its shadows, its apprehensions, the early stages of the English Oratory were, in still greater measure, attended by disappointments for its founder. Hardly had he got back to Birmingham with the brief authorising its establishment, when a most grievous set-back occurred. Wiseman took his departure for London—and for good. In spite of his slap-dash style, his rather frothy enthusiasms, he had been not only the most understanding, but also the most helpful and encouraging of all the Catholic prelates Newman had had to deal with. As we have seen, it had never entered into Newman's scheme of things to commit either himself or his associates to any sort of undertaking unless under Wiseman's auspices. That, in fact, was Newman's sole reason for

[1] W. Ward, Vol. I, p. 158.

coming to Birmingham at all, And now, just when things were beginning, and only beginning, to get into working order, this invaluable patron and ally was transferred elsewhere, and the terms of the brief did not allow Newman to follow him.

Nevertheless, the Oratory was canonically instituted on the 2nd February, the Feast of the Purification and of the Presentation in the Temple of the Infant Jesus. Besides Newman, the original community consisted of St John, Dalgairns, Perry, Stanton, Coffin, Knox the novice, and three lay brothers. The brothers Gordon, Philip and Joseph joined them almost immediately afterwards.

To begin with, Newman's time was wholly taken up with getting things into running order. On the 9th March he wrote:

> We are very busy, as you may think. I, as Superior, as Novice-Master, as Lecturer in theology, have enough to do—besides chance matters and going to Birmingham. We have, I believe, 18 priests in fact or *potentialiter*.[1]

The numbers of the community were notably increased by the addition of another group, the community that Frederick William Faber had gathered around him, and who were known as the Wilfridians. The recollections set down in the *Journal* make it very clear how galling he found this unlooked-for development, and that from the very beginning. After the enigmatic note about Santa Croce, we read:

> And then when I came home, at once Faber was upon me, to bully me, to humbug me, and make use of me.

However, no sooner had Faber placed himself, with his associates, under Newman's authority than we find him writing in this strain. The date is the 17th February.

> Since my admission it seems to me that I am no longer bound to anything unless it be to obedience; I could dance and sing the whole day long I am so merry.[2]

It might almost look, at any rate to begin with, as if Newman shared in this enthusiastic state of mind, seeing that, less than six months later, he appointed Faber to the important post of Novice-Master.

The fact of the matter is that, within the Church—indeed, within the Congregation itself—a divergence of views—we might almost say a rift—was developing, similar to the split we have already noted between the younger and the older groups in the Tractarian Move-

[1] W. Ward, Vol. I, p. 201. [2] *Life and Letters of W. Faber*, p. 337

ment. Faithful to the train of ideas which had led him from Anglicanism to Rome, Newman then, as always, beheld in Catholicism nothing more and nothing less than the prolongation into our own times of the Church of the New Testament and of the Fathers. The very aim and purpose of the *Essay on Development* had been to demonstrate how this continuity, this identity, had been preserved unbroken despite all seeming changes. But, as we have already pointed out, there arose before very long, even among the so-called Anglo-Catholics, a party of young enthusiasts whose admiration for contemporary Catholicism seemed to concentrate on whatever was newest and least easy to reconcile with ancient tradition. Such people as these, put on their mettle by the encroachments of rationalistic scepticism, evinced an almost frenzied admiration for the authoritarian, we might call it the autocratic, tone adopted by the post-Tridentine Church in regard to Protestant heresy. Now that they had become Catholics, what they hoped for (and they were soon directing all their efforts to that end) was that the Church should take up the position of an absolute monarchy and interpose her *fiat*, not as a sovereign merely, but as a dictator, and that, in every sphere, not excluding the remotest fields of human activity. Children of the Romantic era, they were greatly attracted by the sensuous, the sentimental, elements in certain modern forms of public worship, whereas the older, more traditional usages of the Church, which they thought bore too close a resemblance to the now despised Anglicanism, failed to move them. The liturgy did, indeed, please them, but they must have it presented in a ceremonial full of pomp and circumstance and rich in ornament and colour. In dogma they took no interest unless it were conveyed in coloured picture-book style, caring little how they grated on people surfeited beyond all limits by the fanciful knights and troubadours, concoctions of which the works of Faber offered such a constant succession of disconcerting examples.

Faber, a warm-hearted individual, but something of a dreamer, and a rather fantastic one at that, had fallen in love with a brand of Catholicism that was not merely Italian, but super-Italian. When he entered the Church, he made a vow, and blithely he fulfilled it, to manifest as clearly as he possibly could what he considered to be the essence of Catholicism as contrasted with Protestantism. This, however, often enough turned out to be not its essence, but its most modern outward adornment. It was concerned almost wholly with externals. He and his friends came, with due humility of spirit, to place themselves under

Newman's direction, but soon, with the guileless impetuosity of children, and rather spoilt children you might sometimes think, they began to wheedle, to urge, and finally almost to force him to adopt their ideas about anything and everything.

Dazed and bewildered by their exuberance, yet compelled in spite of himself to admire their youthful outspokenness and enthusiasm—and that, be it noted, just when he was beginning to feel vaguely disturbed about himself and about his mission, his work—Newman allowed himself to be swept off his feet by these *giovani* as he came to call them.

They succeeded—Faber with his glowing and expansive temperament carried the position almost at once—not only in influencing Newman, but in putting him on a wrong track. Little as the idea appealed to him, Newman thought it his duty to fall into step, to take his tone from them, and to hold up the Anglican system to scorn and ridicule, and, at the same time, to refer to the hereditary English Catholics with lofty disdain, calling them timorous and half-hearted. So, during the closing weeks of 1848, we are treated to the astonishing spectacle of Newman doing his best to assume a tone of provocative persiflage and lofty rapture, and not doing it quite as to the manner born. It was then that he wrote some things which we might be tempted to look upon as the one and only blemish on a life, and a life's work, of such sincere and genuine simplicity, did we not realise that he was but striving, unhappily but heroically, to substitute for his own ideas, the ideas of men whom he held to be better and saintlier than himself. This accounts for his defending, in opposition to the old Catholics, the really quite indefensible *Lives of the Saints*, which Faber had begun. It accounts, too, for his references, almost cruel in tone, to the collected edition of Keble's religious poems which had then newly appeared.

The first of these matters brought him into collision with the new Vicar-Apostolic, Wiseman's successor at Birmingham, Dr Ullathorne, a Benedictine and one-time missionary. Neither of them had any idea that this not very promising beginning was the prelude to long years of mutual regard and, for Newman, to the closest and most enduring friendship of all those he was destined to enjoy with the members of the English Hierarchy. It is painful to note, in regard to the matter at issue between them, the contrast between the clear and profound understanding, the delicacy and charity so conspicuous in Ullathorne's letters, and the superior tone which Newman, egged on by Faber, adopted, if not in his answers to those letters, at all events in his references to them. Very soon, however, Newman came to recognise to which side the truly saintly and Catholic spirit really belonged, to recognise that the wise and conciliatory Bishop had a better title to it than the young man whose ardour was perhaps almost equalled by his presumption.

With regard to Keble, it was a different matter. Greatly disturbed by Newman's conversion, and all the others that had followed, unable, for his own part, to cut himself adrift from Anglicanism and from all the memories of his beloved ones it would always retain for him, Keble had sought refuge in a consolation with which Newman, too, had for a time beguiled himself. Were there not, he asked himself, within the Anglican fold, souls as saintly as any that one could conceive or hope for? Why, then, seek elsewhere for what they there had found? And how could he bring himself to forsake them? To all such beguiling pleadings of the heart, Newman, we may remember, had found himself compelled to answer that what others might hold in good faith could in no way govern our own beliefs and actions, and the fact that God had not withheld His grace from some who had not been able to read His will, in no way dispensed those to whom it had been made clear, from obeying it.

When poor Keble brought out his *Lyra Innocentium*, which contained the finest and most moving of his poems, he thought, by strengthening others, to strengthen himself, by means of these fallacious pleadings of the heart. It is perfectly understandable, therefore, that his friend of former days, did not hesitate to answer the subtleties of this saintly but timid soul with a bold statement of the truth, and what the truth demanded. What is not so easy to understand is how, if he had listened to the dictates of his heart, and to those alone, he could have done so with the remorseless rigour he displayed on this occasion.

All these painful endeavours to enter into sympathetic communion with minds so remote from his own, with men whose respect for his authority, though sincere, was no more than theoretic, left him in a state of strange uneasiness. With them, as well as with the other young men who had followed them into the Oratory, he seemed quite unable to establish anything like the easy and happy relations he had enjoyed with his students at Oriel. All this brought on a renewal of that feeling of premature old age which had come over him when he was going through that process of conscience-searching during his stay in Rome. In a letter to St John dated the 12th July, he gives poignant expression to his feelings,

> My great trouble is some of the giovani—not that anything new has occurred, but they have so repelled anything between us but what is external, shown so little kindness when I have done things for them, treated me with so little confidence, as to throw me back upon myself—and now I quite dread the fortnightly chapter day, when I have to make them a little address, as being something so very external, when I have no means of knowing what is going on in their minds. In consequence I feel as if I were not doing my duty to them, yet without any fault. I don't know what influence I am exerting over them. It is as if my time of work were gone by.[1]

Wilfrid Ward mentions a moving incident recorded by Philip Gordon about his own noviciate. After some weeks of silence and constraint between them, Newman one morning put a note into the hands of the astonished young man. It read:

> My dearest Brother,—It is strange to write to you and write about nothing; but such is my fate just now and for some time, that, since I have nothing to say to you, I must either be silent or unseasonable.
>
> Many is the time I have stood over the fire at breakfast and looked at you at Recreation, hunting for something to talk about. The song says that "love cannot live on flowers"; not so, yet it required material, if not for sustenance, at least for display—and I have fancied too that younger and lighter minds perhaps could not, if they would, care much for one who has had so much to wear him down.
>
> All blessings come on you my dear Brother—in proportion to my waning.
>
> Ever yours affectionately,
>
> John H. Newman.[2]

As if to add to these depressing circumstances, Wiseman, without taking any preliminary soundings, abruptly rushed the Oratorians into an undertaking to deliver a series of Lenten addresses in the various London churches. The result was a complete fiasco. Hardly anyone troubled to put in an appearance. In an entry subsequently recalling all this in his *Journal*, Newman speaks of this reverse and says it reminds him of his experience when he preached his unlucky sermon at St Isidore's, Rome.

> To please Dr Wiseman, I made the wretched throw off in London against my will, of the Oratorian Lent preaching at Passiontide—a blunder and a failure which even now I cannot think of without a raw sensitiveness.

[1] W. Ward, Vol. I, p. 203. [2] *Ibid.*, p. 204.

Meanwhile, on the 31st October, Newman left Maryvale and took up his residence at St Wilfrid's, Cheadle, while the new Oratory in Alcester Street, Birmingham, was being got ready for occupation. It was opened early in the following year. Now, however, increasing numbers, and the ever-growing incompatibility of outlook between the two groups composing the community, pointed unmistakably to the desirability of opening a separate house, and that in London.

Faber, who arrived at Alcester Street on the 10th April, was off again on the 16th, bound for London, where a house in King William Street had been secured. Hutchinson and Dalgairns went with him, and the rest of the *giovani* soon followed. They were now free to do as they liked, and by the time one month was out they were the talk of London and had furnished some priceless material for *Punch*. Walking the streets in their cassocks (a thing unheard of in England in those days), despite Newman's repeated warnings, they omitted nothing that was calculated to offend both the old Catholics and the Protestants, the former by their off-hand ways, the latter by their arrogance. Faber protesting that he could not possibly keep his junior colleagues in order unless some sort of superior rank was officially conferred on him, Newman appointed him Rector of the London House. That was just before the formal opening, which was due to take place on the 31st May. Little did he foresee what that appointment was to lead to.

Despite their youthful extravagances, Faber's disciples displayed such zeal, they gave evidence of such a warm and lively faith, that by the middle of June we have Newman writing to them and giving eloquent expression to the joy and confidence with which their conduct had inspired him. Clearly the new foundation was already beginning to show itself worthy of the brilliant future that awaited it.

Meanwhile, home in Birmingham, the Old Guard, if one may be permitted the phrase, was grappling manfully with material problems. The house at Cheadle was imposing an intolerable strain on the Community's budget, without serving any useful purpose. As Newman remarked:

> It was the story of the man who bought an elephant, and was too poor to keep, and too merciful to kill it and was unable to persuade any one to accept of it.[1]

The idea then occurred to him of founding an Oratory school. We

[1] W. Ward, Vol. I, p. 221.

shall see later on how the scheme bore fruit, and how deeply it was rooted in Newman's mind. But his late disciples, though the move to London had put them beyond his control, regarded themselves as none the less bound to tell him the way he should go. Faber, and Dalgairns, who had now completely gone over to his side, condemned the proposal as incompatible with the original Oratorian ideal, saying that it was more suited to Cardinal Berulle than to St Philip. It looked as if they more and more regarded anti-intellectualism as the guarantee of orthodoxy.

Newman was by no means convinced, but for the sake of peace and harmony he once more gave way. A note, very much in St Philip's style, and in pleasing contrast to the prevailing sombreness of that period, tells of all the dreams he had cherished about Cotton Hall, and certainly there was nothing excessively highbrow about them.

> I should like St Wilfrid's to be the Eton of the Oratory—a place where Fathers would turn with warm associations of boyhood or at least youth—a place where they wish to be buried—(where their relics would be kept)—a gin bottle or cayenne phial of the Venerabile servo di Dio, il padre Wilfrido Faber, an old red biretta of His Eminence C. Robert Coffin, and a double tooth and knuckle bone of St Aloysius of Birmingham.[1]

The concluding allusion was to a lay brother who seems to have been a source of unfailing entertainment to the Community.

Notwithstanding all these internal dissensions and cross-currents, which seemed to justify only too completely the unflattering forebodings of the old Catholics regarding this association of converts, there is no doubt whatever that towards the close of the year 1849 both groups were in exceptionally good posture. In London the Brothers had gone forth to evangelise the worthy Protestant folk, even as St Philip—so at least they told themselves—had brought the Roman people back to the fold three centuries before. If they still had a heavy task before them, so far as the people in general were concerned, it could not be denied that they had made some dazzling conquests among the aristocracy, such as Lady Arundel and Surrey, the future Duchess of Norfolk. The little King William Street Church was never empty, and the munificence of the faithful relieved them from all anxiety regarding the future. At Birmingham things were not moving quite so briskly, but they were going very well, all the same. During 1849, Newman drew great crowds to listen to his *Discourses to Mixed Congregations*. They were published shortly afterwards,

[1] W. Ward, Vol. I, p. 222.

scoring a big success, proving that whatever effect his depression of spirits had had on him, it had in no way impaired his faculties. But what a long way they take us from the Oxford sermons of earlier days! One feels that Newman was carried along by the encomiums that were showered upon him by all his disciples, by Dalgairns in particular. Their peculiar brand of Christianity, or as near to it as he could get, replaces the pure simplicity of the sermons at St Mary's. In their general style and structure they aimed—and with undeniable success—at reproducing the great French pulpit oratory of the seventeenth century. But these admirable *pastiches*, whatever their sincerity—and his joy at being a Catholic shines out on every page—cannot make us forget the beauty, far less adorned, but ah! how far more spiritual, of those other sermons that came straight from his heart.

A like contrast between a glittering external triumph on the one hand, and, on the other, a spiritual current bearing in a totally different direction, occurs in the following year, 1850, when at Faber's request, he delivered a series of lectures at the London Oratory. Wiseman was there to hear him, and those present long remembered how his face beamed with satisfaction as the points were driven home. These lectures were rewarded by Rome with a Doctorate of Divinity conferred *honoris causa*.

Their title, *Certain Difficulties felt by Anglicans in Catholic Teaching*, gives no hint of the occasion that elicited them, nor of their full range. On the 8th March the Privy Council quashed a decision of the Bishop of Exeter refusing to induct a certain Mr G. C. Gorham on the grounds that he had declined to subscribe to the doctrine of Baptismal Regeneration. The Bishop was ordered by this civil court, whose authority derived direct from the Crown, to institute the clergyman in question as vicar of the parish of Bramford Speke. The effect of this further indication of Anglican disregard of Catholic tradition was to send yet another batch of converts to Rome, among them Manning, the future Archbishop. Faber, and a number of others, thought the time had now come to press such Tractarians as were still hesitating on the brink to examine their position anew as a means of bringing them to take the final plunge. Newman was thus persuaded, very much against the grain, to draw up a sort of balance-sheet of Anglicanism and of the Oxford Movement. This was the last work of his to be conceived and written in a spirit so foreign to his own, to his real self, a spirit forced in upon him by his quondam disciples. Never before had Anglicanism been the target for such withering criticism, never before had its doctrinal inconsistencies been more pitilessly exposed. Even so eminent a literary critic as Hutton, and he a Protestant, had no hesitation in declaring that these lectures were not only superb examples of Newman's powers of dialectic and irony, never before so brilliantly displayed, but that, taken as a whole, the work, both in form and substance, was one of his most triumphant achievements.

Though he never retracted anything he had said in these lectures, he never again suffered himself to be influenced by the spirit that animates them. He was not one to mistake a dazzling polemical triumph of this kind for a convincing apologetic. He knew well enough that you might strip a man bare of all his arguments and, *ipso facto*, close the way to his heart. While the Catholic world was applauding this brilliant performance, he himself was turning his thoughts to methods of a very different character. His personal correspondence about this time, with the Froude family for example, showed him the risks involved in this all-or-nothing sort of line. To Catholicise the English people, more was needed than to shatter their faith in Anglicanism. That might quite well rush them into stark unbelief. Far better start with whatever residuum of truth still remains in Anglicanism, as Newman himself had done, and then go on till it becomes clear that Catholicism is Christianity in all its richness and plenitude, and not merely a counterblast to Protestantism.

But this wise and sober mode of procedure was not at all to the taste of the *giovani*, and when they saw their leader falling back on ideas like that, more than one of them began to have serious doubts about his orthodoxy. It may perhaps be permissible to see something of the providential in the surprising humility which had led Newman to adopt the spirit of the other converts, a spirit so different from his own. It was well that he had entered so completely into the spirit of this showy Catholicism, exulting so triumphantly over its prostrate foe. It was well, no doubt, that he had devoted himself to works like his latest sermons and lectures, and scored such an unsurpassable success. Better still, perhaps, had it been, if he had felt then, as he felt now, the basic vanity of it all.

For he saw now that triumphs of this nature pay no dividend. They are but golden dreams calculated to promote a dangerous optimism in the Catholic mind. They do but repel the more quickly, not only the unbeliever but, what is far more grave, those men and women of goodwill whose minds and hearts are hungry for sustenance. They ask for the bread of Gospel truth; to throw stones at them, however adroitly, is to score a very paltry triumph. Newman, even when he was composing these lectures—they alone of all his works gave his new coreligionists full and entire satisfaction—seems to have conceived a profound distaste for scoring these debating points. Though he did not renew his proposal to inaugurate a School of Theology, feeling that for the time being at any rate, such a thing was out of the question, he does come back, as the sequel will show, to the one task that he feels is peculiarly his own, a task to which all Catholics would turn their minds if they were clearly aware of the signs of the times. That task was, first to recognise and enter into the difficulties that beset the modern mind in regard to the acceptance of religious belief, and next to provide a solution of them. Never for a moment did it enter his head to minimise, or water down, Catholic truth, though that was precisely what he was taxed with doing by certain budding theologians whose self-assurance was scarcely justified by their knowledge. It was the very fact that his own faith was so firmly rooted that made him feel so strongly that the Church ought not to disregard the problems of the age. Drawing forth both new and old from the treasure-house of eternal truth, her office it was to provide such positive solutions as would reconcile and bring to her fold all those multitudes that stood apart. The failure of people to recognise religious truth is not always due to their lack of spiritual vision, but rather the fault of its guardians too confident, too satisfied with the thought of what they themselves possess, to turn and boldly confront the crying problems of the hour.

Newman was not the only one who took this view of things; there were plenty of others, particularly laymen, who thought as he did. He sympathised with all efforts in this direction even if, though well-meant, they might not always be well conceived. And this sympathy increased as he became more and more dissatisfied with the rough-and-ready methods of the *giovani*.

In January 1848, one of his old Oxford friends, a Mr John Moore Capes, himself a recent convert, started a review, entitled *The Rambler*, in which he did his best to deal with those numerous pressing questions which so many other new recruits to the Church thought it less troublesome, and more becoming, to ignore.

The subjects dealt with by Capes and his contributors were all such as would necessarily be included in an apologetic intended rather to function within a select circle, as it were, for the delectation of its contrivers, than to come to grips with actual, positive unbelief.

To show how Newman always felt the importance and urgency of such measures, we need only quote a few lines from a letter he wrote to Capes on the 8th December, 1849.

> "The proof of Christianity" is just the point on which polemics and dogmatics meet as on common ground. It is in the province of both, and I cannot altogether stand the Italian treatment of it, unless I mistake their words and they mine. They know nothing at all of heretics as realities—they live, at least in Rome, in a place whose boast it is that it has never given birth to heresy, and they think proofs ought to be convincing which in fact are not. Hence they are accustomed to speak of the argument for Catholicism as a demonstration, and to see no force in objections to it and to admit no perplexity of intellect which is not directly and immediately wilful. This at least is their tendency in *fact*, even if I overstate their theory. They have not a dream what England is, and what is the power of fascination which the Anglican Church (e.g.) exerts in the case of many minds.[1]

However Newman entertained no exaggerated ideas as to the value of *The Rambler* articles. We find him warning the editor not to be in too great a hurry to recognise agreements between religion and the conclusions of contemporary science, which latter, in the course of a few years, might have completely to be revolutionised.[2]

On problems such as that arising from the doctrine of eternal punishment, or the eagerness of modern thinkers to explain the existence of evil, he brings the same clarity of vision to bear, avoiding any tendency to minimise the poignancy of the question, on the one hand, or to dilute the truths of revelation on the other. He was in complete agreement with the statements made in the review to the effect that a solution of such problems would require a complete overhaul of Catholic teaching methods. That, however, in no way blunted his counter criticism of the critics themselves, whom he told that their views about Catholic teaching, as it then was, were altogether too one-sided.

Here the foresight of this wonderful intelligence strikes one as nothing short of prophetic. As far back as those days, he saw in the suggestions tentatively put out by *The Rambler*, the sort of impossible positions into which, a generation or two later on, Modernism would go blundering. But, far from being led on that account to the conclusion that such lines of enquiry were dangerous and to be avoided, he considered that they ought to be pursued with a strictness of scientific purpose commensurate with the gravity of the matters at issue.

It was now, in the winter of 1850-1851, that the bomb with which the opponents of *The Rambler* had up to now been harmlessly toying,

[1] W. Ward, Vol. I, p. 247 [2] *Ibid.*, p. 249.

suddenly exploded. Protestant susceptibilities, the Englishman's chronic irritability at the mere mention of anything connected with Rome, had been so sorely tried by the majority of these new converts to Catholicism that one wonders how it was that things had not reached breaking-point before. Now, however, it was reached and with a vengeance, and that as the result of an official measure which the Holy See, put on its guard by Catholics who knew their England, had for a long time thought it prudent to postpone. The measure in question provided for the restoration of the Catholic Hierarchy in England.

Ever since the sixteenth century, when Henry VIII cut off the English dioceses from any further communion with Rome, so making the Church of England a schismatic Church, the Catholic Church in England had existed on the same footing as in any other non-Catholic country—that is to say, on the footing of a mission. The priests who exercised their duties there, did so under the authority of the Holy See as represented by a certain number of Vicars-Apostolic—that is to say, by persons entrusted with episcopal powers, but as delegates, not as Bishops in their own right. But now, in view of the repeal of the anti-Catholic laws, and also of the recent wave of conversions, the Catholic cause in England was in process of undergoing a radical transformation. It followed then, as a natural consequence, that the Church should now resume its normal constitution and be provided with a local hierarchy in communion with the Sovereign Pontiff.

On several previous occasions Rome had appeared to be on the point of acting. When Newman was leaving Italy for home, it was almost decided that he should bring with him the Papal Bull giving effect to the measure. Wiseman had been strongly in favour, but the older members of the Catholic clergy demurred, fearing that the great majority of English people, and first and foremost the Anglican Bishops, would look on such a step as a provocation. Rome, therefore, had been very slow to decide. Meanwhile, a compromise had suggested itself, a compromise that looked as if it might be satisfactory to all concerned. The Hierarchy should be re-established, but Wiseman, whose rashness was such a cause of alarm, should be left out. The difficulty about this was that Wiseman's burning zeal, and his conspicuous success in regard to those Oxford conversions, merited, not a snub, but a very signal reward. To meet this difficult situation, a masterpiece of diplomatic finesse was contrived, and this was to get him out of England by sending him to Rome, and giving him a Cardinal's hat. However, the sincerity with which he pleaded to be spared an honour that would have torn him away from his life's work—that, and the fact that he was clearly the most able of all the Vicars-Apostolic—induced the Pope, whom the urgent representations of the aristocratic section of the English converts were far from leading into the path of prudence, to go about-ship. And so it came to pass that, at the beginning of October, the announcement was made public that the Hierarchy had been re-established and that Wiseman had been made a Cardinal. What was more, he had been appointed head of the Catholic Church in England and was to be known as the Archbishop of Westminster, which was something quite new in the way of titles. All these various decisions might quite well have been explained to the British public without any danger of ruffling their feelings, had not Wiseman, with unconscionable tactlessness, done everything imaginable to antagonise them. From Rome, he issued, to his new diocesans, a pastoral letter couched in terms that sounded a note of almost delirious triumph. Every word in it seemed specially chosen to fire the indignation of every non-Catholic Briton, man or woman, from the Queen down to the humblest of her subjects. Custom lays it down that no Bishop other that the Pope shall date his letters from Rome. In accordance with this usage, Wiseman's declaration was issued with a great flourish, "From out the Flaminian Gate"! John Bull, unacquainted with the niceties of Roman etiquette, scented, even in these opening words, all manner of domineering pretensions, and it must be admitted that the lofty grandiloquence of what followed accounts only too easily for all the subsequent misunderstandings; such a passage as this, for example:

> Till such time as the Holy See shall think fit otherwise to provide, we govern and shall continue to govern the counties of Middlesex, Hertford, and Essex as ordinary thereof, and those of Surrey, Sussex, Hants, Berkshire and Hampshire with the islands annexed as administrator with ordinary powers.

Finally, Wiseman ended in tones of Olympian calm:

> The great work is complete. Catholic England has been restored to its orbit in the ecclesiastical firmament. Truly this is a day of joy and exultation of spirit.

That day witnessed an outburst of unbelievable fury. Wiseman landed on the 11th November, only to find the whole country seething with anger against himself and against what his tactless language had led people to call the Papal Aggression.

It must be confessed that throughout the whole of this business both sides were absurdly wide of the mark. If the British public had taken the trouble to read coolly and dispassionately these high-sounding phrases of Wiseman's, they would never seriously have thought that his rhetorical flourishes envisaged any save a purely spiritual authority, and one concerned solely with Catholics. No one could have seen in the re-establishment of the Catholic Hierarchy in Britain any attempt at a politico-religious conquest, or suspected that, in the wake of these new Bishops, some Invincible Armada was going to rise up from the depths of the sea to cast down from her throne, not Elizabeth, this time, but Victoria! Their own common-sense should have told them that their Catholic fellow-countrymen, being governed as they now were by their own Bishops, and being no longer directly controlled by Rome, were far from forfeiting their allegiance to their lawful temporal rulers. On the contrary, they were now free from the faintest semblance of subjection to a foreign power. The titular sees of the new Bishops had been chosen with the express purpose of avoiding any clash with the old cathedral cities whence the Anglican bishops derived their titles. That, in itself, is enough to show how anxious Rome was not to wound any susceptibilities.

However, Wiseman's tone and bearing were nicely calculated to disendow his fellow-countrymen of whatever *sang-froid* the gratuitously aggressive behaviour of the neo-Catholics had left them, and that was mighty little. The fury aroused by the Flaminian letter was ridiculous, no doubt; but Wiseman was merely getting a Roland for his Oliver. Like many another gifted enthusiast, he drove straight ahead, without heeding where he was going. Fortunately, he possessed the talent for improvising, on the spur of the moment, measures to repair the damage he had wrought, and forthwith he proceeded to do so. No sooner was he back in England than he set to work to explain matters, not only to the authorities but to the public at large. Mobs all over the country had been burning him in effigy, and the Pope into the bargain. Popular indignation, once aroused, spread like wildfire. People may well have wondered whether all this did not portend another era of wholesale persecution for the Catholics. But no; the Cardinal's calm, intrepid bearing, the courage with which he faced the storm he had created, the sound sense and humane feeling to which his words bore witness, allayed the storm as if by magic. He drew up an Appeal to the English People which appeared *in extenso* on the 20th November in five leading dailies. Despite its length—it occupied six and a half columns of *The Times*—it was devoured by a whole host of people, Newman, in a letter he wrote to a recent convert, Sir George Bowyer, in January of the following year, made no secret of his admiration.

> He is made for the world, and he rises with the occasion. Highly as I put his gifts, I was not prepared for such a display of vigour, power, judgment, sustained energy as the last two months have brought.[1]

The fact remains that, if Wisemen had gone to work a little more cautiously, if he had taken a more realistic view of things, he might have spared himself a deal of trouble, and the English Catholics a world of vexation. The actual storm had blown over; all the same, people's feelings, too long exacerbated by a needlessly provocative presentation of Catholicism, still clung to their old prejudices, which had now been given a new lease of life. The wound was still there; now the time had come to heal it. That was a task hardly in Wiseman's line. Still less did it appeal to the young fire-eaters whom the storm had taken unawares, though they had done all they could to raise it. If any there were who could do any good in the matter, it was the scanty few who held that a man's becoming a Catholic did not necessarily compel him to vilify and misrepresent everyone who declined to follow his example. Evidently the time was ripe for Capes and Newman to take up their cue.

Newman had not waited for the new Archbishop's monumental blunder before giving expression to his disapproval of a policy of beating the big drum and venting a flood of empty verbiage about victory. Faber it was whom he had had more particularly in view, but more than one of the expostulatory letters he wrote to him would have furnished salutary doctrine for many another. What seemed to him ever more and more to be the need of the hour was to assemble and set in order the resources of Catholicism, spiritual and intellectual, as well as material. Until the Church in England had regained a firm foothold, and that time was still far off, attacks on Anglicanism seemed to him not only useless, but harmful. Capes, who was busily organising a series of lectures on the Catholic position, he strongly recommends not to take that—the anti-Anglican—line. In his letter to Capes, he justifies his own King William Street lectures on the ground that they were addressed, not to Anglicans in general, but wholly and solely to those members of the Tractarian Movement who, though accepting

[1] W. Ward, Vol. I, p. 256.

Catholic doctrine, had not joined the Catholic Church. His object had been to extricate them from the slough of inconsistency. As regards the rest, Anglicans in general, he plainly declared that to weaken Anglicanism at that particular moment would be to strengthen, not the Catholic cause, but the forces of unbelief.

Capes, having been taken ill, had been obliged to suspend his lectures; Newman resolved to step into the breach himself. On the 30th June, in the Birmingham Corn Exchange, he began the series of lectures which were subsequently gathered together into a single volume and published under the title, *The Present Position of Catholics in England*. Here, as in the King William Street lectures, the weapon of irony was again employed, and with even more devastating effect, but its object was something very different. Here there is no desire to disparage the Anglican establishment. The lecturer's sole aim is to free Catholicism from the mass of travesty and falsehood with which the distortions of the controversialists and the inventions of popular prejudice had encumbered it.

In connection with this new undertaking, there is one point to which we must draw special attention, throwing, as it does, a revealing light on what was at the back of Newman's mind. When Capes first announced his lecturing intentions, some rather disdainful ecclesiastics disapproved, saying that such things were no concern of a layman. Newman, however, speaking from the strongest personal conviction, had vigorously supported the principle on which Capes's scheme was based. It was his idea that laymen—educated laymen, capable of taking a clear, intelligent view of their own judgments and convictions—had an important part to play in restoring Christianity and the Church to their due position in the world of modern thought.

What we of today may regard as a perfectly normal proceeding, was looked on then as a scandalous innovation, and nothing, we imagine, helped more to make Newman's own orthodoxy suspect among certain members of the Hierarchy than his attitude to these lectures.

A kindred idea it was that now prompted him, very much in the spirit of St Philip, to busy himself with the creation of an *Oratorium Parvum*, a Little Oratory—that is to say, a group of laymen gathered together by the Oratorians with the object of developing their spiritual life. For them these Corn Exchange lectures were primarily intended, and through them it was that they gained a wider public.

Newman quite recognised that the work on which he had just been engaged was no more than a preliminary clearing of the ground.

Clearing away from Catholicism the grotesque ideas which people entertained about it was well enough in its way, well enough so far as it went, but nothing of a positive nature would be achieved unless Catholics were in a position to follow up the initial spade-work with a reasoned statement of their religious beliefs, so conceived and so presented as to suit the requirements of the time. But for such a purpose it would be needful to bring into being a regular system of training for Catholics, and particularly for Catholic laymen. And now, just at this very moment, an event occurred which may well have made Newman think that Providence had intervened to offer him a marvellous opportunity for the fulfilment of his designs. On the 8th July, 1851, Dr Cullen, the Archbishop of Armagh, and, as such, Primate of Ireland, called at the Birmingham Oratory. He informed Newman that the Irish Episcopate had decided to establish a Catholic University in Dublin, and he had come to enquire whether he would be willing to undertake its organisation, and to become its first Rector.

XVII

THE CATHOLIC UNIVERSITY

WHAT happened in regard to the setting up of the proposed Catholic University in Dublin constitutes probably the most astonishing episode in Newman's career. It was certainly one of the most exasperating. One is amazed at the utter fecklessness with which, throughout the whole affair, Newman's time and energies were wantonly thrown away. It almost looked as if these people had waited for him to reach that time of life which, in the normal way, should have witnessed the full expansion of his powers, with the express purpose of doing all they could to stultify his efforts, to exhaust his strength, and to make him lose heart, and then to cast him aside like a tool that had been worn out to no purpose.

However, there is no doubt that, looked back upon over a certain distance of time, the affair had its ironic side; and that Newman was aware of it his notes and stories abundantly testify. All this, however, was a sorry consolation for having the best years of his life so utterly thrown away.

The prospect held out by this new work, which had come to him quite unsought, must have inspired him with immense hope. The enthusiasm with which he expressed this hope and built upon it shows clearly enough what he might have achieved, despite the effect of his many disappointments, if only he could have counted at long last on even a modicum of trust and understanding.

Nevertheless, from the very outset his hopes cannot have been wholly free from apprehension. Dr Cullen called and disclosed his plans on the 8th July. The visit, however, had been preceded by a letter dated the 5th April which made no reference whatever to the University proposal, but merely asked whether Newman would be willing to come to Dublin and deliver a series of addresses against the principle of "mixed education", as it was called—that is to say, the system by which Catholics and Protestants were taught together. The sequence of these two events, the letter and the visit, was not without significance. The April request had a direct bearing on the one that followed in July.

It all meant that Newman's discomfiture was already written in the book of fate.

The whole scheme for founding a Catholic University in Dublin had been conceived and set going more or less in order to thwart the plans of the British Government. Sir Robert Peel, who had championed the cause of Catholic emancipation for Ireland, brought in a measure providing for the establishment of Queen's Colleges, as they were called, for the higher education of the Irish people. These Colleges were to be entirely undenominational. That, however, implied no anti-Catholic prejudice on the part of Peel. On the contrary, we must remember that hitherto all the British Universities had been bound up with the Established Church, which Church, though in Ireland it had no more than a phantom existence, was the only one which the British Government consented to recognise there. This new scheme, then, would make it possible for Catholics to obtain an advanced education and to qualify for degrees, without in any way compromising their religious beliefs.

In point of fact, there was some reason to foresee that what had happened in regard to the primary schools recently set up by the same Government would be repeated in the case of these colleges, and that was that these latter, in which teachers and students would almost all be Catholics, would therefore be *de facto* Catholic educational establishments. At all events, that was the view which the most wide-awake of Irish Catholics took of the matter, men like Dr Russell of Maynooth, an old friend of Newman's, and Dr Murray, the Archbishop of Dublin himself. However, Rome, from the first, had been opposed to the project, and at the recent synod of Thurles a motion against it had been brought forward by Dr Cullen and adopted. The terms of this resolution were that the most uncompromising opposition should be offered to Peel's colleges, and that Catholics should be forbidden to attend them. In view of all this, one might well be tempted to ask oneself whether the decision rather to set up a Catholic University, as suggested by Rome, had really any other object than to torpedo the official scheme, and whether Newman's name had been bruited abroad for any other purpose than to ensure the success of the manoeuvre by launching it under such impressive colours.

If we carefully examine the facts, and especially their subsequent development, we can arrive at no more credible supposition. That the projected University might serve a few useful purposes of minor importance Dr Cullen was in no way disposed to deny. But these secondary aims were of little moment compared with the main purpose which, though never overtly defined, was, none the less, never lost sight of.

Of these events, in all their very revealing detail, Fergal McGrath's book *Newman's University* (London, 1951), gives us such a full account that it would seem impossible to add anything substantial to his story. It has rendered obsolete W. Ward's previous account. There will be no need for us to repeat what he has made clear, but, after a brief statement of the facts, for which we are indebted almost entirely to him, we shall do our best to get some clear idea of the effect they had on the mind and soul of Newman.

In spite of what we have said, we should be taking an altogether inadequate view of Dr Cullen's attitude if we described it as that of an obscurantist run mad. The fact is the situation was extremely complicated, so much so indeed that we doubt whether the clearest-minded person imaginable would be able to disentangle all its various threads. Between the adoption of Sir Robert Peel's measure for the Queen's Colleges and its being put into practical effect, things had been happening in the political world, and not only in the political world. Peel was no longer in power, having been succeeded by Lord John Russell, who was a Liberal. An open letter addressed by Russell to the Bishop of Durham at the time of, and in connection with, the Wiseman letter, revealed such a fanatical anti-Catholic spirit that the Irish Bishops certainly had some solid grounds for disquietude. The way in which, despite their legitimate remonstrances, the professorial staff at Queen's College, Cork, had been filled up—that is to say, with an overwhelming preponderance of Protestants, whereas all, or very nearly all, the students were Catholics—justified only too thoroughly their apprehensions.

But, above all, we must bear in mind the circumstances of the period. The year 1848 had just seen the whole of Europe shaken to its foundations by revolutions inspired by the spirit of Liberalism. Everywhere political liberalism which, following in the steps of Lammenais, the leading spirits of the Catholic and Ultra-montane renaissance had gone forth to greet, was now assuming a decidedly anti-clerical and anti-religious complexion. It is not surprising, therefore, that Pius IX's change of front, after all he had been through, was followed by a similar change on the part of the great body of the episcopate. Moreover, in Britain, in the advanced educational sphere, something had occurred that seemed to promise important consequences. The revolutionary changes which had threatened Oxford when Newman was there, but which had been hindered by the Tractarian Movement, were now being carried out, and carried out with a force all the greater from having been dammed up for a time. The abolition of religious tests, the early stages in the secularisation of college staffs, the introduction of regular scientific studies loudly advocated as something that was going to put the Christian tradition in the shade—all this will make the Oxford of the fifties a very different place from what it had been when Newman left it, in 1845. To get an idea of the change that had taken place, we should read the *Memoirs* of Newman's one-time pupil, Mark Pattison, the future Rector of Lincoln, who had exchanged Tractarianism for the most thoroughgoing brand of liberal agnosticism. When he tells us that Science had been banished from Oxford till then because the theologians felt instinctively that it was fatal to their speculations,[1] he is ingenuously confessing that what we call the scientific mind, opposed as it is to positive religious belief of any sort, seemed, to the great majority of scientists of those days, inseparable from Science itself. Small wonder, then, if Dr Cullen and his *confrères* in the Episcopate had become sceptical in regard to new institutions which, in a different atmosphere, would doubtless have been of benefit to Catholics. The serious part of the matter was that the rationalism which opposed not only dogma, but the very idea of religion, and which was professed by the scientists whose triumph Pattison proclaims, was destined to furnish only too plausible a ground for the reproach of narrow-mindedness which not a few Churchmen undeniably incurred.

It was in these unpromising circumstances that Newman undertook responsibility for a task in regard to which he was soon led to wonder what positive advantage its promoters expected to flow from it.

By September 1851, he had returned Dr Cullen's summer visit. Knowing that the Archbishop of Dublin, Dr Murray, the most distinguished member of the Irish Episcopate, was irreconcilably opposed to the scheme, he had made every endeavour to see him, but without success. This was anything but an auspicious beginning, and the idea of founding in Dublin a University which the ecclesiastical head of that city would not hear spoken of, was by no means encouraging.

Added to that, the whole thing was in the air, and very much in the air. It was not until the 12th November that the Irish Bishops

[1] Mark Pattison, *Memoirs*, p. 238.

formally invited Newman to fill the post of Rector of this still non-existent University, reserving for themselves collectively the supreme controlling authority.

In May 1852, in view of the projected foundation, Newman returned to Ireland in order to deliver a course of lectures to outline its programme. They were to be entitled *Scope and Nature of a University Education.* Whereas, however, what he wanted to do was to develop the idea of a Christianised humanistic culture such as he had tried to realise at Oxford, and which he was hoping to resume in Dublin, Cullen had a very different plan for him. That plan meant coming back, with a sort of blind obstinacy, to what he had first wanted him to do, and that was to hold forth against "mixed education". Cullen dragged a promise from Newman to the effect that he would demonstrate how impossible it was for Catholics to take advantage of any sort of university education that was not centred on theology. Newman agreed, but with a very wry face, to this distortion of his basic idea. The composition of these lectures (they make up the first part of the book afterwards entitled *The Idea of a University*) gave him a deal of trouble. What he would have liked to do was to establish a scheme of higher education based on the Hellenic concept, and to show how, on that foundation, a Christian might be trained and fitted for social life. But what Cullen wanted to do was to shut the mouths of people like Murray who held that there was no harm in a Catholic attending a neutral university, provided his religious beliefs were not interfered with.

Newman made the best of the matter and set to work to show the inevitable deficiencies of a system of education which was not centred on theology. So dissatisfied was he with the result of his labours that he thought these lectures were bound to prove a failure. Their success went some way to brightening his outlook, and of that he was in sore need.

Since November he had heard nothing, either from Cullen or anyone else, and he had begun seriously to wonder whether the whole scheme had been abandoned. What was more, Dr Murray had died on 24th February and Cullen had recently been transferred to Dublin. Newman was innocent enough to think that this would help to hasten matters on a little. Shortly after the new Archbishop's enthronement, which took place on the 29th June, and which Newman had been invited to attend, he tried to get into closer touch with people, to get to know more about Ireland and the Irish. For that purpose he undertook to do a round of preaching, beginning with the Limerick district. However, worn out with the lawsuit he was obliged just then to carry on in England, he had to give up at the end of a fortnight or so. To that lawsuit we shall presently return. Meanwhile, this unpleasant business, coming as it did on the top of his preliminary work in Dublin, which had been thankless enough, was like a millstone round his neck, and it necessitated his going back to Birmingham and London.

When he was in England, he wrote a number of letters to Cullen about the various things that would have to be done in order to make a start. Without in any way taking an unrealistic view of the possibilities of the situation, what he would have liked to do would have been to gather together in Dublin the most gifted representatives of Catholicism in England. As soon, therefore, as he received his formal invitation from the Irish Episcopate, he proceeded to sound all the most brilliant men among the Oxford converts, such as W. G. Ward, Henry Wilberforce, Northcote, Healy Thompson. All those to whom he first applied excused themselves on one ground or another. He was particularly disappointed that Manning had been unable to accept the vitally important post of Vice-Rector. That office, the holder of which would necessarily be brought into the closest touch with the Rector himself, he thought a great deal about. He had twice written to the Archbishop, leaving the appointment of the professorial staff to him, but insisting, in return, that he should be allowed to select his own Vice-Rector. Cullen never took the trouble to reply to either of these letters, but, more than that, without taking the slightest notice of so reasonable a request, without even sending any formal advice to Newman of what he was doing, he appointed, one after the other, Dr Taylor as Secretary to the Organising Committee, and Dr Leahy as Vice-Rector.

This very off-hand and discourteous proceeding nearly took the heart out of Newman. In an account of this affair which he set down on the 25th November, 1870, he says:

> First Dr Taylor, then Dr Leahy were appointed, and both of them in the intention of the appointment, rather as the four Archbishops' representatives and their security and safeguard against me, than as my own helper and backer-up.[1]

What happened later, while revealing Taylor and particularly Leahy in the most favourable light, amply confirmed what he here

[1] W. Ward, Vol. I, p. 323

says regarding the real intentions of the authorities. Things were looking less and less engaging; but this was only a beginning.

The Bishops' invitation had reference to the University-to-be. But although practical steps had been more or less decided upon, although a committee had been formed, although Dr Cullen was busy with plans for purchasing land and premises, although he had appointed people to various posts, not only was Newman himself left completely in the dark regarding these latter, in which he had expressly asked to be consulted, but, what was still more extraordinary, he himself had not been officially appointed, and no steps had been taken to install him in his sphere of duty. His earlier letters regarding the eventual appointment of a Vice-Rector also stressed the desirability that he himself should take office and be put in control without delay, so that he might set to work as soon as possible. A further letter, dated January 1853, was no less barren of result, so was another he wrote in February, and yet another in March. Dr Cullen still failed to reply.

The situation was getting really beyond belief. He had been approached and asked to assume responsibility for an immense undertaking, and here were people taking on the work of organisation themselves without the slightest reference to him. In spite of his reiterated reminders, they persisted in ignoring his advice, if not his very existence.

People in England all thought the scheme had been given up. There was even some talk of Newman's being appointed Bishop of Liverpool or Nottingham, neither of which suggestions greatly appealed to him. However, when October came, the Committee threw off its trance, invited Newman to come into residence, and put two thousand pounds at his disposal so that a practical start might be made.

However, his troubles were not yet over, for no public announcement had been made regarding his appointment and he had the uncomfortable sort of feeling that he had got to address himself, as on his own personal responsibility and without any official mandate, to a task he was really undertaking at the express demand of the Irish Bishops.

Wiseman, whom, at the beginning of the affair, he had tried, and tried in vain, to get appointed Chancellor of the prospective University, now found, as usual, a splendid solution of the whole problem. Newman himself would have to be made a Bishop. He could then speak on equal terms to these Irish Bishops and be master in his own house. Meanwhile, Wiseman set out for Rome in January 1854, and on his way, at Amiens, encountered Dr Cullen. What passed between the voluble Cardinal and the taciturn Archbishop on this occasion we shall never know. Wiseman came away from the interview quite under the impression that he had won over Cullen to his ideas. Being in excellent odour at Rome, he had no difficulty in getting the appointment approved in principle. He let Newman know at once, and shouted the news from the house-tops, as though it was a *fait accompli.*

Meanwhile, on the 7th February, Newman took up his official quarters in Dublin. His first visit next day was to Father Curtis, the Superior of the Jesuits. The latter received him most affably, but he also made it his business to dispel any illusions he might still be cherishing, assuring him that there could not possibly be any public for the University he was about to found. The middle-class people, he said, were too poor. The gentry, he went on, wanted a proper degree, and would go on sending their sons to Trinity College, Dublin, as they had done in the past. As for the titled people and the like, they would still continue to send theirs to Oxford or Cambridge. What he might hope for, he added, by way of offering him a scrap of comfort, was that a few women, with nothing else to do, would turn up at some of the evening lectures.

The eminent Jesuit summed it all up in these words: "That's my advice to you; go and see the Archbishop and say to him, 'Don't attempt this University scheme; give up the whole idea'."

It did not take long for the unlucky Rector to find out that the Jesuit's views were shared by all the intelligent Churchmen. As for the more influential laymen, he soon found out that it was hopeless to try to interest them in the matter at all. Why that was, he was soon to discover.

As regards Dr Cullen, when he showed Newman the Papal Brief, the fruit of Wiseman's intervention, which arrived the following month, and which, solemnly instituting the University, conferred on Newman the title of Rector, he drew special attention to some of the Curia's flattering phrases, saying, "This is the mark of honour which was promised you." When he came to think over this later on, Newman must have appreciated the grim humour of the remark. All through the spring and summer, everyone, on the strength of what Wiseman had said, treated him as a Bishop-elect. The Duke of Norfolk presented him with a massive gold chain, Mrs Bowden with a pectoral cross, Hope-Scott with a morse for a cope, etc. His own Bishop, Dr Ullathorne, addressed him as Right Reverend. And Wiseman himself, had he not written to him in the Pope's own words, "*E manderemo a Newman la crocetta, lo faremo Vescovo di Porfirio, o qualche luogo*"? On his return to England he began to feel genuinely anxious about the Rector's delay in getting himself consecrated. He was doubtless only waiting for the Papal Bulls.

These were in no great hurry to arrive. Newman must then have remembered how anxious Cullen had been, on the eve of his coming to Ireland, to dissuade him from making the journey to Rome before the Brief arrived. Obviously, the Irish Episcopate had taken due care to make it clear in that quarter that this suggestion about making Newman a Bishop was his own idea and no one else's, and that the Archbishop of Dublin was not at all anxious to see any crozier in his diocese, other than his own.

At last it was decided that Newman should be formally installed as Rector, and this took place on the 3rd June. Despite his many setbacks and disappointments, Newman at the beginning of November opened the school of Philosophy and Letters. So the University was established, notwithstanding all the obstacles, though not very firmly, it is true. He was to keep it going and widen its scope, until May 1857, with a tenacity of purpose that deserves all praise. But then, completely worn out by a series of rebuffs to which those we have recorded were merely the prelude, he at last gave in his resignation. Some eleventh-hour representations led him to reverse his decision in theory, but the following year, after a brief stay in Dublin, he departed for good.

In the notes he afterwards set down concerning these various events, Newman copied out some words from a pastoral letter of Cullen's written in August 1854. In it there is an allusion to the lawsuit in which Newman had been involved and of which we have previously made mention. Dr Newman, said the Archbishop, is,

> One of the most accomplished scholars and profound divines of the age in which we live, whose merits are only brought forward more prominently by the persecutions to which he is subjected and under which he deserves our sympathy and support.

No wonder Newman added after that,

> Considering what has happened since, words like these in the mouth of a person of Dr Cullen's ecclesiastical connections, sound like irony, or at least provoke on reading an ironical smile.

Bearing all these things in mind, one can hardly imagine how Newman could have gone on as long as he did performing so thankless a task. Perhaps that is putting the thing too mildly. Persistently obstructed as he was by the very man who had called on him to take the post of Rector, he displayed, all through those Dublin years, a creative activity, a youthful diversity of enterprise that remind one of his best Oxford days.

In November 1854, Newman, as we have said, opened the Faculty of Philosophy and Letters. To this, in 1856, against the all-but-unanimous advice of the Bishops, he added a School of Medicine. He would have liked to add laboratories and a complete Faculty of Science, but for that he had no time. Persuaded, moreover, as he was that the teaching side was only one part of a university, he set about creating colleges on the Oxford pattern, in which the undergraduates would dwell in community under the direction of graduates who would guide them in their work and be responsible for their religious training. He established, one after another, three houses on these lines. How heartbreaking a task it was, it would take too long to relate in detail.

At the same time he set forth his ideas on what a university is and what it should be, in a series of articles which were the chief items of attraction in the *University Gazette*. This had been founded by him as an organ of university news and opinion. It had a companion later on in the learned *Atlantis*. These articles were afterwards gathered together in a volume entitled *Office and Work of Universities*. With certain modifications, and under a new title more appropriate to the contents, they make up volume III of *Historical Sketches* in the collected edition of Newman's works.

Written without any claims to erudition, these studies, over and above those brilliant and oft-quoted passages about Athens and Rome, and the essay on Discipline and Influence, are of great value as being, if not a synthesis of the historical development of universities, at least as an analysis of the different elements that play their several parts therein, and their subtle reactions one upon another. They complete the great work which is contemporary with them, *The Idea of a University*.

This latter volume brings together the pre-inaugural lectures delivered by Newman to which we have already referred, and the speeches Newman was called on to make on various public occasions during his office as Rector. Despite their composite character, so exacting a critic as Walter Pater looked on them as an example of the perfect handling of a theory. If the articles in his *University Gazette* attempted to explain the mechanism of a full university life, the deeper studies of *The*

Idea define its *raison d'être*—to wit, culture, what the Greeks called παιδεία. It is what the author of one of the greatest books of our generation has recently so described, from the purely historical point of view, it is true, but in a spirit very close to Newman's.[1]

It has been said, and it is hardly an exaggeration, that this book in itself makes up for the years spent by Newman in Ireland. It is certainly one of his greatest books, and one of the most revealing. As well as the idea of culture, so difficult to crystallise in a single definition, we discover in these pages some of his most felicitous *dicta*. The problem of the bearing of the Christian life on the life intellectual is discussed with an originality and a vigour equally lucid, and equally characteristic of their author.

We may recall how he explained the spiritual crisis he went through during the winter of 1827-1828 in these simple words, "I was beginning to prefer intellectual excellence to moral excellence." A few years subsequent to the period at which we have now arrived, Ward was to take a different view, when, in one of the phases of anti-intellectual exaltation to which he was prone, he appeared to see in the functioning of the intellect nothing but an earthly pleasure, whereas Newman regarded it as emphatically one of the austerest tasks this world imposes on a Christian soul. Between Newman's earlier and later ideas about the matter is the lively complexity of the attitude which *The Idea* reflects.

In Newman's view of the matter, it is beside the mark to enquire what useful purpose is served by culture, not because it serves none at all, but because it is its own reward. It does not form the specialist, it forms the man; and, if it did not do that, the specialist would be but a human tool working in the dark. To put it more accurately, its aim is to train the good member of society, and to fit him to undertake his responsibilities as such.

> It is the education which gives a man a clear, conscious view of his own opinions and judgments, a truth in developing them, an eloquence in expressing them, and a force in urging them. It teaches him to see things as they are, to go right to the point, to detect what is sophistical, and to discard what is irrelevant. It prepares him to fill any post with credit, and to master any subject with facility. It shows him how to accommodate himself to others, how to throw himself into their state of mind, how to bring before them his own, how to influence them, how to come to an understanding with them, how to bear with them.[2]

[1] We refer, of course, to Werner Jaeger's *Paideia*.
[2] *The Idea of a University*, pp. 177–178.

If we ask what useful bearing this "humanism" can have on the Christian life, Newman will tell us that to humanise mankind, lapsed, since the Fall, below their own level, is to pull in the same direction as Christianity. Culture is a powerful ally of religion because it leads in the same direction, even if it does not lead so far. But here the critic is on the watch.

In becoming Christian, human culture, the humanities, become permeated with what the Christian feels about things, with Christian sentiments, with Christian customs and ways of life, so that, even if religion disappears from the scene, this culture will retain for some time the power to produce men who are apparently endowed with all the Christian virtues, without any help from Christianity itself. And here we have what, in Newman's view of it, constitutes the great danger of liberalism. The argument for preferring this liberalism to Christianity proper is that it forms the *gentleman* (or as we in France should say, *l'homme du monde*), a type very superior to the Christian. Doesn't he do all that a Christian does, and doesn't he do it without any slavish ideas about reward and punishment, but simply because he thinks he is doing what it becomes him to do?

There we recognise Newman's one-time temptation, that of putting virtue before holiness. But the answer is that the whole idea is a delusion. The very meaning, the very office of religion, as of creation, is to be a personal link between ourselves and God. Properly understood, fear—religious fear—far from being servile, is seen to be something infinitely greater than respect for the proprieties, which, in reality, is respect for oneself, self-respect. The first implies belief in the reality of a divine Someone, and the need for getting away from ourselves that we may go to Him. The second means that we remain proudly but barrenly self-centred, killing that Love which gives life all its meaning.

These disquisitions on Culture, and on the aim and significance of a university education, must have taken Dr Cullen's breath away, if he ever heard, or read them. Once those Queen's Colleges were out of the way, it was his idea that the University's sole function would be to keep everyone in leading-strings. As one of his colleagues used to put it, he thought it a very clever move to harness a thoroughbred to an old hackney-carriage; but, then the thoroughbred turned out before his very eyes to be a Pegasus!

For us, this synthesis and this criticism, one as admirable as the other, explain in the first place why Newman insisted that the constitution of a university should not be merely intellectual, merely a matter of teaching, but that it should educate in the deepest and truest sense of the word, combining the influence of the tutor with the discipline of college life. After that, it is easier for us to understand why it was his desire that a church should be the centre of his University, a church in which the undergraduates should be taught the Christian faith and be made acquainted with its mysteries.

Dr Cullen, however, for whom a university meant a bigger sort of seminary—bigger, but not broader—proved quite incapable of entering into any such idea. He certainly did give the Rector leave to make use of the neighbouring parish-church, but towards the building of a special university church, such as Newman had in mind, he refused to contribute a single halfpenny. Newman, however, had the idea so much at heart that he undertook then and there to find the money himself. In the very nick of time, and in a manner completely unexpected, the Achilli affair was the means of placing a considerable amount of money at his disposal, and this he devoted in full to the work in question. Summoning to his aid J. H. Pollen, an architect with original ideas on church decoration, and of whom he thought so highly as to appoint him professor of Fine Arts, he built the very beautiful church on St Stephen's Green which stands today as the most tangible memorial of his sojourn in Ireland.

Bearing in mind what Newman has put on record regarding the Gothic and the Classical styles of architecture, it will cause us no astonishment to learn that he sturdily refused to have anything to do with those mediaeval imitations which Pugin was then so busily strewing up and down the British Isles. Seeing that the nineteenth century had no distinctive style it could call its own, Newman decided on a church which would combine the order and symmetry of the ancient basilicas, so uniquely answering to liturgical needs, with the further advantage that it would be possible to make use of the labour and material locally available. What he wanted to find in the church, and in the manner of its decoration, was that impression of joy and triumph which seems to emanate from the Byzantine mosaics, and, in its general atmosphere, that effect of serenity and light which, in his eyes, was far more representative of the Christian spirit than the dim shadows of Gothic.

Beneath a renaissance dome and amber-tinted windows, frescoes representing the Virgin, *Sedes Sapientiae*, enthroned amid the Saints, were enshrined in settings of Ireland's many-coloured marble. Newman, who had taken a deep interest in the minutest details of the building, bestowed the same care in the choice of the sacred ornaments, and in all the ceremonial arrangements. He aimed at having a church which, in its simplicity, should be the most beautiful of all the Catholic churches within the British Isles. It is no extravagant eulogy to say that he perfectly succeeded. The church only lacked an audience, a congregation, to make it the successor of St Mary's, and the propagator of its influence.[1]

The undergraduate population of the budding university was of the scantiest. Father Curtis's gloomy prognostications were not completely realised, but they were not far out. Newman, it is true, with what he himself called his Englishman's innocence, had had dreams of bringing all the Anglo-Saxon Catholics of the world within its precincts. That is why he was so anxious for Wiseman to be Chancellor, and for his old Oxford friends or pupils to be on the teaching staff. But he soon realised that anyone who took such ideas as that into his head could not know much about the Irish situation. Long experience of unwanted English rule made the Irish more than suspicious of the introduction of many Englishmen into the staff of the new University.

It was hard to blame them. Newman quite understood that. The queer thing was that, notwithstanding his miscalculation, he fell in with the situation only too completely. After some weeks had elapsed, Dr Cullen was greatly astonished to discover him fraternising with certain cliques whom that worthy man was very much inclined to suspect of lawlessness and treason. Cullen's clerical career had been spent wholly in Rome, and though his psychology was very distinctly Irish, he had no sympathy whatever with those of his fellow-countrymen who were out for independence, no matter what it might cost. Although one of his uncles had been hanged by the English, his respect for order and for constituted authority allowed him to go no farther than to indulge the hope that Her Majesty's Government would vouchsafe permission for an ecclesiastical administration to be set up in Ireland. His loyalty would have known no bounds the moment he got leave to regiment *ad majorem Dei gloriam* the persons of those whose souls he already had in his charge.

Cullen was therefore not a little astonished when he saw Newman striking up an acquaintance with some of the most conspicuous figures in the "Young Ireland" party, a separatist group which included among

[1] Cf. C. P. Curran, *John Hungerford Pollen and University Church*, in *A Tribute to Newman*, Dublin, 1945.

its numbers most of the leading intellectuals of the younger generation. Newman did not stop there. As soon as he could manage it, he gave a practical turn to his interest in Celtic studies. A first-rate scholar, O'Curry, had flung himself, without financial backing or support of any sort, into the task of bringing together all the existing relics of the ancient Irish literature. No sooner did Newman get wind of this than he appointed him to a professorship specially created for him. Not content with that, he provided money for the publication of his works, and, in order to give him every possible encouragement, he himself put in a regular appearance at his lectures.

Things like that, his unfailing adaptability, his old familiar fascination and personal charm, soon won the hearts of the Irish, even of those who were anything but friendly towards England. Without any seeking on his part, he found himself on terms of the closest friendship with people who had been, and still were, most antagonistic to the project to which Dr Cullen had called on him to give practical effect. He himself described what happened at a big ecclesiastical dinner when a Bishop, after telling him straight out that his University was a mere farce, declared in stentorian tones, that, as a token of his friendship and regard, he appointed him then and there Vicar-General of the diocese. The announcement was greeted with an uproar of the wildest applause, accompanied by cordial slaps on the back of the Rector; after which the assembly began singing with all the force of their lungs songs that Dr Cullen would have considered highly seditious.

Never was Newman's correspondence so rich in amusing anecdotes as during his travels about Ireland. Take, for example, his account of a visit he paid to a girls' school, when he was asked to make a speech to the pupils. Standing up and facing this imposing battalion of the daughters of Erin, he made a few kindly remarks which, however, to judge by their uniformly impassive countenances, had little or no effect on them. When he had finished, the Mother Superior asked him to make the promised speech, evidently considering that this friendly chat did not count as a speech. He simply could not say any more, and tried to smooth things over by asking for a holiday for the girls. This the Mother Superior flatly refused to grant. Perhaps to make up to him a little for this downright rebuff, she offered him a glass of raspberry-vinegar, he said, which was like a nun's anger, being both sweet and acid. This was not the only time he puzzled these loquacious and excitable Celts by the brevity and simplicity of his addresses.[1]

[1] W. Ward, Vol. I, p. 340.

The conclusion he came to, after all these various experiences, was, as he himself put it, that the promoters of the University were, like Frankenstein, scared at their own monster.[1] The incompatibility between his views and the Archbishop's was complete. In Newman's opinion, the aim of the Catholic University should be to fit laymen duly to discharge their responsibilities both to Church and to State, and, in particular, to provide themselves with the weapons necessary to combat the agnostic intellectualism of the times. With this aim before him, it was his object and desire to recruit his professorial staff from men of mature judgment, men who were the most conversant with the problems of the day, and to encourage scientific research in an atmosphere of profound but enlightened belief. Dr Cullen's ideal was to have an exclusively clerical staff, whose academic qualifications would be a purely secondary consideration provided they could keep the laymen under proper control, and restrain them from bringing up any troublesome questions.

When it became quite obvious to him that he was not to be allowed to make the appointments which he considered essential, while Dr Cullen went on, as he had begun, appointing whom he chose, without so much as a word to say what he had done, Newman gave in his resignation.

All this affair gave Newman his first inkling how great was the opposition on the part of the Bishops of the time to the idea, which he cherished so dearly, to the idea, that is to say, of forming an educated and enlightened laity. Nor were the Irish Bishops alone in their attitude. Having noted "the absolute refusal with which my urgent representations were met, that the Catholic laity should be allowed to co-operate with the Archbishops in the work", he adds in his memorandum, "So far as I can see, there are ecclesiastics all over Europe, whose policy it is to keep the laity at arms-length." As a matter of fact, he would soon be hearing his own Bishop saying disdainfully, "The laity? What are they?" He answered, that *the Church would look foolish without them!*

[1] W. Ward, Vol. I, p. 387.

XVIII

"OPERA INTERRUPTA"

We have already mentioned that the earlier and probably the most thankless period of Newman's work in Dublin was darkened still further by an additional trouble, and that was an action at law. In this matter the neglect or indifference on the part of the Catholics who should have stood by him and rallied to his aid, strikes one as no less revolting than the fanatical bias displayed by the Protestants.[1]

In the course of his Corn Exchange lectures on *The Present Position of Catholics in England*, Newman, by way of illustrating the sort of baseless accusations brought by Protestants against the Catholics, had referred by name to a certain champion of the Protestant cause whose charges against Rome had caused a wave of indignation to sweep the country. The individual in question was an unfrocked Italian priest named Achilli who had recently been warmly welcomed in England as a victim of the Holy Office. He had been spreading abroad the most hair-raising accounts of the terrible sufferings which the institution in question had inflicted upon him. Wiseman, however, who had had the necessary information from some friends of his in Italy, had written an article in the *Dublin Review* showing up the man as a thorough-paced impostor. He had, it is true, made acquaintance with the inside of Roman prisons, not, however, for being a heretic, but for acts of gross misconduct, breaches of trust, and other similar trifles.

The *Dublin Review* being little read outside Catholic circles, the article in question had had no great publicity, and Achilli, of course, had taken good care to say nothing about it. Newman, however, had referred to it in his lectures. These lectures were a very considerable success, and Achilli felt he had no alternative but to bring an action for libel against Newman, who, of course, requested Wiseman to let him have his documents. Wiseman, unmethodical as usual, declared that he was unable to put his hand on them. Perhaps the fact of the matter was he didn't want to burn his fingers. Newman then asked him to help in getting the necessary depositions from the Italian magistrates. Whether out of carelessness, or caution, both equally inexcusable on

[1] On all this, see W. Ward, Vol. I, pp. 273 et sqq.

Wiseman's part, seeing that he had started the whole affair, the letters Newman ultimately got were so vague as to be utterly useless.

If Newman was to avoid a most humiliating condemnation, there was only one thing for him to do, and that was to go and seek out witnesses on the spot. That undertaking he would never have successfully fulfilled without the help of his staunch ally, Miss Giberne. Without the slightest hesitation, she started right away to discover the whereabouts of the unfortunate women who had been Achilli's victims, and bring them to England. The extraordinary thing is that by dint of indomitable energy and patience she achieved her purpose.

Newman, of course, incurred enormous expenses over these off-stage proceedings. He had to pay the fares of the witnesses, sometimes of their whole family; then he had to pay for their keep as long as they were in England, for, in the hope of making it impossible for them to appear at the hearing, Achilli, who had got some influential people to back him, tried to get the case put off as long as possible.

In the end, an iniquitous verdict declared that the charges brought by Newman were not supported by sufficient evidence. He was condemned to pay a fine; not, as at one time had been feared, to undergo a prison sentence. *The Times* immediately declared that the verdict was a disgrace to British justice. And public opinion in general, despite its religious prejudices, held that Newman was completely justified, and Achilli utterly discredited. That gentleman immediately disappeared from the scene.

All this time, Wiseman had been lying low.

Meanwhile, Catholics the world over had got up a subscription in Newman's favour. As we have said, this appeal on his behalf met with a response so generous that it enabled him, not only to recover the heavy expenses he had incurred in connection with the lawsuit, but also to finance the building of the Church on St Stephen's Green.

When we take into account the mental anguish the lawsuit must have caused him, as well as Wiseman's most unhandsome behaviour; and when we add to it all the worries, the perplexities, and the rebuffs that were the sole reward for his devoted labours in Dublin, we cannot but admit that only a saint could have borne it all as he did, with his patience unexhausted, and his trust in God unshaken.

These events were the prelude to the darkest hours of his existence. No period of his life has come in for more careless and superficial comment than this. Expressions of sorrowful complaint, though always expressed in terms of unfailing moderation, flowed plentifully enough from his pen. Some of them, never before made public, are given here. It would be a very sorry judgment that should see in them anything to mar the image of him which we carry in our hearts. Yet some there are who have seen in these expressions of a sorrow as bitter as any recorded in the annals of Christian sainthood, the proof that Newman could never be held to merit canonisation. They are the signs, these people tell us, that Newman suffered from an acute, an almost morbidly acute, sensibility. Well; grant that Newman's nervous constitution was in fact as exquisitely sensitive as we are asked to believe, whence comes the idea that sanctity, or the lack of it, is a matter of temperament? Is it only such hardy spirits as are by nature more or less inured or impervious to human sorrow, who are to be judged worthy of being honoured as saints? How are we to judge of sanctity if not by merit? Where, then, is the greater merit? In those whom an equilibrium easily acquired and readily retained preserves from suffering? Or in those who suffer, and suffer, some may deem, too bitterly? Admit that Newman had a morbidly sensitive temperament—well, then, if, notwithstanding his temperament, he was able to maintain an inflexible loyalty to duty, ought the price which that virtue cost him to increase, or to lessen his merit? The qualities that go to make a saint are not measured by his temperament; what he wrings from nature, nature that is rebellious in us all, by his obedience to grace—that is what makes the saint! This much being said, and it hardly admits of discussion, those critics display a truly wonderful lightheartedness who, when they hear a cry of sorrow unusually profound, exclaim, "Oh, what a morbid state of mind!", never stopping to ask themselves whether what is extraordinary about the matter is in the intensity of the pain, or in the sensibility of him who suffers it. Julian the Apostate, be it remembered, mocked at the sufferings of Jesus on the Cross, and judged them pitiable in comparison with those saints who suffered the pains of death with a song upon their lips. Therefore, in what we shall now go on to relate, we shall have no hesitation in reproducing, without abridgment or omission, all those mournful plaints which make the *Journal* sound like an echo of the Book of Job. But, so doing, we shall be mindful also of the other side of the account, of all the sufferings whence those plaints arose, and of the resolute determination of him who suffered them to resist and rise above them; to combat and to conquer. Then shall the reader judge on which side were the sinners, and on which the saint.

The events which filled the years from 1857 to 1878—that is to say, from the end of his ill-starred labours in Dublin to the time when a great-hearted Pope made him tardy but glowing amends—have been recorded in great detail by Wilfrid Ward, at least in their outward aspect; while Thureau-Dangin has made them accessible to French readers.[1] There is scarcely anything to be added to these accounts; we shall therefore content ourselves with noting only the more salient points. But, relying on documents recently given to the public, such as the complete text of the *Journal*, or on passages from it here for the first time quoted, we shall make it our best endeavour, in the pages which follow, to bring out the inner significance of all that these events provoked or accompanied. Before, however, proceeding to do so, we must quote a description of Newman as he was in those Dublin days, a description for which we are indebted to one of the truest of the friends he ever made there, to Aubrey de Vere, one of the minor poets of the Romantic Movement, who had been appointed by Newman to the chair of literature. Portraying him in this, his middle age, de Vere tells us that his countenance bore the imprint of "a tenderness marked by a smile of magical sweetness that had in it nothing of softness . . . a decided severity in his face, that severity which enables a man alike to exact from others, and himself to render whatever painful service or sacrifice justice may claim." Aubrey de Vere puts the finishing touch on this portrait when he says that the face was one that betokened "the rare union of the contemplative mind and the heroic soul".[2]

Seated with him at dinner in Harcourt Street, or strolling in his company through Phoenix Park, some of the older men, such as de Vere, as well as many of their juniors, finding in him even now all the old charm, all the old fascination as potent as ever, might well have thought that, after all, despite all that had happened, Dublin even now might offer him a home. But he knew otherwise; he knew now that Dublin could never be for him, as for a brief space he had hoped it might be, a second Oxford. The only home he craved for now was the Oratory, from which his Dublin appointment had for the time removed him, but to which he longed with all speed to return.

Alas, it was not long before he perceived that there, too, fresh troubles awaited him. He had asked that, during his absence, Dalgairns might be spared from the London house to take his place in Birmingham. And now it soon became only too evident what had

[1] In his *Newman catholique*.

[2] Quoted by Roger McHugh, *The Years in Ireland*, in *A Tribute to Newman*, p. 167.

happened. For a long time Dalgairns had completely identified himself with the views and methods of Faber and his followers, and had now, consciously or unconsciously, influenced a section of the Birmingham community against their founder. The full extent of all this, however, did not become apparent till 1856, when Rome, in the perfectly natural order of things, made an announcement which surprised those who had been in the secret of the matter, quite as much as it did Newman, who had received from the Holy See a document informing him that the modifications in the Oratorian rule which had been petitioned for by the English house had been duly approved. In particular, Oratorians were henceforth empowered to act as religious directors to nuns.

For the moment, Newman was completely thunderstruck. He had never for an instant dreamt of such things; far less asked for them. Clearly Rome had been approached by some other person, and Rome, quite naturally, and in perfectly good faith, thought she had been approached by the accredited representatives of the lawful Superior, to whom she naturally sent her reply. Pulling on this thread, Newman brought to light a whole skein of things he had never even dreamt of.

This unhappy affair seems to have been marked by a series of misunderstandings heaped one upon another. The London Oratorians had asked of Rome something which their Birmingham brethren were anything but desirous of having, and Rome, it seems, under the impression that the two English Oratories were in no way distinct, had given a ruling applicable to them both. This made Newman apprehensive, perhaps unduly so, that all sorts of changes might be imposed on his own community without their having any say in the matter. He consequently requested the London community, since it was they who had started the affair, to make it clear at Rome that they had neither the wish nor the power to involve anyone but themselves. This the London Fathers declined to do, not fully realising the effect that their refusal would have at Birmingham. At the same time, some people had been saying things calculated to prejudice Newman in the eyes of the Prefect of Propaganda, Cardinal Barnabò, and the Italian Oratorians. Newman, when he went to Rome in 1856, determined to do everything in his power to make it henceforth quite clear that the two Oratorian communities were completely autonomous and wholly distinct, one from the other. A single detail will suffice to indicate the gravity of what was taking place. So great was Newman's state of anxiety that, as soon as ever he arrived in Rome, he betook himself barefooted to St Peter's to pray at the tomb of the Apostle. Barnabò, for his part, treated him as a person of no account, not only unworthy of respect, but of being treated with the most elementary politeness.

Concerning all this we have a comment in the *Journal*, the bitterest thing ever recorded therein:

> First in 1853, came my mistake in asking for Dalgairns from the London House, then my going to Ireland, in order to impinge upon Dr Cullen, while Dalgairns intrigued at home in my absence. Then the great plot of him Faber etc,—and my going to Rome—and the treatment I met at Propaganda. Then the thousand whisperings against me at the London Oratory, which have succeeded in prejudicing the Catholic body to a great extent against me.

In all this, neither the good faith of Dalgairns nor of Faber is in question. They had come to think, in all sincerity, that Newman, since he did not accept their conception of what Catholicism was in its entirety, was on the road to heresy. No doubt it pained them to go against him by adopting measures which they, nevertheless, regarded as the acid test of true Catholicism. But, when it is for the glory of God and the salvation of souls that we are striving, is it not our duty to disregard our personal feelings in the matter, however difficult and distasteful that may be?

Back again in Birmingham and settled in at the Oratory, now at last by a formal brief separated from the London house, Newman, by no means out of heart, prepares to devote himself in peace and quiet to a fresh task. His relations with John Moore Capes, the editor of *The Rambler*, were becoming increasingly cordial. Then there were his interchanges with Catholic men of learning like W. K. Sullivan, men whom he had tried to get together into a group in Dublin. All this made him feel more and more strongly than he ought to get back to the work he had begun at Oxford, the attempt, that is to say, to define the relationship between Faith and Reason. It was not a question, and for him it never would be, of any theoretic adjustment of the domain of natural philosophy to that of supernatural faith. On that point, the Thomist synthesis, harmonising a modified Aristotelianism with Revelation, he found completely satisfactory. It will be remembered that his most serious grievance with theological circles in Rome was that they so largely neglected St Thomas and Aristotle. The problem that presented itself to him was something quite different. It was the relation between Faith and Reason in the concrete, not the abstract, in the psychological context in which they actually encountered each other in this present world of ours, not in the world of eternal principles. At Oxford he had attempted to adjust his attitude as a Christian to Reason as it then was, working, that is to say, in the framework which it had inherited from eighteenth-century deism, and which still survived in the Oxford liberalism of the 1840s. Now, his aim was to tackle the question of Reason as it then presented itself, in the atmosphere, namely, of historical criticism, and of the nineteenth-century naturalists and physicists.

It happened, however, that just about that time a new school of thought was beginning to take shape. Veuillot and the *Univers* were its accredited representatives in France. They had an enthusiastic following in England among the Faber group and elsewhere, but more among the converts than among hereditary Catholics. This new school, thinking to imitate Pius IX's change of front after 1848, in regard to liberalism, insisted on having it that the right thing for really orthodox people to do was just to turn a deaf ear to everything the modern world had to say. Criticism, Science—these were the works of the Devil, not merely in some of their more extravagant aberrations, but in their very principle. To apply the methods of historical criticism to the stories of the Saints and still more to the Bible itself, to lend an ear to these newfangled ideas about geology and biology consequent upon some recent discoveries, merely to ask about the evidence for a miracle—all this was to abjure one's faith, or to be getting very near to doing so. That being so, there was only one thing for the genuine Catholic to do, and that was to have recourse to authority. Not only what the Pope and the Church prescribed, but, to put it plainly, whatever passed current in Rome, or in Catholic conservative circles in general, was to be regarded as the absolute rule of faith and morals. Sometime later Ward declared that he would like to see a Papal Bull, as well as *The Times*, on his breakfast table every morning.

In saying that, of course, he was merely caricaturing himself. As a matter of fact, as regards the question of attaining Faith through Reason, he had been too thoroughly imbued with liberal ideas not to agree with Newman that the usual apologetic left a great deal to be desired, and that to be made effective it would have to be something far less elementary, something more on the lines favoured by his one-time leader. But once inside the Church, everything, in his view, became purely and simply a matter for authority to decide. What it was necessary to hold concerning the martyrdom of St Cecilia, or the different geological eras, was a matter to be decided once for all by the documents at headquarters. Even so, it never occurred to him that those documents would necessarily be the work of theologians. The sort of fairy-tale theology he had constructed for himself showed him a uniform stream of oracles flowing from a source of permanent inspiration.

There were some, however, who regarded this betwixt-and-between position as falling below the acceptable minimum. In the eyes of such a man as Talbot, the Papal chamberlain, an Englishman very much in the confidence of the Sovereign Pontiff, and playing an increasingly influential role in the *Curia*, or for a man like Faber, and we might soon add, like Manning, it looked as if Ward still retained something of the old Adam in him; pardonable enough, but disquieting, all the same.

It would be somewhat wearisome to go into details; the thing is clear enough. This so-called super-orthodoxy was but another and final example of intellectual defeatism concealed behind a mask of traditionalism, which, in its various romantic theological manifestations, the Church consistently condemned throughout the nineteenth century. In Newman's eyes, this tendency, which he saw becoming increasingly marked in the minds of the *giovani*, was as dangerous in the pastoral field as it was in the theological. He knew too many men of science, he had too much of the instinct for scientific research in him, not to feel, and to say, that the sort of intellectual suicide to which scientists were to be condemned if they wanted to become, or to remain, Catholics, was an impossible absurdity. It was no good trying to justify such a line by bringing the word "sacrifice" into the matter. In the realm of science there is only one thing that can require us to make a sacrifice, and that is Truth. But Newman had penetrated too deeply into the real meaning of Catholic tradition to see in this spurious orthodoxy any mark of authenticity.

It never occurred to him for a moment that revealed truth dispensed a man from thinking things out for himself, even in realms where its light shone the brightest. Nor did he hold that the guarantee of infallibility bequeathed by Christ to His Church covered the whole mass, all and sundry, of those infinitely varied and varying human ideas and opinions which she sweeps along with her in her train. Had he not, in 1847, made acquaintance with Roman schools, where any sort of systematic theology was suspect, where the Schoolmen were looked down upon, and where positive[1] theology alone was taught, no one

[1] The traditional meaning of this phrase is a theology which limits itself to expounding whatever is revealed, in accordance with the documents of Revelation and Ecclesiastical tradition in general.

realising how ill-equipped it was? The position now was that things were moving in the direction of a rigid systematisation thoroughly steeped in post-Tridentine theology, and, in regard to human science, taking a stand of splendid isolation. If ten years had sufficed to bring about such a change, what was going to happen in another ten? If you canonised and put the seal of the absolute on the theological fashion of your day, might you not find yourself in the painful position of having to unsay it all a decade later?

Considerations of this nature prompted Newman to try to put the matter to rights, not by entering into useless controversy, but by a piece of constructive work designed to show that science may be Christian without having to give up any of its principles, and that a scientist can use his brains without having to renounce his religious faith. He was just starting on this work, when Wiseman broke in with another of his sensational proposals, and he had to put it aside. At the instigation of the ebullient Cardinal, the English Bishops had suddenly made up their minds to furnish the Catholic world with a new English version of the Bible. The old Douai translation was undoubtedly archaic, and it urgently needed revision in some places. What was really wanted was an entirely new version. With his learning and his brilliant literary gifts, Newman towered so conspicuously over all his Anglo-Saxon brethren that it seemed impossible that a work like this should be carried out under any other supervision than his. So important was the task that, loath as Newman was to interrupt his other labours, urgent as they, too, appeared, he at once agreed, and in a letter to Wiseman dated the 14th September, 1857, said he would undertake this new responsibility.

However, he did not wholly abandon his earlier project. The *Atlantis*, a review he had just started in collaboration with Sullivan, made this possible. The *Atlantis* was the last product of his Rectorship.

Meantime, letting no grass grow under his feet, he straightway set about getting together all the collaborators he would be needing for the translation work. All the most intellectually distinguished among the English Catholics, and, first and foremost, men like Dr Newsham and Dr Maguire, who represented the highest traditions of the older clergy, he sounded, and asked to take part. Ward, whom he requested to translate the Psalms, replied at great length, and in the warmest of terms, but emphasised how important it was Newman should not relinquish his project of formulating a new apologetic, and made a most happy suggestion. As editor, he, Newman, would have to write a preface to the new version. Now, why, in these *prolegomena*, should he not combine the two enterprises in one? Where, indeed, could the problem of Faith and Reason be more appropriately dealt with than in an introduction to Holy Writ? So taken was Newman with this proposal that he kept on the stocks until the year 1877, what, in the first instance, he had drafted merely as a preface, then, despairing apparently of ever getting his contemporaries to listen to him, it seems that he destroyed the manuscript, little foreseeing the change of circumstances which, one year later, was to give him the right to speak with an authority which none could disregard. A few of his notes afford us some inkling of the main idea of the composition. It was his aim to show, viewing the history of Israel as a whole, how inescapable is the conclusion that God both speaks and acts. For that purpose he would have taken a line something like the one he afterwards followed in his *Grammar of Assent*, where his aim was to explain how the individual mind comes to embrace revealed truth. When we think of the fresh treatment which a man like Newman might have given to the problems of revelation and Biblical inspiration by handling them anew, with his eye on the difficulties of the modern mind, of the far-reaching theology based on the historical evolution of God's People, we cannot but lament our loss.

However, this new translation, for the sake of which he had once more been torn away from the work he had in hand, was destined to suffer the same fate as had befallen the University of Dublin.

Whilst Newman was lavishing his time and his money in organising this great undertaking, the Bishops and the Cardinal, who had involved him in it, said never a word. He had been at work on it, and so had his collaborators, for a whole year, when Dr Ullathorne informed him that he had just received through Wiseman two letters from America. The first, issued by the whole body of American Bishops, protested against Newman's being entrusted with the work in question. They claimed to be first in the field, saying that a like task had already been entrusted to Archbishop Kenrick of Baltimore, who had started on the work, and had indeed already published a part of it. The second, issued by the Synod of Baltimore, suggested a compromise. It was that the English and American collaborators should combine and produce one single version under the joint superintendence of Newman and Kenrick.

Wiseman and his English colleagues neither then nor later sent a single word about all this to Newman, nor did they reply to the

Americans, being unwilling no doubt to burn their fingers in such an embarrassing situation. Meanwhile, Newman, at the start, seeing that the work was going to involve him in considerable expense, had expressed the desire that the copyright should be made over to him. This, Wiseman, who thought the copyright might be worth a good deal of money, had declined to do. Now, however, when it looked as if the scheme was going to fall through by reason of the American intervention, and when Newman had already involved himself in some heavy expenditure, the Cardinal changed his mind. Still making no allusion to the American affair, he wrote to Newman offering him the copyright, which was now worth little or nothing. On that, it would be superfluous to comment.

Meantime, in the absence of any reply from England, first the Bishop of Charleston, and after him the Archbishop of Baltimore himself, wrote direct to Newman. The only thing he could do was to refer them to the English Bishops, which really meant to Wiseman, seeing that they merely did what Wiseman told them to do. But Wiseman took no notice, nor did he take the trouble to tell Newman what he thought of doing. One of the Irish Bishops, the Bishop of Dromore, who had a friendly regard for Newman, wrote a letter to the Cardinal in which he told him, politely but firmly, that Newman's work, seeing how far he had already got with it, ought to be kept going at all costs. This prelate had no better luck than the other people. He never got a word in reply. It really began to look as if the English Bishops had never heard of this Father Newman and his translation of the Bible.

Newman, without a word of protest, just wrote and told his collaborators to hold up their work, while he himself put his *Prolegomena* on the shelf. So magnanimous was he that he even tried to find excuses for Wiseman in a letter he wrote to Kenrick:

> The Cardinal's many anxieties and engagements, and his late and present illness, doubtless are the cause of a silence which I am sorry you should have felt to be an inconvenience.

Something Faber said on his deathbed, and an article in the *Union Review*, gave him the idea, later on, that what had been at the bottom of the whole business had been carefully concealed from him. One of the big London booksellers, who, it seems, had a large stock of Douai Bibles on hand, appears to have brought pressure, and effective pressure, to bear on Wiseman, so that Newman and his translation should be quietly extinguished.

Forthwith he went back to the old problem, the relations between Faith and Reason. Alas, and to his great repugnance, he was to find himself compelled to deal with it in circumstances very different from the calm and peaceful ones he had hoped to enjoy.

He had kept up all along his correspondence with Capes, the editor of *The Rambler*. Still as alive as ever to the acuteness and actuality of the problems which the review set forth, he was no less so to the defects of Capes, and more particularly to those of Simpson, who had succeeded him in 1858. Richard Simpson, an Oxford man and a converted Anglican clergyman, had always displayed great intellectual brilliance, but also great impatience of authority. His principles were uncompromising, and his application of them fearless. Under his influence, the paper took on an increasingly independent tone, not merely critical but aggressive, in regard to the Bishops and, indeed, to all those Catholics who did not share the views of the editors. At the same time, a sort of arid intellectualism reduced the gravest of religious problems to the level of mere logic-chopping. In his correspondence with the editors, Newman animadverted freely and sometimes pretty sharply on both of these matters. On the other hand, whenever they achieved something really useful and illuminating, he was just as prompt to commend them.

About the same time, *The Rambler* began to increase in prestige. This was due to the fact that one of its contributors was fast gaining for himself a foremost place among international historians. Young Sir John Acton, soon to become Lord Acton, a pupil of the great German historian Döllinger (Sir John himself was of German descent), bore a distinguished name and was the nephew of a Cardinal. In fact, he was eminently and typically representative of the sort of thoughtful Catholic laity whom Newman said it would be folly to muzzle; far better employ them in furthering the cause of God and the Church.

On the 30th December, 1858, an interview took place between Acton and Newman. The former was greatly surprised at the way Newman cast aside his reserve. The outcome was a decision between the two to act in close co-operation. One of the subjects discussed was an article contributed to *The Rambler* by Döllinger himself. Acton had told Newman, to the latter's indignation, that people had been found to denounce this article to the authorities at Rome because it drew attention to the link between Jansenist ideas and St Augustine. In a letter to Simpson, Acton gives an amusing account of Newman's behaviour when he was told about the matter. "He was quite miserable when I told him the news, and moaned for a long time, rocking himself backwards and forwards over the fire like an old woman with a toothache."

In the course of their conversation, Newman insisted, as he afterwards did, again and again, that *The Rambler* should avoid all strictly theological questions, limiting itself to raising, surely and steadily, the intellectual level of the English-speaking Catholics. That was what seemed to him the most prudent line to take. It would be but commonsense to adopt it; moreover, it would provide the atmosphere in which the laity would find themselves most at home.

Despite all the promises that were made to him, number after number appeared without any appreciable modification in the style or substance of their contents. There was the same flippant tone towards authority and, what made matters worse, some very off-hand references to the fundamental data of religious belief.

In 1856, Wiseman had set to work to look for a counterblast to *The Rambler*, and this he found in the *Dublin Review*, which was now refloated fully manned, with Ward at the helm. The bellicose temperament of the latter did not augur a smooth passage despite Newman's efforts, and painful they sometimes were, to mediate between the opposing reviews, despite, too, the whole-hearted admiration (at least, Ward himself believed it was whole-hearted) which the quondam disciple still entertained for his erstwhile leader.

Ullathorne knew and encouraged, even if he did not fully understand, the role that Newman was playing behind the scenes. He wrote on the 16th June, 1859, telling him that *The Rambler* would certainly be censured by the Bishops unless some change were made in it. In Ullathorne's opinion there was only one thing that could be done at the moment to ward off this blow, and that was that Simpson should give up the editorship. To that move, Newman readily agreed. He advised Simpson to resign, and Simpson did so. On the 21st, Ullathorne wrote to thank him for helping to bring about this peaceful solution.

Meanwhile, Burns, who published the journal, as well as Acton, Döllinger, and Simpson himself, all agreed to beg Newman to take over the editorship. No one but Newman had the intellectual prestige, and the personal authority, to maintain the essential character of the Review, to correct its defects, and to set the minds of the Bishops at rest. Through Ullathorne, Wiseman and the other Bishops had definitely asked Newman to take the matter in hand and to adopt whatever measures he might deem fit. At the same time, they did not want Acton as editor, any more than they did Simpson. He hesitated a long time and said many prayers. Then he asked Ward himself what he thought about it all. At last he came to the conclusion that he could not possibly refuse.

But what Ward wanted Newman to do was not only to alter the tone and principles of the Review from top to bottom, but to change its very title. As to the tone, Newman readily agreed; with regard to the principles, he would have liked to have some definite particulars, which, however, Ward did not give him. As for the title, that could not possibly be changed. It would be tantamount to bringing out a new paper. It would look as if the old one had been suppressed because of the censure, which was the very impression they wanted to avoid. Newman stated clearly what his own idea had been in something he wrote long afterwards, on the 24th May, 1882. What he had in mind was to change the general line of the Review, and, more important still, the tone of its editorial matter, wherever such changes were called for by the criticisms he himself had made about it. But, said he,

> I had no wish to damage the fair fame of men who I believed were at bottom sincere Catholics, and I thought it unfair, ungenerous, impertinent and cowardly to make in their behalf acts of confession and contrition, and to make a display of change of editorship and (as if) so virtuous a change

However, the Bishops did not see in the May number—the first that followed this transaction—the prompt and radical change they had expected and they were not satisfied. Ullathorne took the trouble to go and see Newman in order to talk the matter over with him. There was goodwill on both sides, but the conversation showed plainly what a tremendous gap there was between the general standpoint of the English Bishops and that of Newman. Newman often repeated what the Bishop said on that occasion, and the words are highly characteristic. "The Catholics of England were a peaceable people; the Church was peace. Catholics never had a doubt; it pained them to know that things could be considered doubtful which they had always implicitly believed. *The Rambler* was irritating." In answer to that, Newman says, "I stated my own view strongly." It was only too clearly a case of the ostrich hiding its head in the sand, the sort of thing Newman and Ward, yes, even Ward—had always deplored, ever since they became acquainted with Catholic teaching. Did it then come to this, that in order not to disturb the intellectual repose of unenquiring, easy-going Catholics, there was to be no facing up to the questions and arguments put by unbelievers to the more thoughtful Catholics? This presentation of the case had no effect whatever on Ullathorne and his colleagues.

"He did not allow the weight of anything I said," was Newman's only remark. The conversation admitted of only one sequel, and that was that Newman should give up his connection with *The Rambler*. Ullathorne himself suggested the step, and thought that if he resigned in July, that would give the proprietors ample time to look about them. Newman, who had felt such great difficulty in undertaking this responsibility, felt none at all in resigning it. So now, once again, the authorities, having entangled him in an enterprise that was not at all to his taste, tell him they are not at all pleased with his efforts, and leave him to sink or swim in midstream. In a note he had pinned to *The Rambler* correspondence, Newman contented himself with this humorous comment on the change in the editorship which had been made expressly to please the Bishops, "Perhaps the Cardinal, &c., were seized with a panic lest they had got out of the frying-pan into the fire."

However, his troubles with *The Rambler* were not yet over. In an earlier article, Newman had upheld the idea that there was no disrespect to episcopal authority in expressing the hope that the Bishops would take counsel with the laity before committing themselves to certain measures of great practical importance to the latter. (He was thinking of such problems as that involved in the attendance by Catholics at non-Catholic universities.) Among the instances he adduced was the up-to-date one of the consultations which had preceded the definition of the Immaculate Conception. In that case the Holy See had been quite ready to seek the views of the laity. Well, then, thought Newman, if, even in doctrinal matters, the Pope takes the views of the laity into account, the Bishops would not possibly be derogating from their own authority if they listened to what the laity had to say, before they finally committed themselves in regard to matters that were not doctrinal, but purely practical in their nature.

This line of argument must have been very disturbing to some readers. In order to explain and justify it, he wrote another article in which he took up somewhat wider ground. This article appeared in the July number, the last for which he was responsible. It was entitled: "On consulting the Faithful in matters of Doctrine". Little did Newman foresee the outcry which this article was fated to create. After all, it was an extremely moderate affair, almost purely historical in its approach, and adducing only such facts as were familiar to every competent historian. Reminding his readers of the confusion that had followed hard upon the Council of Nicaea, he went on to say, "The episcopate did not, as a class or order of men, play a good part in the troubles consequent on the Council, and the laity did. The Catholic people in the length and breadth of Christendom were the obstinate champions of Catholic truth, and the Bishops were not." The truth of these statements was incontestable, but the article stirred up a more violent reaction than anything else that had appeared in *The Rambler*. One prelate, Dr Brown, Bishop of Newport, took it upon himself to delate the article and its author to Rome. Taking his stand on a sentence divorced from its context, "there was a temporary suspense of the functions of the *Ecclesia Docens*", he formally accused Newman of heresy. To the sequel of that incident we shall return in due course.

Meantime, Newman, seeing the deplorable effect which the shilly-shallying policy of the episcopate was having on the editors of *The Rambler*, was clearly convinced that he ought not to leave them to shift for themselves. He therefore kept in touch with them, after he had resigned the editorship. He did more, he continued to send them contributions. These articles he did his best to make serene and objective in tone and substance, avoiding all controversy, or anything that might lead to it; the sort of thing, in fact, that he had recommended. This put him in a position to express, without any excessive mincing of his words, his disapproval of the extravagances, the errors, the infelicities for which, not only Simpson, but Acton himself was to blame.

Thus, one day, when he was correcting the proofs of an essay on St John Chrysostom, he discovered on the back of them an article by Simpson on Toleration in which the encyclical of Gregory XVI regarding Lamennais was very roughly handled. He said that if that article was printed, he would withdraw his own.

One cannot praise too highly Newman's kindliness and forbearance in these matters, but what could he do, situated as he was betwixt the hammer and the anvil, but displease both sides? He had hoped to withdraw from the editorship with as little noise as had attended his acceptance of it, but as people went on saying openly that he was still responsible for it, he had nothing for it but to write to *The Tablet*, making it quite clear that this was not the case. Acton was greatly offended at this disclaimer, saying that it looked as if Newman was repudiating his former colleagues. However, it was not this, but quite another affair that set the seal on Newman's break with *The Rambler*.

This time it was not the education of the laity, but the training of the clergy that was the question at issue. One H. N. Oxenham, a layman, who for a time had studied at St Edmund's with a view to the priesthood, sent a letter to *The Rambler* criticising the seminary training of the clergy. It was Ward who, although he was a layman and the father of a family, taught dogmatic theology there. Published over the signature X. Y. Z., this letter, though temperate in tone, amounted to an attack on the whole seminarist system: the separation in boyhood of candidates for the priesthood from future laymen, the strict surveillance, the limitations imposed on the reading of the seminarists, and so on. The letter made abundant references, in support of its writer's views, to Newman's Dublin Lectures, applying to the special case of the clergy all that Newman had said about general culture being the best preparation for a strictly professional career.

Ward, when he read the letter, knew perfectly well who had written it and therefore read into it a more fundamental attack on the whole priestly ideal than it would have conveyed to others. Ward, in a letter to *The Tablet* which he signed A. B. C., hit back with all the force at his command. As for Newman, he had been profoundly displeased by the article. Its author was, or pretended to be, unaware of the decisions of the Council of Trent regarding the organisation of seminaries, and entirely disregarded the spiritual preparation necessary for those who were training for the priesthood. Moreover, if there was any matter on which a layman's competence to offer an opinion was at least doubtful, and the adoption of a dictatorial tone quite intolerable, it was this one.

Choosing by a mere accident the signature H. O.—Oxenham's own initials—and quite unaware that Oxenham was the author of the letter on which he was animadverting, Newman wrote to *The Rambler*. He merely pointed out that the passages quoted by X. Y. Z. from *The Idea of a University* had been absolutely divorced from their true context. What Newman had been concerned with in his Dublin lectures was the training of laymen destined to live in the world. Furthermore, he himself had drawn attention to the danger attending culture in general, the danger, namely, of providing the temptation, as well as the means or occasion, of putting oneself on a level with God. Of all this, the writer of the article had taken no account.

It should be added that Newman would have wished that in England as in Germany, a certain number of priests should go through a course of university training. Nevertheless, as he shortly afterwards said in a letter to Ward, he realised that the uneducated among the laity being the many, and the refined, the accomplished, and the large-minded being the few, it would be preposterous that the *clerus universus* should be trained on the model of the few, and not so as to fit him to deal with the capacities and characteristics of the many.

At this juncture, something most amusing and quite unforeseeable happened. Oxenham, greatly annoyed by A. B. C.'s letter in *The Tablet*, thought he discerned the same pen under the initials H. O. Never dreaming for a moment that it was Newman himself who had been playing the scholiast to Newman, he answered as if he took the document to be the work of some fanatic or imbecile, or both; anyhow, someone quite incapable of understanding the meaning of what he quoted. Needless to say, this tickled Ward immensely. At his request, Newman explained his attitude in a letter which he authorised Ward to make public. For his own part, he was glad to have the opportunity of dispelling any false ideas about what he himself really thought.

This story is just another instance of what so often turns out to be the case, and that is that fanaticism and stupidity are not always where we expect to find them. This affair put the final extinguisher on his connection with *The Rambler*. That periodical, having given some further causes for offence to conservative-minded Catholics, and to other Catholics as well, came to an end in 1862, after taking up the question of the temporal power of the Pope.

It is difficult at this date to form an idea of the passionate interest which the question of the Papal States at that time aroused. Practically no one would listen to any half-way or reasoned opinion. Yet, if there ever was a case when a reasoned view of things was imperatively demanded, it was this one. How it could profit the Holy See to maintain the government of a State in the world, now in the process of political development, in the heart of an Italy in which the spirit of nationalism was being so passionately aroused, was indeed a problem. The criticisms, the too-unanswerable representations which Cardinal Antonelli and his policy provoked, did not contribute to facilitate its solution.

Newman agreed with Manning, who was now Provost of the Chapter of the Pro-Cathedral of Westminster, that Acton should be advised to suspend publication of *The Rambler*, that being the only way to ward off the condemnation that was otherwise bound to follow, condemnation not only by the Bishops but by Rome as well. However, simple honesty compelled him to make it quite clear to Manning, the future Archbishop, that he could not possibly regard, as he, Manning, did, the defence of the temporal power, as it then was, as a matter of faith. Little did he foresee the effect which that letter, in which he stated this view in carefully guarded terms, was to have on his relations with Manning. From that moment, in Manning's eyes, he was judged and condemned, without appeal.

The Rambler, then, disappeared; but that same year another periodical, of much wider scope, took its place. It was called the *Home and Foreign Review*. Acton was editor, and all the old *Rambler* group were back again. Newman, in view of the general state of people's minds at the time, would rather this new venture had not been launched, and that Acton had concentrated all his energies on his great historical work. No sooner was this new publication started than Ward, now the official editor of the *Dublin Review*, began, in its columns, a campaign of complete opposition to everything that men like Acton and his friends were advocating. It seemed to Newman, in the light of all this, that he ought once more to assume the role of mediator and peacemaker between the two extremes. It was now that he began a singularly fruitful correspondence with Acton. These letters were intended to sustain and encourage but also to inculcate moderation. Wilfrid Ward has reproduced them almost *in extenso*. There is perhaps no more eloquent testimony than that which these letters furnish to the clarity and firmness of Newman's ideas in regard to those questions on which the Catholics of the nineteenth century found it so difficult to form a clear and balanced judgment.

The *Home and Foreign Review*, incited by Ward and the most intolerant members of the group around him, failed to profit by these great and salutary lessons. In 1864 came the famous scientific congress at Munich, and the speech of Döllinger, who held that scholastic theology should be complemented by a scientific study of the Bible and of the history of theology. The editors of the Review were among those who interpreted this discourse as the manifesto of a new Catholicism, designed to take the place of what they deemed to be a senile and out-of-date tradition. This was very certainly not what Döllinger had had in mind. The Papal Brief, addressed to the Archbishop of Munich, which followed was careful not to condemn the great historian himself, though it did condemn, and most severely, the use that had been made of his words. The *Home and Foreign Review*, thus directly censured, ceased publication.

We may take it as certain that those barren years of difficulty and frustration which Newman had spent in Dublin bore nothing like so heavily upon him as the years that now follow. It may be said, however, that he himself was not so personally involved in *The Rambler* affair, and still less in that of the *Home and Foreign Review*. But that only shows how utterly without foundation is the reproach of self-centredness which some people have levelled against him, because of the note of sadness which pervades some of his most intimate notes and avowals from this time onwards.

The Dublin conflict might quite well be accounted for as the result of a clash of temperaments and ideas between Newman and Cullen. For the Archbishop to have taken him away from what he was doing in order to set him to a task which he was under no obligation to undertake, and then to have quarrelled with him because he had discharged it so faithfully—this was indeed deplorable, though it was just an ordinary enough bit of meanness. But now the conflict was of a very different nature, involving things far beyond Newman and the personalities with whom he found himself in collision. With Ullathorne, the first and, for Newman, the principal, representative of the episcopate, his relations, far from being strained, were almost every day growing closer and closer. But the truth, truth to which Newman had devoted his life, the light against which he prayed he might never sin, this it was that was now at stake, this it was that caused him such agony of mind.

There is a touch of the tragic about the humour with which he says that, when he was in Rome in the years 1846 and 1847, what he felt, when talking to more than one theologian, was that his gravest fault was to have discovered Catholicism, and kept to it in the way he had. This conception of an integral Christianity, of a Church, exacting indeed, but infinitely broad and deep, baffled them, made them feel at a loss. Now, it was no longer a case of a transient impression. The apathy, the total inability of the English Bishops to appreciate what he, with painful conviction, felt to be the crying problem of the time, was enough to fill him with dismay. But now, behold, a party was getting together and taking shape, another group of converts, with Ward, to begin with, as their centre, and, after him, Manning, whose lineaments, for a long time but dimly discerned, were now at length becoming legible. This party, already very sure of itself, declared that it alone was loyal to Rome, and that at the very moment when, with great coolness, it was claiming to be acknowledged as the interpreter of Rome's intentions. First, they tried to make use of Newman, but, failing in that, they realised that in him they had to deal with something far more than an adversary; they had to deal with a conscience, of whose judgment they stood in awe, denounce it as they would. Since they could not bend him, they would take good care to gag him.

But it was now, just when Newman was growing more and more aware of the gulf that was deepening around him, and of all that was signified thereby—it was at this very moment that a certain scatter-brain thought well to deal him a foul and clumsy blow. It was in 1864 that Kingsley's article appeared, that notorious article which was destined, not only to call forth the *Apologia*, the greatest piece of psychological religious literature of all time, but to give rise in Newman to a feeling of confidence such as nobody, least of all Newman himself, thought possible.[1]

[1] To show how true this is, we have only to compare the tone of the *Journal* immediately before and immediately after the Kingsley affair.

XIX

SHADOW AND SUNLIGHT

AFTER his conversion, Newman seemed to have been forgotten by Anglicans and, indeed, by Protestants in general. He himself, very unlike some of the new converts, had no desire whatever to turn back and renew the conflict. Had it not been for the pressure of circumstances and the urgent demand of certain ecclesiastical authorities, which he thought he could not disregard, he would certainly never have written the lectures *On Anglican Difficulties*, or those on *The Present Position of Catholics*. As we have seen clearly enough, it was not by attacks on their Church that he thought Anglicans might be brought back to Rome, but rather by such a presentation of Catholicism as would lend it a new radiance, a fresh attraction.

For nearly ten years he had been devoting his energies to this end, and of those efforts of his, one set-back after another had been the only visible result. All this was bound to attract attention. What is more, the way in which he was misunderstood by at least some of the highest Catholic authorities in England, was bound to strike those who, some with sorrow, some with indignation, had seen him sacrifice everything for the sake of becoming a Catholic. Manning had now begun spreading it abroad that he had taken his stand against the temporal power of the Pope. Either Manning, or some of his *entourage* (Mgr Talbot without a doubt), went the length of asserting that he was preaching in favour of Garibaldi (some even declared that he was helping to finance his campaign), and took care to point out the denial of the faith that such an attitude implied. Nor, furthermore, were people unaware of the rift that had occurred in the Oratory, the Oratory which he himself had founded.

All this was well calculated to give Protestants the idea, which they were only too eager to welcome, that Newman had been misled by the Church. From that, it was but a single step to making the triumphant announcement that he was about to return to the Protestants. That step was taken by the *Stamford Morning Advertiser* in July 1862. This paper gave out the sensational piece of news, which was forthwith repeated by the *Globe*, that Newman had just left the Brompton

N.—23

Oratory [*sic*], which could be taken as the prelude to his forthcoming return to the Church of England.[1]

There had been instances of such things happening among some of the Oxford converts. Speaking generally, they occurred among those who hastily, without due reflection, had identified themselves with a Catholicism of an extremist and provocative form. This sort of thing, in Newman's eyes, made it all the more important to discourage hasty conversions, and those people who were bent on making converts at any price. But it was gravely to misjudge him to suppose that he had been led to the Church from any human motive, and that, because the Church had refused to fall in with it, he had become estranged from her. He therefore lost no time in sending a stinging denial to the *Globe*, a denial such as he hoped would put an end once for all to any hypotheses of the kind.

> I have not had one moment's wavering of trust in the Catholic Church ever since I was received into her fold. I hold, and ever have held, that her Sovereign Pontiff is the centre of unity and the Vicar of Christ; and I have ever had, and have still, an unclouded faith in her creed in all its articles; a supreme satisfaction in her worship, discipline and teaching; and an eager longing, and a hope against hope, that the many dear friends whom I have left in Protestatism may be partakers of my happiness.
>
> This being my state of mind, to add, as I hereby go on to do, that I have no intention, and never had any intention, of leaving the Catholic Church and becoming a Protestant again, would be superfluous, except that Protestants are always on the look-out for some loop-hole or evasion in a Catholic's statement of fact. Therefore, in order to give them full satisfaction, if I can, I do hereby profess *ex animo*, with an absolute internal assent and consent, that Protestantism is the dreariest of all possible religions; that the thought of the Anglican service makes me shiver and the thought of the Thirty-nine Articles makes me shudder. Return to the Church of England! No! "The net is broken and we are delivered." I should be a consummate fool (to use a mild term) if in my old age I left "the land flowing with milk and honey" for the city of confusion and the house of bondage.
>
> I am, Sir,
> Your obedient servant,
> John H. Newman.[2]

Borrowing his expressions from the hymn of dedication, in which the Church is called Vision of Peace, Newman, at the end of his *Essay on Development*, had summed up all that his conversion had brought him. But no one was more safely preserved than he from any danger of confounding the peace which is given by Christ with the peace

[1] W. Ward, Vol. I, pp. 568 et sqq.

[2] *Ibid.*, Vol. I, pp. 580–581.

which the world gives. So there was little cause to fear that the world, while refusing him the tranquil enjoyment of the divine graces, would be able to mar for him the inward serenity which accompanies them. He knew that the Cross is the sign of union with Christ, and if anything could have made him doubt whether he still was so united, it would have been a life that was free from tribulation. At the end of 1852, the Oratory was still in process of getting into working order. Difficulties, of course, there were, but, on the whole, the outlook was exceedingly promising. It is therefore somewhat remarkable that Newman, who was then in Scotland, should have written to the Birmingham Fathers in such a strain as this,

> It is then the very constitution, as it may be called, of the Kingdom of Grace, that its children must all suffer. If they do not suffer here they will suffer the more hereafter; and they suffer little hereafter, in proportion as they suffer much here. The Apostles have laid down the rule, that "through many tribulations we must enter into the Kingdom of God". If then we have no trouble here, either we shall have a long purgatory, or, what is infinitely worse, we are not the children of grace at all, and are going straight for a worse place.

Writing to them again a few days later, he makes his meaning quite clear. The idea he enunciates is perhaps a little startling, but its significance is far-reaching. What he says amounts to this; conversion, in its deeper implications, is not a mere solution, or smoothing away, of doubts and difficulties; not a period of restfulness and calm. To imagine that, for the Christian, life has no burdens for him to bear, is to take a very superficial view of things. The gifts and graces bestowed on the Christian are not of this world, and they bring with them obligations and demands hitherto undreamt of. If he is called to partake of joy and peace, if he is nevermore to know discouragement, this does not mean that his trials are at an end. It is but the necessary introduction to another ordeal of a kind, inconceivable to any but a Christian. Either he must undergo that trial, or risk being the dupe of a perpetual illusion.[1]

This sense of a struggle, not only always inevitable, but becoming more and more of a spiritual necessity as we progress along the Christian way of life, forms the theme of a story which he wrote when in Dublin, the story of *Callista*. Few are the pages in that book in which

[1] We have here made use of certain manuscript notes entitled *Chapter Discourses*, which are really letters sent from Abbotsford on the 22nd December, 1852, and 2nd January, 1853.

his own reactions to the world, to life in general, to the cross which every convert must needs take up, are not visible beneath the thin veil of fiction. If we would realise to the full the rich humanity of his heart, as well as the very delicate but very healthy sensibility which was ever his, it is to this book that we should turn.

Agellius, who has long been a Christian, but whose early ardour has much abated, falls in love with a young pagan, Callista. He is anxious to win her over to the Christian faith, but, little by little, it is borne in upon him that it is for his own sake that he is so eager to convert her. There is but one way of bringing her to God and of finding his own way back to Him, and that is to renounce all hope of the human happiness which, for him, she represented.

This little drama, sketched in quiet, simple tones, is set in surroundings which reveal Newman's conception of the Universe with marvellous clearness. All the allurements of the world of sense, which grow the stronger the more clearly they are seen, are here portrayed in happier terms than in any of the Oxford sermons. But here, too, the magical, demoniac fascination of the Enemy of God is seen veiled in the most transparent attractiveness. But over against this, on the other side of the picture, are the agony of the Crucifixion, the triumph of martyrdom, the Divine Presence victorious, joy and peace untold.

In the middle of those sad years which were to follow, he wrote a poem which Wilfrid Ward did well to set over against some of the reflections he made when his spirits seem to have reached their nadir. In it, we have again the old theme of the two worlds and their bewildering juxtaposition. This world, with all its freshness and beauty, speaks to us of the world to come, ere it becomes its rival; then, at last, by the cross it imposes on us, after cheating us with the promise of happiness here and now, it becomes, once more, the herald of that other world.

The Two Worlds

Unveil, O Lord, and on us shine
In glory and in grace;
This gaudy world grows pale before
The beauty of Thy face.

Till Thou art seen it seems to be
A sort of fairy ground,
Where suns unsetting light the sky,
And flowers and fruit abound.

But when Thy keener, purer beam
Is poured upon our sight,
It loses all its power to charm,
And what was day is night.

Its noblest toils are then the scourge
Which made Thy Blood to flow;
Its joys are but the treacherous thorns
Which circle round Thy brow.

And thus when we renounce for Thee
Its restless aims and fears,
The tender memories of the past,
The hopes of coming years,

Poor is our sacrifice, whose eyes
Are lighted from above;
We offer what we cannot keep,
What we have ceased to love.[1]

Nevertheless, it is not in utter loneliness that Newman yet again comes into the presence of his Creator. The Church is now the place at long last discovered where he may find Him, that shining home already his by the power of faith which outstrips sight, that home so bright amid the shadows of this world. The Church is no unincarnate society, no *Civitas Platonica* without any counterpart on the earthly plane. No; it is a daily and most joyful reality. When disappointments are heaped upon him at the hands of her human representatives, at those terrible moments when he is forced to cry, in the words of the Psalmist, *Imposuisti homines super capita nostra*, it is beautiful to see how the reality, the divine reality of the Church of God existing in this present world, is for him a truth whereof he never entertains a doubt. Nay, it is rather his overflowing consolation. And this, be it noted, in circumstances demanding an act of faith, is perhaps an act of faith beyond compare. Faith is ever a struggle, but a struggle in which we appeal for help to God, so that to God we may attain. What his thoughts were concerning these things, nothing could more clearly reveal than the words of a prayer which belongs to those years:

Let me never for an instant forget that Thou hast established on earth a kingdom of Thy own, that the Church is Thy work, Thy establishment, Thy instrument; that we are under Thy rule, Thy laws and Thy eye—that when the Church speaks, Thou dost speak. Let not familiarity with this

[1] Cf. W. Ward, Vol. I, p. 592.

wonderful truth lead me to be insensible to it—let not the weakness of Thy human representatives lead me to forget that it is Thou who dost speak and act through them.[1]

Nor is that act of faith a blind one. When he asks God always to reveal Himself behind those erring and fallible men who represent Him in the Church which is holy and infallible, Newman prays also that he himself may be enlightened. May he never stumble nor fail in that individual personal effort after truth from which the Church, once more be it said, in nowise dispenses us.

> Come, O my dear Lord, and teach me in like manner. I need it not, and do not ask it, as far as this, that the word of truth, which in the beginning was given to the Apostles by Thee, has been handed down from age to age, and has already been taught to me, and Thy Infallible Church is the warrant of it. But I need Thee to teach me day by day, according to each day's opportunities and needs. I need Thee to give me that true Divine instinct about revealed matters that, knowing one part, I may be able to anticipate or to approve of others. I need that understanding of the truths about Thyself which may prepare me for all Thy other truths—or at least may save me from conjecturing wrongly about them or commenting falsely upon them. I need the mind of the Spirit, which is the mind of the holy Fathers, and of the Church, by which I may not only say what they say on definite points, but think what they think; in all I need to be saved from an originality of thought, which is not true if it leads away from Thee. Give me the gift of discriminating between true and false in all discourse of mine.[2]

This encounter of immutable truth and human frailty, within us and around us, wherein is the whole mystery of the Church, was henceforth to be enacted for Newman in just such a setting as he himself would have wished. It comes, in fact, to suit him more and more as the years pass on, years outwardly so sad and sombre, but inwardly, in the depths of his being, illumined with an evergrowing light. The Oratory, which to begin with he had taken up as a result of the elimination of other plans, rather than because it presented any positive attraction in itself, had now become very dear to him. Following its rule, it is himself that he finds again, as Catholic and priest, in St Philip's ideal, and ever more and more, as that ideal becomes the very texture of his own existence. Slowly and surely, without his knowing it or consciously willing it, the form and figure of the saint who created the Oratory grows clearer—to his eyes shall we say? or to his inward vision?

Philip, for him, now takes his place beside those great figures of the

[1] W. Ward, Vol. II, p. 365. [2] *Ibid.*, Vol. II, p. 366.

Bible—Abraham, David, Jeremiah—who were always familiar friends, and beside those who were dearest to him among the Fathers of the Church—Athanasius, Gregory Nazianzen, Chrysostom—as though he were his second self. He reveals to him possibilities, till then hidden within the depths of his being, and illumines his everyday countenance with a calm and tranquil light, in striking contrast with the shadows that encompass him.

Back once more in Dublin after that agonising journey to Rome which the events of 1856 had driven him to undertake, he sent the Birmingham Fathers a series of letters concerning the Oratorian vocation. So important did their recipients consider them, so germane to their present needs, that they had them printed at their own expense in a little booklet, which, however, was never offered to the public. The little volume opens with a moving prayer addressed by Baronius to St Philip. Then follows this exquisite litany in honour of the Saint,

> Vir prisci temporis,
> Sanctus amabilis,
> Heros umbratilis,
> Pater suavissimus,
> Flos puritatis,
> Martyr caritatis,
> Cor flammigerum,
> Discretor spirituum.

And again,

> Lux sanctae laetitiae,
> Imago pueritiae,
> Forma senectutis,
> Piscator fluctuantium. . . .

Then follow the seven letters which, together, throw an invaluable light on what the Oratory meant to him. The several ideas which he unfolds in them all link up with the definition of the Oratory as set forth in the first Bull of Institution, in which it is described as a congregation of secular priests. Nothing, indeed, is more essentially characteristic of the Oratorian rule than this living in community, with the object which is that of all religious communities, the object, that is to say, of aiming together at achieving Christian perfection but remaining all the time indistinguishable from other secular priests.

Newman begins by showing how this paradox is possible, by analysing the connection between such perfection and what are called the Gospel precepts. Perfection is a thing for which the Christian is bound to strive. It forms the sum-total of all the precepts of the Gospel as described in the concluding words of the Sermon on the Mount: "Be ye therefore perfect, even as your Father which is in heaven is perfect." The precepts, such as those which inspire the three monastic vows "namely, Poverty, Obedience, Chastity," are but means put into action in order to achieve that aim. It is impossible to achieve it unless we have recourse to some extent to those Gospel precepts. But all those precepts are not universally applicable. We must not in consequence so idolise them as to exalt them above the end to which they are but the means. While, therefore, we strive with all our might after perfection, we may, wherever the nature of our mission so prescribes, omit to observe this or that precept, if it would hinder that particular work.

Thus it came about that the priest's immediate presence in the modern world seemed to St Philip to be an essential part of his vocation and of his disciple's vocation. That he might be all things to all men in the Rome of his day, Rome whose Apostle he was, he dispensed with the breastplate of vows, even as David put aside the armour of Saul. Speaking broadly, all manner of precepts that may be of the greatest service in the achieving of sanctity, were discarded by him for the sake of the apostolate to which God had called him, in which, and nowhere else, was perfection attainable by him.

Newman dwells long and insistently on the point, on which, from the outset, Faber, Dalgairns, and the *giovani* had opposed his wishes. To put aside the culture of the mind, to disdain all intellectual pursuits, may be in some cases a highly meritorious act of humility. But, in spite of the childlike simplicity so dear to the heart of St Philip Neri, this means to an end, this instrument, for such it is, was never one that he encouraged his followers to adopt.

Dalgairns would have it that for them to address themselves to the consideration of matters intellectual, as well as to the education of children and young folk, would constitute a departure from the original character of the Oratory, a deviation of the sort for which certain Frenchmen of the seventeenth century, such as Berulle and Condren, were answerable. This was by no means the case. To begin with Baronius; he was not only encouraged, but deliberately prompted, by St Philip to take this line, which is definitely in the Oratorian tradition. It betokens no worldly leanings; no abatement of Christian ardour. What it does betoken is a sense of duty. Just as St Philip succeeded in winning back to God the dissolute youth of the Renaissance by sharing, so far as he could do so without sin, in their interests, their enthusiasms, and even in their amusements, so did it behove the Oratory to win back the intellectuals of the day who had strayed so far from Christ, by sympathising with them, not from afar, but in their actual lives, sharing in all their researches, all their endeavours, and all their expectations.

This is in no way to abandon the pursuit of perfection. It means seeking it along another road, a more difficult road, a more perilous road, but one that wins us the greater merit, provided we remain faithful to our aim. However, if it be true that the seekers after perfection, though free to adopt or discard this or that particular precept as circumstances may require, can by no means dispense with them all, which are those to which the Oratorians will have recourse? They will choose those least likely to hinder them in their sacerdotal ministry, yet those also best calculated to ward off the dangers to which that ministry might be specially exposed. Living in the world, mingling with the world in a manner no regular could do, they found their safeguard in community life. Sacerdotal community, the common task sustained in common, all this never obligatory, but always the more freely agreed to in that it needs constant renewal in order to be carried on, this for them was the great, the salutary rule. And since, for them, community is not imposed on them once for all by a solemn vow, it must needs be a sort of supernatural friendship or family group. And so, brotherly charity, as Bossuet clearly saw, becomes the safeguard of charity, charity unqualified, but it does so because it tends to mingle with "the love of God poured into our hearts by the Holy Ghost."

One could scarcely fail to recognise in these indications the final efflorescence of some of Newman's earliest intuitions. That gentle captivity, gentle but inexorable, in the love of God, which, once it is recognised, subdues the most freedom-loving spirit more effectually then any external constraint could have done—is not this identical with the deep religious intuition by which he was visited when he was a boy of sixteen? And this intellectual vocation harnessed to the service of Apostolic charity—what is it but the final adjustment, so long and so hesitatingly sought, between intellectual and spiritual excellence?

The image of Philip, as Newman came to see it, can alone give to these few traits the gentle and radiant warmth of life which makes them harmonise in his own countenance. The Florentine subtle and candid; smiling to others, austere to himself; the most simple-hearted and the most perfect of humanists, but also the wielder of a disconcerting irony, who called the Fathers of the desert, "old fellows of my kidney," could have found no more speaking likeness of himself than in these lines of Newman, who, however different he was from his subject, seems sometimes to project himself unwittingly into the portrait:

This is the Saint of gentleness and kindness,
Cheerful in penance, and in precept winning;
Patiently healing of their pride and blindness,
Souls that are sinning

This is the Saint, who, when the world allures us,
Cries her false wares, and opes her magic coffers,
Points to a better city, and secures us
With richer offers.

Love is his bond, he knows no other fetter,
Asks not our all, but takes whate'er we spare him,
Willing to draw us on from good to better,
As we can bear him.

When he comes near to teach us and to bless us,
Prayer is so sweet, that hours are but a minute;
Mirth is so pure, though freely it possess us,
Sin is not in it.

Thus he conducts by holy paths and pleasant,
Innocent souls, and sinful souls forgiven,
Towards the bright palace where our God is present,
Throned in high heaven.

In another version of the same hymn, three stanzas bring together Philip, Mary, and the Angels, Mary the Queen of Oriel in whom he had already put his trust to bring him to Jesus, among those other "angel faces . . . loved long since and lost awhile."

This is the Saint, with whom our hearts, like Moses,
Find o'er the waste that Tree, so bright and beaming,
Till 'neath her shade the sobered soul reposes,
After its dreaming.

And then he shakes the boughs where it is lying,
Nor of their fruit are those sweet branches chary,
May the tree, Jesus the fruit undying,
Jesus and Mary;

Jesus and Mary, Philip and high Heaven,
Angels of God the glorious reflexion,
To you be praise, to us from you be given
Peace and protection.

The long and patient work involved in the building of the Oratory took up more of Newman's time than one would have thought his public engagements and preoccupations would have allowed. In 1852, in the very middle of the Achilli trial, the Community, giving up their temporary and inconvenient quarters in Alcester Street, came and settled at Edgbaston, a suburb of Birmingham, in the premises which Newman had had built, and where so many things still today remain exactly as he left them. In spite of the omnibuses which ply continuously up and down the Hagley Road, in spite of the development of a thickly populated industrial quarter on the very fringe of the Oratory site, Edgbaston, with its many parks, its quiet, shady avenues, still remains an oasis of silence, notwithstanding its proximity to so vast and busy a commercial centre.

Newman at once took up his quarters in the little room, its walls lined with books, its cupboards stuffed with manuscripts, whose three windows look out on to the end of the small garden and a street corner, where you rarely see a passer-by. He had but a little way to go, no more than a few steps, to reach the magnificant collection of books which had been brought from Oriel to Littlemore, from Littlemore to Maryvale, and now from Maryvale to Birmingham, to find itself at last comfortably installed in the handsome oblong chamber that had been designed to receive it. Beside it was the little community chapel where was always the Blessed Sacrament, and whither he loved to withdraw for prolonged and peaceful meditation.

Here, in this home of peace, where many a memento of his Oxford days was to be seen mingled with pictures connected with Rome and with St Philip Neri, a new group of friends gradually gathered about him under the aegis of the Oratory. Old friends who came to see him refused to admit that these new surroundings of his bore any comparison with the old. No doubt there was no one among this later group to be put on a par with men like Pusey, Froude, or Keble, to say nothing of Whately and Hawkins. If, from the purely intellectual point of view, this new society was not so brilliant as the other, it made up for it by its supereminent moral qualities. That is not to say that it did not also include some most highly gifted minds. His dearest companion, friend, and disciple in one, whose filial devotion and lavish affection were the best of human consolations amid the many trials he had to suffer, was one to whom he always referred as, "My dear Ambrose St John". He had got to know him in 1843, when St John was devoting himself with passionate interest to the study of Oriental languages, one of Pusey's most industrious pupils. St John, who was twenty-eight, was not then at Oxford. For two years, he had been a curate of Henry Wilberforce's at Walmer in Kent. It will be recalled that in 1846, when Newman had just settled in at Maryvale, he wrote to his former pupil, the most beloved because the most loving of them all, saying, "And that is the reason perhaps I love St John so much, because he comes from you and from your teaching".

Soon after being introduced to Newman by Morris, Pusey's assistant, St John came to Littlemore to try to clear up some of his doubts. After that initial visit he wrote to ask permission to come again "for about three months, perhaps a longer time." Newman agreed, but at the same time warned him that he would not attempt to solve his difficulties for him, but merely to afford him the atmosphere of peace and prayer in which he might be able to settle them for himself. As Fr Tristram writes, "The anticipated visit 'for about three months, perhaps a longer time', was destined to endure for thirty-two years".[1]

He was received into the Church at Prior Park by Dr Brindle on the 2nd October, 1845, returning to Littlemore just in time to be present at Newman's own reception. Newman and he were students together at Propaganda, and he won the affections of the warm-hearted Italians by the kindnesses and attentions he showered on his companion. They called him his Guardian Angel. He was quite a young man and looked still younger than he was, decidedly English-looking, fair-haired and blue-eyed, with a very cheerful expression, altogether a striking contrast to Newman with his expression of mingled gentleness and austerity. One can understand how it was that, when they saw him, the Romans quoted St Gregory's saying, *Non Angli, sed Angeli.*

Thereafter, he continued to devote to his Semitic studies all the time he could spare from his duties, which consisted largely in visiting the sick, and afterwards, from 1861 until his death, in looking after the school of which we shall speak hereafter. St John began to age very early. Pius IX, when he saw him again in 1867, playfully taunted him with being a *vecchione*. The handsome young man had become an

[1] H. Tristram, *Newman and his friends,* p. 255, London, 1933. From this exquisite book, most of the details which follow are taken.

elderly gentleman with a decided tendency to *embonpoint*. The contrast with Newman, who, if he had changed at all, was slimmer than ever, was no less marked, and certainly no less comical. According to Fr Tristram, the differences between the two were not confined to their physical characteristics. St John, it seems, took no interest at all in patristics or in philosophy, and he had no ear for music. On the other hand, he was by no means unappreciative of the merits of a good cigar, whereas Newman simply could not bear the smell of tobacco. Over and above the religious interests they had in common, the only thing St John had to offer was his heart. As to the worth of that offering, we have only to remind ourselves of the inestimable value Newman set upon their friendship.

St John died in 1875. It was William Paine Neville who succeeded him as Newman's secretary, right-hand-man, and, to some extent, his confidant, Newman being by this time quite an old man. Neville, too, had been at Trinity, but he had arrived too late to come under Newman's direct personal influence. However, his ideas had been largely moulded by a prominent Tractarian, John Hungerford Pollen, then a fellow of Merton. Later on, Pollen became a convert, and he it was who was the architect of the University Church, Dublin. It was Newman who received Neville into the Church, at Leeds, at the same time as a number of others. That was on the 2nd April, 1851. He was Newman's devoted assistant and rendered him every possible help. He was also Newman's literary executor, and on him fell the task of collecting all his letters and papers.

A far more striking personality was one who was destined to succeed Newman as Superior of the Birmingham Oratory, Henry Ignatius Dudley Ryder. Fr Ryder came of a family of some note. An ancestor of his had been a member of Pitt's cabinet, another a Bishop, the first to be chosen from the ranks of the Evangelicals. His father, an Anglican clergyman, had become a convert to the Church of Rome in 1846, he and his whole family. For a time, Henry, together with some other boys, was at Maryvale. Afterwards, he put in some time at the Catholic University, Dublin. In 1856, he entered the Oratory, and was ordained priest in 1863. Henceforth the main part of his time was occupied by his clerical duties, especially those entailed by the parochial charge of an extensive suburban district. Totally devoid of ambition though he was, caring nothing about writing or publishing, he was a man of exceptional intellectual gifts and culture. A few years later, when Newman was thinking how he could best tone down some of Ward's more extravagant utterances regarding Infallibility, Ryder, who was then barely thirty years of age, brought him a little essay of his own on the subject. Newman judged so highly of its merits that he forthwith had it printed, and wrote no more on the subject himself.

The mother of this tall, handsome young man, was one of the four granddaughters of John Sargent, Rector of Woolavington-cum-Graffham in Sussex. All four were famous for their beauty, and married, respectively, Samuel Wilberforce, Bishop, first of Oxford and then of Winchester, his younger brother Henry, H. E. Manning, and G. D. Ryder. It was doubtless from his mother that Ryder inherited at least some of his disarming fascination. The impression was increased as soon as one realised that he was possessed of a mind at once strictly logical and at the same time delicately poetical. He was, without a doubt, the ruling personality at the Oratory.

After Ryder, some mention at least must be made of Fr John Joseph Gordon. He was at Rugby, just before Arnold became headmaster. From there, he went on to Oxford with his younger brother. This was when the Tracts were beginning to go the round. To begin with, he made considerable fun of them, but after hearing some of Newman's sermons, he changed his tune. For a brief period he was a clergyman in the Church of England, and, then, in 1847, he became a Catholic. He began his Oratorian noviciate a year later, together with his brother, afterwards known as Fr Philip Gordon of the London Oratory. It was his admiration for Newman, when he saw him for the first time, that made, first, a convert of him, and then a priest. Newman who, as a rule, hated being made an object of veneration, was nevertheless completely disarmed by the generous confidence with which the young man committed himself to him. Unhappily, Joseph Gordon's life was fated to be cut short. Shortly after the Achilli trial, during which he had proved himself one of Newman's stoutest supporters, on the 13th February, 1853, he died. Newman wrote a beautiful memorial tribute to him which Fr Tristram quotes in full. In 1865, when *The Dream of Gerontius*, the poem of a Christian death, came to be written, it was to Fr Gordon that Newman inscribed it.

We saw how, at Oxford in the 1840s, that Oratorian-like community in which Newman seemed to visualise the pattern of an Oxford college enriched with all its pristine Catholic and religious character, drew so many converts to the Movement into its orbit. So was it now at the Oratory itself. One of the main problems of these visitors was the difficult and delicate one of their children's education.

The great English public schools, as well as the older universities, were closed to them. When Newman founded the University of Dublin, of all the high hopes that had attended that event, nothing had rejoiced them more than the idea that they were going to find in Dublin another Oxford. The idea naturally came about that their boys would receive their early training in Birmingham, under the shadow of the Oratory, after which they would go across St George's Channel to the Father who would put them through their final stages, as he had done their fathers before them.

The *giovani*, we know, regarded this plan, the plan of starting a school, as something of a corruption, French in its origin, of the true Oratorian ideal. Newman, however, bearing in mind that St Philip had spent a great part of his time educating young people, by no means shared their view. But the sort of little school that appealed to him was something very different from the general run of Catholic schools in those days. In it, the spirit of St Philip would prevail, his gentle firmness, his warm-hearted trustfulness, and that service which was perfect freedom. That meant that all the best of the public school tradition would be preserved, but purified, and illumined by the light of grace.

Such a project as this could not even begin to be put into effect without coming into collision with prejudices that were more or less calumnious in their implications. In Ireland, people had been terribly alarmed when they realised that Newman was firmly against modelling university discipline on that of an Italian seminary. What would such laxity as that lead to in a school for quite small boys? Whereto Newman very sensibly replied, "It does not logically follow, because I think in matters of discipline a University should not be like a School (which I *do* think), that *therefore* in those same matters a School *should* be like a University."

It proved impossible to open the school till 1859, and by that time Newman had already relinquished his post at the University. He exercised the greatest care in selecting the teaching staff, and personally saw to all the details of organisation. Fr Nicholas Darnell was the first headmaster. But Newman, while anxious to keep the actual school-work up to the highest level, was also concerned, especially in the case of the younger children, with their out-of-school training, as distinct from what was taught them in class. With this in view, he wanted a lady of wide experience, a Mrs Wooten, who had become a Catholic through his influence, to be something more than an ordinary matron; he wanted her to be, in a special sense, mistress of the house. This was opposed by Darnell and the other masters, and, as Newman stood firm, they resigned in December 1861. The school apparently suffered no great ill from this crisis. Darnell's place was taken by Ambrose St John, and there he stayed throughout the fourteen years that still remained to him. Dr Arnold's son, Thomas Arnold, he too a convert, became senior classical master.

This little school, amid all those many great undertakings that had had to be abandoned, was always a great solace and comfort to Newman. He never ceased to take an interest in it, and a very active interest. He even took over for a time the duties of director of studies. No doubt such occupations brought back the memory of his own early days with singular vividness, especially on those occasions when he would spend whole days rehearsing some play of Terence, making his pupils repeat their parts till they were word-perfect, even contributing topical prologues in the best style of the Latin author. One day when the school orchestra was playing over some chamber music, he was seen to be moved to tears as the strains of one of his favourite pieces of Beethoven fell upon his ear.

It would, however, be a great mistake to take it that his appearances in the Oratory School were uniformly idyllic in character. He took an interest in the work of each individual pupil, and was by no means averse to putting them through some pretty stiff interrogations. These latter spread a feeling of holy terror throughout the house, followed as they sometimes were by painful retribution punctually administered by the mild Ambrose St John.

Newman was always prone to reminiscence, and these dealings with schoolboys brought back to him the memory of days long past. If he was little, or perhaps not at all, tempted to regret his associations with the Anglican Church, he certainly did look back with longing on his days at Ealing and at Oxford. Indulging in memories of the past had always seemed justifiable to him because they enabled him the better to order and provide for the future. But now he feared lest he should despair alike of the present and the future; feared, indeed, that, for him, there was no future. This apprehension runs all through the first entry in the *Journal*, a sort of diary of the spirit, which is dated 15th December, 1859.

Nemo, mittens manum suam ad aratrum, et respiciens retro, aptus est regno Dei. I am writing on my knees and in God's sight. May He be gracious unto me! As years go on, I have less sensible devotion and inward life. I wonder whether it is, or rather whether it is not, so with all men, viewed as apart from the grace of God. The greater part of our devotion in youth, our faith, hope, cheerfulness, perseverance, is natural—or, if not natural, it is from a *εὐφυία* which does not resist grace, and requires very little grace to illuminate. The same grace goes much further in youth as encountering less opposition—that is, in the virtues which I have mentioned. The Greek poet, himself an old man, speaks (in the Chorus of the *Oedipus Coloneus*) of the unamiable state of the aged. Old men are in soul as stiff, as lean, as bloodless as their bodies, except so far as grace penetrates and softens them. And it requires a flooding of grace to do this. I more and more wonder at *old* saints. St Aloysius, or St Francis Xavier or St Carlo, are nothing to St Philip. O Philip, gain me some little portion of thy fervour. I live more and more in the past, and in hopes that the past may revive in the future. My God, when shall I learn that I have so parted with the world, that, though I may wish to make friends with it, it will not make friends with me?

Three weeks later, he returns to his *Journal* again, and makes quite clear the sort of temptation he feels. Here again, it is not his conversion that he is sorry for. What he does regret, what he does look back upon with longing, is the life that he lived before his conversion, when things on the human plane seemed to go so well, the life which his obedience to the Light seemed to have taken from him for ever.

8th January, 1860.

When I last wrote, I had something to say, but I lost my thread, and got on a different line of thought, far away from what I had intended,—and I will now recover it, if I can. Circumstances have brought a special temptation upon me of late. I have been exerting myself, labouring, toiling, ever since I was a Catholic, not I trust *ultimately* for any person on earth, but for God above, but still with a great desire to please those who put me to labour. After the supreme judgment of God, I have desired, though in a different order, their praise. But not only have I not got it, but I have been treated, in various ways, only with slight and unkindness. Because I have not pushed myself forward, because I have not dreamed of saying: "See what I am doing and have done"—because I have not retailed gossip, flattered great people, and sided with this or that party, I am nobody. I have no friend at Rome, I have laboured in England, to be misrepresented, backbitten and scorned. I have laboured in Ireland, with a door ever shut in my face. I seem to have had many failures, and what I did well was not understood. I do not think I am saying this in any bitterness.

"Not understood"—this is the point. I have seen great wants which had to be supplied among Catholics—especially as regards education,—and of course those who laboured under those wants, did not know their state,—and did not see or understand the want at all—or what was the supply of the want—and felt no thankfulness at all, and no consideration towards a person who was doing something towards the supply, but rather thought him restless, or crotchety, or in some way or other what he should not be. This had naturally made me shrink into myself, or rather it has made me think of turning more to God, if it has not actually turned me. It has made me feel that in the Blessed Sacrament is my great consolation, and that, while I have Him Who lives in the Church, the separate members of the Church, my Superiors, though they may claim my obedience, have no claim on my admiration, and offer nothing for my inward trust. I have expressed this feeling, or rather implied it, in one of my Dublin sermons, preached in 1856. [*Occasional Sermons*, pp. 64, 65, p. 57, edition 4.]

So far well—or not ill—but it so happens that, contemporaneously with this neglect on the part of those for whom I labour, there has been a drawing towards me on the part of Protestants. Those very books and labours of mine, which Catholics did not understand, Protestants did. Moreover, by a coincidence, things which I had written years ago, as a Protestant, and the worth or force of which were not understood by Protestants then, are bearing fruit among Protestants now. Hence some sympathy is showing itself towards me on the part of certain persons, who have deliberately beat me down and buried me for the last ten years. And accordingly I have been attracted by that sympathy to desire more of that sympathy, feeling lonely, and fretting under, not so much the coldness towards me (though that in part) as the ignorance, narrowness of mind, and self-conceit of those whose faith and virtue and goodness, nevertheless, I at the same time recognised. And thus I certainly am under the temptation of looking out for, if not courting, Protestant praise.

And now I am coming to the meaning of the text with which I began on Dec. 15th. "No man putting his hand to the plough, etc." I am tempted to look back. Not so, O Lord, with Thy grace, not so! What I had meant to say then, to ask of Thee then, I ask of Thee now. What a shame that I should fear to ask it. I have asked it often in time past, I think, long before I was a Catholic. Yes, I have referred to it above, as in the words above thirty years ago. "Deny me wealth", etc. It has been my lifelong prayer, and Thou hast granted it, that I should be set aside in this world. Now then let me make it over again. O Lord, bless what I write and prosper it,—let it do much good, let it have much success; but let no praise come to me on that account in my lifetime. Let me go on living, let me die, as I have hitherto lived. Long before I knew St Philip, I wished *nesciri*. Let me more and more learn from Thy grace *sperni*, and *spernere me sperni*. . . .

Three years went by before he again took up the little notebook with the mottled cover, in which he recorded the innermost workings of his mind. One month before his sixty-second birthday, on the 21st January, 1863, he turned to it again. By this time he had come to feel so utterly useless that he felt like giving up all attempts, up to now unremitting, to keep himself in good health, so that he might be able to master any task that came along. What was the good of it all? Then came these notes which sum up and explain all those inward impressions which the preceding pages had recorded.

O how forlorn and dreary has been my course since I have been a Catholic! here has been the contrast—as a Protestant, I felt my religion dreary, but not my life—but, as a Catholic, my life dreary, not my religion. Of course one's earlier years are (humanly speaking) best, and again events are softened by distance—and I look back on my years at Oxford and Littlemore with tenderness. And it was the time when I had a remarkable mission—but how am I changed even in look! Till the affair of No. 90 and my going to Littlemore, I had my mouth half open, and commonly a smile on my face,—and, from that time onwards my mouth has been closed and contracted, and the muscles are so set now, that I cannot but look grave and forbidding. Even as early as 1847, when I was going through the Vatican with Dalgairns, stopping before a statue of Fate which was very striking and stern and melancholy, he said: "Who *can* it be like? I know the face so well." Presently he added: "Why, it is you!"

Then, sadly but calmly, and that very calmness is perhaps the saddest thing about it all, he proceeds to review all the uncomprehending rebuffs which, one after another, in unbroken succession, had been heaped upon him. The blaze of glory, which the sudden revelation of the great supernatural attributes of the Church had at first seemed to cast over the sorry shortcomings and petty meannesses of mankind, was now pierced with a discerning ray which did not, and henceforth could not, fail to distinguish the gift of God from the poverty of the human envelope which enshrouded it.

How dreary my first year at Maryvale when I was the gaze of so many eyes at Oscott, as if some wild incomprehensible beast, caught by the hunter, and a spectacle for Dr Wiseman to exhibit to strangers, as himself being the hunter who captured it! I did not realize this at the time except in its discomfort; but also, what I did realize, was the strangeness of ways, habits, religious observances, to which, however, I was urged on to conform without any delicacy towards my feelings. J. B. Morris undertook to lecture me. This has been the way with those who had been Protestants, and who felt themselves (seemingly) on a level with me now. Morris lectured me as the organ of Dr Wiseman, Dalgairns lectured me still more from France, as the organ of M. Laurent, John Walker lectured me, from the inspiration of Dr Acqueroni, Capes had lectured us from Prior Park, as put up to it by Dr Baggs. A smaller fry afterwards presumed to cut at me, and at a later date others, whom just now I cannot call to mind. I was made an humiliation at my minor orders and at the examination for them; and I had to stand at Dr Wiseman's door waiting for Confession amid the Oscott boys. I did not realize these as indignities at the time, though, as I have said, I felt their dreariness.

And then when I went to Rome, my first act was a mistake, and a presage and specimen of my after course. Much against my will, as an act of duty, I made a speech over Miss Talbot O'Brien at St Isidore. O, I was a sort of sucking child, just as much knowing what I should say, what I should not say, and saying nothing right, not from want of tact so much as from sheer ignorance. The sermon or oration (!) was the talk of Rome, and the Pope expressed a sort of sorrow for it.

Then, after some notes regarding the difficulties which attended the starting of the Oratory, he goes on:

> Then my taking the Rambler came—I did it, at the wish of the Cardinal and our Bishop, and after as good consideration as I could give—but here again I made a blunder—and then in consequence I got into trouble at Rome. From that time all sorts of suspicions and calumnies have attended my name. And, since we began the School, have been both increased, and directed against it.

What follows is of capital importance. It shows that the root of his sadness was not, in the words of the Apostle, according to this world, but according to God. It was not the sadness of one who had suffered offence, though that he might justly say he had, but the sadness of one who was fain to offer his services for the furtherance of God's work and had seen them turned irremediably to naught.

> Now I say again, I am noticing all this opposition and distrust, not on their own account, for St Philip had them abundantly, but because they have (to all appearances) succeeded in destroying my influence and my usefulness. Persons who would naturally look towards me, converts who would naturally come to me, inquirers who would naturally consult me, are stopped by some light or unkind word said against me. I am passed, in decay; I am untrustworthy; I am strange, odd; I have my own ways and cannot get on with others; something or other is said in disparagement, I am put aside on the ground that I *ought* to be put aside; and then men make statements of which their very words bring about the fulfilment. Nor is it wonderful that all this slight and scorn reacts upon my own mind. I shrink from a society which is so unjust towards me. I must say, that the converts have behaved to *me* much worse than old Catholics, when they might have had a little gratitude, to say the least.

But he immediately goes on:

> I should be very ungrateful if I did not bear in mind what God has vouchsafed to do by me.

He then mentions the foundation of the two Oratories, the University and the Oratory School. Nevertheless, he has too much insight not to add at once:

> This is another matter altogether. They are works of my *name*; what I am speaking of is what belongs to my own person; things, which I ought to have been especially suited to do, and have not done, not done any one of them.

What follows, and it has been quoted at length by Ward and Thureau-Dangin,[1] gives a detailed account of the reproaches levelled against him by other Catholics, especially by the converts. They concerned his languid interest in what they held to be the great Catholic cause—a cause, that is to say, in which nothing counted but conversions, more and more conversions, conversions by the score, and preferably in the higher ranks of society. All this leads up to a conclusion in which he brings the full weight of his judgment to bear, all his insight into men's souls, all that saintly exercise of the intellect which is, in a way, his most distinctive characteristic:

> To me conversions were not the first thing, but the edification (building up) of Catholics. So much have I fixed upon the latter as my object that up to this time the world persists in saying that I recommend Protestants not to become Catholics. And, when I have given as my true opinion, that I am afraid to make hasty converts of educated men, lest they should not have counted the cost, and should have difficulties after they have entered the Church, I do but imply the same thing, that the Church must be prepared for converts, as well as converts prepared for the Church.

Now, have we not here, a century in advance, an adumbration, a preliminary foreshadowing, of the very policy, that of preparing for the reception of converts, which the hierarchy, from the Holy See downwards, seem to regard as one of the crying needs of the age? A further paragraph makes his position perfectly clear. For Newman, there is no question of making any addition to, still less any change in, the store of gifts bestowed by God once for all on the Church, a treasure which can neither be impoverished from within, nor augmented from without. But is there not a great temptation for Catholics to think that, having got the truth, no further effort is required of them whether in their lives, or in letting their light shine before men. That is the drift of the criticism of which Newman so frankly delivers himself, and which we are fain to hope is now no longer called for. Such, above all, is the aim of the constructive educational effort to which he would have liked to devote his powers, before they began to decline, a time that was not so very far off.

> How can this be understood at Rome? What do they know there of the state of English Catholics? of the minds of English Protestants? What do they know of the antagonism of Protestantism and Catholicism in England? The Cardinal might know something, were he not so one-sided, so slow to throw himself into other minds, so sanguine, so controversial, and unphilosophic

[1] W. Ward, Vol. I, pp. 583 et sqq.

in his attitude of mind, so desirous to make himself agreeable to authorities at Rome. And Catholics in England, from their very blindness, cannot see that they are blind. To aim, then, at improving the condition, the status, of the Catholic body by a careful survey of their argumentative basis, of their position relatively to the philosophy and the character of the day by giving them juster views, by enlarging and refining their minds, in one word by education, is (in their view) more than a superfluity or a hobby, it is an insult. It implies that they are deficient in material points. Now from first to last, education, in this large sense of the word, has been my line, and, over and above, the disappointment it has caused as putting conversions comparatively in the background, and the offence it has given by insisting that there was room for improvement among Catholics, it has seriously annoyed the governing body here and at Rome;—at Rome on the side of the philosophy of polemics. I should wish to attempt to meet the great infidel etc questions of the day, but both Propaganda and the Episcopate, doing nothing themselves, look with extreme jealousy on anyone who attempts it, and giving him no credit for what he does well, come down with severity on any point in which he may have slipped. And secondly, especially at home, because I have set up a school and so interfered with the vested rights, as they may be called, of this and that College or Seminary. Hence the keen sensitiveness of Dr Grant and the two Dr Browns, not to say the Cardinal, and the multitude of slanders which have been spread and are believed, about our boys and our treatment of them. And last of all, since from first to last, there have been the two objects of the Rambler,—to raise the status of Catholics, first by education, secondly by a philosophical basis of argument,—and the Rambler has attempted it injudiciously, intemperately, and erroneously, at least at times, I come in for the odium of all the Rambler's faults, and that the more because for a little while I was the Editor of the Rambler, &, when such, shared in my measure in the imperfections of the preceding & succeeding Editors. The consequence is, that, so far from being thought engaged in any good work, I am simply discouraged and regarded suspiciously by the governing powers, as doing an actual harm.

One other circumstance there is, peculiar to the time, to give a special intensity to this feeling of suspicion. At present the Temporal Power is the all important point at Rome—I, thinking that they would be obliged to rely more on reason, a truer defence, than on the sword, if they had it not, am lukewarm on the point; and this lukewarmness [h]as been exaggerated into a supposed complicity with Garibaldi! The Cardinal some years ago said that I had put myself on the shelf. But the position I occupy at the moment is, in his mind, a less harmless one.

A question here suggests itself. How are we to account for this revival of interest in him on the part of the Protestants? Falling in as it did with the longing glances he had been casting back over the past, it constituted the major temptation of this period of his life. Thanks to what we learn from his correspondence, the enigma is easily solved. Liberalism, now on the march and triumphant, had opened the eyes of many an Anglican, who, up to then, had regarded the Oxford Movement merely as a piece of theological romanticism. Such Christians as there still were among the more thoughtful and cultivated class were alarmed when they realised that scepticism, or downright atheism, was becoming, as Newman long ago declared it would, the sole possible alternative for those who rejected the Catholic tradition. The Dublin lectures, which had all along been neglected, if not regarded with suspicion, among Catholics, suddenly began eagerly to be devoured by a multitude of readers outside the Church.

People who, still in the Anglican fold, had some time since, under Newman's leadership, opened the campaign against what he called "the infidelity of the day", were now of a mind to come back to him, to seek him out once more. They had a dim idea that he had by no means withdrawn from the fight, and that his conversion, though they could not account for it, was a fulfilment, not a contracting-out. So they found him again, with all the plenitude of the Church's might to support him, far ahead of them, fighting doughtily, almost single-handed, with arms which they possessed not, and which others, and they Catholics who did possess them, disdained to use.

Copeland, his curate at Littlemore, whom he had chanced to run across in London, came to visit him at the Oratory. Others followed suit; Frederic Rogers, for example, a former pupil of his at Oriel. Keble, too, wrote him, and the correspondence between the two men entered on a new phase.

This is not to say—far from it—that hostility against him had died down in all Anglican circles. It was, indeed, a sudden and unlooked-for eruption of that hostility which, a little later, was to call forth the *Apologia*. An interesting thing about that event was that it revealed how great and complete were the general ignorance and incomprehension concerning both the Tractarian Movement and the Catholic Church. In combating this state of affairs, Newman found himself provided with a unique opportunity, not only of defending the Church against the grave slanders of which she was the object, but also of justifying the line of thought that had drawn him to her fold. Thus, at a stroke, he won for himself an invaluable and indisputable title to the gratitude of Catholics and Tractarians alike.

Charles Kingsley, who was now to attack him so lightheartedly, and so incautiously, was a writer of great popularity, the author of *Westward Ho!*, *Hypatia*, and many other books, most of them imbued with the spirit of what has been well called "Muscular Christianity".

The phrase is a perfect expression of the Victorian brand of Christianity to which, it is not too much to say, all the unworldliness implicit in Newman's religious ideas had been opposed since his earliest Oxford days. According to Kingsley's ideas, and those of innumerable other English folk, whose subconscious convictions he expressed with innocent candour, Christianity was nothing more or less than the art of so ordering the service of God and Christ as to promote the aims of a human society which was evidently on the best of terms with itself. In return, that society, the England of the 1850s, virtuous, energetic, and very much of the earth earthy, stood out in its own estimation as the perfect example of the Kingdom of God upon earth.

For Christians of that mould, one may readily imagine how utterly distasteful the Christianity preached by Newman must have been. Still it argues an astounding degree of recklessness on Kingsley's part to attack Newman as he did, evidently never dreaming of the crushing retribution he was to bring upon himself. In a review of J. A. Froude's *History of England* which appeared in *Macmillan's Magazine* for January 1864, he said this:

> Truth, for its own sake, had never been a virtue with the Roman clergy. Father Newman informs us that it need not, and on the whole ought not to be; that cunning is the weapon which heaven has given to the Saints wherewith to withstand the brute male force of the wicked world which marries and is given in marriage. Whether his notion be doctrinally correct or not, it is at least historically so.

The article was not signed. No sooner had his attention been called to it than Newman wrote to the publishers to draw their attention to a grave and gratuitous slander, and demanding an immediate apology. Kingsley made matters worse for himself by the cool effrontery with which he sought to justify himself. His only reparation was to insert in the next number of the magazine a statement which, under cover of what purported to be an apology, gave the impression that Newman had withdrawn the statement to which he had pretended to allude. At the same time, when Newman called on him to name the passage on which he had animadverted, he merely referred him to one of his Anglican sermons, entitled *Wisdom and Innocence*, taking very good care, for obvious reasons, not to go into further detail.

Newman felt that he had no other course than to publish the correspondence, which he did, together with an incisive commentary on the "straightforwardness" of which this doughty champion of the truth therein gave proof. Hutton drew attention in the *Spectator* to the telling nature of Newman's reply, and of the hopeless quandary in which Kingsley was bound to find himself.

The hapless victim thought to extricate himself by a sudden elevation of tone. The mere title of the pamphlet which he now flung back at Newman was nothing more or less than a thinly veiled insult: *What then does Dr Newman mean?* His pseudo-retractation was abandoned, and all the old calumnies which had stirred Newman to such a pitch of indignation were produced again, precariously poised on the flimsiest of Protestant gossip about Catholics and the Oxford Movement.

Unless Newman was going to allow himself to be regarded as a liar, and all other Catholics with him, he had no alternative but to make people understand what the Oxford Movement really was, what part he himself had played in it, and the reasons that had finally led him to Rome. No more distasteful task could possibly be imagined for a man so averse to putting himself in the limelight. Still, it might afford him an unequalled opportunity of dispelling the misunderstandings which had attended his conversion. Not only that, it would enable him to explain what his feelings were in regard to the inward and incommunicable essence of Catholicism, an attitude already implicit in that conversion, but almost as ill-understood by the majority of Catholics as by the majority of Protestants.

Having taken counsel with his friends, and especially with Rogers, in whose advice he had the utmost confidence where sound worldly judgment was called for, and with the assurance that all the Tractarians, whether converts or not, would place such documents as he might require at his disposal, Newman plunged into his task. On the 21st and 22nd April, there appeared two pamphlets, in which Kingsley's behaviour throughout the whole affair was described with a keenness of insight and a passionate indignation that make these pages one of the most outstanding examples of polemical writing to be found in the English language.

In the weeks that followed, the public, whose interest in the controversy immediately reached white heat, eagerly seized upon the pamphlets in which, as they appeared in swift succession, Newman recounted the full history of his religious opinions. Once again, and as never before, all England hung upon his every word. At last, in June, the work, which had cost its author such a terrific effort, was finished. Some time later, the pamphlets appeared in a single volume which had an enormous sale, and which was destined to stand out as the greatest religious classic of the nineteenth century. It concluded with a passage which George Eliot, little as she had in common with its author, could not read without tears:

I have closed this history of myself with St Philip's name upon St Philip's feast-day; and, having done so, to whom can I more suitably offer it, as a memorial of affection and gratitude, than to St Philip's sons, my dearest brothers of this House, the Priests of the Birmingham Oratory, Ambrose St John, Henry Austin Mills, Henry Bittleston, Edward Caswall, William Paine Neville, and Henry Ignatius Dudley Ryder?—who have been so faithful to me; who have been so sensitive to my needs; who have been so indulgent to my failings; who have carried me through so many trials; who have grudged no sacrifice, if I asked for it; who have been so cheerful under discouragements of my causing; who have done so many good works, and let me have the credit of them; with whom I have lived so long, with whom I hope to die.

And to you especially, dear Ambrose St John; whom God gave me when he took everyone else away; who are the link between my old life and my new; who have now for twenty-one years been so devoted to me, so patient, so zealous, so tender; who have let me lean so hard upon you; who have watched me so narrowly; who have never thought of yourself, if I was in question.

And in you I gather up and bear in memory those familiar affectionate companions and counsellors, who in Oxford were given to me, one after another, to be my daily solace, and relief; and all those others, of great name and high example, who were my thorough friends, and showed me true attachment in times long past; and also those many younger men, whether I knew them or not, who have never been disloyal to me by word or deed; and of all those, thus various in their relations to me, those more especially who have since joined the Catholic Church.

And I earnestly pray for this whole company, with a hope against hope, that all of us, who once were so united, and so happy in our union, may even now be brought at length, by the Power of the Divine Will into One Fold and under One Shepherd.

XX

THE CLOUD IS LIFTED

THE publication of the *Apologia*, and the warmth of its reception, began to bring about a change in Newman's position. It looked as if the dawn was breaking. The uncomprehending attitude of Protestants, and, what was still worse, of Catholics, was not dispelled all at once. But the tide began to turn in his favour, and, slowly and surely, pursued its course. Not only was the ever-growing neglect he had suffered at last made up for, but it soon became clear that in him the Church had one of the most gifted of her children, and perhaps one of the most saintly.

Some very hard struggles still lay ahead, but the steadily deepening oblivion, the unfriendly indifference which had been his lot, were now necessarily things of the past. When you could not agree with him, there was nothing for it but to do battle with him. And there was no doubt on which side the victory would lie.

The English Catholic clergy in particular, with almost one voice, saluted in Newman the vindicator of their moral dignity, and, more than that, one whose sentiments and character, no less than his genius, reflected the greatest honour upon them. On the 2nd June, the diocesan synod, under the presidency of its Bishop, presented an address offering him a tribute of respect and gratitude. Letters from individuals and from the clergy of other dioceses, notably an address from the Westminster clergy, gave expression to sentiments which were those of nearly all Catholics. On the Anglican side, a letter from his sister Jemima gave utterance, in terms of loyal sisterly affection and pride, to a joyful satisfaction scarcely less widely shared:

> Dear John
>
> I have waited till the whole series was complete to thank you very much for your kindness in sending me the "Apologia"—it has been very interesting indeed to me, though I have not quite read the Appendix yet. I am very glad you have made the effort of writing it—for the sake of truth generally, and also for your own sake—for many people from ignorance have, without intending to be unfair, misrepresented you.[1]

[1] Unpublished letter dated 20th June, 1864.

The necessity he had been under of appealing to Keble and Rogers, and through Rogers to Church, for leave to have recourse to their correspondence and their memories of the times, so that he might give an accurate account of the Tractarian Movement as it really was, completed the restoration of friendships which had already begun to revive. Rogers himself took the initiative by suggesting a meeting of all of them with Church. Newman at once showed hesitation. He did not conceal how unnerved he felt at the idea of meeting them again after twenty years of separation. Then he wrote to Church telling him that it would be too much for him, too great a tax on his emotions, to renew contact with two such friends as Rogers and himself both at once. However, he invited Church to come and see him the following spring at Rednal, where the Oratorians had recently acquired a country house.

As it turned out, it was at Manning's consecration as Archbishop, in succession to Wiseman, who had died that winter, that the meeting actually took place. Newman went up to London for the ceremony and stayed with Rogers, and there Church came to join them. A few days later, Church and Rogers clubbed together to present Newman with a violin. For years, Newman had given up playing, lest it should interfere with the graver duties of life. He returned to it with delight, for he knew the solace that music would bring him, and how greatly it would enhance his powers of work. The letter he wrote to Church on the 11th July to thank him, told him, in terms of almost boyish glee that recall those happy times at Oxford, how delighted he was at thus regaining his friend and his music.

A little while before, he had been to see Isaac Williams, who like Copeland, was one of his former curates. Williams, although he was suffering from a disease that carried him off a week later, was so moved by this visit that he insisted on driving back with Newman to the station to see him off.

In September of that same year, he at length saw Keble again, and Pusey too, on the same occasion, though he had dreaded beforehand the prospect of meeting them both together. We must let him tell in his own words what took place on that pathetic day. It was spent at the parsonage at Hursley, where Keble had been living for many years. In a letter to Ambrose St John dated the 13th, Newman writes:

> I had forgotten the country, and was not prepared for its woodland beauty. Keble was at the door; he did not know me, nor I him. How mysterious that first sight of friends is! for, when I came to contemplate him, it was the old face and manner, but the first effect or impression was different.

His wife had been taken ill in the night, and at the first moment *he*, I think, and certainly *I*, wished myself away. Then he said: "Have you missed my letter?" meaning, "Pusey is here, and I wrote to stop your coming." He then said: "I must go and prepare Pusey." He did so, and then took me into the room where Pusey was.

I went in rapidly, and it is strange how action overcomes pain. Pusey, being passive, was evidently shrinking back into the corner of the room, as I should have done, had he rushed in upon me. He could not help contemplating the look of me narrowly and long. "Ah," I thought, "you are thinking how old I am grown, and I see myself in you,—though you, I do think, are more altered than I." Indeed, the alteration in him startled, I will add pained and grieved, me. I should have known him anywhere; his face is not changed, but it is as if you looked at him through a prodigious magnifier. I recollect him short and small, with a round head and smallish features, flaxen curly hair; huddled up together from his shoulders downward, and walking fast. This as a young man, but comparing him even as he was when I had last seen him in 1846, when he was slow in his motions and staid in his figure, there was a wonderful change in him. His head and features are half as large again; his chest is very broad, and he is altogether large, and (don't say all this to anyone) he has a strange condescending way when he speaks. His voice is the same; were my eyes shut, I should not be sensible of any alteration.

As we three sat together at one table, I had a painful thought, not acute pain, but heavy. There were three old men, who had worked together vigorously in their prime. This is what they have come to—poor human nature! After twenty years they meet together round a table but without a common cause or free outspoken thought; kind indeed, but subdued and antagonistic in their language to each other, and all of them with broken prospects, yet each viewing in his own way the world in which those prospects lay.[1]

We remember how Pusey, speaking one day about the Oxford converts, said they had all deteriorated, adding, "Except Newman, who had always been so good that he couldn't be spoilt, and Ward, who was so bad that he couldn't be worse". In that letter, and in other accounts of the meeting, what strikes us most forcibly is how, despite the passage of the years, each of the three friends was the same as he always had been. Newman still had all his old mental elasticity, his ardour, his reserve. Keble was the same as he had always known him, thoroughly kind and gentle, but unable to make up his mind, scared at the world in general, afraid to look problems in the face. Pusey was more than ever like a man walled up in his own opinions, stubbornly bent on building, even if it had to be in the middle of the desert, a house without windows.

[1] W. Ward, Vol. II, p. 95.

At this time, Pusey's obstinate determination to be himself, to remain what and where he was, was beginning to win him an influence among Anglicans such as no one could have counted on in 1845. Insensible alike to censure, calumny, and misrepresentation, with a purely bookish theory of the Church; as little put out by contemporary Anglicanism as he was by those facts of history which had been such a revelation to Newman, he remained immovable. Amid the confusion created by the triumph of Liberalism, following the failure of the Oxford Movement, people again began to look towards him and his friends. Did they not offer the one stable anchorage for those to whom abandoning traditional belief or quitting the Church with which all their past, all their upbringing, all their memories were bound up, represented alternatives equally unwelcome?

Pusey continued to console himself for Newman's defection by clinging to the branch theory, according to which the Church of today was divided into three branches, each imperfect in itself, but all alike true heirs of the One Church: Rome, Constantinople, Canterbury. In consequence, he gave his support to the *Association for Promoting the Unity of Christendom*, which for some time now had been gathering people perhaps more generous than clear-sighted into an association in which the extremest form of Anglicanism was combined with a very special brand of Catholicism. Of this latter, a layman belonging to an old aristocratic family, Ambrose Phillipps de Lisle, and Father Lockhart, who had lived with Newman, then still an Anglican, at Littlemore, were the most zealous representatives. Newman, while entertaining profound respect for the sentiments which animated them, regarded them as Utopian dreamers. It was not merely that he looked on the branch theory as pure fantasy. They themselves could scarcely have taken a different view without ceasing to be Catholics. The main obstacle, however, which stood in the way of the corporate reunion of Anglicans with Rome seemed to him to lie in its semi-political and hopelessly composite character.

We have a letter of his in which he deals with these matters at considerable length.[1] Nevertheless, it was his great desire that the exchanges between Anglicans and Catholics should be carried on in an atmosphere of perfect charity but, at the same time, with the utmost frankness. That, he conceived, was the only way to get rid of vexatious misunderstandings, and thereafter to open up the way to a future whereof God alone possessed the secret.

[1] W. Ward, Vol. II, pp. 115 et sqq.

As for Pusey, he, when they met at Hursley, had been full of a projected book which was, in fact, already on the stocks. The work in question was the *Eirenicon*—that is to say, it, too, was designed to open up the way to a reconciliation and it, too, was to employ the weapons of sympathy and outspokenness. After talking the matter over with Newman face to face, he continued the discussion by letter. He made no secret of his intention to indicate, as the two great obstacles to reunion, one, the excessive honour paid to the Saints, and to the Virgin, as exemplified in the writings of people like Faber; the other, the interpretation of the doctrine of the infallibility of Church and Pope which Ward, in *The Dublin Review*, was urging with ever-growing exaggeration. Newman replied with equal frankness that in his opinion the ground for the discussion had not been well chosen. Neither the type of devotion represented by Faber, nor the theological views of Ward, were representative of Catholicism as such.

Pusey, with his customary stubbornness, persisted in his design, and the *Eirenicon* appeared in due course, but it was so taken up with argument on those lines that Newman declared in his *Letter to Dr. Pusey* that Pusey had discharged his olive-branch with a catapult.

There was no lack of replies on the Catholic side, but it soon seemed to Newman that they all erred in the same way, they all failed to recognise how sincere was Pusey's effort and the real difficulty created for people like him by views such as those to which he took exception. It would not do to say that Pusey was caricaturing Catholic doctrine, if, as was, alas, only too plain, the caricature was furnished him by Catholics, and by those who thought themselves more Catholic than their fellows.

Newman, for his part, did not think that a mere, and wholly negative repudiation of the extreme views of the *giovani* and their sympathisers would suffice. It would carry no weight unless it were supported by a positive exposition of a really helpful and conciliatory nature, which should deal, in the spirit of a true *eirenicon*, with the doctrines and practices to which objection had been taken. Such was the task to which he addressed himself in his long *Letter to Dr Pusey concerning his "Eirenicon"*. This little booklet, which was eagerly read and discussed by the vast number of people who had devoured the *Apologia*, confined itself to the problem of Mariology. The last chapter of the *Apologia*, explaining his views on the Church and Revelation, had already set forth all that he thought necessary to say on the other problem.

Far from holding, as did Ward, that Papal Infallibility was to be regarded as a kind of permanent inspiration which dispensed people from thinking for themselves, Newman had made it sufficiently clear in what he had recently written on the matter, that Infallibility was in the nature of a providential safeguard. It was not a substitute for intellectual activity; what it did was to keep the Church from the danger of obscuring in the eyes of the world the Word which had been entrusted to her. At this time, when the Holy See was seriously threatened by the course political developments in Europe were taking, Newman thought it useless to hark back to these matters and, in the circumstances then ruling, painful to stress them. On the other hand, Pusey's book offered an opportunity not to be missed of differentiating between Catholicism in its true guise, and the presentation of it given by over-eager or over-fanciful writers. Nor must it be forgotten that one of the points which up to the last had held him back from Catholicism was the feeling he so long retained that the cult of the Saints, and of the Virgin in particular, amounted to nothing less than idolatry. He therefore readily appreciated how important it was that such false impressions should be removed.

Pusey quoted a number of breath-taking extracts from modern spiritual writers. Here are some specimens:

> That the present disposition of Our Lord towards sinners, as well as His Father's, is to reject them, while the Blessed Mary takes His place as an Advocate with Father and Son.
>
> The Saints are more ready to intercede with Jesus than Jesus with the Father.
>
> As we are clothed with the merits of Christ, so we are clothed with the merits of Mary.
>
> As He is Priest, in a like sense is she Priestess.
>
> As He is present and received in the Eucharist, so is Mary present and received therein.

That such statements are in no way expressive of Catholic practice, still less of Catholic dogma, Newman makes absolutely clear. He stresses the fact that they were unheard of in England, until certain converts of recent times had made it their aim to exaggerate still further the already extravagant outpourings of Southern sentimentalism. But what is truly remarkable—and it shows how genuinely Catholic, how remote from any hint of the party-spirit he really was—is that he was not content with this negative task of clearing away error. Behind the criticisms, justified though they may have been, which Pusey directed against certain extravagances in the cult of the Virgin, he detects and brings to light a sort of mistrust and reticence in regard thereto which are no less out of key with true tradition. The honour paid to Mary is not, as it were, a sort of permissible vagary, permissible but dangerous, which the Church has to keep an eye upon, to see that it does not go beyond certain limits. It belongs, on the contrary, to the essence, to the very heart of Catholicism, and, if it needs must be preserved from distortion and deformity, that is not because it is in any way equivocal in its nature, but rather because it is the efflorescence, the blossoming forth of the most consoling of Gospel truths, the Incarnation of the Son of God in our humanity.

All that was but continuing the task so splendidly begun by the *Apologia*; the task of revealing to England the true lineaments of Catholicism of which a misguided, and growingly irrational, faction seemed determined to rob it. Needless to say, the *Letter to Dr Pusey* was no more pleasing than the *Apologia* to those who were denied therein the right to speak for Catholicism in all its fullness, or to be, as they regarded themselves, its sole authentic spokesmen. Manning, though keeping to himself, generally speaking, his dissatisfaction with a Catholic apologetic which drew a distinct line between Catholicism in the real sense, and the school with which he was more and more identifying himself, did pour forth his bitterness to a few bosom friends.

He was, however, far too politic a person to display his displeasure at a success like that which had greeted the *Apologia*, and he was among the hundred and ten signatories of the address of gratitude and respect presented to Newman by the Westminster clergy on the occasion of its publication. Still more astute, a courtier if ever there was one, was his Roman correspondent, Mgr Talbot. Passing through England during the summer of 1864, he thought it would be the correct thing to call at the Birmingham Oratory and invite Newman to come to Rome and deliver a course of sermons in his church there.

Newman, however, was not at home, and the Fathers, anything but anxious to commit themselves, sent Fr Caswall, the wariest of their number, to deal with the visitor. Fr Caswall, who, like Elpenor in the *Odyssey*, was destined never to have another opportunity of showing his talents of diplomacy, displayed a wiliness that was too much, even for Talbot. Talbot was anxious to find out all he possibly could about the life of the Community, what sort of people Newman was mixed up with, what he talked about, what his influence was. The conversation lasted a long time, but at the end of it, all that the crafty prelate took away with him was that large numbers of books were received at the Oratory, that these, in the ordinary way, were stacked in the library, and that Newman was pretty often to be found there.

Talbot then repeated his invitation by letter. Newman wrote in terms of frigid politeness, declining it. Talbot had put it about that the invitation virtually came from the Pope himself. In a letter to Miss Bowles, Newman expressed himself pretty wholeheartedly about the invitation and the statement about its origin:

> Monsignor Talbot, who had been spreading the report that I subscribe to Garibaldi, and said other bad things against me, had the assurance to send me a pompous letter asking me to preach a set of sermons in his church. . . . When Talbot left for England he said, among other things, "I think of asking Dr Newman to give a set of lectures in my church" and the Pope, of course, said, "a very good thought", as he would have said if Mgr Talbot had said, "I wish to bring Your Holiness some English razors".[1]

Events were soon to show how completely well founded had been Newman's mistrust, and how right he had been the following year, when Manning was appointed Archbishop, to decline the offer of a bishopric *in partibus*, which the latter had dangled before him as a means of binding him to his triumphal chariot.

In view of the Protestant "come-back" in his favour, and of the fact that Catholics, won over willy-nilly by the *Apologia*, had offered him an expression of their esteem and gratitude, Newman for a time considered the possibility of a renewed connection with Oxford. It was quite impracticable for English Catholics to send their sons to Dublin, even if that University had not been already almost in its death-throes. It was still more out of the question that a Catholic University should be started in England within the foreseeable future. All this left them no option but to fall back on Oxford or Cambridge. Besides, had not the religious tests been abolished?

Of course, this would be only a second-best solution, a *pis-aller*. As Newman had taken abundant pains to demonstrate in his *Idea of a University*, Catholicism, for those who profess it, should not only be an accompaniment to education, it should penetrate and dominate it. However, as the ideal was for the time being, unrealisable, was it not better to make the best of things as they were than to take up an uncompromising, "All or nothing" attitude? Oxford was now open to Catholics. Would not the wisest thing be to open Halls or Hostels, where, under the best conditions available at the moment, they might

[1] W. Ward, Vol. II, pp. 47–48.

acquire the culture necessary to enable them to take their proper place in the community? For Catholics to reject this course would be to refuse to come out of the Ghetto, to decline to take their proper place in public life and so to exert their influence on the governing classes.

Moreover, seeing the reception that had been accorded to the *Apologia*, Newman began to feel conscious of the authority which his words, if heard anew in Oxford, might regain for him there. He had no desire to wage war on the Church of England in her old stronghold; but rather to encourage her in the efforts she was making to stem the tide of Liberalism, now sweeping all before it. It seemed to him that quiet, peaceable witnessing to the truth would, in the long run, be of far greater benefit to the Catholic cause than a policy of active opposition to the Establishment. We know that he entertained no illusory expectations about the latter; but if he did not look for corporate reunion, he considered the risk of flinging men's minds into unbelief by undermining Anglicanism was far greater than the likelihood of winning them over to Rome. On the contrary, he thought that the more the remnants of true tradition in Anglicanism were fostered and upheld, the more likely Catholicism would be to find a responsive echo in Anglican hearts.

> While I do not see my way to take steps to weaken the Church of England, being what it is, least of all should I be disposed to do so in Oxford, which has hitherto been the seat of those traditions which constitute whatever there is of Catholic doctrine and principle in the Anglican Church. That there are also false traditions there, I know well: I know too that there is a recent importation of scepticism and infidelity; but, till things are very much changed there, in weakening Oxford, we are weakening our friends, weakening our own *de facto* παιδαγωγὸς into the Church. Catholics did not make us Catholics; Oxford made us Catholics. At present Oxford surely does more good than harm. There has been a rage for shooting sparrows of late years, under the notion that they are the farmers' enemies. Now, it is discovered that they do more good by destroying insects than harm by picking up the seed. Is there not something of a parallel here?[1]

Dr Ullathorne's proposal that Newman should take charge of the Catholic mission in Oxford came, as though providentially, to encourage Newman's plan. But no sooner had that plan taken shape than Ward, Manning, and Vaughan all combined to bring their adverse pressure to bear in Rome. In their eyes, to have any association with Oxford, and to inject heresy and unbelief in their most virulent form into the minds and souls of Catholics, were one and the same

[1] W. Ward, Vol.II, p. 75.

thing. Rome, on receipt of their urgent communication, duly sent to the various notabilities indicated to them (neither Newman, of course, nor any of his friends were included) a list of questions to be answered. It was worded in such a way as to imply that Oxford was on a par with Brussels, and that to send young Catholics there was like handing them over to the forces of militant atheism.

Newman, however, got to know about this document and its contents through a Mr Gaisford, whom Manning and his party had mistakenly supposed to be of their own way of thinking. As he remarked to Gaisford, "They might as well have been summed up in one—viz., 'Are you or are you not, one of those wicked men who advocate Oxford education?' "[1]

The sequel was a foregone conclusion. Propaganda, misled as to the true facts of the situation, early in 1865, sent instructions to the English Bishops couched in terms that left them no alternative but to forbid parents to send their sons to Oxford. That being so, Newman saw no further object in founding an Oratory in Oxford. He sold the piece of land that he had bought, and looked on the scheme as dead and buried. His *Journal*, which he took up again at this juncture, gives us the conclusions he drew from this latest experience of his. The success of the *Apologia* and the *Letter to Dr Pusey* gave him the lasting certainty that his views on all these questions would finally carry the day. But these latest events left him in no doubt that he would have to give up all hope of personally witnessing that triumph, let alone of bringing it to pass himself. Well; what matter? So long as truth prevailed, he resigned himself sadly, perhaps, but without fuss, to seeing his own part in the matter misjudged or ignored.

February 22nd, 1865.

I have just now looked over what I wrote on January 21st, 1863. My position of mind now is so different from what it was then, that it would require many words to bring it out. First, I have got hardened against the opposition made to me, and I have not the soreness at my ill-treatment on the part of certain influential Catholics which I had then,—and this simply from the natural effect of time—just as I do not feel that anxiety which I once had that we have no novices. I don't know that this recklessness is a better state of mind than that anxiety. Every year I feel less and less anxiety to please Propaganda, from a feeling that they *cannot* understand England. Next, the two chief persons whom I felt to be unjust to me are gone,—the Cardinal and Faber. Their place has been taken by Manning and Ward; but somehow, from my never having been brought as closely into contact with

[1] W. Ward, Vol. II, p. 66.

either of them as with the Cardinal and Faber, I have not that sense of their cruelty which I felt so much as regards the two last mentioned. Thirdly, in the last year a most wonderful deliverance has been wrought in my favour, by the controversy of which the upshot was my "Apologia". It has been marvellously blest, for while I have regained, or rather gained, the favour of Protestants, I have received the approbation in formal Addresses, of good part of the [Catholic] clerical body. They have been highly pleased with me, as doing them a service, and I stand with them as I never did before. Then again, it has pleased Protestants, and of all parties, as much or more. When I wrote those sharp letters, as I did very deliberately, in June 1862, in consequence of the reports circulated to the effect that I was turning Protestant, I at once brought myself down to my lowest point as regards popularity, yet, by the very force of my descent, I prepared the way for a rebound. It was my lowest point, yet the turning-point. When Crawley wrote to remonstrate with me on the part of my Protestant friends, I answered him by showing how unkindly they had treated me for 17 years,—so much so that they had no right to remonstrate. This touched Keble. Moreover, it happened just then that, independent of this, Copeland, having met me accidentally in London, came to see us here, and he spread such a kind report of me that Keble wrote to me, Rogers visited me August 30th, 1863, and Church proposed to do so. Williams too wished to come and see me,—but *he* had never lost sight of me. The kind feeling was growing, when (Copeland accidentally being here) I began the Kingsley controversy, the effect of which I need not enlarge on. I have pleasant proofs of it every day. And thus I am in a totally different position now to what I was in January 1863. And my temptation at this moment is to value the praise of men too highly, especially of Protestants—and to lose some portion of that sensitiveness towards God's praise which is so elementary a duty.

On all these accounts, though I still feel keenly the way in which I am kept doing nothing, I am not so much pained at it,—both because by means of my "Apologia" I am (as I feel) *indirectly* doing a work, and because its success has put me in spirits to look out for other means of doing good, whether Propaganda cares about it or no. Yet still it is very singular that the same effective opposition to me *does* go on, thwarting my attempts to *act*, and what is very singular, also "avulso uno non deficit alter". Faber being taken away, Ward and Manning take his place. Through them, especially Manning, acting on the poor Cardinal (who is to be buried tomorrow), the Oxford scheme has been for the present thwarted—for me probably for good—and this morning I have been signing the agreement by which I shall sell my land to the University. Bellasis told me that, from what he saw at Rome, he felt that Manning was more set against *my* going to Oxford, than merely against Catholic youths going there. And now I am thrown back again on my do-nothing life here—how marvellous! yet, as I have drawn out above, from habit, from recklessness, and from my late success, my feeling of despondency and irritation seems to have gone.

So Newman, now a man of sixty-four (that entry was made the day after his birthday) considers that nothing now remains for him but to prepare for his departure. There were certain signs of oncoming age that seemed to him—and he always kept a sharp eye on himself—to be a warning of Providence. He detected, or he thought he did, a progressive benumbing of his mental and physical faculties. He resigned himself with perfect calmness to saying farewell, not only to his earthly interests and preoccupations, but to earth itself.

That year, more than ever before, he courted solitude, or, rather, sought to be alone with God. The Oratory had recently acquired a small estate at Rednal, well out in the open country. Newman took great interest in arranging things in this unpretentious abode, which is situated on the side of a hill, and commands an extensive view over a rolling landscape of woodland and meadow. Quite near to the house, the garden—a quiet, meditative retreat—leads into the burial ground where he expected one day—and that no distant one—to be laid to rest. As in the old Oxford days, he was not afraid of long, lonely walks, and, as often as he could, he went there on foot. And there it was that his meditations on the Eternal bore fruit that summer in the poem which he entitled *The Dream of Gerontius*. His unfailing submission to the judgment of God, in the light of divine holiness is merged in this, which he deems his final hour, in the perfect serenity of his religious faith. All speaks of love, even his trials. The Christian soul will find its purgatory in that very love which burns but to enlighten, rendering it pure and transparent. The man who could write such a poem certainly was not one to flinch or falter in the face of trial. He kisses the hand that strikes him, for he sees in it nothing but the love which saves him from himself in order to deliver him wholly to God. Does this mean that he wilfully shuts his eyes, nor tells what he sees. No; following the Light to the very last, he will never come to believe that truth is a thing to be sacrificed. But now, to quote the conclusion of his *Essay on Development*, we may be sure it was not "disappointment, or disgust, or restlessness, or wounded feeling, or undue sensibility, or other weakness" that inspired his words.

The world to which he deemed he had said farewell for ever was not to let him go so readily as he thought. Despite all that the Mannings, and the Talbots could say or do, his influence, all through those years, though he never sought to exercise it, continued to grow and grow.

Meanwhile, the problem concerning higher education for Catholics became so pressing that, prohibitions notwithstanding, even some of the best-intentioned people could not bring themselves to forgo Oxford, now that it was open to them. Their sole choice lay between that, or resigning all hope of their sons' playing any worthy part in the public life of the nation. To condemn them, only meant that such Catholics as did go there, which they had to do if they were to prepare themselves for a career, would be deprived of all religious support at the University. It became clear, from 1866 onwards, that this stringent ruling, based as it was on a misunderstanding, could not go on much longer.

Dr Ullathorne himself again intervened in the matter. Although this time there was no question of starting any undertaking officially connected with the University, he urgently enjoined on the Oratorians that they should build a church and establish a house in Oxford. Newman needed a deal of persuasion. Once before, he had experienced the pain of giving up a project which, of all others, was dearest to his heart. He was loath to rekindle hopes which, if they proved illusory, would cause him a bitterer disappointment than any he had yet experienced, and bring on him fresh reproaches and renewed suspicions.

But the Bishop, convinced that he was right, clung to his idea. Everyone with any common-sense saw, as he did, what a gross error it would be to hinder Newman from undertaking a work of the highest importance and one which he alone was able to fulfil. In the end, he allowed himself to be talked over. A formal authorisation from Propaganda, obtained by Ullathorne, gave leave to the Oratorians to establish themselves at Oxford. This put an end to his hesitations, but not to his misgivings.

On this latter point, his presentiments did not mislead him. Manning and Talbot—Talbot more especially—made one supreme effort to compass his undoing. What they never dreamt was that the utter folly of their machinations was to bring ruin on all the plots they had laid to achieve that end.

One Saturday in April 1867, when Fr Neville was about to set out for Oxford to see that everything was ready for the move, Newman and he went for a stroll along a quiet Edgbaston road beneath the shade of some fine trees, then in their full springtime luxuriance. Newman seemed to have got back all his hopes. He spoke with a delight and a buoyant confidence, that were something quite new, of the work he had at last been called upon to fulfil. Then they both went back to the Oratory. The servant who opened the door gave Newman a letter which he said had just come from the Bishop. Newman opened and read the letter, then, turning to Neville, he said quietly, "All is over. I am not allowed to go".

Dr Ullathorne's letter told him what an article in the *Weekly Register* was, by some unexplained indiscretion, proclaiming to the world at large. An Oratory might be opened at Oxford, but Newman was not to go there. Cardinal Barnabò had sent a secret instruction to the Bishop saying, in a phrase that deserves to be handed down to posterity,

> *Patrem Newman si forte de sua residentia in urbem Oxfordensem transferenda cogitantem videris . . . blande suaviterque revocare studeas.*

The Bishop judged that it was useless to try to conceal from him what had been said, seeing that the *Weekly Register* was already proclaiming to the house-tops that the project of an Oratory at Oxford had been quashed by the Holy Father because, to put it plainly, Fr Newman's orthodoxy had come under suspicion.

In publishing this article, the party, who thought they had scored a resounding triumph, had committed the grossest of blunders. But, before all this, Newman had had an idea that some sort of a move against him was going on in Rome. He had recently had a queer kind of communication from Barnabò about the Oratory school, taxing him with preparing young Catholics for the University. Well,—he said to himself, how can I help doing so unless I teach them their Greek and Latin all amiss? So Ambrose St John found himself at Rome, his mission being to state the facts about this unlucky little school, whose great fault was that it was proving more and more of a success.

In view of this new turn of events, Newman sent an urgent message to St John asking him to protest on his behalf to Propaganda. The extraordinary way he had been treated, which that indiscreet announcement in the *Weekly Register* ascribed to doubts as to his orthodoxy, gave him a right to ask what error it was that had incurred censure, what he had said or done to account for such mistrust.

Meanwhile, the unblushing machinations of the *Weekly Register*, which were quite unconcealed, had created such disgust in the minds of all decent-thinking people that, to make up for it, an address of respect and esteem was sent to Newman by the leading Catholic laymen of the country, beginning with the Earl Marshal.

The correspondence that passed between Manning and Talbot in regard to this affair leaves no doubt as to the part they played in it and how they looked upon their respective roles. The wild and whirling words in which the Papal Chamberlain imagines he is pointing the moral of the whole business, opens with this wonderful phrase which he doubtless thinks will put the laity in their place once and for all, in regard to matters ecclesiastical:

> What is the province of the laity? To hunt, to shoot, to entertain. These matters they understand, but to meddle with ecclesiastical matters they have no right at all, and this affair of Newman is a matter purely ecclesiastical.

Then he proceeds to come down on Newman very heavily indeed:

> Dr Newman is the most dangerous man in England, and you will see that he will make use of the laity against your Grace. You must not be afraid of him. It will require much prudence, but you must be firm, as the Holy Father still places his confidence in you; but if you yield and do not fight the battle of the Holy See against the detestable spirit growing up in England, he will begin to regret Cardinal Wiseman, who knew how to keep the laity in order. I tell you all this in confidence, because I already begin to hear some whisperings which might become serious. I am your friend and defend you every day, but you know (Cardinal Barnabò) as well as I do, and how ready he is to throw the blame of everything on others. . . .

As regards this last point, Talbot's presentiments were not so far out. Being cornered by St John, Cardinal Barnabò made no bones about stating that Newman's orthodoxy had been under suspicion at Rome ever since 1860. His article in *The Rambler* about consulting the laity had been delated to the Holy Office as heretical, and he had been asked to explain it. He had not done so. Small wonder, therefore, if he was under a cloud at Rome.

St John lost no time in reporting this conversation to Newman. Newman had noted at the time in his *Journal* how Dr Ullathorne had brought him the news about his article and how upset he had been, though he made up his mind to say nothing about it to anyone. He had written straight off to Wiseman, who was then in Rome, asking him to hand in without loss of time the explanatory comments he was then sending him, and saying that he was prepared to furnish any further elucidations that might be called for. Wiseman did not answer. Later on, he asked Manning about the matter, and Manning told him that the whole thing was settled and that he need not worry himself any more about it. Newman sent all these particulars to St John and, with them, a copy of the letter he had written to Wiseman.

Barnabò, on being told about all this, had a tremendous shock. Wiseman had not handed in any letter at all. The Cardinal stated in the most positive terms that whatever mistrust may have been entertained about Newman at Rome, this omission (if omission there had been) was the cause of it. As to Wiseman, he added this reflection, "Well; he is dead now; *Requiescat in pace!*" And no more need be said.

When the Pope was informed about it all, he was extremely anxious that Newman's mind should be completely set at rest. Barnabò, after that, had to sing the same tune; even Talbot thought it prudent to fall into step, and if possible to sing loudest of all. The worthy Ambrose St John saw the sky suddenly clear. Newman, not so near the scene of action, pleased though he was that matters had been cleared up, took the news more coolly. His trust in Pius IX had never wavered. He had never doubted the kindly disposition of the Pope towards him. But he was happy to have such a striking proof of it. For the rest, there was no doubt in his mind that Rome now saw that the *zelanti* had committed a monumental blunder. For all that, the clouds even now were not completely dispelled.

Two events soon happened to confirm his way of looking at things. After what had occurred, Barnabò could not go on keeping him at arms-length about the question of Catholics going up to Oxford, and he now embarked on a lengthy correspondence with him, which Newman unhappily thought it fit to destroy. However, his *Journal* shows clearly enough how unsatisfactory had been this exchange. It also shows the absolutely frank and realistic manner in which Newman said what he thought about the matter.

Oct. 30, 1867. What I have written in the foregoing pages, has been written as a sort of relief to my mind, if that were the only reason for writing, I should not write now, for I have no trouble within me to be relieved of. I will put myself under the image of the Patriarch Job, without intending t[o] liken myself to him. He first strenuously resisted the charges of his friends, the[n] he made a long protest of his innocence, & then we read, "The words of Jo[b] are ended". Mine are ended too—I have said to Cardinal Barnabò "Vide[rit] Deus". I have lodged my cause with Him—and, while I hope ever by His grace to be obedient, I have now as little desire as I have hope, to gain the praise of such as him in any thing I shall do henceforth. Faber and others have been too much for me. They have too deeply impressed the minds of authorities at Rome against me, to let the truth about me have fair play while I live; and when one ceases to hope, one ceases to fear. They have done their worst—and, as Almighty God in 1864 cleared up my conduct in the sight of Protestants at the end of twenty years, so as regards my Catholic course, at length, after I am gone hence, Deus viderit! I did not use the words lightly, though they seem to have rested most unfavourably on his mind (C. Barnabò's)—nor do I dream of retracting them. For many years I tried to approve myself to such as him, but it is now more than ten years, that, from failing to do so, I have been gradually weaned from any such expectation or longing. I have recorded the change in the words of my Dublin sermon of Novr 23, 1856, though covertly and only to my own consciousness. "There are those who . . . think we mean to spend our devotion upon a human cause, and that we toil for an object of human ambition. They think that we should acknowledge, if cross-examined, that our ultimate purpose was the success of persons and parties, to whom we are bound in honour, or in interest, or in gratitude; and that &c. . . . They fancy, as the largest concession of their liberalty, that we are working *from the design*, generous but still human, *of the praise of earthly superiors*, and that, after all, we are living on the breath, and basking in the smile of man", &c, &c.

And now, alas, I fear that in one sense the iron has entered into my soul. I mean that confidence in any superiors whatever never can blossom again within me. I never shall feel easy with them. I shall (I feel) always think they will be taking some advantage of me—that at length their way will lie across mine, and that my efforts will be displeasing to them. I shall ever be suspicious that they or theirs have secret unkind thoughts of me, and that they deal with me with some arrière pensée. And, as it is my happiness so to be placed as not to have much intercourse with them, therefore, while I hope ever loyally to fulfil their orders, it is my highest gain and most earnest request to them, that they would let me alone—and, since I do not want to initiate any new plan of any kind, that, if they can, they would keep their hands off me. Whether or not they will consent to this is more than I can say, for they seem to wish to ostracize me. But, in saying this, I repeat what I said when I began to write, I am now in a state of quiescence, and fear as little as I hope. And I do not expect this state of mind to be reversed. God forbid I should liken them to the "Scribes and Pharisees"—but still I obey them, as Scribes & Pharisees were to be obeyed, as God's representatives, not from devotion to *them*.

Meanwhile, the authorities at Rome were bent on clearing up, once for all, this business about Newman's orthodoxy. With this end in view, they thought the best thing they could do, in order to come to some definite conclusion, would be to refer the question to Dr Cullen, the Archbishop of Dublin. One might well have thought that this time it would be all over with Newman and his credit with the Holy See. Not at all. It was quite the contrary that happened.

Cullen was a man of narrow views, and he was an ardent conservative. He had given abundant evidence that there was nothing of the *gentleman* about him, not, at least, as the *Idea of a University* defines that term. He was, however, perfectly straightforward; no one could deny that he had plenty of common-sense, so far as it went, and he was, up to his lights, a thoroughly sound and honest person. Having been trained at Rome on the lines of the old school, he may have been rigid, narrow in his outlook, but his narrowness was of a very different brand from Ward's and, still more, from Manning's. Their romantic theology, to use no stronger term, had nothing about it which he, any more than Newman, could possibly mistake for orthodoxy.

We do not know the precise terms of his reply to Rome, but we are entitled to assume that he authoritatively and definitely treated as utter nonsense the suspicions cast upon Newman by the faction of which Talbot was the mouthpiece. Henceforth, the case was over and done with, not only for the Pope himself, but for everyone else of any consequence. A few years later, when the Vatican Council was convened, Cullen suggested to Newman that he should accompany him thither in the capacity of theologian. This invitation Newman declined, but it was subsequently renewed direct by the Holy See. Such pressure was highly encouraging, and if it failed to bring about Newman's acceptance, it was that, in view of the incredibly chaotic state of ideas that preceded the Council, he was above all things anxious not to be involved. The various parties that were confronting one another all seemed equally remote from the true theological position. Taking a more or less general view, one would be inclined to conclude that, of the three parties—namely the Infalliblists, the anti-Infalliblists, and the Opportunists (that is to say, those who believed in the Infallibility of the Pope but thought the moment an unpropitious one for its definition)—it was the first that carried the day, and the third that was supported by Newman. A closer examination of the facts shows that none of the contending parties could claim to have had the last word in this Council, as indeed in a number of others. But the definition was almost exactly what Newman and a few other theologians of his calibre had desired it should be, without being very hopeful that their desire would be fulfilled.

What the Infalliblists, Ward among them, most ardently desired was an infallibility virtually co-extensive with all the public declarations of the Holy See. In Manning's view, it was a positive inspiration, putting the Pope's utterances on a level with the words of Holy Writ. In Veuillot's case, we may well ask ourselves whether it was not something completely off the lines that was in view. Did he not publish in the *Univers*, among other productions on similar lines, a revised version of the hymn for Nones, which was to replace the familiar line:

Rerum Deus tenax vigor

by another, which, it was thought, was more up-to-date, viz.

Rerum Pius tenax vigor.[1]

[1] See *Univers*, 2nd October and 8th November, 1869.

As for Manning, he astounded the Fathers of the Council by proposing that the Church should be defined as the Incarnation of the Third Person of the Trinity.[1]

Exaggerated statements of this kind, far from sealing the triumph of those who for the past five-and-twenty years had been identifying the cause of their rough-and-ready theology with that of the Holy See, did but ensure their own lasting discredit. They were more anxious than anyone that the Infallibility of the Sovereign Pontiff should be proclaimed. And proclaimed it was, that is true enough, but in terms annihilating their own presentation of it, and supporting what Newman, starting with the concluding portion of the *Apologia*, had ever since presented as the true Catholic doctrine in the matter. It had come to pass exactly as Newman had foretold it would in his *Letter*[1] to Pusey in 1865. What had happened was that true Catholicism had disowned its caricature. That was all.

For instance, the way in which the *Univers* party in France, and the *Dublin Review* across the Channel proclaimed, in spite of all evidence to the contrary, that theirs was the interpretation that had been solemnly adopted by the Council, was the cause of the wave of indignation which swept Europe from end to end. Then it was that it fell to the lot of men like Fessler in Germany in his stand against Bismarck, and Newman in England in his controversy with Gladstone, which elicited his famous *Letter to the Duke of Norfolk*, to set Catholic truth on its base again, Catholic truth which had fallen into such disrepute as a result of the activities of those who boasted of being its defenders. It would serve no useful purpose to go into all these things in detail. It would take us too far away from Newman, who deemed it sufficient, in these circumstances, to say over again what he had been saying for a long time past. As he had always hoped, with a confidence that never wavered, the truth triumphed in the end.

Some years later, Ryder, in a letter to Ward's son about Papal Infallibility (a subject on which Manning had had to adopt the interpretation which he, Ryder, and Newman had shared since 1867), said, "I am like those old Whigs, who see themselves outdone by the young liberals". Newman was the last man in the world to take any credit to himself for such turns of Fate. But at last, in a saner atmosphere, in 1870, he was to bring out his final great work, *The Grammar of Assent*, containing a matured version of his Oxford sermons on Faith

[1] Letter dated 15th November, 1865. Cf. Mersch, *Le Corps mystique du Christ*, Louvain, 1933, p. 33, note 2, Vol. II.

and Reason. And then, when that was completed, the idea comes over him again that his work is done, and his sole thought is to give thanks that his life is ending with hope dawning in the sky.

Meanwhile, in 1878, Pius IX had been succeeded by Leo XIII. The task of buttressing the supernatural authority of the Church against the encroaching tide of Liberalism being now safely accomplished, the new Pontiff found himself free to encourage the development and due presentation of Catholic ideas. When he was asked what would be the policy of the new Pontificate, he said, "You will see that by my first Cardinal". Soon after that, news was brought to the old man at Edgbaston, news as overwhelming, but far more unexpected, than the news which sent the young scholar of Trinity into such transports of joy that day the bells rang out to summon him to Oriel. The tidings this time were that the Successor of Peter desired to invest with the Roman purple the misunderstood, be-slandered priest that the hapless leader of the Oxford Movement had now become.

But now, when it seemed that amends for all he had endured were at long last to be made to him, the old fatality, which had so relentlessly piled misunderstanding after misunderstanding on his head, seemed even now, for one last time, to be at work again. Manning, who was at the head of the Hierarchy in England and himself a Cardinal, was naturally chosen to make the Pope's intention known in the proper quarter. What was it that happened now? Lytton Strachey, who does no more than say out bluntly what Purcell, Manning's official biographer, merely hints at, accuses him of wilfully garbling Newman's reply to the Pope, making what was really an acceptance look like a refusal. One is reluctant to admit the possibility of such a piece of frigid and deliberate treachery. But obviously it implies some extraordinary wishful-thinking on Manning's part to make him imagine that Newman's answer amounted to a "No". What is more, he did not quote the actual words of Newman's reply.

The Pope, naturally hurt at what seemed to him an inexplicable slight, said no more. As for Newman, he took it that once more a hope, which he had not courted, had been awakened in him for the sole purpose of inflicting upon him yet another disappointment. But others there were who were not so ready to give in to circumstances. For one thing, reports of the Papal proposal had leaked out. *The Times* published the news of the proffered honour, and stated that Newman had declined it; another piece of information whose source again was obvious. The Duke of Norfolk wrote straightway to Manning, saying that if Newman did not receive the dignity which had been promised him there would be a public scandal. All Manning could do was to make abject excuses for his "error", and blossom forth into exaggerated praises of the man he had done all in his power to discredit and humiliate. About this time, Mgr Talbot, stricken with general paralysis, was peacefully ending his days in a nursing-home at Passy.

Some few months before, Trinity College had conferred on Newman an honorary fellowship, the first they had ever bestowed. His old tutor, Sharp, still at work, though he must have been now nearly ninety, was in hall to welcome him, the hall which he had not seen since the days of his youth. Newman now appeared there as the most distinguished of Oxford's living sons. Some weeks later, the Pope conferred upon him the highest honour it was in his power to bestow. John Henry Newman, priest of the Oratory, was created Cardinal Deacon of the Roman Church, with the title of "San Giorgio in Velabro".

XXI

"EX UMBRIS ET IMAGINIBUS IN VERITATEM"

THE last pages of the *Journal*, written in 1874 and 1876, are devoted to lamenting over the uselessness of what he is doing. True, one of the earlier entries dwelt on the hidden blessings that all the disappointments and trials of his life had really been to him. Nevertheless, an active life spent wholly in trying to serve God, and, as it seemed, spent wholly in vain, could not but seem a sorrowful mystery to one who, now an old man, turned his gaze over the years gone by.

Newman was under no illusion as to the unfavourable verdict that might be passed by anyone reading this *Journal* of his in times to come, for it is but one long lament; but before God and before posterity, faithful to the truth, he did not shrink from risking even this final misunderstanding. Penetrating, pitilessly penetrating, as was the light he turned upon himself, now, as at all the other periods of his life, he knew well that it was not for himself that he had made his plaint, but for what he had tried to do for God, which despite all his efforts, had proved in vain.

September 10, 1876.

> I notice the following, lest the subject should turn up when I am gone, and my friends be perplexed how to deal with it.
>
> I have before now said in writing to Cardinals Wiseman and Barnabò, when I considered myself treated with slight and unfairness, "So this is the return made to me for working for the Catholic cause for so many years", i.e. to that effect.—
>
> I feel it still, and ever shall.—But it was not a disappointed ambition which I was then expressing in words, but a scorn and wonder at the injustice shown me, and at the demand of toadyism on my part, if I was to get their favour, and the favour of Rome.

Only once more did he open his *Journal*, and this was what he wrote in it:

> Since writing the above I have been made a Cardinal!

Nevertheless, it would be yet another misunderstanding to see in these words any slight upon the Holy See. Yet there is no denying the irony of them. They were aimed at those who had done everything in their power to paralyse his work, but now flew to the aid of the winning side, and hailed as a pillar of the Church the very man whom they had denounced and relentlessly hounded down as her direst foe.

Coming so late upon the scene, Leo XIII could do little but offer him a purple shroud. It was not the fault of this great Pope that he did not make the recompense more effective by making it earlier. Even so, it was the sanctifying seal set on a life of unwearying endeavour, of sacrifice endured with the help of grace to the very limits of human endurance. Maybe it was the more precious for not wearing the appearance of an earthly reward. It was not the last few years of life that still remained to him that could reap the blessed harvest of so long and sorrowful a sowing-time.

The fruits of his labour, the testimony of his life, are beacons whose light extends beyond the vision of any save a posterity so distant that even now it is scarcely coming into being. He remains, in the history of the modern Church, the shining light of an era of whose sad plight his prophetic vision had been the first to gauge the miseries and the needs.

We catch some final glimpses of him there in the great room at Edgbaston, or at the country retreat at Rednal, or maybe, on some rare occasions, swathed in that Roman purple which reminds us that the sanctification of martyrdom transcends all other marks of sanctity in the Church's eyes. But all these pictures of him fade and melt away in the light of the celestial vision. *Ex umbris et imaginibus in veritatem.* When he was invested with the purple, to make that journey had long been his sole desire. But now that he has made it, we find it harder and harder to believe that he has left us. In our perplexities, in our hopes, in our unshakable trust in the Church, no voice from beyond the grave speaks to us like his, for there is none other that speaks so clearly to our hearts, none other that comes so directly from his own. *Cor ad cor loquitur*, such was the motto of his Cardinal's coat-of-arms, such is the final comment on the life of a man for whom truth and charity were always one.

Among the enormous pile of letters that came to him from those numberless people whose hearts he had touched with a ray of light since it was also a ray of love, one in particular merits quotation here:

Clare,
Suffolk,
7 June, 1890.

Dear Sir,

I do not know the style in which I ought to address you but I am sure that you will forgive any informality that springs from my not knowing the usages of your people; especially do I think you will be ready to overlook any infringement of the outward laws of reverence due to your position when you know that I am writing this expressly to inform you as I think it is my duty to do, how much I owe to you.

The question of whether I should acknowledge my spiritual debt has been on my mind for some months. I have at last decided it in the way this letter shows.

And now I am at a loss to say what I feel towards you. Were it not for the perfect confidence established by your writings I should leave unsaid what I want so much to say. But that confidence begotten in me towards you leads me to endeavour to say quite simply what is in my heart.

About four years ago I came by the first three volumes of your *Parochial and Plain Sermons* and some time afterwards I bought an odd volume of selected sermons adapted to the seasons of the ecclesiastical year. These sermons, with the hymn "Lead, Kindly Light" (so frequently sung by my congregation), are all that I have read of your writings. But—how poorly should I say it if I attempted to put down how much I have received from those four volumes. Surely it is right that I should tell you, if I could, how my life has been changed, how my spirit has been fashioned, how the mind that was in Christ Jesus has been communicated to me by the reading of your sermons.

If I were to allow in myself a perfectly free and natural expression of feeling I should say with a feeling of grateful tears about my heart—"God bless you Cardinal Newman, God bless you!"

When I tell you that I am a minister of Jesus Christ to a congregation of those who are called "Independents" you will know at once, much better than I know, what an ecclesiastical gulf separates me from you. These matters I fail to understand, and I have, I must confess, very little wish to understand them. I only know that I desire most sincerely to live the life of our Lord Jesus Christ, to do His will, to have His spirit to take hold of my tasks and duties and carry them forward as He would have me, and I know that you have helped me as no one else has, to be distinctively in aim and spirit, a Christian. Therefore I cannot see, notwithstanding our religious positions, that I am doing anything but what is loyal to Him and what you will not regard as presumption in thus writing out of the fulness of my heart.

I feel that I have very inadequately stated my experience of benefit, but that precious and profound doctrine which you teach us, viz. that the best part of the Christian life remains hidden, leads me to hope that from this very impoverished utterance you may be able to understand how rich and, I hope, lastingly rich you have made me in that inward life according to which we are accepted.

I am yours faithfully and gratefully,

W. Wood.

A very old man now, he was given more and more to silence and meditation. Gradually his weakness increased. His sight had almost gone, his limbs were all but paralysed. One after another, he had had to give up the Mass, the Breviary, and the Rosary. One beautiful day in August 1890, the Fathers were astonished to see him walking with upright carriage and a firm step, as of old. His voice was clear and strong. But next day he had to keep to his bed. He had a cough and a high temperature. Scarcely twenty-four hours later his long life had ended. His last conscious act had been to ask for an old silk scarf, which he wrapped round his neck. It was a present some poor woman of the neighbourhood had given him in those lonely years gone by, when he felt as if the whole world had forsaken him.

He rests in that same grave in which, with such heartbreaking sorrow, he had seen his beloved Ambrose St John laid to rest.

And now I know of no better way of drawing these pages to a close than by recalling an incident still fresh and vivid in the memory of him who recalls it. One day, his faithful and beloved Jemima came to see him at Edgbaston bringing with her one of her grandsons. The small boy had quite naturally been told not to worry the old man with a lot of questions. No less naturally the child could not help talking. Charmed as he always was with children, Newman, despite Jemima's protests, encouraged the little fellow to say what it was he wanted to know. Whereupon he came out with, "Which is greater, a Cardinal or a Saint?" The reply was, "Cardinals belong to this world, and Saints to heaven".

INDEX